Critical Ap

to the Study of Higher Education

Critical Approaches
to the Study of Higher Education

A Practical Introduction

Edited by
Ana M. Martínez-Alemán, Brian Pusser,
and Estela Mara Bensimon

Johns Hopkins University Press
Baltimore

© 2015 Johns Hopkins University Press
All rights reserved. Published 2015
Printed in the United States of America on acid-free paper

2 4 6 8 9 7 5 3 1

Johns Hopkins University Press
2715 North Charles Street
Baltimore, Maryland 21218-4363
www.press.jhu.edu

Library of Congress Cataloging-in-Publication Data

Critical approaches to the study of higher education : a practical introduction /
edited by Ana M. Martínez-Alemán, Brian Pusser & Estela Mara Bensimon.
pages cm
Includes bibliographical references and index.
ISBN 978-1-4214-1664-9 (hardcover : alk. paper) — ISBN 978-1-4214-1665-6
(pbk. : alk. paper) — ISBN 978-1-4214-1666-3 (electronic) — ISBN 1-4214-1664-6
(hardcover : alk. paper) — ISBN 1-4214-1665-4 (pbk. : alk. paper) — ISBN
1-4214-1666-2 (electronic) 1. Education, Higher—United States—Research.
2. Educational equalization—United States. I. Martínez-Alemán, Ana M.
II. Pusser, Brian. III. Bensimon, Estela Mara.
LB2326.3.C74 2015
378.007—dc23   2014029356

A catalog record for this book is available from the British Library.

Special discounts are available for bulk purchases of this book. For more information,
please contact Special Sales at 410-516-6936 or specialsales@press.jhu.edu.

Johns Hopkins University Press uses environmentally friendly book materials,
including recycled text paper that is composed of at least 30 percent post-consumer
waste, whenever possible.

CONTENTS

The genesis of this book dates to the Association for the Study of Higher Education's (ASHE) Institutes on Equity and Critical Policy Analysis, funded by the Ford Foundation. The editors are grateful to the Ford Foundation for its support of critical higher education scholarship. While at the Ford Foundation, Jeannie Oakes and Greg Anderson made it possible for us to build a stronger intellectual presence for critical research methods within the community of higher education scholars. We acknowledge their committed leadership to research that aims to make higher education a more equitable institution.

Critical Approaches
to the Study of Higher Education

Introduction

ANA M. MARTÍNEZ-ALEMÁN, BRIAN PUSSER,
AND ESTELA MARA BENSIMON

What does it mean to understand social actions? There is interdependence between the basic concepts of social action and the methodology of understanding social actions. Different models of action presuppose different relations of actor to world; and these world-relations are constitutive not only for aspects of the rationality of action, but also for the rationality of interpretation of action by, say, social-scientific interpreters.—*Habermas (1981, p. 102)*

As higher education researchers and scholars, we seek to provide explanation and enlightenment on the vast constellation of issues that broadly affect American higher education. We seek to provide for policymakers, the public, and institutional actors clear, reasonable, and authoritative information about higher education as it is experienced in a democracy. We seek to offer trustworthy accounts of multifaceted and complicated issues that determine access to, enrollment in, and graduation from our many institutions. We explore and explain the nature of work and labor at higher education institutions. We account for the university's past, we interpret its present-day forms, and we forecast its future.

The researcher's account of higher education phenomena, whether retrospective or predictive, analytic or descriptive, is by nature interpretative in that these products of our investigations present a particular view of social relationships framed and filtered through our epistemological partiality. We consequently make meaning of phenomena through methodological norms that regulate our view of actors, their relations to the world, and the benefits and costs of their actions. In higher education research, our methods determine what and whom we study; how we study actors, functions, and projects; and what purpose(s) inquiry should serve. As social inquiry, higher education research reflects views of social action that are undeniably determined by what and how we investigate, and how we choose to interpret and communicate our findings. Our methods, then, effectively interpret social relationships and actions, invariably positing an assumed, implied, or articulated purpose. As higher education researchers, how our findings shape social action is a matter of epistemological translation.

It is therefore not surprising that higher education researchers interested in identifying and correcting sociocultural inequities would utilize social science research methods produced by an "emancipatory" epistemology whose principal aim is to foster greater social freedom. Among Western theoretical frameworks, critical theory has uniquely positioned scholars and researchers to explain and decode inequitable social relations and action in higher education. Focusing on educational equity, for example, higher education researchers and scholars have employed critical theories to identify and explain the sources of "racial gaps" in higher education (Chesler & Crowfoot, 1997). In particular, they have used critical discourse analysis to identify the social and operative attributes of how language—as a medium for social power—is used to control individuals and groups (Allan, Gordon, & Iverson, 2006).

These and other studies present views that in one way or another point to the paradox of inequity in a democratic society. Fundamentally, critical interpretations of American higher education endeavor to bring social science inquiry to identify the causes and causalities of inequitable access to higher education, as well to craft a view of the discriminatory and unjust experiences of actors in higher education. A public declaration, critical research, and scholarship have sounded the clarion of equity under the banner of democratic social justice, seeking to animate our institutional and public policy debates and our educational practices. Designed to effect democratic change, critical studies animate research with theory that detects democratic inconsistencies so that our practices and policies can better serve democratic society.

Bohman (1999) put forward the assertion that critical inquiry is consonant with democratic principles, especially the primacy given the public's group and individual agency. Anchored in democratic ethics, critical inquiry suits democratic social arrangements because it combines theory and research with "intellectual and moral responsibility within a well-integrated interpretive and explanatory framework and a political practice aimed at human emancipation" (p. 472). This is John Dewey's pragmatic view of the social sciences' value, that inquiry can critically inform and reconcile abstract democratic principles and social practice. In this view, democratic societies as cooperative social arrangements need critical inquiry to make evident the historical narratives that have shaped past and current limitations on individual freedoms and communal growth. Identifying normative beliefs and practices that contradict the aims of democratic living—

cooperative living and freedom—is the central value of critical theory and its application: social inquiry. All critical inquiry is grounded in lived experience, and power relations and social justice are central concerns. The agency of the subject under study is of paramount importance in critical examination, a historical snapshot of subjectivity that gives texture to phenomena and their effects. As one example, feminist methodology epitomizes the ontological and epistemological concerns of critical inquiry regarding subjectivity. How feminist research should be conducted—its methodology—requires a view of the nature of being as well as reality (its ontology) as composed by social relations, and thus what counts as knowledge (its epistemology) is socially constructed. Consequently, how subjects and subjectivity are treated in inquiry matters to the meaning derived from analysis. For feminists, social relations are understood as relations of power in which gender is central, and so feminist research methodology employs methods (techniques and procedures) that will elicit knowledge about the complex ways in which women's lived experiences reveal their subjugation as gender caste. Because of their commitment to revealing gender discrimination and inequity, and to bringing about women's empowerment, feminist researchers choose critical methods that ensure participant subjectivity. In choosing these methods, feminist researchers adopt the same stance as critical researchers in that denying subjectivity breaches its emancipatory commitment. Choosing research methods in which women's interpretation of their lived experiences is irrelevant or immaterial, thereby rejecting their subjective claims, would make such inquiry uncritical. Thus, like all other variations of critical inquiry, feminist research must acknowledge subjectivity—that subjects are experts and authorities of their own experiences—recognizing that consciousness of one's privilege or disenfranchisement is imperfect and impure.

Researchers further influence inquiry from their own subjective positions. In critical inquiries, researchers must consider their own subject positions in order to take into account their own preconceptions that result from their own social positions. The decisions researchers make about choice of topic, method, and its production are affected by their own agency, their own positions in relations of power and in disciplinary discourses (Harding, 1987). In sum, if the objective of critical inquiries (like feminist research) is to reveal hegemonic practices and to better understand the ways in which these practices are resisted (or not) and can be overturned, then such inquiry must always keep subjectivity—the researchers' *and* the researched—in critical view.

This volume presents a number of specific critical theories and models for conducting research in higher education, with examples of the ways in which

critical approaches have begun to change scholarly approaches to the postsecondary landscape. It presents original research that uses critical models and theories to better understand central problems in higher education. This collection
of essays is intended to aid teaching in education and public policy doctoral and
master's degree programs in the United States and internationally. In the chapters
that follow, higher education scholars and researchers present approaches, techniques, and methods intended to serve as models of critical research in higher
education for graduate students and faculty. This book presents research in postsecondary education as informed and shaped by critical approaches to theory,
history, discourse, standpoint, and advocacy. The foundation of the book grows
from an emerging body of research that argues that critical frameworks can position scholars to effectively analyze inequities in organizations, social relations,
and actions in higher education in ways that traditionally functionalist, rational,
and increasingly neoliberal approaches do not.

The book focuses on the ways in which higher education researchers can use
a critical research design and critical theories to see beyond the normative models and frameworks that have long limited our understanding of students, institutions, organization, governance, and the policies that shape the postsecondary
arena. Given the mix of theory building and original research presented here, a
book of this scope can be a practical guide for beginning researchers as well as
instructors, who can incorporate the lessons of critical approaches into their syl-
labi, curricula, and pedagogies. The contributors to this volume—scholars whose
own work has often set the standard for critical work in a particular domain of
research in higher education—present theoretically and methodologically rich
chapters.

The idea for a book on critical research methods dates to the Association for
the Study of Higher Education's (ASHE) Institutes on Equity and Critical Policy
Analysis, funded by the Ford Foundation and directed by the Center for Urban
Education at the University of Southern California's Rossier School of Education.
The institutes' purpose was to build a community of scholars who could ask critical questions about higher education policies and practices while learning new
research methods and techniques for studying issues related to race and ethnicity
in American higher education. The practical intent of the ASHE Institutes on
Equity and Critical Policy Analysis project was (1) to encourage research that asks
critical questions and creates new knowledge to support equity-oriented changes
in policy and practices; (2) to start a dialogue to frame issues in higher education
that are at the forefront of policy agendas from the perspective of equity; and
(3) to create a community of scholars throughout academe who understand the

challenges and need for critical work focused on equity. To that end, the core activities of the institutes included a series of intensive research methods workshops focused on quantitative and qualitative data from critical perspectives as well as workshops on critical policy, scholarly publishing, and participatory action research. Several contributors to this book served as directors of the institutes, including Brian Pusser (Critical Policy Analysis), Anna Neumann and Aaron M. Pallas (Critical Qualitative Methods), Sylvia Hurtado and Mitchell J. Chang (Critical Quantitative Methods), and Alicia C. Dowd and Estela Mara Bensimon (Participatory Critical Action Research). The institutes commissioned Ana M. Martínez-Alemán's chapter. For more information on the institutes, see http://cue.usc.edu.

Despite the widespread understanding of critical standpoints and research methods in other areas of the social sciences, the study of higher education, particularly in the United States, has only recently begun to develop research using such essential approaches as critical feminist theories, critical race theories, critical discourse analysis, state theoretical approaches, or theories of power and marginalization. At the same time, as the contributors to this volume argue, intertwined with the lack of critical perspectives has been a dearth of work addressing key topics in higher education that are central to critical work elsewhere in the social sciences: race, gender, social class, power, discourse, privilege, and inequality. The fundamental premise in this book is that by linking critical theories, models, and research tools with a critical vision of the central challenges facing postsecondary researchers, we can make a significant—and long overdue—contribution to the development of scholars and scholarship in higher education.

While the chapters presented here will address many of the central domains in the study of higher education—students, institutions, and knowledge creation—we are particularly interested in turning attention to the importance of critical research design for understanding politics and policy making in higher education. Policy is a central area of contemporary research interest in higher education, as governments, foundations, and institutions around the world increasingly demand research to guide the transformation of higher education in a globalized context. To a far greater extent than in past decades, however, much of the contemporary policy research in higher education today is driven by scholars working in disciplines traditionally at some remove from the majority of work in the field: economists, political scientists, demographers, legal scholars, public policy analysts, and scholars of business and management. We argue that these fields are also the areas in the social sciences that have made the least use of—and, arguably, resisted—the forms of critical scholarship. We thus contend that the use of critical research design and the application of critical vision in higher education are in danger of being "crowded out" before they have had a chance to thrive.

We find this situation untenable not as an ideological or personal affront, particularly since the authors brought together here reflect a broad range of training and standpoints, but because—as the mass of postsecondary research and scholarship increasingly relies upon functionalist, rational, and normative theories and models—we find ourselves at a distance from discovery, less likely to solve the pressing problems in higher education and society. We argue for critical research designs, theories, and standpoints because they stand as a viable alternative to the largely ineffective approach to postsecondary research that has dominated the field for nearly five decades. Authors present possibilities for equity that have been shaped by critical vision and intelligence. We intend for this book to reshape thinking in those fields that have not traditionally applied critical perspectives to higher education, and also for the work to appeal to scholars in anthropology, women's studies, sociology, and other fields that have made more significant use of critical approaches to research and scholarship.

In the twenty-first century, the intensification of class stratification; the heightening of racial, ethnic, and religious persecution and conflict; and the neoliberal turn in the acquisition of wealth and power have challenged the capacities of individuals and groups to engage freely and fully in American higher education. It is our hope that the lessons offered in this book serve as citadels for equity research and practice. Through critical insight and imagination, we believe, higher education research can engender equitable change.

REFERENCES

Allan, E. J., Gordon, S. P., & Iverson, S. V. (2006). Re/thinking practices of power: The discursive framing of leadership in *The Chronicle of Higher Education*. *Review of Higher Education, 30*(1), 41–68.

Bohman, J. (1999). Theories, practices, and pluralism: A pragmatic interpretation of critical social sciences. *Philosophy of the Social Sciences, 29*(4), 459–80.

Chesler, M., & Crowfoot, J. (2000). An organizational analysis of racism in higher education. In M.C. Brown II (Ed.), *Organization and governance in higher education*. (ASHE Reader Series, 5th ed., pp. 436–69.) Boston: Pearson Custom.

Habermas, J. (1981). *The theory of communicative action* (Vol. 1). *Reason and the rationalization of society*. Boston: Beacon Press.

Harding, S. (Ed.). (1987). *Feminism and methodology*. Bloomington: Indiana University Press.

CHAPTER ONE

Critical Discourse Analysis in Higher Education Policy Research

ANA M. MARTÍNEZ-ALEMÁN

Though critical theory has been used in higher education scholarship and research, little (if any) clear articulation of its foundation and purpose has been put forth to help guide higher education's empirical inquiry. Often in higher education research, critical theory is deployed haphazardly through methodologies loosely tied to their theoretical underpinning. Critical race theory research, for example, often catapults the articulation of critical theory in order to apply methods designed to identify racial and ethnic discrimination or subjugation.

In this essay I present a brief overview of critical theory and its relevance to higher education research and policy, with the caveat that the breadth and depth of critical theory are much too wide in scope for one chapter. A list of suggested readings on critical theory appears at the conclusion of this chapter to encourage readers to deepen their understanding. But no discussion of critical theory can be complete without deliberation on its methodologies. I offer critical discourse analysis (CDA) as one analytical tool for higher education research and policy, and suggest examples of how CDA can be applied to higher education research and policy.

Critical Theory: An Overview

According to Max Horkheimer (1993), a founding cultural theorist of the Institute for Social Research at the University of Frankfurt (or Frankfurt School), the goal of critical theory is to develop interdisciplinary research that is both empirical and historical as a means for solving "socio-philosophical problems," or more specifically, those problems that are the consequence of domination within and across human communities. Human subjugation characterizes society, and thus liberating individuals requires that we should "impart knowledge, on the basis of observations and of a systematic study of facts as to how one achieves domination and how one maintains it" (p. 316). Clearly, then, critical theory's central conceptual distinction is that it unites theory (philosophical thinking) with the social sciences (application), and in so doing provides us with normative criticism, explanatory analysis, and practical solutions. As social criticism, Horkheimer reasoned, theory must seek to identify and explain the underlying causes of social problems in order to make positive transformation possible. A theory is really only valuable to the extent that it can use social science research as a means for resolving social problems and facilitating the public good. Horkheimer (1972) saw the need to integrate traditional, abstract theory with social science inquiry grounded in concrete and tangible concerns so that social inequities could be actively transformed. Abstract theorizing, in this view, could not adequately inform or explain reality because it lacks the "systematic study of facts as to how one achieves domination and how one maintains it" (p. 316). The study of facts or the gathering of data is a necessary condition for theory to be effective at engendering social equity.

Horkheimer's assertion that critical theory should be used "to dispel myths, to overthrow fantasy with knowledge" (Horkheimer & Adorno, 2002, p. 1) frames the broad and diverse conceptualization and applications of what we now understand as critical theory in the West. Since its genesis in 1923 at the Frankfurt School, the arts, humanities, and social sciences have employed critical theory to de-center grand narratives of social and political subjugation, particularly those of colonialism, race and gender, sexuality, and class broadly conceived. As a consequence, its criticism of culture is now far reaching and comprehensive (Wheatland, 2009). Marxists, feminists, gender and queer theorists, structuralists, and poststructuralists all utilize critical theory to identify and locate the ways in which societies produce and preserve specific inequalities through social, cultural, and economic systems. The uninterrupted production and preservation of structures that reproduce social inequalities—whether material or cultural—are targeted by theory and research to increase the freedom of individuals. Cultural values, which are most often unconsciously assumed, govern individuals, whether independently or in communities. Individuals' experience of reality, then, is greatly determined by the meaning that these cultural values carry either explicitly or implicitly. Over time, these meanings become accepted, reproduced, and standardized, thereby replicating structures of domination and suppression. Consequently, the desired objective of critical theories is to emancipate individuals from what has been socially regulated and thus assumed "natural" or "normal"— Foucault's (1980) "regimes of truth"—whether it is one's economic position in a capitalist market or gender identity, for example. By isolating and assessing critically those normative structures in language, and social and economic practices that curb and control individual lives, critical theories aim to liberate individuals from humanly constructed and socially reproduced restrictions.

Undeniably created by the impulse of the Frankfurt School's cultural theorists' desire to articulate an emancipatory Marxism free of orthodoxy, the foundation of critical theory was situated in an era of rising capitalist power. From this perspective, capitalism was identified as a humanly constructed and reproduced social structure that challenged individual autonomy. Capitalism had proven to be a primary yoke of social subjugation for masses of individuals by the early twentieth century, and critical theory was conceived as a basis for social inquiry that could end capitalism's suppression. In Horkheimer's (1982) view, the transformation of capitalist society into a democratic or consensual community free of the repressive structures of capitalism could be achieved through critical social inquiry. The "real democracy" that he envisioned demanded the power of social science investigation, coupled with Marxism's liberatory hermeneutics, so that capitalism could be transformed both in theory and practice (p. 250). Thus, in its earliest conceptualization and iteration, critical theory was a normative social theory concerned primarily with the effects of capitalism and all its structures. Its advancement into the twenty-first century does not discount this primary principle, but the conceptual development and advancement of the means of critical analysis have been broadened and expanded since the establishment of critical theory as a post-Marxist consciousness.

Language and Semiotics

As a hermeneutics, critical theory since the latter decades of the twentieth century has centered on two intricately related dimensions: (1) the analysis of how our realities are arranged and systematized by and through language and (2) semiotics studies. Early critical theory was primarily sociological in nature until Jürgen Habermas posited a reconsideration of critical theory *as* philosophy. Arguing that critical inquiry could reconcile "theory" and "practice" and that a philosophy of language could provide the means to cultural and artistic innovation that would disturb oppressive modernist structures, Habermas formulated his "Theory of Communicative Action" as a framework through which to move critical theory beyond the epistemological limitations of the norms of social science methodology outlined in earlier decades of the twentieth century (Habermas, 1981, 1987). Habermas's communicative action focuses on the interpretation of the meaning of texts, symbols, and language through literary studies. Michel Foucault's expositions on power, identity, sex, and sexuality, for example, offer a critical view of language as a historically situated structure through which subjectivity is constituted. Together with Ferdinand de Saussure's foundational work on the structural study of language and thought, theorists like Roland Barthes, Jacques Derrida, Julia Kristeva, Jean Jacques Lacan, and François Lyotard contribute to this semiological turn in critical theory, a turn that brings critical theory to the analysis of discourse. In the work of Claude Lévi-Strauss, critical theory is used to study the anthropology of institutions, cultural practices, and mores.

As formulated by Saussure (1974), semiotic studies centers on the proposition that the nature of language is arbitrary, that things have meaning because of values that conceptualize our thinking and ways of being in the world. Language signals meaning and is used to construct our understanding of events, persons, relationships, and being. As a result, how we experience things is often governed by the meaning that language coveys to us and that we interpret. Language and images too convey meaning and thus act as systems of social organization. As a system of signs, language and images combine with sound and vision to denote meaning or "signification." Take the case of gender as a system of sociocultural organization. Whether I say *niña* or *fille* or "girl," signification occurs, and ideas and concepts are formed. In the case of English, the signifier "girl" has represented some connotation and implication because language has organized a concept for us. We make sense of things through language and images, which serve to regulate meaning. In this way, when we read the word "girl," we draw upon its signification to us in order to understand it. So when we read "The girls went to lunch," we interpret through conceptualizations of subjectivity ("girls"), action/behavior ("went"), and activity/event ("lunch"). The problem, of course, is that as signifiers these words are historic and reflect the social constructions of meaning. For some, the gender semiotics of the sentence reflects a conceptualization of several possible subjectivities: prepubescent, young female humans, adult females or "women," and perhaps "feminized" men. If we change the sentence to read "The *guys* went to lunch," the signification changes. Perhaps the subjectivities are male, young, matured or old, or they could be a group of young women, or both. Most importantly, however, it is the signified—the concept denoted by the signifier, its assumed or unconscious meaning to us—that matters most.

What language and image communicate has bearing on how we conduct ourselves and structure our societies. Taking this same example, the organizing, implicit conceptualization is that of gender. Who and what constitute "female" (which is itself a signifying referent) and what characteristics we ascribe to them is the signification. What they are not—men, boys, masculine forms—is also encased in the signification. Language's primary property is that it differentiates and defers meaning. In this example, the difference is sex and, arguably, gender; the difference is between what we conventionally understand to mean either a male form or a female form. But it is a difference that matters socially and culturally, and so we create language to structure this difference. If sex and/or gender did not matter to us, if it was not a category of social and cultural distinction, then the structure of language would not reflect this difference. This is Derrida's (1973) most important contribution to semiotics: that the signifier essentially refers to the idea from which it is different. Girls are neither boys nor men, are they?

The signifier/word carries with it social convention and its associated historic power. In this example, the dichotomization of sex and gender in Western cultures and the construction of adult male and masculinity as the idealized form bring us to an unconscious signification about the infantilizing (negative adulthood) of female and feminine forms. This conceptualization of women as incomplete and imperfect men, as lesser men, as able to reason only in childish ways, is carried in language when we use the word "girl" to denote the subjectivity of adult females. And recall that when the subjectivity was changed to "guys," the signification altered our understanding; that is, the signifier deferred its meaning to the positive ideal. It is acceptable conceptually to subsume women's and girls' subjectivity under the ideal of masculinity, and we can only refer logically to men or boys as girls when we mean to diminish them, when we mean to connote a negation of their ideal male form. The signification in this latter case is a pejorative one—to call men or boys girls means that they are less than what they *should* be.

As critical theory, then, semiotic studies give us a means through which we can recognize and comprehend the foundations of culture and social convention so that we may change those principles and practices that dominate and suppress communities of individuals. Through language, semiotics gives us a view of cultural assumptions and systems that organizes our consciousness; it is an analysis of a regulatory practice that normalizes behavior—women can be infantilized, or treated as children; they are not men's equal; and their autonomy (if such autonomy can in fact be conceptually accepted) can be conceded. Critical theorists argue that from the normalization of consciousness, institutions, policies, and behaviors are formed, in turn reproducing and reinforcing the normative assumptions. In this case, the normalization of the claim that women are not men's equal makes possible historical social and political conventions that have restricted women's freedom to vote, to own property, to earn equal wages, to access educational and leadership opportunities, and so on. How we experience our realities—how we experience the term girls when used to denote adult women— is really shaped and governed by our confidence or blind faith in the meaning or signification transmitted and communicated by the signifier, girl. Through critical analysis of the signification, our conceptual confidence is shaken because we "see" (perhaps for the first time) a system that produces oppression, in this case, sex and gender discrimination. Through a semiotics, we engage in a critical analysis of the cultures and principles that inhabit and produce meaning, in this case, the acceptance of the subjugation of women in a sex and/or gender hierarchy. Such gender disparity bears out clearly in higher education research on the climate for women on college and university campuses where women's salaries, laboratory spaces, and job promotions have historically lagged behind men's (e.g., Massachusetts Institute of Technology, 1999; Perna, 2001; Sandler & Hall, 1986).

Semiotics Applied

There is obvious correspondence between those critical analyses that focus on hermeneutics (the signification of the word girl) and those that center on actual social phenomena (sex-based wage discrimination). Each of these directions in critical theory can guide scholars and researchers in assessing how meanings are constructed as well as the implications of their application in our lives. In these traditions, the medium of communication—whether textual, visual, or regulatory policy and practice—captures the varied and broad character of human experience and enables us to deliberate on the messages communicated intentionally and unintentionally, consciously and subliminally. The medium through which signs are arranged and through which signification happens is important. Signs conveyed visually point to sociocultural constraints that are typically normative. Restroom signs, for example, often signal cultural conventions such as men wear pants, not dresses; women wear dresses (figs. 1.1 and 1.2). If the words "MEN" and "WOMEN" did not appear below the symbolic figures, many in Western cultures would assume the sex differentiation. Here the regulatory cultural "truth" is that sex is an important category of difference, and within the regulation of that difference are conventions about appropriate attire. In cultures in which this sign has meaning, we become compliant in our thinking; that is, we experience no quandary or predicament with the sign. We "know" which door to enter. We know which door we are *supposed* to open and walk through, and most continuously consent to the convention. Many of us have unwittingly experienced the critical analysis of these signs when young, preliterate children are not confused by the signs; they know which is for boys and which is for girls. When signs appear simply as words or letters that read "MEN" or "GENTLEMEN" on one door and "WOMEN" or "LADIES" on the other, our preliterate toddlers and kids are baffled because the medium (text) is unintelligible and therefore meaningless.

Transgender and genderqueer persons have a much more injurious experi-

Figure 1.1.   *Figure 1.2.*

ence with such signage. To these individuals, though the sociocultural convention may be "known," their bodied, experiential realities are in opposition to the
signification. To a critical theorist, such incongruity is evidence of a society's
need to challenge what is passively recognized as natural and in so doing question and confront our passive sanctioning of social regulation—in this case the
regulation of gender. As many college and university administrators can attest,
the sex and/or gender designation of bathroom facilities is a site of critical contestation on campuses with transgender students (Marklein, 2004; Russell, 2003).
Through challenges to the convention and institutionalization of sex and/or gender distinction and dichotomization, transgender students in these cases unsettle
what Foucault (1972) would term the "discursive formation" of sex and gender.
Transgender students challenge the "truth" of a social practice; they confront and
dispute a priori ideas about the nature of subjectivity. The discursive practices of
sex and/or gender dichotomization and segregation—as historically situated—
are tested and new forms of discourse are created.

The critical analyses and inquiries by Pierre Bourdieu and Michel Foucault are
particularly enlightening for critical education research and scholarship. Both
Bourdieu and Foucault engaged in sociological, anthropological, and philosophical inquiry to explore and explain repressive social structures that ultimately
establish and reproduce subjectivity. Each, though not in precisely the same way,
engaged in critical social inquiry and analysis to ascertain the varied dimensions
of power and their impact on subjectivity and the sociology of identity. Bourdieu (1993) rightly identified education as a structure or "field of cultural production" through which socioeconomic class distinctions are perpetuated. Bourdieu
(1984) asserted that social stratification occurs through the accrual of cultural,
social, and symbolic capital that then transfers from one generation to another as
a means to preserve class privilege. Examining how societies teach and inculcate
"strategies of distinction" (Bourdieu, 1993, p. 66) across generations is a respon-

sibility of critical scholars because it is through this generational transfer that we perpetuate class oppression. The accrual of cultural capital, for example, enables individuals to attain certain capabilities, valuable experiences, and credentials that preserve class distinctions, privilege, and access to a broader range of society's goods. As a noncompulsory social institution, for example, higher education in the United States is a vehicle for reinforcing class stratification. In awarding degrees or verification of qualifications (aesthetic as well as technical), higher education as a social institution confers cultural capital.

Michel Foucault (1984) brings to critical inquiry a view of language as social practice and consequently as a means and exercise of power that is helpful in our consideration of the role of critical theory in higher education policy research. Foucault recognized that language is entrenched in the performance of subjectivities and that as "discourse" it was integral to social structures like education. Discourse in this way is understood as comprising knowledge and the group of people who possess it, or who are believed to possess it. Determining discourse necessarily signifies power; or, in Foucault's treatise, discourse *is* power. In Foucault's critical analysis, knowledge is a means of supervision, regulation, and discipline. Knowledge shapes who we are and who we are not. We are the knowledge we possess, suggesting, of course, that if individuals have ownership of discourse, they assert power, and in so doing control and in turn are controlled by their experiences. Institutions with power determine what can be known and who is to know it. Knowledge and power are inextricably linked in that we can control social reality through knowledge, and through controlling that reality we capture knowledge (Foucault, 1977). All this to say that, as a social structure in which knowledge is currency and credentials are capital, higher education (especially because it is not compulsory) is fertile ground for the exercise of power and for its realization. Higher education is a place where disciplinary discourse is produced and that "produces domains of objects and rituals of truth" (Foucault, 1977, p. 194). The university is a place where power is created and through which reality is shaped.

Perhaps even more salient with contemporary concerns about higher education is Foucault's claim that power is used as social discipline. Power, according to Foucault, disciplines through the imposition of norms or the normalization of behavior, dictating and enacting standards of compliance or distinction. Standards for performance by faculty or students, normalization of research or scholarly practice among the faculty, and restrictive orthodoxies with regard to faculty and student comportment all exemplify the ways in which power in higher education regulates individual actors and groups. The penalty or punishment that individuals face is transformation and assimilation. We must become normal; we should correct our deviant behavior and assimilate into convention in order to avoid categorization as abnormal, consequently being shut out of privilege. Those individuals who do not conform to normative standards or models are marginalized. Thus, in order for a woman member of the faculty to possess the discursive power of her profession, she must take on the subjectivity of the "academic man" (Wilson, 1942); students of color must abide by the cultural norms of "whiteness" or risk social and academic marginalization; researchers must not breach the methodological paradigms of the dominant discourse unless they are unconcerned with their professional status and future acquisition of power and capital and their reproduction. Understood in this way, power defines, conditions, and manipulates individual and groups.

But changing or contesting discourses is possible. Counterdiscourses can be communicated widely, but only by those who possess the means of communication. Foucault's (1977) critical view of contesting discourses begins with his observation that the modern subject self-regulates because she internalizes the means of regulation and control through "technologies of power." Self-regulation is commanded in several ways, but especially through knowledge and belief systems. The relationship between power and knowledge is such that social viewpoints, attitudes, and values (discourses) can regulate knowledge and thinking. We come to "believe" what is normal, what is tolerable, and act either in accordance or in contradiction to it. We may comply or resist completely or just partly in some measure. We can internalize sexist and ethnocentric beliefs about ourselves; we can internalize homophobia and change or alter our behavior accordingly, because these belief systems have become hegemonic. We regulate our behavior because we perceive that our subjectivities are monitored and scrutinized and that any transgression from normality is punishable. But we may also contest certain or all conditions of a regulatory discourse and defy compliance and complicity.

Foucault (1984) makes room for resistance in his conceptualization of power in this way. The seat of struggle, power comes about because we resist or refuse to accept discourses; we refuse the regulation of presumptive truth or and standardization, what Foucault (1977) called "continuous and uninterrupted processes which subject our bodies, govern our gestures, dictate our behaviors, etc." (p. 97). Women faculty and faculty of color do attain tenure and leadership positions in male-dominated fields and do shift the discourse away from adherence to the sexist and ethnocentric norms of the academic man and toward their own evolving professional subjectivities. Once in possession of discourse, these "marginalized" actors acquire the means of self-representation. Often disciplined to understand themselves only as heterosexist discourse tolerates, gay, lesbian, bisexual, and transgender students do appropriate the means of communication and self-representation and in so doing break free of normalizing models of identity. In a Foucauldian analysis, this is an example of the nonstatic nature of power, the ways in which power shifts as a consequence of resistance to oppressive structures, and view of the asymmetrical and multidimensional character of power that enables social and cultural transformation. In fact, resistance to regulation and control demarcates power and subsequently makes critical social change possible.

In sum, in critical theory there is the assertion of the need and value of interdisciplinary research and the reconciliation of theory and empiricism in order to change societies' oppressive and hegemonic structures that capitalist and other exploitive and suppressive forces formulate and ground. Critical theory is aimed at identifying those structures that create, produce, and reinforce mythic beliefs about natural or normal ways of being, and detecting and undoing discourses with regulatory power that dominate and suppress subjectivity. The goal of critical theory, then, is to emancipate individuals and communities from repressive and hegemonic ideas, practices, and policies by identifying the ways in which these "technologies of power" regulate subjectivity and behavior through language expressed in varied media (e.g., text, image), and by identifying and analyzing power relations that create generate social stratification and compulsory segregation. So what is critical theory's relevance to higher education policy? What role can it play in the production of higher education? How can critical theory inform higher education policy making?

Critical Theory's Relevance to Higher Education Research and Policy

Critical theory's bearing on higher education research and policy is significant. As theory, it demands the integration of the empiricism of the social sciences with philosophy's aim to understand the nature of knowledge, life, and systems of beliefs. Critical theory enables the researcher and policymaker to inform decisions about methodology and course of action with epistemological thoroughness. Its interdisciplinary character draws knowledge from many scholarly sources, allowing us to more completely explore and examine the wide array of higher education problems and issues. Because it is epistemologically diverse, researchers are better able to more scrupulously investigate the many multifaceted and knotty issues that mark the landscape of higher education in the United States—

the disparity between men's and women's rates of tenure, the achievement gap between races, and the difference in access between racial and ethnic groups, as examples.

Understanding the underlying causes of such complex problems is what some would argue is the objective of "good" educational policy. As Anyon (2005) correctly reasoned, any effort like research and policy making that seeks to solve complex social problems equitably requires "an understanding of underlying causes" (p. 65). To identify and analyze the multiple layers and intersections of social systems and structures will require that critical theory frame research design. Critical theory provides research design with the analytical power to link multiple causes and effects of structural inequities and, most importantly, to provide the framework for pragmatic change.

In the case of higher education policy making, we can anticipate that critical research could identify and explain much more thoroughly and intricately those structural inequities that are and have been root causes of attrition rates among historically marginalized college student groups. The goals of critically informed higher education policy—educational equity and social justice—would be to target those specific root causes of disparity—for example, decreasing federal funding + increasing pricing + low-asset family base + cultural norms, and so on—and articulate the ways in which each root cause can be addressed *in relation* to the others. The greatest challenge of critical higher education policy making is to map the graph of causes and the valance interactions (relationships) between causes. Each source of inequity, each cause or node, links and networks in one or multiple ways to other causes. In this view, critical higher education policy's functionality is to attend to the nodal locations of social injustice as well as their structural interactions. This graph may indeed reveal that current or past policies have themselves been responsible for the introduction of a new causal relationship, or perhaps the exacerbation of historic causalities.

Critical policy making should then entail the construction of such a complex and contextually rich graph of inequity but, more importantly, provide directives and means for attending to causes. Because of the complex nature of social inequality and the likelihood that the interaction between nodes is intricate and multifaceted, however, to be effective, critical policy should be understood not as a singular macropolicy but rather as one of several critical practices within a consortium of critical social policies. For example, the federal government can enact policy that expands financial assistance to needy students. But doing so without putting in place effective mechanisms for access to these funds renders the policy critically impotent. Students may not know how to access information, or even that expanded benefits exist. A critical policy would include budgeting and strategies for expanding the advising and guidance services of schools to better improve the likelihood of getting information into the hands of students.

Applying critical theory to higher education concerns bringing the social sciences into interdisciplinary communicative action, effectively allowing explanation as well as interpretation. In this way, a critical theory approach can simultaneously explain phenomena (the researcher's aim) and interpret phenomena (the policymaker's task). As practical scholarly exercise, critical theory positions the researcher as a communicative actor who advances meaning to the policymaker, closing the gap between theory and practice, research and application. As in Habermas's (1988) conceptualization of communicative action, researchers and policymakers are engaged in dialogical inquiry in which information is gathered and directed to attain reasonable and practical social objectives. In this way, critical theory locates the researcher in a dialogical relationship; he must engage in the practical assessment of experience, identifying *and* communicating expert knowledge for the purposes of democratic progress. Serving as proxy for the public, the policymaker verifies the expert/researcher knowledge. Bohman (1999) thus reasons that research truly becomes a social process meant to improve decision making in a democratic society. Democratic societies, after all, are well suited for critical social inquiry. Democracy demands cooperation as a fundamental principle, and the critical inquiry and communication of knowledge of social institutions are "precisely the analysis of the basic terms and norms of cooperation" (p. 462). Through the dialogical relationship between researcher and policymaker, critical inquiry is carried out, and as a consequence democratic societies can attend to domination and oppression.

Critical Inquiry

As an analytical tool, critical inquiry brings together varied and diverse methods and assumptions of the social sciences and philosophic traditions. As Habermas (1987) explains in his *Theory of Communicative Action*, the role of critical theory is to elucidate the particular limitations and strengths of social science methods and to identify productive empirical strategies. It is then the responsibility of the researcher to fashion a complete and inclusive framework for analysis that is relevant to the subject of inquiry, keeping in mind that the means and aims of critical inquiry must correspond and must always be scaffolded by their sociocultural and historical context. Researchers engaged in critical inquiry must have knowledge of the context, of the ways in which the phenomenon under study is historically situated, in order to identify the structures that regulate and control social freedoms. Additionally, as critical inquiry, any endeavor must situate human participants as "subjects of inquiry," as "equal reflective participants," and as "knowledgeable social agents" (Bohman, 1999, p. 474).

This last point demands some attention. If the goal of critical analysis is the undoing of hegemonic structures and the liberation of subjugated and exploited individuals and groups, then subjectivity—how individuals interpret the world—must be taken in to account. If, as Foucault and Bourdieu argue, "subjects" are social constructions of the consequence of power and discourses that discipline, then their emancipation through inquiry is only possible if they are conceptualized and actualized as knowing agents. Representing subjugated classes through research—that is, not involving participants in the meaning making that is research—is a means to their further subjugation. To critically examine society, then, to conceive of individuals and communities as *objects* of study, is epistemologically faulty.

The critical view is one in which subjects of study are participatory in that their interpretation of phenomena is integral to the inquiry. Subjects participate in meaning making and are not objectified; that is, they are not denied agency or the capacity for self-determination and they are not seen as interchangeable objects of examination. Making persons and communities objects of study, whether in research or policy making, entails "making into a thing, treating *as* a thing, something that is really not a thing" (Nussbaum, 1995, p. 258). If the goal of critical inquiry is to develop policy and practices that have emancipatory social ends, it cannot treat participants as a means for further or different subjugation; it cannot own or put forth a singular view of their experiences uninformed and even co-constructed by participants. Critical inquiry by definition must take into account the experiences of those individuals or communities under examination; it cannot reify participants. And because critical researchers cannot conceptually frame inquiry with normative criteria and principles, they must be methodologically flexible enough to capture the complexity of singular and collective subjectivity. For example, critical researchers cannot judge subjugated classes' experiences using normative/privileged behavioral criteria. We see this in research that labels disenfranchised students' experiences as deficient or lacking because they fail to match normative standards. Cultural deficit models used by educational researchers, for example, can stipulate that because minority parents/students do not appear to assimilate the educational values of white parents/students, they are uninterested in educational success (see Valencia & Solorzano, 1998).

For the educational researcher, the epistemological claims of critical theory and inquiry require a break from traditional research methods and agenda, from objectification and normalization. First and foremost, normative research typologies are incongruous with critical theory. Conceptualized and developed out of "discourse(s) of exclusion," the means and aims of traditional, rationalistic research reflect "discourses of exclusion" that are inconsistent with critical theory and critical social science inquiry (Young, 1999, p. 680). Research methods cannot be grounded in normative assumptions about behavior or existence; the social phenomena under scrutiny cannot be viewed as either standard or deviant, or from one singular position. As a guiding principle for conducting investigations and analyzing data, value neutrality is discredited. What data are gathered, how data are gathered and by whom, and what meaning is made of them fundamentally constitute a series of subjective exercises. In effect, critical inquiry challenges the ontological and epistemological bases of traditional social science research. An illustration of critical inquiry is feminist research's challenge to the "objective" claims of science.

Though critical inquiry can take many forms in the field of education and in education policy in particular, discourse is its most common target of inquiry. Discourse presented in text as well as other media is often examined through critical inquiry in order to reveal systematic and disparate distributions of power. The analysis of text, whether in the form of official policy documents by organizations or governments, or advertisements or visual media, is a method through which we can begin to understand the complex layers of prescriptive "grand narratives" (Lyotard, 1984). In text reside the disciplinary social structures that inhibit agency. As a "functional text," policy (of any kind) will limit as well as facilitate meaning between the authors and the readers. In their analysis, we can name the macrostructures that give reality what we perceive as a rational order (Luke, 1995). Through text, meaning is shaped to preserve or modify cultural significance and convictions about reality (e.g., Disney's reinforcement of traditional views of the nuclear family). The lexicon of the text will expose social power and prevailing orthodoxies, as in children's school forms that require only the names of "Father" and "Mother" and in that order, as well as university policies for "maternity" leave but not "paternity" leave.

As an example of the investigative application of critical theory, critical discourse analysis, or CDA, is often applied to text intended to describe and investigate educational phenomena so that we can better understand the ways in which dominant discourses construct realities that support and advance their world views and convictions that are inherently unjust.

Critical Discourse Analysis Defined

Broadly understood, CDA is a method through which we can expose in text (words or images) the metanarratives of hegemonic structures in society (Fairclough, 1993). Researchers use CDA to determine the relationships between text and discursive practices and the social circumstances that informs each. The processes of writing, reading, and viewing images—and what meaning we make of them—characterize the analysis. In CDA, we are most concerned with how text presents discursive practices or the ways in which we are in the world (Gee, 1990), because it is in and through this presentation that our social identities are formulated and regulated. This is the manner in which text in all its forms signifies. Texts present ideologies, beliefs, and messages about subjects of study. Their critical analysis proposes to illuminate these messages, how they are framed, and how they can be resisted and usurped (Fairclough, 1993). As the unit of analysis in CDA, text is understood as a means to perpetuate hegemonic power relations and norms (Foucault, 1980).

In the last forty-plus years, critical researchers have applied CDA to education in an effort to identify those discursive practices in schools, colleges, and universities that signify the ideologies and values that produce educational and social inequity (Gee, 2008). Applied primarily to phenomena in elementary and secondary education, CDA has been used to understand the nature of learning a second language, cognitive processing of text, and socialization and enculturation through language, and to disturb discourses of deficit among nonmajority populations of children. Feminist critical inquiry has used CDA to identify subject positions in textbooks that stereotype sex and gender hegemonies. In the latter part of the twentieth century, CDA was applied to contest the lexical preference in word choice (e.g., "colonization" instead of "invasion"); preference for descriptions of indigenous peoples that promulgated discourses of difference and deviance (e.g., natives as "savage" and colonizers as "civilized"); and the presumptive positioning of the reader as having the experiences of a privileged class (e.g., use of "we" as the all-inclusive experiential standpoint; Luke, 1995). In higher education, Ayers (2005) uses CDA to reveal a neoliberal discourse that reconfigures the community college's historic democratic mission to one that powers social inequality.

We can see clearly the power of educational discourse in the phenomena of Indian boarding schools in the late nineteenth century. A critical analysis of the discourses embedded in their curricula, textbooks, and rules for student behavior reveals a framework of lexical preferences and enculturation designed to "kill the Indian and make the man" (Official Report of the Nineteenth Annual Conference of Charities and Correction, 1973/1892). Designed to "civilize" and "save" Indians by educating and training them in an attempt "to civilize them with the idea of taking them into the nation," these schools were formulated by a functional discourse: US federal policy. Its catchphrase, "kill the Indian and make the man," signals the essence of the ideological underpinnings of federal policy at the time, that "Indian" is not human in the Anglo-Saxon construction—he is not a subject and therefore has no agency or natural right to self-identify; it must be done for him.

The text of Captain Richard H. Pratt's speech, given in 1892 to the Annual Conference of Charities and Correction (note here the lexical choice of the word "correction"), in which he lays out the rationale for the need for federal policy that will institute Indian boarding schools, is a good example of federal policy as functionally discursive. Just in this excerpt, for example, we can note the discourse of the assimilation of deviance to normalcy through education, the power of "civilized" nurture over "savage" nature, so to speak. We are told to believe that the "transfer" of ways of being through socialization is a reliable truth, that cultural assimilation can triumph over "biology as destiny," that the unfortunate event of Indian birth into an uncivilized social order (in this case the generalization, "Indian") could be transformed through Anglo-Saxon edification. In other words, the federal policy that Pratt outlined was a presentation of ethnocentric and assimilationist ideology, a discourse not surprisingly familiar to critical researchers of African American education (e.g., see Ferguson, 2001; Fryer & Torelli, 2005). Below I underscore the signs to which I refer in this paragraph but suggest that a more thorough CDA would yield further discursive elucidation. Note the gender discourse and the lexical choice of developmental images that signal natural possibility (e.g., each powerful hegemonic contrivance).

It is a great mistake to think that <u>the Indian</u> is born an inevitable <u>savage</u>. <u>He</u> is born a blank, <u>like all the rest of us</u>. Left in the surroundings of savagery, he grows to possess a savage language, superstition, and life. <u>We</u>, left in the surroundings of <u>civilization, grow to possess a civilized language, life, and purpose. Transfer</u> the infant white to the savage surroundings, he will grow to possess a savage language, superstition, and habit. Transfer the savage-born infant to the surroundings of civilization, and he will grow to possess a civilized language and habit. Th<u>ese results have been established over and over again beyond all question</u>; and it is also well established that those advanced in life, even to maturity, of either class, <u>lose already acquired qualities belonging to the</u>

side of their birth, and gradually take on those of the side to which they have been transferred.

In addition to text, images of schooling and university life are also the object of CDA. We are generally aware that colleges and universities market and "sell" the institution through print media and online media, but CDA of images identifies the implicit signification meant by the selection of images as well as their placement and production. A dramatic example is the selling of the success of the Carlisle Indian Industrial School noted above. In an effort to "show" how Indian children could "lose already acquired qualities belonging to the side of their birth," headmaster Pratt required "before and after" photographs of students.

In the photographs of Navajo boy "Tom Torlino," he first appears as he did when he arrived at the Carlisle Indian Industrial School in 1882. He then appears as he looked three years later (fig. 1.3). CDA of these images would first identify the presentation of ideology and beliefs about the purpose of education; that is, to assimilate students into Anglo-Saxon Christian culture and values and in so doing rid the student of the deviance and inferiority of his birth culture. The discourse of ethnic, racial, and cultural superiority frames this message—to "kill the Indian and make the man" not only involves cognitive assimilation, but also a physical one. Through federally sponsored education like that found in Pratt's Carlisle Indian Industrial School, the message is that full subjectivity is only pos-

Figure 1.3. Tom Torlino: 1882 and 1885. *Source:* Cumberland County Historical Society (n.d.). http://explorepahistory.com/displayimage.php?imgId=1-2-C2F.

sible through identification with and appropriation of dominant-class norms, mind *and* body.

To more completely conduct CDA, however, researchers must attend to other elements and components in particular ways. Below I explain strategies used to conduct CDA, giving examples from higher education research and higher education policy documents. I also refer the reader to appendices that contain a worksheet to conduct CDA (appendix A) on sources identified in appendix B.

Conducting Critical Discourse Analysis

Before setting out to apply CDA to any text, researchers must keep critical principles in mind. First, my position as analyst here is important to note. I am an educational philosopher by profession and a pragmatic theorist by specialty. For this reason I deeply value the empirical and its contribution to our understanding of phenomena, yet my pragmatic inclinations enable me to appreciate and value the richness and complexity of research and scholarship, especially those that are emancipatory in mission. Next, CDA as a research method has certain fundamental goals: (1) to reveal the ideological foundation of discourse so that hegemonic power relations can be identified and (2) to provide evidence (data) necessary to support corrective action. These goals are principally affected by core ideas in critical theory articulated by Marx, Foucault, and Bourdieu. Marxist theories' identification of texts as discourses of economic subjugation; Foucault's ideas on the connection between discourse and power relations; and Bourdieu's assessment of text as a form of cultural capital comprise the theoretical core of CDA (Luke, 1997).

To reveal the ideological foundation, researchers conducting CDA must keep in mind those aspects that construct and restrict discourse: (1) culture, (2) social identity (race, gender, class, sexuality, etc.), and (3) language (Fairclough, 2000). The critical relationships that must be kept in view in CDA are the connections between the text (which carries the discourse) and the discourse and the social context (Fairclough, 2000). Texts are spaces in which "cognition and representation of the world, and social interaction" play out (Fairclough, 1995, p. 6). Identifying and explaining their interactions are goals of CDA.

Having identified these connections, CDA researchers need to be mindful of the linkages between the text, structural power, and context. Additionally, as McGregor (2004) reminds, the CDA researcher must always bear in mind that because discourses are contextual, their meaning can have varied interpretations, and thus "the 'right' interpretation does not exist whereas a more or less plausible or adequate interpretation is likely" (para. 10). An individual researcher's culturally bound context will affect the analysis. So reliable causality is not the endgame of CDA; rather, validity derivative of interpretive analysis becomes the objective.

With this conceptualization is the necessity of the "ensemble of techniques" to examine texts (Luke, 1997, para. 22). Because text mediates social practice, it necessarily tells us who "we" "are" and "are not"; the text tells us how to relate to or what meaning we are to make of self, others, and things (Fairclough, 1995, p. 133–34). As Fairclough (1995) points out, the CDA researcher must be vigilant of the "content of texture" or the form and organization of the text, must note that what is absent from the text is significant, and must understand that what is implicit is also analytically germane. In Fairclough's (1995) estimation, "implicit content" (p. 6) is critically significant. What is socially and culturally understood as normal and natural gives the critical researcher a view of presumed normative structures whose power need not be declared. Their totality is presumed.

Because CDA is derived from an array of social science techniques, it is not a singular method that can be outlined in a step-by-step way. The development of a "template" is thus impossible, making the critical researcher's task even more complex. McGregor's (2004) primer on CDA does, however, provide researchers new to discourse analysis with a set of guidelines to begin the critical task of unmasking hegemonic dialogues. McGregor (2004) advises that the researcher should first engage the text or simply read the text without probing it, making note of the text's genre. The researcher should ask herself: Is it a research article bound to the discourses of social science style and intent? Is it an institutional directive made public only to employees? Is it a funded research report published for sponsors or for marketing purposes? Is it an electronic memo between superior and subordinate? Is it an example of a course examination? All of these modes of textual communication have rules and conventions that will affect their construction, arrangement, content, and language, and that convey the point of view intended by the text. This process of assessing the context is referred to as "framing" the text. McGregor (2004) suggests that we can frame texts by keeping the following *guidelines* in mind:

- *Choosing and placing* specific photographs, diagrams, sketches, etc.
- *Using headlines and keywords* to emphasize certain concepts by giving them textual prominence (*foregrounding* if the text is emphasized and *backgrounding* if text is there but de-emphasized).
- *Leaving certain things out completely.*
- *Using certain words that take certain ideas for granted*, as if there is no alternative (presupposition).

- *Manipulating the reader by using selective voices* to convey that certain points of view are more correct, legitimate, reliable, and significant while leaving out other voices. (para. 8)

Below I excerpt a strategy for CDA presented by McGregor (2004) that is useful and that I will employ on higher education texts in the pages that follow. I underscore key practices. Here are suggested *techniques* consistent with the guidelines above:

1. Just as text can be framed, so can a sentence, called *topicalization*. In choosing what to put in the topic position, the writer creates a perspective or slant that influences the reader's perception.

2. Sentences can also convey information about power relations! Who is depicted as in power and over whom? Who is depicted as powerless and passive? Who is exerting power and why? This property of the text is referred to as *agency* and can remain at the subconscious level unless made visible by the analyst or critical reader.

3. Again, as with the text in general, omission of information about agents of power can occur at the sentence level and is most often achieved by nominalization (converting a verb into a noun) and the use of passive verbs.

4. Many readers are reluctant to question statements that the author appears to be taking for granted; presupposition can also occur at the sentence level in the form of persuasive rhetoric that can be used to convey the impression that what an agent of power says carries more weight.

5. Insinuations, another tool, are slyly suggestive, carrying double meanings. When the facts, or the way the facts are presented, are challenged, the originator of the discourse can readily deny any culpability. This ability to deny any intention to mislead gives the originator of the discourse a lot of power.

6. Even one word can convey strong meaning—connotations! These connotations are not always, or seldom, in the dictionary, but often assigned on the basis of the cultural knowledge of the participants. Connotations associated with one word, or through metaphors and figures of speech, can turn the uncritical viewer's mind.

7. The tone of the text is set with the use of specific words to convey the degree of certainty and authority (called modality). The tone of doubt or surety is introduced by using words such as may, might, could, will, can, must, it seems to me, without a doubt, it's possible that, maybe, or probably. Moods of heavy-handed authority (don't challenge me) or deference can be created

simply by choice of verb or modal phrases, which assert or deny the possibility, impossibility, contingency, or necessity of something.
8. Finally, as with the full body of the text, single words can convey *register—
do the words spoken ring true*? Writers can deceive readers by affecting a
phony register, one that induces mistrust and skepticism. Register can be
affected by choice of person—first person (I, me, my, we, our), second (you
and your), and third (he, she, they, their, his, hers, him, her). (para. 10)

What does the application of this CDA strategy reveal for higher education
texts? I have chosen to examine text from and about the National Survey of Student Engagement (NSSE). The selection is motivated by the fact that these documents represent several frames in higher education discourse: funded research,
the marketing of funded research results, and the role of data-driven policy initiatives in a system of noncompulsory regulation and accountability. The NSSE
documents chosen were: (1) "Promoting Engagement for All Students: The Imperative to Look Within, 2008 Results"; (2) "The College Student Report" survey;
(3) "Executive Snapshot 2008: NSSEville State University"; (4) "The NSSE Institute for Effective Educational Practice" overview; and (5) "NSSE 2008: Exclusive
Focus on Average Scores Misses the Mark when Comparing Colleges and Universities, Survey Finds" press release. Links to these documents appear in appendix C.

In table 1.1, I briefly sketch the CDA applied to these documents. My intent
here is to give a cursory view of how and where the techniques that McGregor
(2004) presents can be employed to ascertain the ideology grounding this text
and frame its policy implications. A complete and exhaustive CDA of these documents is beyond the scope of this particular chapter, but table 1.1 serves as a
simple illustration of the ways in which researchers can begin to apply CDA to
higher education documents. I use such tables or charts to keep a more precise
record of the analysis and to keep track of the details. Because CDA requires both
the macro and the micro view, some form of cataloging or indexing is advisable.
For me, charting and detailing the elements of the analysis allow me to "see" the
forest as well as the trees.

What does CDA of the documents listed in table 1.1 suggest? What characterizes the discourse in these documents? Does the evidence revealed by CDA suggest any particular corrective action?

Let me address the first concern of CDA, the uncovering of metanarratives (the
macro view) that reinforce and reproduce power relations and hegemonic structures. An early indication of the discourses that frame NSSE documents is found
in the foreword to "Promoting Engagement for All Students: The Imperative to

TABLE 1.1. The National Survey of Student Engagement and critical discourse analysis

Source	Quote/section	CDA type / comments	Page number
NSSE Promoting Engagement for All Students	"NSSE may well have achieved an eminence that requires no foreword. The acronym is everywhere."	Presupposition (framing): tone = authority	3
	The Power of a Big Idea	Foregrounding; tone again suggests authority	3
	"769 institutions participated in 2008, bringing the total to more than 1,300 college and universities . . . NSSE is an amazing success story."	Tone = everybody's doing it, act now, get on board!	3
	"the idea of a tool"	Tone? Or presupposition? Privileging the quantitative	3, 4
	"NSSE has made a special contribution by taking the general concept of student engagement and giving it legs and language. Oh, yes, and scores."		
	"part of a larger commitment to improvement driven by evidence and understanding"		
	"engagement"	Word choice (connotations); framing	4, throughout
		Why not use "assessment"?	
		Does not assess student learning but the student learning environment; equates engagement with quality	
	Many of the large selected/highlighted quotes from national educational leaders, professors, and researchers	Foregrounding; using selective voices (experts for legitimacy and authority)	throughout
	"the really hard work has already been done: systems have been developed to ensure smooth operation of a very complex enterprise, a capable and dedicated staff is in place, the quality of our work is well-established, and we have a solid base of committed users"	Presupposition; tone	8
	Figure 1: NSSE 2008 Participating Colleges and Institutions	Insinuations / implicit referencing; omission of information or backgrounding—scale only goes from 0 to 30%, making usage look greater	9

		What's missing from benchmarks?	
	Benchmarks of Effective Educational Practice	What's missing from benchmarks?	10
	Promising Findings	Many of these findings assume causation and do not consider other mitigating factors (omission of information)	11, 16
	"Online courses seem to stimulate more intellectual challenge and educational gains."		
	Using NSSE Data	Although there are different examples, most institutions are using such data for state reporting requirements or for accreditation purposes	23–26
	References	Who is being cited? (e.g., George Kuh, who is involved with NSSE)	30
Survey	"In a typical week, how many homework problem sets"	Assumes quantity = quality	
	"Number of written papers or reports"		
	"Which of the following have you done or do you plan to do . . . independent study or self-designed major?"	Two very different things yet grouped together; why?	
	Select your year of birth	Options only go to 1983, after which one must enter birth year. Overall, the survey privileges or assumes "traditional" college students. What about nontraditional and other students?	throughout
	What is your racial or ethnic identification?	Gives "other" as an option; gender given in male, then female, order; power relations	
	Since graduating from high school, which of the following types of schools have you attended?	Presumption about how everyone gets to college	
	Are you a member of a social fraternity or sorority? Are you a student-athlete?	What about other extracurricular activities? Foregrounding athletics and Greek life	
	Which of the following best describes where you are living now while attending college?	What about living with parents? Again assumes the "traditional" college student experience . . . many low-socioeconomic status students live at home (class and power)	
	Highest level of education for father and for mother	Assumes two-parent mother/father household; father (male) is listed before mother (female)	

(continued)

TABLE 1.1. The National Survey of Student Engagement and critical discourse analysis (*cont.*)

Source	Quote/section	CDA type/comments	Page number
	Attended college but did not complete degree	What type or level of college? What about trade degrees/licenses/certificates?	
Executive Snapshot 2008	"student experiences and outcomes are more varied among students *within* institutions than *between* institutions"	Presupposition; this finding is supposed to be surprising	1 (also in other reports)
The NSSE Institute for Effective Educational Practice	"The first [objective] is to identify, document, and disseminate the institutional policies and practices used by educationally effective colleges and universities that promote student learning."	As defined and determined by NSSE; student learning is not what they are measuring, but here they claim they are (insinuation)	1
	Sidebars throughout report list organizations/partners	Legitimacy (foregrounding)	2–4
	"seeking practical solutions"	What about theory?	3
	Campus audits, consultations, workshops	Word choice (business language); corporatization of higher education	3
Exclusive Focus on Average Scores Misses the Mark	"more than 90% of the variation in undergraduate education quality occurs *within* institutions, not between them"	Presupposition—this finding is supposed to be surprising	1
	iceberg metaphor	Connotations	1 (also p. 7 of Promoting Engagement for All Students)

Note: In the larger social context, the accountability movement in higher education equals assessment. None of the NSSE reports mentions gaps or weaknesses with NSSE, representing omission. The pictures throughout the reports depict diversity of students and faculty. Overall, the reports presuppose or privilege the "traditional" undergraduate experience as being "quality," which in turn privileges those individuals likely to fit into this category (e.g., white, middle-high socioeconomic status). Power relations. What's missing from NSSE?

Look Within, 2008 Results." Written by the vice president of the Carnegie Foundation for the Advancement of Teaching, a patron and stakeholder in NSSE research, it begins by announcing to the reader in strong and authoritative first-person language that NSSE "needs no introduction," that

> NSSE may well have achieved an eminence that requires no foreword. The acronym is everywhere: on institutional Web sites and the lips of parents and students selecting a college; the pages of *USA Today, the Chronicle of Higher Education, Change* magazine, and *The New York Times*; the 2006 report from the National Commission on the Future of Higher Education, and now on the template for the Voluntary System of Accountability being developed by several education associations. In fact, go to Google and you'll find "about 299,000" entries that deal with NSSE. (p. 3)

The tone and lexical choice here are certainly those of authority and superiority, corroborated by the empirical, quantitative claim that a Google search of NSSE will yield "about 299,000" entries, as well as by having received cultural validation from other cultural authorities (the *New York Times, USA Today,* the *Chronicle of Higher Education,* and *Change*). Both of these attributes are presumptive capital in the text's discursive logic, and that capital is further strengthened by the belief in the value of the federal government's oversight of higher education (through the National Commission on the Future of Higher Education) and its derivative, the Voluntary System of Accountability. Note that invoking the seal of approval from the federal government manipulates the reader by conveying a corroborative substantiation from the highest civil authority. Minimally, the critical analysis here is that this phenomenon—the NSSE projects—cannot be subject to challenge because, simply stated, it makes a universal claim: anybody who knows anything knows about NSSE and its prominence and importance. Additionally, the marks of authoritative weight in the twenty-first century (number of search engine / Google entries and public exposure) prove this statement to be an unconditional truth.

In this short foreword I identify an example of the power of disciplinary discourse to frame consciousness. At first blush the introductory remarks read rather harmless, but once I scrutinized the text for topicalization, once I identified the tone of the text and the presuppositions (that what is perceived to be ubiquitous is valuable; that what makes something "good" or "right" is the number of Google entries, etc.), the critical inquiry revealed discourse intended to rationalize the appropriation of the NSSE framework and its products on the grounds that they are unquestionably valued standards. Critically, however, this is simply a manipulation of the reader, carried out by using the appeal of popularity and alleged status (a cultural value) to discipline the reader's behavior. If I am a college dean of student services, for example, I may wonder why no one at my institution has heard of NSSE, let alone subscribe to one of its services. Motivated by the desire and concern to have my institution be part of a perceived valued group, will I then take action to introduce NSSE products to my superiors? The group of NSSE-participating institutions is large, according to the text, "769 institutions participated in 2008, bringing the total to more than 1,300 colleges and universities since NSSE's inception" (p. 3). Doesn't that mean something? What is that "something"? This lexical choice to display a number to indicate value reinforces the discourses of popularity, recognition, and normalization. From a CDA of this sentence and its position in the text, however, I elicited other impressions: What proportion of all higher education institutions do the 1,300 comprise? Are all institutions being served equally and effectively by the services provided? Do those services suit the great variety of institutional missions? Does the framework allow for the range and multiplicity of student enrollment and completion strategies? If all the institutions are treated the "same"—that is, that the framework allows for no individualization of institution mission and culture (in CDA terms, ignoring the context)—then are students also assumed to be unitary and singular (in CDA terms, discounting subjectivity)?

Among the more interesting outcomes of the CDA I conducted on this foreword is the invoking of the concept "engagement" late in the text, as if it too were established, known, and accepted universally. In fact, the first substantive mention of the concept "student engagement" comes late in the fifth paragraph, long after an inconsequential mention (i.e., "Community College Survey of Student Engagement"):

> Of course this sea change has many sources, and many people, projects, movements, and organizations have contributed to it. But NSSE has made a special contribution by taking the general concept of student engagement and giving it legs and language. Oh, yes, and scores. (p. 3)

In this sequence of text, CDA reveals at least three techniques used to orchestrate discursive power: connotations, tone, and presupposition. The presumption that resides in this portion of the text is that NSSE is unsurpassed by any other research or policy effort to understand the lived experiences of students. The connotative use of metaphors ("sea change" and "giving it legs") associates the topic with forward movement and power, striking transformation for the better. Pairing the metaphor of giving it legs with "language" is a linguistic device that is meant to remind the reader of the power of the research discourse—that abstraction can be brought down to the concrete; that the expert's knowledge can be distilled for the practitioner; that putting research into words will enable understanding for even the most unsophisticated of intellects among us. In suggesting that a "special contribution" has been made, the meaning that I derive is, again, that NSSE is out of the ordinary, unique, singular, and unrivaled in its production. I interpret the tone in this section of text to be condescending. As intonated by the two introductory clauses, "Of course" and "But," the reader is more or less told to disregard anything other than NSSE, that only NSSE has managed to achieve certainty, and, by implication and lexical omission, that one would be foolish to look anywhere else. The condescending "Oh, yes, and scores" not only reasserts tone but also most importantly invokes the discursive power of performance measurement. "Scores" reflect the empirical and reliable character of NSSE, both conditions historically esteemed in the research discourses of the social sciences and in Western epistemologies. As a reader, the signal I receive is that because NSSE follows a research tradition that is valued above all others, NSSE and its findings must be legitimate and absolutely true.

The CDA that I conducted throughout the foreword's fifty-one pages revealed many instances of standpoint or prominence given to the point of view of selected stakeholders only, as in the case of highlighting remarks by Lee Schulman, president emeritus, and the Carnegie Foundation for the Advancement of Teaching. The foreword foregrounds and emphasizes Shulman's comments, its content reinforcing the presupposition that only NSSE's methodology and methods are "trustworthy" and thus its "results" can be used for "plans for action and strategies for reform and transformation" (p. 30). CDA also revealed throughout the text the privileging of discourses (quantitative assessment over all others; a limited and narrow range of cited authors, overwhelmingly those whose work is used for NSSE products), the foregrounding of text to emphasize presumptive educational values (e.g., in "Writing Matters" and the highlights box of "Benchmarks of Effective Educational Practice"), and many omissions.

My critical analysis of text, as was the case in the documents listed previously, revealed a presentation of ideology and beliefs at the core of the NSSE projects. What constitutes student "success" and how we can best assess and account for it is communicated in these NSSE documents as discourse meant to create, produce, and reinforce ideas about the kind of achievement and how it should be valued. Here the discourse of student success is a regulatory one that like all discourses shapes and normalizes what we are to believe constitutes a social structure or identity, in this case, the "successful" college student and, by implication, the "failed" student. But from a critical perspective, defining and examining "stu-

dent success" is really a question of how we understand and conceptualize subjectivity or, more precisely, how we can capture the experiences of the individual—
not as a singular, autonomous, static entity but rather as an unstable, developing
identity engaged in networks of relationships that have variable, fluid and shifting, and symbolic meaning. My critical view of these NSSE documents is that the
construction of the discourse of student success normalizes certain uncontested
and undisturbed experiences, privileges some identities over others, and restricts
the range of valued student interactions. The actual lived experiences of many
students are not captured by the discourse presented in NSSE products, and its
products and production of normative claims therefore reinforce hegemonic beliefs about what is and is not a valuable experience in college, what is or is not
contributing to a student's definition of "success."

The CDA that I conducted on these various NSSE documents did not suggest a
conceptualization of students as subjects, as agents capable of self-determination,
as persons engaged in autonomous choice making. My CDA also suggested that
if NSSE dictates the grounds upon which we determine whether our educational
practices serve all students well, then it can certainly be understood as a regulatory discourse whose power is strengthened when deployed by institutions as
paid-for policy. Institutions buy in to NSSE (literally and figuratively); they invest
capital for a service or set of services designed to produce a product that is valued
currency in their economies (state policy boards, systems of ranking, accredita-
tion, marketing initiatives, to name a few). In effect, institutions purchase the
means to attain currency that is valued in markets in which accountability is
prized. NSSE provides "scores"; NSSE provides "language." In other words, NSSE
is able to provide institutions with the currency to buy favorable treatment or
perception by stakeholders—state and federal government officials, professional
oversight boards, and consumers. As a consequence of the purchase (motivated
by a desire or pragmatic reality of regulation and government oversight), institutions will then reconfigure and reinforce structures to discipline student experiences to fit the standards set by NSSE. Normalization of student experience will
be the logical outcome.

The discourse of "success" I uncovered through the critical analysis of the
NSSE text—for example, "participating in activities that enhance your spirituality" or "study abroad"—suggests that there is little recognition of the complexity
of relationships in a student's life, relationships that may matter more to student
self-esteem, self-worth, academic confidence, and the like—all psychological constructs we know to play an integral part in academic achievement. The NSSE survey, for example, pays little attention to developmental markers in a student's sub-

jectivity. There is also little attention paid to the developmental or time-sensitive reality of "states of awareness"; that is, to be aware of something making a difference requires knowledge borne of the realization of the connection between things, of the connections between cause and effect. As measured by NSSE, does "engagement" account for the inability of some/many students to recognize the impact of collegiate activities and behaviors? In matters of personal development and achievement, engagement is not a predictable condition in the lives of many undergraduates, and yet NSSE presents a discourse that assumes this is true. The measures used to determine student success are normative, and by that I mean that I am unsure just how well they capture the vast diversity of an accounting of success. Is success the same to all students of all kinds always and everywhere the same? Is success to students who are the products of cultures that highly value interdependence rather than autonomy categorically different from those whose rewards come as a consequence of separation and self-sufficiency? What, if anything, do young women value that will make their definition of success counternormative? The NSSE text addresses none of these subjective concerns.

The inclusion of items that reflect normative assumptions of what it takes to be successful in college is clearly an element of a discourse of power. Items that seek to determine the extent to which students engage in activities to develop spirituality reinforces normative assumptions that ultimately construct nonbelief as deviance. Not all students are raised to value "spiritual" growth, or for that matter know exactly what spiritual growth is. Yet, by inserting the item, the implication is that spiritual growth is an expectation or standard of college participation. Items suggesting that the only educational level that matters in predicting student success is that of a student's "mother" and "father" also reinforce conventions and normalization of families. Certainly, not everyone has a mother and a father. Some students have a parent that does not matter much in their lives or to their success, and some students have two fathers or two mothers, or none at all. Involvement in fraternities and sororities and athletics also appears to be overly important to capture in the survey when figuring out student success. I am not certain that all students everywhere care about having those activities as part of their college experience, or perhaps some students cannot participate because they work to pay for school, or perhaps they are young gay men put off by fraternity culture.

The texts asserted that "student success" instruments measure the "quality of relationships." A critical analysis of this assertion contests this claim by contending that quality is not a measure of "what" and "when" but of "how" and "why," all significations that require much more direct and participatory contact with subjects. Attempts to ascertain the quality of relationships in the NSSE survey (NSSE's Likert scales of "quality of relationships" with "other students," "faculty members," "administrative personnel and offices"), for example, barely get at the how and the why of these relationships. What do any of these characterizations really mean? What can we really say about student–faculty relationships as a consequence of the scores? As I note below, these particular items in the NSSE are critically ineffectual. For example, students are asked to rate their relationships with faculty members in a range where the negative endpoint is "unavailable, unhelpful, unsympathetic" and the positive endpoint is "available, helpful, sympathetic." I see, at minimum, two problems with this item. First, which faculty? All faculty? Are we all the same? What if a student has some real losers as well as two or three inspiring, supportive faculty? And what if some of the faculty are available (a positive score) but unsympathetic (a negative score)? Can't we as faculty all be available to our students during office hours, but can't we also be unsympathetic and insensitive during those same religiously held hours? Aware that incidents of sexual harassment of students by faculty can and do occur during these office hours of "availability" (Paludi, 1996), colleges and universities understand this as a space where harassment can occur. What score do those faculty members get?

The critical analysis I conducted about student success revealed that the discursive impetus to capture empirically those elements of student success in college ignored the subjective, and failed to conceptualize the individual as self-directed. What is absent in the NSSE text and in the discourse is a consideration of the particularities of lived experiences, of subjectivity. The CDA I conducted of these documents leaves me with the following questions: What do all kinds of students in all kinds of institutions think is important in order to be successful? What constitutes their success? Has anyone asked them? Are our measures of student success more often than not about outcomes—those tangible differences important to institutional stakeholders but maybe not to the students themselves? Can students really know *now* or at the moment of measurement what matters for their success? Contemplation and deliberation to see connections and missed connections in our experiences and in our relationships seem to be necessary steps in the determination of success for individuals. How is that factored into this conceptualization? To know what matters to our experiences requires some measure of subjective scrutiny, which I think is missing in the NSSE conceptualization of student success. What constellation of relationships, serendipitous or anticipated, expected and presumed necessary for some valued outcome (some success), can students easily identify as causal? This seems to me to be an unfair expectation of late adolescence—and even of nontraditional students, though I believe that such students have a better idea of what is necessary for success—but this does not matter because it is not the student who defines her success but rather institutions that, like all well-intentioned, well-meaning parents, compose the one narrative, the one discourse of success for students, forgetting that aspects of that discourse will and must be coauthored by those subjectivities making their way in the postsecondary world. As a critical educator, I need to know—really know—*how* and *why* students attain self-authored achievements; *how* and *why* particular institutional action contributes to or hinders *each* student's success. As a teacher, I need to know, for example, when sympathy is useful, when disbelief or a lack of understanding of the lived circumstances of students is inconsequential. In my view, these are the questions that possibly yield the evidence that can critically inform policies, in turn transforming institutions into more equitable environments. But these questions require inquiry that attends to subjectivity, and that takes notice of concerns communicated by individuals.

Conclusion

The ultimate purpose of critical inquiry, according to its primary architect, Max Horkheimer (1982), is to bring to light the social structures that create, maintain, and perpetuate inequity in order to cultivate true democracy. Despite Horkheimer's (1947) rejection of American pragmatists' conceptualization of democracy (because he perceived pragmatism to be too allied with liberalism's acceptance of capitalism's structures), the vision of democratic ethics put forth by both critical theorists and pragmatic theorists, especially John Dewey, should appeal to those among us who choose to marshal the power of critical inquiry for the purposes of greater and richer social participation by all in our democracy.

Dewey challenged the social sciences to engage in inquiry that was not "clumsy," that was context specific and artful (Dewey, 1946/1927, p. 181). Dewey asserts these two claims—that social science inquiry be grounded in lived experience and history and be motivated by the artist's function in a democracy—must "break through the crust of conventionalizes and routine consciousness" (p. 183). Social inquiry, like art, is the means through which democratic societies touch the "deeper levels of life," enabling individuals to communicate aspirations, needs, desires, and ideas about life and its realities (p. 184). In effect, social inquiry is the process through which and in which individuals in a democracy can critically reflect on life's conditions.

But it is the responsibility of social inquiry to communicate these subjective assessments. Like artists in a democracy, reasoned Dewey (1946/1927), social inquiry's primary purpose is to communicate the "deeper level(s)" of lived experience (p. 184), and to do so requires appropriating methodology, method, and public discourse. Such communication would guarantee that social inquiry could ensure the reassertion of subjectivity, and the breakdown of social conventions and habits contradictory to democratic living. Thus effectively communicating the subjective realities of individuals should be the essential motivation of social inquiry in a democracy, communication whose primary purpose is to inform public policy. NSSE, as an example, does not communicate a full range of subjective realities and simply keeps students as objects of study. Public policy, then, is a direct communication of the historic context and desires of individuals; it is the communication of democratic knowledge (not myth) for the purpose of engaging in intelligent action.

Young's (1999) assessment of traditional educational policy studies highlights this very issue. Concerned with superficial understanding at the policy level and the need to "increase trustworthiness of research findings" (p. 679), Young argues that traditional approaches to educational research typologies are developed from a "discourse of exclusion" (p. 681) that produces policy incapable of addressing inequity. Young charges that traditional policy studies are limited by their inability to view subjectivity outside of normative frames, and as a result aim, perhaps counterproductively, to discipline or reshape individuals, Young warns social science researchers that generalizable models for policy initiatives derived from such research will ultimately fall short because such models cannot capture the multiplicity of subjectivities nor resistance to such normalization, thus perpetuating the myth that equitable change is possible through standardization. We see this in policy analyses like the one by Shaw & Bailey (2007), in which researchers "test" a model for policy change "across six diverse states" and conclude that "it does not appear that the model of change that drives the Bridges Initiative is a generalizable model of state policy change" (p. 49) because context matters—students differ, their life experiences are not all the same, and not all stakeholder relationships behave identically. Yet educational policy informed by social science research continues to rely on epistemologically narrow frames and the standards for social change that they create. The desire to apply policy models or change paradigms derived from social science inquiry that failed to consider and communicate subjective realities and the nature of relationships and interactions between individuals and structures (e.g., NSSE) will not, as Horkheimer warned, "dispel the myths" and "overthrow fantasy" that democratic social change is possible through normalization of practice (Horkheimer & Adorno, 2002, p. 1).

What does it mean to understand and communicate social actions? Pragmatically speaking, in our democratic arrangements, it requires the critical inquiry and communication of subjectivity. It requires us as social science researchers to engage in analyses that presuppose the value of differing subjective claims, analyses that seek to understand the complexities of human relations and their many effects, analyses that enlighten the construction and relevance of public and institutional policy for all individuals and groups. For this reason, the charge to social researchers by critical theory is to disclose and interpret subjective discernment and to pass on intricate conclusions so that intelligent social action can be taken. Critical discourse analysis is but one means to this essential democratic need, one method to attain this democratic end.

APPENDIX A: CDA WORKSHEET

Source	Quotes/sections	CDA type / comments	Page number
Spellings Commission Report (Summary)			
NSSE 2009 Brochure			

APPENDIX B: SUGGESTED SOURCES FOR THE CDA WORKSHEET

"A Test of Leadership: Charting the Future of U.S. Higher Education," Spellings Commission Report, US Department of Education (see the summary section for analysis, 6 pages): www.ed.gov/about/bdscomm/list/hiedfuture/reports/final-report.pdf.
"National Survey of Student Engagement 2009 Invitation to Participate" (7 pages): http://nsse.iub.edu/pdf/2009_NSSE_Invitation.pdf.

APPENDIX C: SELECTED DOCUMENTS FROM NSSE

"Promoting Engagement for All Students: The Imperative to Look Within, 2008 Results," http://nsse.iub.edu/NSSE_2008_Results/docs/withhold/NSSE2008_Results_revised_11-14-2008.pdf.

"The College Student Report" (survey), http://nsse.iub.edu/pdf/US_web_09.pdf.

"Executive Snapshot 2008: NSSEville State University," http://nsse.iub.edu/NSSE_2008_Results/docs/NSSE08%20Executive%20Snapshot%20(NSSEville%20State).pdf.

"The NSSE Institute for Effective Educational Practice" (overview), http://nsse.iub.edu/pdf/2003_inst_report/NSSE_Institute.pdf.

"NSSE 2008: Exclusive Focus on Average Scores Misses the Mark when Comparing Colleges and Universities, Survey Finds" (press release), http://newsinfo.iu.edu/news/page/normal/9214.html.

SUGGESTED READINGS IN CRITICAL THEORY

Allan, E. J., Gordon, S. P., & Iverson, S. V. (2006). Re/thinking practices of power: The discursive framing of leadership in *The Chronicle of Higher Education*. *Review of Higher Education, 30*(1), 41–68.

Appiah, K. A. (1992). *In my father's house: Africa in the philosophy of culture*. New York: Oxford University Press.

Ayers, D. F. (2005). Neoliberal ideology in community college mission statements: A critical discourse analysis. *Review of Higher Education, 28*(4), 527–49.

Barthes, R. (1993). *Mythologies*. (A. Lavers, Trans.). London: Vintage.

Bhabha, H. K. (1994). *The location of culture*. London: Routledge.

Bourdieu, P. (1993). *The field of cultural production: Essays on art and literature*. Cambridge: Polity Press.

Butler, J. (1990). *Gender trouble: Feminism and the subversion of identity*. London: Routledge.

———. (2004). *Undoing gender*. New York: Routledge.

Daly, M. (1973). *Beyond God the father: Toward a philosophy of women's liberation*. Boston, MA: Beacon Press.

Derrida, J. (1973). Difference. In J. Derrida, *"Speech and phenomena" and other essays on Husserl's theory of signs* (D. B. Allison, Trans.). Evanston, IL: Northwestern University Press.

———. (1993). *Monolinguism of the other: Or, the prosthesis of origin*. Stanford, CA: Stanford University Press.

Foucault, M. (1980). *Power/knowledge: Selected interviews and other writings, 1971–1977*. New York: Pantheon.

Habermas, J. (1981). *The theory of communicative action* (Vol. 1). *Reason and the rationalization of society*. Boston, MA: Beacon Press.

Hall, D. E. (2003). *Queer theories*. Basingstoke: Palgrave.

Horkheimer, M. (1993). *Between philosophy and social science: Selected early writings*. (G. F. Hunter, M. S. Kramer, & J. Torpey, Trans.). Cambridge: Massachusetts Institute of Technology Press.

Horkheimer, M., & Adorno, T. W. (2002). *Dialectic of enlightenment: Philosophical fragments*. Stanford, CA: Stanford University Press.

Laclau, E., & Mouffe, C. (1987). *Hegemony and socialist strategy: Towards a radical democratic politics*. London: Verso.

Lévi-Strauss, C. (1963). *Structural anthropology* (C. Jacobson & B. G. Schoepf, Trans.). New York: Basic Books.

Lyotard, J.-F. (1984). *The post-modern condition: A report on knowledge*. (G. Bennington & B. Massumi, Trans.). Manchester: Manchester University Press.

Reuther, R. R. (1983). *Sexism and God-talk*. Boston, MA: Beacon Press.

Royle, N. (2003). *Jacques Derrida*. Manchester: Manchester University Press.

Said, E. (1978). *Orientalism*. New York: Vintage.

Sedgwick, E. K. (1990). *Epistemology of the closet*. Berkeley: University of California Press.

Spelman, E. (1988). *Inessential woman*. Boston, MA: Beacon Press.

Williams, P., & Chrisman, L. (Eds.). (1994). *Colonial discourse and postcolonial theory: A reader*. New York: Columbia University Press.

REFERENCES

Anyon, J. (2005). What counts as educational policy? Notes toward a new paradigm. *Harvard Educational Review, 75*(1), 65–88.

Ayers, D. F. (2005). Neoliberal ideology in community college mission statements: A critical discourse analysis. *Review of Higher Education, 28*(4), 527–49.

Bohman, J. (1999). Theories, practices, and pluralism: A pragmatic interpretation of critical social sciences. *Philosophy of the Social Sciences, 29*(4), 459–80.

Bourdieu, P. (1984). *Distinction: A social critique of the judgment of taste* (R. Nice, Trans.). London: Routledge.

———. (1993). *The field of cultural production: Essays on art and literature*. Cambridge: Polity Press.

Derrida, J. (1946/1927). *The public and its problems: An essay in political inquiry*. Chicago: Gateway Books.

———. (1973). Difference. In J. Derrida, *'Speech and phenomena' and other essays on Husserl's theory of signs* (D. B. Allison, Trans.). Evanston, IL: Northwestern University press.

Fairclough, N. (1993). Critical discourse analysis and the marketization of public discourse: The universities. *Discourse and Society, 4*(2), 133–68.

———. (1995). *Critical discourse analysis: The critical study of language*. London: Longman.

———. (2000). *Language and power* (2nd ed.). New York: Longman.

Ferguson, A. A. (2001). *Bad boys: public schools in the making of black masculinity*. Ann Arbor: University of Michigan Press.

Foucault, M. (1972). *The archaeology of knowledge* (A. Sheridan Smith, Trans.). New York: Harper and Row.

———. (1977). *Discipline and punish: The birth of the prison* (A. Sheridan, Trans.). New York: Vintage.

——. (1980). *Power/knowledge: Selected interviews and other writings, 1971–1977.* New York: Pantheon.

——. (1984). *History of sexuality* (Vol. 1). *An introduction.* (R. Hurley, Trans.). London: Penguin.

Fryer, R. G., Jr., & Torelli, P. (2005). An empirical analysis of "acting white." Working Paper 11334. Cambridge, MA: National Bureau of Economic Research.

Gee, J. P. (1990). *Social linguistics and literacies: Ideologies in discourse.* London: Falmer.

——. (2008). *What video games have to teach us about learning and literacy* (rev. ed.). Basingstoke: Palgrave Macmillan.

Habermas, J. (1981). *The theory of communicative action* (Vol. 1). *Reason and the rationalization of society.* Boston, MA: Beacon Press.

——. (1987). *The theory of communicative action* (Vol. 2). *Lifeworld and system: A critique of functionalist reason.* Boston, MA: Beacon Press.

——. (1988). *On the logic of the social sciences* (S. W. Nicholsen and J. A. Stark, Trans.). Cambridge: Massachusetts Institute of Technology Press.

Horkheimer, M. (1947). *The eclipse of reason.* New York: Continuum.

——. (1972). Traditional and critical theory. In M. Horkheimer, *Critical theory: Selected essays* (pp. 188–243). New York: Herder & Herder.

——. (1982). *Critical theory.* New York: Seabury Press.

——. (1993). *Between philosophy and social science: Selected early writings* (G. F. Hunter, M. S. Kramer, & J. Torpey, Trans.). Cambridge: Massachusetts Institute of Technology Press.

Horkheimer, M., & Adorno, T. W. (2002). *Dialectic of enlightenment: Philosophical fragments.* Stanford, CA: Stanford University Press.

Luke, A. (1995). Text and discourse in education: An introduction to critical discourse analysis. *Review of Research in Education, 21,* 3–48.

——. (1997). Theory and practice in critical discourse analysis. In L. Saha (Ed.), *International encyclopedia of the sociology of education* (pp. 60–92). New York: Pergamon.

Lyotard, J.-F. (1984). *The post-modern condition: A report on knowledge* (G. Bennington & B. Massumi, Trans.). Manchester: Manchester University Press.

Marklein, M. B. (2004, June 21). Gender neutral comes to campus. *USA Today.* Retrieved from http://usatoday30.usatoday.com/life/lifestyle/2004-06-21-lgbt-gender-neutral-housing_x.htm.

Massachusetts Institute of Technology (1999). A study on the status of women faculty in science at MIT. *MIT Faculty Newsletter, 11*(4) [online]. Retrieved from http://web.mit.edu/fnl/women/women.html.

McGregor, S. L. T. (2004). Critical discourse analysis: A primer. *KON Forum, 15*(1) [online]. Retrieved from www.kon.org/archives/forum/15-1/mcgregorcda.html.

Nussbaum, M. C. (1995). Objectification. *Philosophy and Public Affairs, 24*(4), 279–83.

Official Report of the Nineteenth Annual Conference of Charities and Correction (1973/1892). Reprinted in Pratt, R. H. (1973). The advantages of mingling Indians with whites. In *Americanizing the American Indians: Writings by the "Friends of the Indian," 1880–1900* (pp. 260–71). Cambridge, MA: Harvard University Press.

Paludi, M. A. (1996). *Sexual harassment on college campuses: Abusing the ivory power.* Albany: State University of New York Press.

Perna, L. (2001). Sex differences in faculty salaries: A cohort analysis. *Review of Higher Education, 21*(4), 315–42.

Russell, J. (2003, July 27). Finding a gender-blind dorm: Most schools lack specific housing. *Boston Globe,* C1.

Sandler, B. R., & Hall, R. (1986). *The campus climate revisited: Chilly for women faculty, administrators and graduate students.* Washington, DC: Association of American Colleges and Universities.

Saussure, F. de (1974). *Course in general linguistics* (W. Baskin, Trans.). London: Fontana.

Shaw, K. M., & Bailey T. (2007). Can access to community colleges for low-income adults be improved? Testing a model of the policy change process across six diverse states. In K. M. Shaw & D. E. Heller (Eds.), *State postsecondary education research: New methods to inform policy and practice* (pp. 37–54). Sterling, VA: Stylus.

Valencia, R., & Solorzano, D. (1998). Contemporary deficit thinking. In R. Valencia (Ed.), *The evolution of deficit thinking in educational thought and practice.* Bristol, PA: Taylor & Francis.

Wheatland, T. (2009). *The Frankfurt School in exile.* Minneapolis: University of Minneapolis Press.

Wilson, L. (1942). *Academic man.* Oxford: Oxford University Press.

Young, M. D. (1999). Multifocal educational policy research: Toward a method for enhancing traditional educational policy studies. *American Educational Research Journal, 36*(4), 677–714.

CHAPTER TWO

Sense and Sensibility

Considering the Dynamic between Scholarship and Lived Experiences

MITCHELL J. CHANG

The main thing is the YOU beneath the clothes and skin—the ability to do, the will to conquer, the determination to understand and know this great, wonderful, curious world.—*Du Bois (1903)*

In her book *Sense and Sensibility* (1811), Jane Austen's main characters, Elinor and Marianne, struggled with the tension between their logic, or common sense, and their inner feelings or sensibility. Both characters experienced great pressure to choose one over the other to guide their life decisions. The older and more prudent Elinor placed the welfare and interests of her family and friends above her own, suppressing her strong emotions. By contrast, the younger Marianne tended to be more expressive and emotional. As Austen noted, "Marianne Dashwood was born to an extraordinary fate. She was born to discover the falsehood of her own opinions, and to counteract, by her conduct, her most favorite maxims." Marianne's failings eventually led her to reject her old self and to become more like Elinor. Arguably, the lesson Austen imparted to her female contemporaries in the 1800s was that it is more prudent to choose *sense* over *sensibility*.

A similar struggle occurs among some emerging scholars, especially those from groups that have been historically excluded from fully participating in academic scholarship. These "minority" or "underrepresented" scholars often struggle in the course of their study with the tension between the common sense that governs their field, which is informed by a well-established and venerated body of scholarship, and their sensibility, which is informed by their cultural background and lived experiences. Should emerging scholars adopt Austen's lesson to resolve this tension? In other words, is it better to choose the established sense that governs one's field over the sensibility informed by one's personal development? Must sense necessarily triumph over sensibility?

This chapter explores the tension between sense and sensibility. I provide personal insights that position a critical approach to research as a way to negotiate this tension and to address inequitable social relations and actions in higher education. This chapter is written primarily for those who are still emerging as scholars, curious about employing critical research and policy analysis. It can also help more established scholars to better appreciate and support their students' critical standpoints. I argue that this tension between sense and sensibility can be an asset, and when scholars draw from it to take a critical approach, they increase their potential for providing new knowledge that extends beyond the normative models and frameworks that might limit our understanding of students, institutions, organizations, and governance as well as the policies that shape the postsecondary arena. For new knowledge to be created, however, we must first recognize and then embrace our own struggle between sense and sensibility, as it may well compel us to take a critical approach to research.

I use the term "critical approach" loosely, not in reference to particular methods, theories, or frameworks, which are addressed in other chapters in this volume. Instead I use the term in a generic way to refer to a broad set of approaches to critical research and policy analysis that critically engage scholars by enabling them both to challenge their fields' current paradigms and to be challenged by those paradigms. These systematic and rigorous approaches also make room to critically engage one's own lived experiences in research, which raises the potential for rethinking one's own perspectives, views, and a field's dominant paradigm.

Being Shaped

My struggle between sense and sensibility significantly shaped my own development in the academic profession. One of my core areas of research concerns diversity-related issues in higher education, which I approach as an extension of the broader yet unfinished civil rights agenda of the 1960s. A large portion of this work addresses claims about the educational benefits associated with attending a campus with a racially diverse student population, which was an important consideration in deciding the constitutionality of race-conscious admissions practices (see, e.g., Chang, 1999, 2013; Chang et al., 2003; Denson & Chang, 2009). In the course of study that prepared me to empirically examine diversity, I regularly experienced a disconnection between existing research and my lived experiences, creating an uneasy tension between my intellectual world and emotional self shaped by lived experiences. My struggle with this tension almost steered me away from an academic career.

But it turns out that my unique journey in life was an asset for my research. I did not appreciate this fact until I embraced the tension and adopted a critical approach to research, helping me recognize that I possessed unique expertise informed by my personal journey. My introduction to "diversity" started long ago, in 1971, when I landed at San Francisco International Airport from Taiwan when I was nearly six years old. My father, who completed an engineering degree in Missouri, sent for us (my mother, two sisters, and me) once he found a job in Silicon Valley. Three days after arriving in this new country, I started kindergarten knowing only a handful of English words. At the time, the Northern California valley was beginning to transform from a largely rural area to an urban one, eventually becoming the technological capital of the world. Developers were quickly converting farmlands into what would become suburban sprawl. After a brief residence in Santa Clara, our family settled into a new tract development on the south side of San Jose. Each week, new families moved into this neighborhood as homes were built.

Unlike older and more established neighborhoods, my childhood community was built shortly after Congress passed the federal Fair Housing Act, Title VIII of the Civil Rights Act, in April 1968, only one week after the assassination of Martin Luther King. This legislation made it unlawful to refuse to sell, rent to, or negotiate with any person because of race, color, religion, sex, or national origin. Whereas more established neighborhoods continued to practice housing discrimination through covenants, preventing families of color from purchasing homes, those bankrolling our modest, yet new, tract home development seemed unconcerned about racial exclusivity. Thus our neighborhood became a natural experiment for diversity. Instead of slowly integrating older communities, racially diverse communities in different parts of San Jose were literally being built from the ground up in the 1970s. Although I did not realize it at the time, I had the unique experience of being among the first ever to grow up in such a community.

Consider our neighbors when we moved in to our newly built home on Vistapark Drive. Next door lived an older African American couple, the Pressleys, with a grandson who regularly visited for long weekends and played with me and other neighborhood kids. He told us that his family came from the East Coast and that his father had once played for my favorite basketball team at the time, the Harlem Globetrotters. Next door to the Pressleys lived a Mexican American family, the Alvarez family, who had a son I did not know because he was about ten years older. But, like me, he would later earn a doctorate degree in education. To the other side of us lived an older white couple, the Hildebrands, who owned an auto body shop, and next to them was another Asian family, the Kongs, who were third-generation Chinese Americans. Mr. Kong worked as a butcher at a local supermarket and would pass on to his son, who was a regular childhood playmate of mine, a love for fishing. Several houses down from them lived a family who were recent immigrants from Denmark, with a boy who would also occasionally play with us and spoke with an accent different from mine. This racial mixing was repeated throughout the block.

To accommodate our growing neighborhood, brand-new schools were built at the elementary, middle, and high school levels. Exposure to diversity was an inescapable reality in this community. The school cafeteria, for example, served enchiladas and tacos, prompting me to come home one day and ask my mother to replicate those meals that were considered my favorite "American food." In turn, my mother cooked fried rice or chow mein for my Cub Scout potlucks, which were always well received, and even introduced the group to sushi, which was not as well received. For this newly formed Cub Scout "pack," Admiral Johnston, an active commanding naval officer, served as the scout master. My close childhood friends included Silvano Bernardi, whose parents were recent Italian immigrants, and Doug Tatsui, whose US-born parents were forced by their own government to spend part of their childhood during WWII in an internment camp in Topaz, Utah. To me, they were all Americans with roots in the national fabric, and I was the curious Taiwanese kid with the funny accent and cultural practices. Our family tried earnestly to "fit in" without knowing exactly what we were trying to fit into, given the unique composition of our developing community.

But such diversity, created almost overnight, also gave rise to thorny challenges that are still being studied by researchers and were certainly not well understood at the time. Certain encounters would prompt some residents to withdraw from, or leave altogether, the community. One day our next-door neighbor Mr. Hildebrand, for example, got into an argument with a relative of the Kongs' who regularly visited them. Mr. Hildebrand told this American-born visitor to go back to China, after explicitly referring to his Asian features in unflattering ways. In another incident, Mrs. Pressley, our African American neighbor, sat on her porch one winter Saturday afternoon holding her garden hose and proceeded to spray down neighborhood kids as they rode by on their bikes. The parents and their children used racial epithets to refer to her while condemning this inexplicable behavior. We later learned that she had been grieving over a family member who had recently passed away. Both Mr. Hildebrand and Mrs. Pressley moved out of the neighborhood before I started high school. While those specific encounters might not have led to their decision to move, they still stand out in my memory. Needless to say, I too was a target of racial antipathy, and there are too many incidents to recount here. Oddly, the most hurtful ones were not inflicted by strangers but by my friends. Yet we somehow managed to remain friends despite those incidents, some of which turned into physical altercations. Likewise, I engaged in racial antipathy, employing negative stereotypes and racial slurs in my everyday actions. So, despite the diversity, we could not escape the broader context of overt societal racism and did not always get along.

I experienced other collateral damage while growing up during that historical moment and in that neighborhood. In my determination to fit in, I stopped speaking my native language and can now hardly communicate with my relatives when I travel back to my birth country. My family hid our "un-American" ways and only privately practiced our cultural heritage, which slowly washed away. By the time I became a teenager, we had already paid a heavy price to become "Americans." I subsequently came to resent immigrants of all stripes who were unwilling to pay the same price and actively cleanse themselves of their "foreign" ways. I especially resented those who openly practiced and celebrated their heritage, which in my adolescent mind undermined my own chances of ever fitting in. Curiously, anti-immigrant organizations such as James Gilchrist's *Minutemen Project* would have appealed to me as a teenager, even though, ironically, I would have been a target of those organizations' scorn.

When I left San Jose to attend college, my childhood experiences provided a backdrop to gauge what I would be learning, although the interpretations of community shaped in my formative years left me with a naïve set of assumptions. In other words, I was equipped with a set of unique experiences to help confirm or disconfirm what I was learning, and I was prepared to confirm or disconfirm my beliefs on the basis of what I learned. I would later discover that the experiences and perspectives associated with having lived through a natural residential integration experiment were highly unusual. After all, the community that shaped them was made possible by the Fair Housing Act, which was signed just three years before my family moved into that development. I was therefore among the first to test the modern-day benefits and challenges of growing up in a racially diverse community. This world was still unfamiliar to most scholars at the time, who generally grew up amidst de facto racial segregation. Yet these scholars established the bases for understanding racial diversity in their fields and legitimized their fields' problems and methods. Because the world in which I grew up was qualitatively different from the world most scholars knew, studied, and documented, critical frameworks allowed me first to interpret my own world, and then to help others understand it.

Shaping

I share my own narrative to point out the importance of recognizing what our past personal journey might bring to our professional development, which other researchers have addressed well (see, e.g., Delgado & Stefancic, 2001; Magolda, 2004). That body of work makes clear that scholars' unique backgrounds provide them with a special set of tools to engage with their studies. For those backgrounds that are underrepresented in a particular field of study, the experiences can be an even more valuable asset. My academic studies both informed my early development and also bumped up against it. When the latter occurred, it heightened the pressure to choose between *sense* and *sensibility* as the tension between the two mounted. Rather than choose one over the other, as Austen's characters had done, I embraced this tension by applying a critical approach to inquiry.

It is well known in the study of higher education that going to college can be a life-changing experience. With respect to how I engaged with my background, leaving my hometown to attend college had two especially profound effects. First, being exposed to a wider range of backgrounds and viewpoints through my coursework and interactions with peers significantly challenged my worldview, especially concerning race and ethnicity. I changed my perspectives about immigrants and immigration, for example, and became more aware of the limitations of assimilation. My coursework and my peers also helped me to better appreciate my unique upbringing, as most of my classmates had been raised in racially segregated environments, some interacting meaningfully with Asians for the first time while in college.

Even though the acquisition of knowledge was helping me reinterpret my development, the bulk of assigned academic materials did not fully explain my childhood experiences or the context that shaped them. I had taken sociology and psychology courses that addressed immigration, integration, and policy intervention, for example, but the research that informed those topics seemed to depict a world different from the one that I knew while growing up. My sense and sensibility, however, became less disconnected after taking a couple of Asian American studies courses. The scholarship presented in those courses not only challenged what I had learned, but also further clarified some of my developmental experiences and the community that shaped them. Although the class materials were not presented to me as having a critical approach, what I digested helped me critique both what I was learning and my lived experiences. This type of scholarship resonated with me because, unlike what I picked up in some of my other courses, it helped me make sense of my realities and what I was learning.

After seeing the world in this way, I had great difficulty embracing my first graduate studies program. It was a traditional psychology program with a heavy emphasis on behaviorism and experimental methods. I was learning to place individuals into discreet categories in order to generalize lived experiences. I was, as Thomas Kuhn described it in his classic book *The Structure of Scientific Revolutions* (1970), learning the "rules and assumptions" of this scientific paradigm and proceeding through a "process of professional initiation" (p. 47). According to Kuhn, the existence of the paradigm requires a "strong network of commitments-conceptual, theoretical, instrumental, and methodological," which "provides rules that tell the practitioner of a mature specialty what both the world and his science are like" (p. 42) and "sets the problem to be solved" (p. 27). I soon learned that the world of this scientific paradigm did not resonate with my lived experiences and there was little room to address this contradiction, as the paradigm did not recognize such anomalies as a priority. In order to succeed in this program, I would have to resolve this contradiction by choosing sense over sensibility. W. E. B. Du Bois famously described a similar personal struggle in his classic book *The Souls of Black Folk* (1903): "One ever feels his twoness—an American, a Negro; two souls, two thoughts, two unreconciled strivings; two warring ideals in one dark body, whose strength alone keeps it from being torn asunder." Having been exposed to other possibilities during my undergraduate studies, choosing one soul over the other was simply not a satisfying solution for me, so I considered abandoning my studies altogether. Fortunately, I was urged to explore other options and found another psychology program with a different orientation. Unlike my first graduate program, this one was situated in a school of education. It took a critical approach and did not divorce the researcher's own background from academic inquiry.

In this new graduate program, I took a course with Carol Gilligan and was exposed to one example of this critical approach. In it, I read her groundbreaking book on moral development, *In a Different Voice* (1982), whereby she challenged a body of research in developmental psychology that held that girls on average reached a lower level of moral development than boys. This well-established view in her field, Gilligan told us in class, conflicted with her own experiences and worldview. She discovered that one problem with this body of research was that the standards for determining the levels of moral reasoning privileged a principled way of reasoning that is more common among boys. Her research showed that when it came to moral reasoning, girls tended to focus more on relations, which was considered a lower form of development. The privileging of a form of reasoning more common among boys, she argued, was based largely on the exclusion of girls from the research that animated the levels of moral development.

Gilligan's willingness to challenge the assumption that girls are morally inferior to boys, which conflicted with her own sensibility, enabled her to advance both the research in her own field and her position as a woman. In other words, she did not just adopt the demeaning common sense that guided her discipline, which contradicted her own lived experiences and views, but instead critically approached this tension between existing scholarship and self, subsequently improving the life circumstances of those negatively stigmatized by a dominant paradigm in her discipline.

This dynamic between self and one's field appealed to me because what I was learning in graduate school was helping me rethink my own perspectives and challenge existing knowledge informed by my lived experiences. As James Joyce wrote in *A Portrait of the Artist as a Young Man* (1916), "This race and this country and this life produced me . . . I shall express myself as I am." By making room for my classmates and me to place our lives within the academic discourse and to critique it, inquiry that embraced a critical approach also allowed us to develop a greater appreciation for different experiences. My diverse group of classmates expressed themselves through lived experiences, which made even clearer the limitations of the academic literature, especially certain widely documented educational realities. I subsequently became more concerned with the educational inequities and racial divides that shaped the experiences and perspectives of my classmates.

The greater premium that I was starting to place on experiences—and my growing interest in educational disparities informed by taking a critical approach— steered me out of graduate school and into the workforce. There I spent two years getting a firsthand look at the challenges facing schools. My work in the schools raised more questions than answers, so I returned to graduate school armed with new insights based on those experiences. This time around, I was even better prepared to take a critical approach in conducting education research. Working in the schools was indeed valuable, but when I began my dissertation, I found myself returning to those childhood experiences living on Vistapark Drive.

During the course of my studies in the early 1990s, one highly controversial issue in higher education concerned the application of race-conscious admissions. At the time, a court case challenging this practice at the University of Texas at Austin (*Hopwood v. Texas*, 1996) appeared to be headed for the US Supreme Court. As I studied the arguments concerning affirmative action in general and race-conscious admissions practices in particular, I came across a discourse that had significantly guided how the concept of diversity is understood in the current social and political context. This discourse, which is often referred to as the "diversity rationale" (see Moses & Chang, 2006), had played a central role in the defense of race-conscious admissions practices. Given my racial minority and immigrant background, diversity has always been a way of life, so it struck me as odd that it would serve as a legal argument—and, subsequently, that it needed to be defended—which further drew me into this area of research.

The diversity rationale has had a unique course of development in Supreme Court deliberations. Judicial recognition of diversity as a compelling state interest is often attributed to former Justice Lewis Powell, but Goodwin Liu (1998) argued that the Supreme Court recognized the educational value of racial diversity even before the landmark 1954 *Brown v. Board of Education of Topeka, Kansas*, decision. In any case, Powell's opinion came to play a critical and arguably determining role in the case of *Regents of the University of California v. Bakke* (1978), which is widely regarded as the cornerstone of the affirmative action debate. In his opinion, Powell wrote in support of the broad-based interest in pursuing the educational benefits that flow from a racially diverse student body and considered it to be a constitutionally permissible goal for an institution of higher education. Explaining the decision, Powell stated that the First Amendment allows a university the freedom to make its own judgments about education, which includes the selection of its student body. He argued that the attainment of a diverse student body broadens the range of viewpoints held collectively by those students and subsequently allows a university to provide an atmosphere that is "conducive to speculation, experiment and creation—so essential to the quality of higher education." This type of atmosphere, he believed, enhances the training of the student body and better equips the institution's graduates. Because such goals are essential to the nation's future and are protected under the First Amendment, Justice Powell concluded that race-conscious admissions practices, when narrowly tailored, serve a compelling educational interest (see *Regents of the University of California v. Bakke*, 1978).

According to Justice Powell's reasoning, those educational benefits are products of an intellectual atmosphere that is enhanced by racial diversity. Powell claimed that bringing together racially diverse students broadens the range of experiences, outlooks, and ideas of the student body. A diverse student body, he believed, is conducive to speculation, experimenting, and creativity and can thus enhance the education of students and better equip the institution's graduates. But the Fifth District Court of Appeals rejected Powell's argument in its 1996 *Hopwood v. Texas* ruling, in part because it charged that the "use of race, in and of itself, to choose students simply achieves a student body that looks different" and thus "is no more rational on its own terms" than considering "the physical size or blood type of applicants" (*Regents of the University of California v. Bakke*, 1978). Likewise, Judge B. Avant Edenfield of the District Court of the Southern District of Georgia noted in his *Tracy v. Board of Regents of the University of Georgia* (1999) decision that there is no reliable evidence that "an increase in racial diversity . . . leads to a more diverse collection of thoughts, ideas and opinions on campus."

Given my background, I was quite drawn intellectually, politically, and experientially to this controversy. When I conducted the literature review for my dissertation—*Racial Diversity in Higher Education: Does a Racially Mixed Student Population Affect Educational Outcomes?* (Chang, 1996)—there was a dearth of empirical research that addressed the two competing claims. Curiously, neither set of claims was satisfying to me (see my critiques, e.g., Chang, 2002, 2005; Chang & Ledesma, 2011). Neither one fully reflected nor adequately explained my own lived experiences, with the many facets and nuances presented by growing up in diverse communities and interacting with a range of people of different racial backgrounds. Clearly, I possessed important knowledge informed by my unique background. Rejecting those possessions would have weakened—not strengthened—my capacity to address this important issue. Taking on the educational potential of diversity with a critical approach enabled me to mediate established scholarship and my own lived experiences, which subsequently provided the foundation for a long-term research agenda. My scholarly work and its capacity to make an impact would certainly not look the same had I not adopted a critical approach. I will examine further in the next section how both scholarly careers and an entire field might look different today in the absence of a critical approach.

Taking Flight

As James Joyce so eloquently said in *A Portrait of the Artist as a Young Man* (1916), "When a man is born . . . there are nets flung at it to hold it back from flight. You talk to me of nationality, language, religion. I shall try to fly by those nets." Likewise, when students begin their academic journey, most of them earnestly try to absorb the knowledge and ways of knowing that their professors metaphorically fling at them. Further applying Joyce's metaphor, the widely regarded knowledge of a discipline or field of study that students are expected to master can end up serving as "nets." When emerging scholars are further expected only to "fly by those nets," might this exact certain personal and societal costs? Rejecting *sensibility* and choosing *sense* by metaphorically choosing to fly within the nets can potentially prevent a scholar from taking flight or from making significant contributions to a field specifically and to human understanding generally. Taking a critical approach mediates the tension between sense and sensibility, providing scholars with greater intellectual freedom.

According to Thomas Kuhn, academics regularly get trapped in their field's dominant paradigm, which can lead them to overlook anomalies in the real world that are not well explained by, or contradict, that rigidly held paradigm. Such narrowness of focus limits what C. Wright Mills (1959) called a "sociological imagination." For Mills, this type of imagination seeks to develop "lucid summations of what is going on in the world and of what may be happening within [our]selves," which in turn assist in combating "contemporary uneasiness and indifference" and increase "involvement with public issues." According to Mills, the sociological imagination has the quality to "grasp the interplay of man and society, of biography and history, of self and world," and to advance the lesson that one "can know his own chances in life" only by becoming aware of the circumstances of all individuals. My upbringing in San Jose, for example, has in part shaped my sociological imagination, providing me with unique insights into diversity and a distinctive capacity to facilitate social interactions across racial and ethnic differences. This imagination inspired a different sense of what is going on in the world, which enabled me to better grasp a wider range of possibilities for addressing public issues concerning diversity. Such reimagination in academe, however, typically begins as an anomaly that conflicts with established summations of the world and is often rejected prematurely without undergoing more rigorous testing.

Rather than seriously consider those anomalies, Kuhn argued that scholars have a tendency to grip too tightly to a paradigm that subsequently constrains their imagination and estranges them from the important happenings of the real world. Stephen Steinberg in his book *Race Relations: A Critique* (2007), for example, pointed to a case of what he called an "epistemology of ignorance" and failure of imagination in the social sciences. Steinberg recounted Everett Hughes's presidential address at the 1963 meeting of the American Sociological Association, which occurred on the same day as the historic March on Washington, the largest civil rights demonstration in the nation's history. According to Steinberg, Hughes issued a public confession of intellectual failure—indeed a failure of his discipline to anticipate the civil rights revolution. As strange as it may sound, the so-called giants of sociology overlooked this broader movement, and certainly did not expect it to change the course of history. In his presidential speech, Hughes asked, "did social scientists—and sociologists in particular—not foresee the explosion of collective action?"

Why did sociology suffer such a major intellectual failure? According to Steinberg, the sociological enterprise became too insulated from what was really happening in society. In other words, they were blind to this collective movement because they became trapped in their own tightly woven net and subsequently became too removed from the shifts taking place outside their overly intellectualized world. Steinberg noted that the field was being directed largely from the vantage point of elite institutions of higher learning, with researchers engaged in collecting narrow and limited "bundles of fact applied to small hypotheses." By contrast, the civil rights movement was widespread and more bottom–up than top–down, challenging powerful institutions including universities. Steinberg also added that his field's "narrow empiricism" became "stubbornly detached," "remote," geared toward seeing the "world wrongly," and created an "epistemology of ignorance" and failure of imagination. According to Steinberg, sociology in the late 1950s through mid-1960s was "part of the problem and not part of the solution."

In addition to societal costs, there are personal costs to consider when it comes to choosing sense and rejecting one's sensibilities. By making such a choice, sense does not necessarily triumph over sensibility, but may instead contribute to a chronic psychological duality that fuels a restlessness of the conscience. W. E. B. Du Bois described this duality and uneasiness in *The Souls of Black Folk* (1903) as a "longing to attain self-conscious manhood, to merge his double self into a better and truer self. In this merging he wishes neither of the older selves to be lost . . . He simply wishes to make it possible for a man to be both a Negro and an American."

How can scholars reduce the risk of becoming estranged from themselves and the world they seek to document, explain, and advance? As my own story suggests, adopting a critical approach may enable a better balance of sense and sensibility, allowing for mediation of the dynamic tension between scholarship and self. On one hand, taking a critical approach enabled me to apply my life journey as an intellectual asset to make sense of academic knowledge and, subsequently, to address a knowledge base that did not align with my lived experiences. On the other hand, this approach also exposed me to alternative explanations that operated at the margins rather than at the core of a field, which challenged my own assumptions and worldviews. In the classroom, instructors who embraced critical inquiry broadened the range of perspectives and opinions, which were enhanced by the diversity of students' lived experiences. Critically engaging with the diversity of ideas and worldviews then contributed to a conscientiousness that made me less likely to overstate my own positions or to become too self-involved in ways that could potentially ignore and even oppress other realities.

Conclusion

In thinking about how to do critical research, perhaps one of the first steps is to examine closely one's own personal journey. By doing so, we develop a better sense of why we are drawn to taking a critical approach. Such an approach can reconcile a scholar's developmental and philosophical discords, mediating the tension between scholarship and self. By reflecting on my own personal journey, I also developed a stronger appreciation for my life experiences. Adopting a critical approach enabled me to apply those experiences in my scholarship, shaping my interpretation of the existing knowledge base and vision of higher education.

Before adopting a critical approach, however, it is important to understand that this approach carries certain personal and professional risks. For example, it requires asking difficult questions that challenge deeply held beliefs and conventions, which can rub up against the ways in which an academic program approaches education and the manner in which a discipline or field of study produces knowledge. Likewise, a critical approach forces scholars to refrain from holding tightly onto their own practices, perspectives, and worldviews, because it encourages others to critique them and offer stronger counterpositions that can unsettle what we know. Even as critical scholars become more aware of and engaged with the interplay between biography and history, we can never become fully sure of or overly confident about ourselves or our fields. For us, what is familiar can quickly become strange. So the risk of becoming unsettled should be considered when adopting a critical approach, especially for emerging scholars who may well have more at stake when they take on such risks.

Even with those and other personal risks associated with adopting a critical approach, for some scholars, taking another path is simply not a viable option. The disconnection between one's lived experiences and a knowledge base that fails to document and explain important realities fuels an intense and potentially debilitating tension that can estrange us from both ourselves and our research. This uneasiness will compel some of us out of anonymity as we exercise self-knowledge to bring attention to overlooked problems and communities, transforming the unfamiliar into the core concerns of the field and policy priorities. Yet, by amplifying a scholar's voice in a way that better balances self and scholarship, a critical approach also prevents us from becoming too self-interested and self-involved, ensuring that the center or core of our field of study remains a moving target guided by active scholarship that operates on the margins.

While applying a critical approach to one's studies may not be appropriate for every scholar, it has certainly served me well. My perspectives and research continue to be shaped by those who occupy common intellectual and physical space but who also arrived there from different paths or who often orbit multiple spaces. Such dynamic engagement and exposure, mediated through a critical approach, raise the probability that the study of higher education will remain relevant. It may also better link scholarship to what is actually going on in the world, as C. Wright Mills hoped, in a way that will increase public involvement in contemporary issues. Although Jane Austen's lesson to choose *sense* over *sensibility* may have been appropriate for her female contemporaries in the 1800s, adopting that lesson today can hold back a scholar and a field of study from taking flight.

REFERENCES

Austen, J. (1811). *Sense and sensibility.* London: Thomas Egerton.

Chang, M. J. (1996). *Racial diversity in higher education: Does a racially mixed student population affect educational outcomes?* (Unpublished doctoral dissertation). University of California, Los Angeles.

———. (1999). Does racial diversity matter? The educational impact of a racially diverse undergraduate population. *Journal of College Student Development, 40*(4), 377–95.

———. (2002). Preservation or transformation: Where's the real educational discourse on diversity? *Review of Higher Education, 25*(2), 125–40.

———. (2005). Reconsidering the diversity rationale. *Liberal Education, 91*(1), 6–13.

———. (2013). Post-*Fisher*: The unfinished research agenda on student diversity in higher education. *Educational Researcher, 42*(3), 172–73.

Chang, M. J., & Ledesma, M. C. (2011). The diversity rationale: Its limitations for educational practice. In L. M. Stulberg & S. L. Weinberg (Eds.), *Diversity in higher education: Toward a more comprehensive approach* (pp. 74–85). New York: Routledge.

Chang, M. J., Witt, D., Jones, J., & Hakuta, K. (Eds.). (2003). *Compelling interest: Examining the evidence on racial dynamics in colleges and universities.* Stanford, CA: Stanford University Press.

Delgado, R., & Stefancic, J. (2001). *Critical race theory: An introduction.* New York: New York University Press.

Denson, N., & Chang, M. J. (2009). Racial diversity matters: The impact of diversity-related student engagement and institutional context. *American Educational Research Journal, 46*(2), 322–53.

Du Bois, W. E. B. (1903). *The souls of black folk: Essays and sketches.* Chicago: A. C. McClurg.

Gilligan, C. (1982). *In a different voice.* Cambridge, MA: Harvard University Press.

Hopwood v. Texas, 78 F. 3d 932 (5th Cir. 1996).

Joyce, J. (1916) *A portrait of the artist as a young man.* New York: Viking.

Kuhn, T. S. (1970). *The structure of scientific revolutions.* Chicago: Chicago University Press.

Liu, G. (1998). Affirmative action in higher education: The diversity rationale and the compelling interest test. *Harvard Civil Rights-Civil Liberties Law Review, 33,* 381–442.

Magolda, M. B. (2004). *Making their own way.* Sterling, VA: Stylus.

Mills, C. W. (1959). *Sociological imagination.* New York: Oxford University Press.

Moses, M. S., & Chang, M. J. (2006). Toward a deeper understanding of the diversity rationale. *Educational Researcher, 35*(1), 6–11.

Regents of the University of California v. Bakke, 438 U.S. 265 (1978).

Steinberg, S. (2007). *Race relations: A critique.* Stanford, CA: Stanford University Press.

Tracy v. Board of Regents of the University of Georgia, 59 F. Supp. 2d 1314 (S.D. Ga. 1999).

CHAPTER THREE

A Critical Approach to Power in Higher Education

BRIAN PUSSER

To have spent time in a particular natural spot—a wilderness, forested park, or open space preserve—to return to it repeatedly or to grow up in such a place, is to think that you know it. By "know" the place, I mean that in your mind you can see the contour of the land, the fullness of the trees, random patterns of leaves on the ground, the texture of lichen on the rocks, the thickness of the underbrush, the color of the sky, what awaits around each bend and over the next hill. If you know the place well, you can conjure images, the quality of the light, the way heat rises from the ground, the sound of the wind soughing in the trees. There are occasionally sensations, aromas, colors, images in your daily life that, wherever you are, will take you to the place you think you know, reinforcing an innate certainty of what it means to be in that place, even when you are far away.

Yet, at some point in time, a fire may burn through one of those sites in nature you know well. If you go there a season or two afterward, you will arrive as a virtual stranger to that place. You may be astonished by how much has changed by the effects of fire, which reduces trees to ash, turns underbrush to dust, and destroys native and invasive species alike. You may also be taken aback by what grows in place of what was there before the conflagration. The bushes and ferns, grasses and nascent trees that begin anew will have a different character, as another landscape emerges, one shaped by a different mix of elemental forces. Where tall trees had shaded the world below, sunlight illuminates, initially nurturing a less vertical flora, one more contoured to the revealed landscape. Not only the amount of light but also its power to illuminate will have changed, as will the strength of the wind that reaches you. In the absence of trees, the sounds the wind makes will be equally transformed.

Upon reflection, what will become clear is that you did not know "the place" so much as you had become accustomed to, and knowledgeable of, "a place"—a place that was the representation of a moment of time, an instant in the cycle of growth, destruction, and renewal. To have placed a definitive claim upon knowing it, or to have taken for granted that it was an immutable landscape, may have been soothing, perhaps even essential, to one's sense of self, but that solace is revealed as a personal construct, an imposed norm that has little to do with the forces of nature and a place on the earth.

Any individual's construction of a place, or the socially constructed version, is just that. It may not be a better or worse place than the one that exists just before or after a moment of transformative illumination. A wildfire, though often a tragic event, does not destroy *the* landscape. Rather, it transforms *a* landscape, altering much that stood in its path and any preconceptions about what was right and permanent in that place. So too do powerful norms of understanding shape the landscape of higher education and the majority of the research that seeks to understand it. What those received constructs lack in attention to power they make up for with a powerful certainty, which in its own right exerts a hegemonic force— the privileging of the status quo.

In this chapter, I use critical theory to argue that our intellectual and conceptual landscapes, the powerful forces that govern postsecondary policy making, and institutional practices in the twenty-first century are received constructions that define the terrains of knowing and inquiry and constitute the dominant norms at a moment in time. More precisely, I use a model of power to understand how these norms come into being, how deeply ingrained they are in our consciousness, and how difficult it is to understand them in the absence of a transformative moment. While there is considerable work on structuralist and poststructuralist approaches to the relationship between language and voice in higher education (cf. chap. 10 by Amy Scott Metcalfe, this volume), surprisingly little work has been done on the ways in which the construction of discourse and the marginalization of voice shape relations of power—and the resultant policies—in higher education (Pusser, 2004). This is a specific aspect of a more general concern that persists today, as it has throughout the history of postsecondary research: we have yet to define and instantiate a theoretical framework for understanding power through critical policy analysis in higher education.

Research on Power in Higher Education

Power has long been an essential topic in the social sciences (Dahl, 1961; Mills, 1956; Weber, 1947), and it has also been a significant concern of critical scholars (Bordieu & Passeron, 1977; Foucault, 1977; Lukes, 1974, 2005). Despite the deep and rich historical attention to power in other fields, scholars of higher education have noted the relative absence of power as a conceptual and theoretical tool in this domain (Parsons, 1997; Pusser & Marginson, 2012; Slaughter, 1990).

While researchers have turned their attention to particular policies or practices in higher education that are shaped by powerful interests and institutions—including selective admissions (Karabel, 2005), the creation and transfer of capital through university activities (Slaughter, 1990; Slaughter & Leslie, 1997; Slaughter & Rhoades, 2004), the gendered nature of institutions (Metcalfe & Slaughter, 2011), student departure (Tierney, 2000), contested governance (Pusser, 2004), the construction of prestige hierarchies (Marginson, 2007a), and the ways in which feminist poststructural perspectives deconstruct understandings of power (Allan, Iverson, & Ropers-Huilman, 2010)—little attention has been paid to applying critical theoretical models of power itself to understanding higher education. In part, this lack stems from a dearth of critical work on the central purposes of postsecondary institutions in the United States. While an important arena of scholarship in the social sciences has been devoted to critiques of key areas of the social and political economy (Bourdieu, 1984; Foucault, 1980; Freire, 1985; Rawls, 1971), the literature on central areas in which power is exercised in higher education—governance, policy making, and resource allocation—emerged largely from functionalist approaches to authority relations as a process of institutional interest articulation (Baldridge, 1971; Kerr, 1963).

In the scholarship of higher education, the turn away from functionalist accounts began in earnest with the introduction of State[1] theoretical approaches to higher education (Clark, 1983; Rhoades, 1992; Slaughter, 1990). More recently, scholars have turned attention to universities as political institutions of the State, and as both sites of contest and instruments in larger political contests (Carnoy & Levin, 1985; Pusser, 2008; Rodriguez Gomez & Ordorika, 2011), as well as to the role of the State in the production of local, national, and global public goods through higher education (Marginson, 2007b; Slaughter & Leslie, 1997; Slaughter & Rhoades, 2004). Postsecondary research using feminist theory, particularly feminist poststructuralism, has created new conceptual models for analyzing identity, the relationship of discourse to power and resistance, and subjectivity (Allan et al., 2010). The work of Foucault (1977, 1980), particularly the analysis of discourse and power, has also been key in expanding the understanding of power as an analytical concept (Iverson, 2010) and as a force in higher education (Suspitsyna, 2010).

This chapter locates colleges and universities—particularly public ones and to a lesser (but important) degree private ones—as politically constituted institutions of the State. Because the study of power is central to the study of political institutions (Dahl, 1961; Weber, 1947), the study of power in higher education should address the role of colleges and universities as political institutions of the State (Ordorika & Pusser, 2007; Pusser, 2008). Treating universities as political institutions and sites of the exercise of power has not been the historically dominant approach, as education in general and higher education institutions in particular have been traditionally studied using models of public administration and institutional theory rather than inherently political ones (Moe, 1996). Here I use Steven Lukes's three-dimensional model of power as a lens for examining the ways in which power shapes norms of analysis in the research and scholarship of higher education, and the role of critical perspectives in reevaluating those norms.

Critical Theory and Lukes's Critique of Power

Steven Lukes (1974, 2005) presents a three-dimensional analysis of power that offers great utility for critical research in higher education (Pusser & Marginson, 2013). The three-dimensional approach to power challenges norms, questions the legitimacy of the dominant discourses of politics and policy, and calls for new imaginaries of the structures and practices of power. Ana M. Martínez-Alemán (chap. 1, this volume) argues that, for nearly three decades, critical theory "has centered on two intricately related dimensions: (1) the analysis of how our realities are arranged and systematized by and through language and (2) semiotics studies." In his critique of power, Lukes focuses primarily on the first of these two frames. This approach embodies an analysis of language that Martínez-Alemán (chap. 1, this volume) presents through the words of Foucault, "a critical view of language as a historically situated structure through which subjectivity is constituted." As Lukes (2005) noted in the original articulation of his model, the three-dimensional approach to power raises questions concerning "the limits or bias of pluralism, about false consciousness and about real interests" (p. 14). Put simply, the first dimension of the model is focused on how we understand observed conflict in the exercise of power through decision-making contests. The second dimension turns attention to the ways in which power is used to shape the context and terms of debate in contests, while the third dimension presents the challenge of imagining a different world in a conceptual universe so constructed and dominated by powerful interests that conflict and contest over many issues are essentially unfathomable.

A One-Dimensional View of Power

Lukes argues that much of the contemporary work on power in political science stems from an instrumental view based on the work of Weber (1947) and Dahl

(1961) that is founded on the belief that power is best understood through the analysis of its exercise in observable conflict between identifiable interests that in turn reflect the decision-making behaviors of legitimate interests in a system, as defined by dominant formations within that system. The instrumental view is central to pluralist models of political decision making. As Cooper, Cibulka, and Fusarelli (2008) present it, "The pluralist perspective tends to define power as an exchange of desired goods among political actors. It emphasizes the role of contradictions, bargaining and compromises among competing interests who work within the existing institutional roles and structures, such as school boards, state legislatures, Congress and executive agencies" (p. 193).

In a pluralist model, it is generally accepted that interest groups have access to decision-making contests and they make their preferences known. As Lukes (2005) notes, "the pluralists assume that *interests*[2] are to be understood as policy preferences—so that a conflict of interests is equivalent to a conflict of preferences. They are opposed to any suggestion that interests might be unarticulated or unobservable, and above all, to the idea that people might actually be mistaken about, or unaware of, their own interests" (p. 19). Lukes's second dimension of power can be used to challenge the notion that all interests are expressed in a pluralist model.

A Second Dimension of Power

Understanding power also calls for a deeper analysis of observable conflict, one that considers the ways in which political contests are framed through the reliance on norms—particularly norms of discourse—that shape what counts as legitimate contest. The two-dimensional view, which draws upon the work of Bachrach and Baratz (1970), moves beyond the pluralist understanding of power by suggesting that the perceived interests in observable political conflicts are a construct. That is, power is deeply shaped by the process of constructing normative understandings of contest in ways that favor certain interests over others. Their explanation of how those constructs are created draws upon the work of E. E. Schattschneider (1960), who argued that "all forms of political organization have a bias in favor of the exploitation of some kinds of conflict and the suppression of others because *organization is the mobilization of bias.* Some issues are organized into politics, while others are organized out" (Bachrach & Baratz, 1970, p. 8).

As one example of the gradual mobilization of bias in a key policy contest, consider the conflict over admission to selective public colleges and universities in the United States. Over the past four decades, state flagship and other elite public universities have become increasingly selective (Bowen, Chingos, & McPherson,

2009). As a result, particularly at the most selective public institutions, considerable attention has turned to the factors that are used in determining whether to admit or reject an application (Karabel, 2005; Lemann, 2000). Both the legality of certain criteria—such as race, gender or legacy status—and the weighting of those criteria in the admission process have been challenged and contested within institutions, legislatures, and the courts. It is worth noting that the degree of competitiveness in the admissions process varies widely. From a one-dimensional perspective, the interests that compete over admissions policy are relatively easily understood as those who support various admissions policies and those who oppose them (Golden, 2006). Likewise, the terrain of contest is understood as access to highly selective universities. From a pluralist perspective, the outcomes of these contests reflect the observed will of a political majority as expressed through ballot initiatives, appointments to governing boards made by governors and legislators, a continuum of legal precedents, or the path dependence of institutional policies.

A two-dimensional analysis challenges the simplicity of this model of contest, suggesting that while pluralist political action has altered the nature of the selective admissions process (Pusser, 2004), the essential rationale for a selective admissions process itself is rarely challenged. In other words, over time the higher education policy community has come to accept selective admissions as a fait accompli. While policies for increasing access through alternative avenues (such as percentage plans) have emerged (Horn & Flores, 2003), these policies do not constitute challenges to the fundamental questions of who should have access to elite public institutions and why. We take for granted that we must have selective admissions in our most prestigious public higher education institutions. This is so, even though such selective and elite public institutions are rare in other spheres of American society, and given that an extremely selective public university admissions process is a relatively new construct that has gathered force in many public universities only over the last half century (Lemann, 2000). The taken-for-granted status of the need for selective admission in public universities is all the more surprising given that there are alternatives, including one that has been implemented to powerful effect in the past: meeting demand through creating new, well-resourced, and highly effective public universities. One of the nation's premier systems of public research universities, the University of California (UC) system, established three such campuses—UC San Diego, UC Irvine, and UC Santa Cruz—in just over a decade in the 1960s (Douglass, 2000; Pelfrey, 2004) and opened UC Merced in 2005. More recently, such a commitment to building capacity in the selective public postsecondary system has become so separated from political discourse in the United States that it practically qualifies as a thought experiment. Yet, from a two-dimensional perspective on power, one could argue that the decline of a comprehensive project to increase capacity predicated on public funding is itself the product of a series of political, ideological, and interest-group efforts, not an immutable law of politics or nature. As such, the resistance to providing state or federal funding to increase the capacity of elite public institutions, and the concurrent contest over admissions, can be understood as a result of the mobilization of bias in favor of neoliberal approaches to the finance and governance of public institutions that conceptualize individuals, not the public, as being responsible for financing postsecondary educations (Pusser, 2011).

That dominant interests shape the scope of contest and decision making by defining the terrain of contest and by determining what is a legitimate matter is a central tenet of the exercise of power. With regard to college access, a number of scholars have noted that the limited capacity of highly selective public institutions creates a zero-sum competition for admissions slots that has become increasingly tilted in favor of those in higher-income brackets (Astin & Oseguera, 2004). While constraints on access to elite public institutions may not be sustainable in the long term, powerful formations are slow to change. Lukes (2005) suggests that the mobilization of discourse may be so profound that the dominant interests themselves do not see alternatives. He notes, "As Bachrach and Baratz themselves maintain, the domination of defenders of the status quo may be so secure and pervasive that they are unaware of any potential challengers to their position and thus of any alternatives to the existing political process, whose bias they work to maintain" (p. 25).

A Third Dimension of Power

Lukes's analysis of the third dimension of power moves beyond *perceived interests*, arguing that the ultimate mobilization of bias occurs when norms and understandings of power are instantiated to such a degree that many potential forms of contest and resistance are inconceivable and thus are never observed or put forth in political decision making. In essence, they become "non-decisions" that legitimize existing norms within the status quo (Lukes, 2005, p. 28).

In each case of political decision making, we can observe the contest from one dimension of observed conflict and pluralist decision making, from a second dimension that turns attention to the forces shaping how the conflict and choices available for resolution are shaped and understood, and from a third dimension that suggests a different outcome might emerge if the unthinkable was thought, the unspoken proclaimed, and critical imagination brought to bear on the conflict. From a three-dimensional perspective, one would try to envision the ways in which new visions, coalitions, technologies, and understandings might reshape the elite admissions process. This perspective might also call for reconsidering the fundamental constructions of resource allocation and merit to ask, for example, whether the greatest social good is achieved through devoting the highest resources per student to those in the most selective institutions.

A Critical View: Power and the Public Finance of Higher Education

Few issues are more prominent in contemporary postsecondary debates than the finance of public universities (Zumeta et al., 2012). Throughout their histories, public colleges and universities in the United States have relied on public subsidies. While these institutions receive funding from a variety of sources, two of the most prominent have been direct funding from state legislatures and, since the passage of the Higher Education Act of 1965 and its amendments in 1972, income-contingent grants and subsidized student loans provided by the federal government (Gladieux & Wolanin, 1976). Many public universities levied extremely low tuition until the early 1960s, with tuition then rising sporadically until the 1980s. In the three decades since, tuition has risen relatively rapidly, exceeding the rate of inflation in most years (College Board, 2014).

Neoliberalism and Public Finance

The rising price of tuition has generally been linked to several concurrent phenomena: increasing costs (Ehrenberg, 2000), the steady reduction of subsidies for public institutions under legislative policies that call for significant limitations on personal income taxes and corporate taxes, and a retreat from support of public institutions in general. In the United States the reduction in state subsidies for higher education is often linked to calls for increased privatization—or "marketization"—of public higher education (Morrow, 2006; Pusser, 2008). Privatization then relates to the ascendance of human capital theory in higher education policy, with a pronounced turn to market ideology in the broader political economy. As Zumeta et al. (2012) put it, "In place of government action, the market (it was argued) was the best vehicle for resource allocation, and private interest should supersede public interest in driving the economy" (p. 70).

More globally, the turn to the market and away from the public is seen as a central tenet of neoliberal ideology. David Harvey (2005) defines neoliberalism as a political economic project, noting that "neoliberalism is in the first instance a theory of political economic practices that proposes that human well-being can best be advanced by liberating individual economic freedoms and skills within an institutional framework characterized by strong private property rights, free markets and free trade" (p. 2). Inherent in neoliberal ideology is the belief that markets are more effective for organizing and regulating institutions than is the State.

The neoliberal economic model in the United States, as prominently conveyed in the work of Nobel Laureate Milton Friedman (1962) and in collaboration with Rose Friedman (Friedman & Friedman, 1980), valorized markets and the role of individual investments in human capital and characterized higher education as essentially a private good, not a public one. As a result, Friedman characterized postsecondary education as an arena in which the student should make the primary investment in her own education, investments in new capacity should be left to the private sector, and most student subsidies should be considered inefficient and possibly counterproductive. Friedman and Friedman (1980) challenged two traditional justifications for public finance of higher education: that the education itself yields significant social benefits and that such benefits could be achieved only through public subsidy. While countenancing the possibility of some public benefits from higher education, they suggested that such gains were of little public concern: "If higher education improves the economic productivity of individuals, they can capture that improvement through higher earnings, so they have a private incentive to get the training. Adam Smith's invisible hand makes their private interest serve the social interest" (p. 179). Through a sustained mobilization of bias and subsequent policy enactments over the past three decades, the neoliberal project has moved so prominently into contemporary discourse that it is hard to recall a time without it.

The tension between markets and universities as well as the contest over organizational forms for universities around the world are not recent developments. Formal universities existed centuries before the birth of Adam Smith, but the majority of the universities in the United States were founded after his death in 1790. Despite the contemporary reverence for his work and the market logics attributed to his vision, for nearly two hundred years after his death, the United States built an elaborate and highly regarded system of higher education. That system was largely composed of nonprofit institutions operating in a nonmarket manner (Leslie & Johnson, 1974), with the majority of enrollments in institutions with public charters, state subsidies, and public oversight. To this day, the majority of postsecondary degrees in the United States are granted in nonprofit, public institutions. Thus, despite the rhetoric of the neoliberal approach to public institutions, its discourse and practices do not fully reflect the structure and history of public higher education in the United States. Critical scholarship has challenged core tenets of the neoliberal model, noting that it promotes a set of beliefs about the utility of markets and public policy for education that are highly contested (Ball, 2012; Pusser et al., 2011; Slaughter & Rhoades, 2004). And yet neoliberal ideology remains a dominant force shaping public higher education in the United States today.

A Model of Power in Practice: The Mobilization of a New Discourse

The debate over the finance of higher education in the United States and globally, like the contemporary contest over the finance of public institutions in the broader political economy, has been posed as a struggle between the traditional model of State subsidy of public and private institutions in the public interest (Marginson, 2007b) and a neoliberal model suggesting that education is essentially a private good. The model of postsecondary education as a private good calls for a sector where consumer demand drives policy and institutional behaviors are organized around market principles and individual finance. The discourse supporting the private-good model of higher education relies upon the claim that public provision and regulation of education are inefficient and ineffective, thus advocating a reduced State role (Friedman & Friedman, 1980). In the neoliberal moment, this discourse is often framed as two competitions. The first is the effort to redirect subsidies in favor of economic development (Slaughter & Rhoades, 2004) and to reduce support for public institutions, essentially creating a referendum on public provision of goods and services. The second competition is over how to allocate the dwindling subsidies between various types of public projects, and whether public funding should go to higher education or elementary/secondary education or health care, national security, infrastructure, and the like. As constructed, the contest is seen as a zero-sum game in which a dollar for health care is a dollar that cannot be spent on higher education, security, or anything else.

To understand the rise of market models and policies in contemporary postsecondary education, it is useful to see the process as driven to a considerable degree by a mobilization of bias in favor of neoliberal approaches to postsecondary finance. In the neoliberal policy framework, demands for entrepreneurial fund-raising, outsourcing, and privatization of public sector functions have supplanted a tradition of tax support for public institutions (Ball, 2012; Harvey, 2005; Singer, 2003). The contemporary standing of neoliberal policies in the United States rests in part on several decades of persistent and bold discursive claims—essentially that the market is a force for good, and the State is a constraint on the market. Such claims are coupled with an argument that regulation and state control are key barriers to markets in education (Chubb & Moe, 1990).

Drawing upon broader neoliberal arguments that public organization and finance are inherently less efficient than market approaches, the notion that state provision of higher education is therefore also less efficient has become widespread in policy and legislative discourse over the past two decades. A passage from a report prepared for the state of Texas summed up this rhetoric: "Obviously, to create a more responsive market for higher education, institutions of higher education must be substantially freed from the state regulation that currently binds them" (Texas State Senate Special Commission on 21st Century Colleges and Universities, 2001, p. 9). This attitude was not unique to Texas. State system reports from across the country stressed entrepreneurship and competition along with the proposition that students should be treated as customers or consumers. At the same time, a wide array of commissions and foundation-funded research projects turned attention to controlling college costs through a variety of measures, including many traditionally associated with private sector organizations. As the beliefs that subsidies should be reduced, market-like behaviors increased, and consumer demand privileged became more thoroughly instantiated, public universities themselves adopted some of the rhetoric of neoliberal tenets. As they sought greater autonomy and new revenue sources, public colleges and universities began to create a rhetorical distance between themselves and the legislatures—and, by extension, the public—with which they had been aligned for centuries. One former college president expressed the frustration of a number of university leaders in stating that public institutions had moved from being "state supported" to "state assisted" and then to "state located" (Folbre, 2009; Olson, 2006.) Public universities also sought to garner greater autonomy from legislatures under the rationale that a shift in revenue sources should be accompanied by lower levels of state regulation and oversight, an argument suggesting that, to some degree, public financial support, rather than public purpose, was the justification for public control of institutions (Pusser, 2008). Similarly, public universities turned their attention toward increasing tuition and developing fund-raising campaigns and branding exercises that set forth the ambitious, albeit counterintuitive, goal of becoming essentially privately funded public universities.

The shift in discourse, and the recognition of neoliberal norms, was apparent not only in institutional rhetoric but also in the scholarship of postsecondary education. Many analyses of policy in higher education noted that public colleges and universities faced an array of financial challenges, including decreased state contributions for higher education (Zumeta et al., 2012), rising costs (Ehrenberg,

2000; Weisbrod, Ballou, & Asch, 2008), and the loss of state and federal funding to other areas of need. Scholars have debated the causes and effects of the shifting financial landscape, but the market discourse is so firmly instantiated in American political and policy debates and legislative actions that few scholars or public institutions offered significant challenges to either the underlying premise—that taxes cannot be raised—or its corollary, the idea that the political resource allocation process must be a zero-sum game, whereby an extra dollar for one public good or service must come from some other public good or service.

Challenging the Narrative

Are political decisions and resource allocation practices timeless, immutable properties like gravity? Critical scholars of politics and of power would argue that they are not. Rather, they can be seen as constructs, the products of power dynamics, history, culture, and context. Lukes (2005) notes "For Bachrach and Baratz, by contrast, it is crucially important to identify *potential issues* which nondecision making prevents from being actual" (p. 23). In this sense, non–decision making is a political space in which contest does not manifest because the issues have not reached the decision-making arena. In the earlier example of college admissions, the possibility of raising tax revenue for new campuses, a staple of the politics of public institution building in the 1960s, is a potential issue that cannot be fully envisioned in the present ideological moment. That is not to say that a contest over building new, high-quality campuses to alleviate admissions pressure would result in those campuses being built, only that without advancing the possibility it cannot happen. At the same time, the reinforcement of neoliberal norms has succeeded to such a degree that they have become a political "reality," limiting the terrain of debate to the most economically desirable solutions to public sector challenges. The essence of a critical approach to higher education policy is to move beyond the taken for granted, to challenge norms, to open space, and to deconstruct the dominant constructs.

A Three-Dimensional Approach: Deconstructing Imaginaries of Power

The taken-for-granted assumptions and discourses shaping public higher education policies are deeply embedded, intuitively familiar, and often repeated. But what are they a case of? From a critical perspective, are they universal truths, or do they reflect a particular standpoint or account of the world? Does the basic contest articulated in a pluralist, one-dimensional account reflect the entire continuum of contest and resistance over resource allocation, redistribution, and economic equity in the finance of higher education? As a two-dimensional view suggests, has a particular narrative been instantiated so insistently and authoritatively that critical alternatives are rarely considered? Or, from a three-dimensional view, are there possibilities for transformation that are essentially unimaginable in the present context?

The most significant challenges in establishing a multidimensional perspective on power are imagining a world that is rarely imagined and asking questions that have not been asked. As Lukes (2005) put it, "Now the classical objection to doing this has often been stated by pluralists: how can one study, let alone explain, what does not happen?" (p. 40). There are several answers, three of which offer particularly useful insight into critical approaches to postsecondary challenges: contextualizing norms, turning attention to historical precedents, and creatively reconstructing the debate over what is possible.

Contextualizing

The first key to deconstructing norms is to accept that what is taken for granted in a particular political or social system is highly contextual (Stone, 2012). As one example, the goals for higher education in the United States and Finland share much in common: to create informed citizens and to promote economic development, security, and social mobility (Valimaa, 2011). Yet even as Finland feels the growing weight of neoliberalism, its approach to financing higher education is quite distinct from that in the United States, relying on relatively high levels of taxation and low tuition.

At the same time that tuition was rising to record levels in the United States at the turn of the twenty-first century, students at the Universidad Nacional Autónoma de México (UNAM), the largest university in Latin America, began a strike that closed the university for nearly ten months. One purpose of the strike was to prevent the administration from increasing tuition from under $1 per semester to a means-tested $100 per semester. The strike was eventually settled without a tuition increase (Ordorika, 2006; Rhoads & Mina, 2001). The events at the UNAM provide additional perspective on the degree to which tuition matters as a symbolic and structural barrier to access. And that understanding is not unique to Mexico. In California, students have protested tuition increases in the state's postsecondary system throughout the last decade, often invoking cultural and symbolic references, such as Día de los Muertos demonstrations in which students used the iconography of the Day of the Dead to symbolically invoke the end of their postsecondary ambitions under tuition increases. In attempting to resist the discourse of inevitability that surrounds tuition setting in the United States and the continuous price increases that discourse enables, the actions at the UNAM and in California serve as a powerful reminder that tuition increases are not inevitable, and that higher education finance can indeed be a contested terrain.

A second force for envisioning new norms for understanding higher education in the United States is history. Much of the finance of public colleges and universities in the United States, for most of the period since the creation of the land-grant colleges, has come from public sources. Tuition was historically quite low until the ascendance of neoliberal policies in the 1980s, when tuition began to increase dramatically. Average tuition calculated in constant dollars for in-state students increased in public four-year universities between 1982/83 and 2013/14 by over 200% (College Board, 2014). While universities have made efforts to use portions of tuition increases to subsidize students with financial need, and federal subsidies for student access such as Pell grants have grown, tuition has increased rapidly in a highly contested policy terrain. Admissions officers have faced mounting pressure to attract highly prepared applicants independent of financial need (Zumeta et al., 2012), and some state legislatures have attempted to end university redistribution of tuition dollars for financial aid, where the process is seen as a form of institutional taxation imposed upon students whose tuition subsidizes those students with greater financial need (Kiley, 2012).

Over roughly the same period of time that tuition has taken a great leap upward (1980–2011) in the United States, income inequality has significantly increased (Piketty, 2014) and the top marginal federal tax rate on individuals has significantly decreased (Krugman, 2013). While the collection and allocation of revenue for public higher education have been largely state-level concerns, neoliberal tax policies have greatly constrained states' abilities to raise tax revenue. There are many forms of taxes that provide total revenue for state functions, and in many instances sales taxes and user fees are rising, but the shift to individual responsibility for the finance of higher education continues. It would be tempting to infer from policy debates over higher education finance that tuition is rising *because* state tax revenue is declining. But while that rationale may be alluded to in universities and state houses, it is not generally the case that declining revenues and increased tuition are linked by specific legislative mandates. Rather, the decision to cut funding to public universities at the legislative level is one choice from myriad options. The decision at the institutional level to seek approval for tuition increases from a legislature is also one of many options. Given that federal tax rates on personal income have dramatically declined and tuition is at historically high levels, however, it is a tribute to the power of the mobilization of bias for neoliberal policies that today in many policy debates over higher education finance it is taken for granted that federal and state income taxes for higher education will not be raised and tuition can be raised.

Reconstructing Possibility through Imagination

While context and history offer important windows into conceptualizing a three-dimensional view of power in higher education, it is also essential to draw upon creativity, imagination, and personal narratives in efforts to reframe norms (cf. chap. 2 by Mitchell J. Chang, this volume). Cass Sunstein (2006) has noted Franklin Delano Roosevelt's visionary effort in the 1940s to create and implement a second Bill of Rights, one that would have added the right to an education. A right to an education is not directly enumerated in the Bill of Rights, and without that status, higher education remains something to be earned, negotiated, or denied. Those opposing tuition increases during the student strike at the UNAM cited the Mexican constitution, which guarantees the right to a free, public education. In the absence of such codified legitimacy in the United States, it takes an act of imagination, a creative leap to envision a right to higher education. The belief that one possesses a right to an education, that claiming an education is one's due (Rich, 1979), reconstructs the normative understandings of access and finance in higher education. The student strike at the UNAM and similar, though less dramatic, contemporary protests at universities around the world point to the power of reconstructing access and finance away from political norms and into the realms of individual rights and social justice.

The work of John Rawls (1971) is also particularly helpful, as it deconstructs norms of justice, equity, and distribution. Rawls calls for rethinking essential understandings of fairness, a process central to reconceptualizing policy norms in higher education, particularly those derived from market models. Elements of Rawls's work can be seen as challenging the degree to which models of equitable income distribution can be applied to every sphere of public and private life, particularly as he points to the difference between economic relations and ties of affection. Paul Graham (2007), in reference to Rawls's work on families, notes, "This difference is significant in at least two ways: it may not be possible to redistribute affection in the same manner as income or freedom, and even if it were possible it would not be *desirable* to attempt a redistribution" (pp. 28–29). Yet, increasingly, the distinctions between purposes, the balance of public goods and private goods through higher education, the right to claim an education as opposed to the opportunity to earn one, the nature of subsidies, and their sources and distribution are all fundamentally debated in the contemporary politics of higher education within the constraints of a neoliberal economic model.

Conclusion

There are a number of historical practices in the United States that over time have been discredited, such as the denial of women's right to vote or the failure to regulate the exploitation of child labor. There is far less accord on policies in place today that will be considered unacceptable one hundred years from now. It is a demonstration of how comfortable we are with norms, particularly those "settled" by historical agreement, and how uncomfortable we are in confronting norms in our own context. At the same time, it is a lesson in power relations, evidencing how familiar we are with settled notions of the appropriate and inappropriate uses of power in historical context and how reluctant we are to challenge contemporary norms of power.

Critical approaches offer a path to change this dynamic. Building on Lukes's model, we can analyze the politics and policies of higher education by studying observable conflict and the decisions that emerge from that conflict. We can look beyond the apparent terrain to conceptualize issues that are not able to rise to the level of policy contest to potential decisions that never reach the agenda, to voices unheard, and to the discourses and practices that instantiate the beliefs and interests of dominant groups. Perhaps most importantly, we can also look beyond the norms of research on power and politics in higher education to seek the representation of power in other domains, such as philosophy, art, and nature. In that process, it will be essential to think not only of new formations, policies, and understandings of society and its institutions, but also of the role of the individual in sense making and contest.

At the core of the critical approach to power are questions about what people believe and how those beliefs manifest in communities, states, and nations. Norms are shaped by history, context, and power but lived, legitimated, and enacted by individuals and groups who make decisions about what is known and what the impact of that knowing will be personally and globally. That latter process—personal and contextual knowing—allows one to acknowledge the importance of norms and the certainty that what one knows can and will change, that understanding comes not only from appreciating a landscape but also from understanding its history and potentials, in order to begin the process of supporting a revitalized and sustainable terrain going forward.

NOTES

1. Throughout this chapter I use the capitalized form, "State," to refer to the State as used in social and critical theory, and the lowercase "state" in reference to the individual states in the United States.

2. All italics in this chapter are original.

REFERENCES

Allan, E. J., Iverson, S., & Ropers-Huilman, R. (Eds.). (2010). *Reconstructing policy in higher education: Feminist poststructural perspectives.* New York: Routledge.

Astin, A. W., & Oseguera, L. (2004). The declining "equity" of American higher education. *Review of Higher Education, 27,* 321–41.

Bachrach, P., & Baratz, M. (1970). *Power and poverty: Theory and practice.* New York: Oxford University Press.

Baldridge, J. V. (1971). *Power and conflict in the university: Research in the sociology of complex organizations.* New York: Wiley.

Ball, S. J. (2012). *Global education Inc.: New policy networks and the neo-liberal imaginary.* New York: Routledge.

Bourdieu, P. (1984). *Distinction: A social critique of the judgment of taste.* London: Routledge and Kegan Paul.

Bourdieu, P., & Passeron, J. (1977). *Reproduction in education, society and culture.* Beverly Hills, CA: Sage.

Bowen, W. G., Chingos, M. M., & McPherson, M. S. (2009). *Crossing the finish line: Completing college at America's public universities.* Princeton, NJ: Princeton University Press.

Bowen, W. G., Kurzweil, M. A., Tobin, E. M., & Pichler, S. C. (2005). *Equity and excellence in American higher education* (Thomas Jefferson Foundation Distinguished Lecture Series). Charlottesville: University of Virginia Press.

Carnoy, M., & Levin, H. M. (1985). *Schooling and work in the democratic state.* Stanford, CA: Stanford University Press.

Chubb, J. E., & Moe, T. (1990). *Politics, markets and America's schools.* Washington, DC: Brookings Institution.

Clark, B. R. (1983). *The higher education system: Academic organization in cross-national perspective.* Berkeley: University of California Press.

College Board. (2014). Inflation-adjusted published tuition and fees relative to 1983–84, 1983–84 to 2013–14. In *Trends in higher education* (fig. 5). Washington, DC: College Board. Retrieved from http://trends.collegeboard.org/college-pricing/figures-tables/published-tuition-and-fees-relative-1983-84-sector.

Cooper, B. S., Cibulka, J. G., & Fusarelli, L. D. (2008). *Handbook of education politics and policy.* New York: Routledge.

Dahl, R. A. (1961). *Who governs? Democracy and power in an American city.* New Haven, CT: Yale University Press.

Douglass, J. (2000) *The California idea and American higher education: 1850 to the 1960 master plan for higher education.* Stanford CA: Stanford University Press

Ehrenberg, R. G. (2000). *Tuition rising: Why college costs so much.* Cambridge, MA: Harvard University Press.

Folbre, N. (2009, October 5). When state universities lose state support. *New York Times.* Retrieved from http://economix.blogs.nytimes.com/2009/10/05/when-state -universities-lose-state-support/?_php=true&_type=blogs&_r=0.

Foucault, M. (1977). *Discipline and punish: The birth of the prison.* New York: Pantheon.

———. (1980). *Power/knowledge: Selected interviews and other writings, 1972–1977* (C. Gordon, Ed.). New York: Pantheon.

Freire, P. (1985). *The politics of education.* South Hadley, MA: Bergin and Garvey.

Friedman, M. (1962). *Capitalism and freedom.* Chicago: University of Chicago Press.

Friedman, M., & Friedman, R. (1980). *Free to choose: A personal statement.* New York: Harcourt Brace Jovanovich.

Gladieux, L. E., & Wolanin, T. R. (1976). *Congress and the colleges: The national politics of higher education.* Lexington, MA: Lexington Books.

Golden, D. (2006) *The price of admission: How America's ruling class buys its way into elite colleges—and who gets left outside the gates.* New York: Crown.

Graham, P. (2007). *Rawls.* Oxford: Oneworld.

Harvey, D. (2005). *A brief history of neoliberalism.* London: Oxford University Press.

Horn, C. L., & Flores, S. M. (2003). *Percent plans in college admissions: A comparative analysis of three states' experiences.* Cambridge, MA: Civil Rights Project at Harvard University.

Iverson, S. (2010). Producing diversity: A policy discourse analysis of diversity action plans. In E. J. Allan, S. Iverson, & R. Ropers-Huilman (Eds.), *Reconstructing policy in higher education: Feminist poststructural perspectives* (pp. 193–213). New York: Routledge.

Karabel, J. (2005). *The chosen: The hidden history of admissions and exclusion at Harvard, Yale and Princeton.* New York: Houghton Mifflin.

Kerr, C. (1963). *The uses of the university.* Cambridge, MA: Harvard University Press.

Kiley, K. (2012, June 8). Who pays for student aid? *Inside Higher Education.* Retrieved from www.insidehighered.com/news/2012/06/08/iowa-proposes-end-use-tuition -revenue-financial-aid#sthash.D4OJScTY.dpbs.

Krugman, P. (2013, May 28). Taxing the rich. *New York Times.* Retrieved from http:// krugman.blogs.nytimes.com/2013/05/28/taxing-the-rich/?_php=true&_type =blogs&_r=0.

Lemann, N. (2000) *The big test: The secret history of the American meritocracy.* New York: Farrar, Straus & Giroux.

Leslie, L. L., & Johnson, G. P. (1974). The market model and higher education. *Journal of Higher Education, 45,* 1–20.

Lukes, S. (1974). *Power: A radical view* (1st ed.). London: Palgrave Macmillan.

———. (2005). *Power: A radical view* (2nd ed.). London: Palgrave Macmillan.

Marginson, S. (2007a). Global university rankings. In S. Marginson (Ed.), *Prospects of higher education: Globalization, market competition, public goods and the future of the university* (pp. 79–100). Rotterdam: Sense.

———. (2007b). The new higher education landscape: Public and private goods in global/national/local settings. In S. Marginson (Ed.), *Prospects of higher education: Globalization, market competition, public goods and the future of the university* (pp. 29–77). Rotterdam: Sense.

Metcalfe, A. S., & Slaughter, S. (2011). Academic capitalism. In B. J. Bank (Ed.), *Gender and higher education* (pp. 13–19). Baltimore: Johns Hopkins University Press.

Mills, C. W. (1956). *The power elite.* New York: Oxford University Press.

Moe, T. (1996). *The positive theory of public bureaucracy.* New York: Cambridge University Press.

Morrow, R. A. (2006). Foreword—Critical theory, globalization, and higher education: Political economy and the cul-de-sac of the postmodern cultural turn. In R. A. Rhoads and C. A. Torres (Eds.), *The university, state and market: The political economy of globalization in the Americas* (pp. xvii–xxxiii). Stanford, CA: Stanford University Press.

Olson, G. A. (2006, May 2). Can you spare a dime? *Chronicle of Higher Education.* Retrieved from http://chronicle.com/article/Can-You-Spare-a-Dime-/46775/.

Ordorika, I. (2006). *La disputa por el campus: Poder, política y autonomía en la UNAM.* Mexico City: Seminario de Educación Superior-UNAM / CESU-UNAM / Plaza y Valdés.

Ordorika, I., & Pusser, B. (2007). La máxima casa de estudios: The Universidad Nacional Autónoma de México as a state-building university. In P. G. Altbach & J. Balan (Eds.), *World class worldwide: Transforming research universities in Asia and Latin America* (pp. 189–215). Baltimore: Johns Hopkins University Press.

Parsons, M. D. (1997). *Power and politics: Federal higher education policymaking in the 1990s.* Albany: State University of New York Press.

Pelfrey, P. A. (2004) *A brief history of the University of California* (2nd ed.). Berkeley: University of California Press.

Piketty, T. (2014). *Capital in the twenty-first century.* Cambridge, MA: Belknap Press of Harvard University Press.

Pusser, B. (2004). *Burning down the house: Politics, governance and affirmative action at the University of California.* Albany: State University of New York Press.

———. (2008). The state, the market and the institutional estate: Revisiting contemporary authority relations in higher education. In J. Smart (Ed.), *Higher education: Handbook of theory and research* (Vol. 23, pp. 105–39). New York: Agathon Press.

———. (2011). Power and authority in the creation of a public sphere through higher education. In B. Pusser et al. (Eds.), *Universities and the public sphere: Knowledge creation and state building in the era of globalization* (pp. 27–46). New York: Routledge.

Pusser, B., & Marginson, S. (2012). The elephant in the room: Power, global rankings and the study of higher education organizations. In M. Bastedo (Ed.), *The Orga-*

nization of higher education: Managing colleges for a new era (pp. 86–117). Baltimore: Johns Hopkins University Press.

———. (2013). University rankings in critical perspective. *Journal of Higher Education, 84*(4), 544–68.

Pusser, B., Marginson, S., Ordorika, I., & Kempner, K. (Eds.) (2011). *Universities and the public sphere: Knowledge creation and state building in the era of globalization.* New York: Routledge.

Rawls, J. (1971). *A theory of justice.* Cambridge, MA: Harvard University Press.

Rhoades, G. (1992). Beyond "the state": Interorganizational relations and state apparatus in postsecondary education. In J. C. Smart (Ed.), *Higher education: Handbook of theory and research* (pp. 84–192). New York: Agathon Press.

Rhoads, R., & Mina, L. (2001) The student strike at the National Autonomous University of Mexico: A political analysis. *Comparative Education Review, 45*(3), 334–53.

Rich, A. (1979). *On lies, secrets, and silences: Selected prose, 1966–1978.* New York: Norton.

Rodriguez Gomez, R., & Ordorika, I. (2011). The chameleon's agenda: Entrepreneurial adaptation of private higher education in Mexico. In B. Pusser et al. (Eds.), *Universities and the public sphere: Knowledge creation and state building in the era of globalization* (pp. 219–41). New York: Routledge.

Schattschneider, E. E. (1960). *The semi-sovereign people: A realist's view of democracy.* New York: Holt, Rinehart & Winston.

Singer, P. W. (2003). *Corporate warriors: The rise of the privatized military industry.* Ithaca, NY: Cornell University Press.

Slaughter, S. (1990). *The higher learning and high technology: Dynamics of higher education policy formation.* Albany: State University of New York Press.

Slaughter, S., & Leslie, L. L. (1997). *Academic capitalism.* Baltimore: Johns Hopkins University Press.

Slaughter, S., & Rhoades, G. (2004). *Academic capitalism and the new economy.* Baltimore: Johns Hopkins University Press.

Stone, D. (2012). *Policy paradox.* New York: Norton.

Sunstein, C. R. (2006). *The second bill of rights.* New York: Basic Books.

Suspitsyna. T. (2010) Accountability in American education as a rhetoric and a technology of governmentality. *Journal of Education Policy, 25*(5), 567–86.

Texas State Senate Special Commission on 21st Century Colleges and Universities. (2001). *Moving every Texan forward.* Austin: Author.

Tierney, W. G. (2000) Power, identity and the dilemma of college student departure. In J. M. Braxton (Ed.), *Reworking the student departure puzzle* (pp. 213–35). Nashville: Vanderbilt University Press.

Valimaa, J. (2011). The corporatization of national universities in Finland. In B. Pusser et al. (Eds.), *Universities and the public sphere: Knowledge creation and state building in the era of globalization* (pp. 101–20). New York: Routledge.

Weber, M. (1947). *The theory of social and economic organization.* Glencoe, IL: Free Press.

Weisbrod, B. A., Ballou, J. P., & Asch, E. D. (2008). *Mission and money: Understanding the university.* Cambridge: Cambridge University Press.

Zumeta, W., Breneman, D. W., Callan, P. M., & Finney, J. E. (2012). *Financing American higher education in the era of globalization.* Cambridge, MA: Harvard Education Press.

CHAPTER FOUR

A Critical Reframing of Human Capital Theory in US Higher Education

SHEILA SLAUGHTER, BARRETT J. TAYLOR, AND KELLY O. ROSINGER

The policy climate in the United States has changed slowly but dramatically as neoliberal actors have mobilized to promote policies that favor markets, quasi-markets, or market-like mechanisms over direct state control. Essentially, over time, the state has been "rolled back" and opportunity for marketization "rolled out" (Peck & Tickell, 2002). The rationale undergirding these market-like strategies has been to reduce costs and make strategic use of limited state support (among others, see Hearn & Longanecker, 1985; Johnstone, 2004; Leslie & Johnson, 1974). Yet costs have continued to increase (Archibald & Feldman, 2011), particularly at research universities, which means that direct state support constitutes a falling share of higher education expenditures even when state support is relatively constant in raw dollars (Desrochers & Wellman, 2011). In this context, US higher education policy reflects a changing understanding of government and its role in providing services such as higher education (Slaughter & Rhoades, 2004).

In this chapter, we juxtapose market-like competition for external resources with human capital discourse. Human capital, defined as "the knowledge, skills, and attributes acquired by investment in education and health throughout the lifecycle" (McMahon, 2009, 41), constitutes a common rationale for public investment in higher education. We argue that market-like competition undercuts higher education's contribution to human capital development because the pursuit of resources turns faculty and university attention away from students' education, the central building block of human capital.

Theory

Elements of two theories guide our analysis. The first comes from Ball's *Global Education, Inc.* (2012), which highlights the neoliberal turn in education policy, and the second is the theory of academic capitalism (Slaughter & Rhoades, 2004).

Ball emphasizes the abrogation of state authority and the growing use of market-like mechanisms in education. He uses neo-Marxian understandings of the economic foundations of social life to highlight power inequalities, conflict, and new opportunities for profit and influence. From the Foucauldian tradition, he considers actors to be self-governing and disciplined rather than ruled by a sovereign. Together, these insights allow Ball to understand neoliberalism as a complex phenomenon that fundamentally alters previous power dynamics by deemphasizing direct state provision of higher education and foregrounding competition between actors within academe. Such competition prompts actors to regulate their own behaviors, as in Foucault's work, but it does so within a context that is inherently unequal and fraught with economic conflict, as in the neo-Marxian tradition (Ball, 2012; Slaughter, forthcoming).

The resulting policy networks blur the borders between state and society. These networks are unstable because they often include competitive elements. Yet—because they allocate power, status, and resources—such networks nonetheless represent a form of governance. Because they are composed of many voices in competition and consultation with one another, they both create and legitimate a kind of shadow hierarchy that mixes bureaucracy, markets, and networks. This hierarchy stimulates policy mobility, facilitating wide-scale changes such as deregulation and increased competition in market-like spaces. As the traditional state and government bureaucracy decline in influence, they are less willing to provide traditional educational services. Instead, governments contract with others to provide various aspects of schooling (Ball, 2012; Slaughter, forthcoming). The state is thus rolled back and the opportunity for contracting and private sector profit making is rolled out (Peck & Tickell, 2002).

We supplement Ball's (2012) work with the theory of academic capitalism, which, while broadly compatible with Ball's analysis, emphasizes different facets of the policy process. Like Ball, academic capitalism casts the narratives and discourse that develop policy agendas as central to the successful creation of legislation or administrative rules (Slaughter & Rhoades, 2004). As these narratives change in the neoliberal direction indicated by Ball's (2012) work, they provide opportunities for deregulation, the reprioritization of public funds for more market-oriented activity, and reregulation that favors marketization.

Despite these broad complementarities between the two theories, the shape of these competitive spaces differs in each account. Where Ball sees education as moving toward the for-profit sector, Slaughter and Rhoades (2011) cast business as drawing on public funds to create the infrastructure for profit. In this account, higher education policy subsidizes the training of students in particular fields, and channels research funding into science and technology endeavors that may yield intellectual property and contribute to economic growth. The most salient feature of academic capitalist policy regimes, in other words, is not an emphasis on existing private-sector markets, but rather the subordination of public priorities and purposes to market-like competition that policymakers create (Slaughter & Cantwell, 2012; Taylor, Cantwell, & Slaughter, 2013). Such competitions steer faculty away from interaction with students and instead reward them for successful competition for external resources, meaning that, in general, faculty members spend relatively little time developing their students' human capital.

Stage 1: Human Capital and Neoliberal Narratives

Gary Becker (1962) and other academic economists in the 1960s developed the theory of human capital to examine the economic outcomes associated with investing skills and resources in people (Kiker, 1966). As these early theorists framed, "human capital" commonly refers to activities—such as health care, formal education, and on-the-job training—that are associated with increased earnings brought about by investments in individuals. Human capital theory posits that the resources and skills resulting from these investments promote economic development by increasing the productive capacity of workers (Becker, 1962; Leslie & Brinkman, 1988; McMahon, 2009; Schultz, 1961). Society benefits from this relationship because more highly skilled workers are prepared for high-skill jobs that are the backbone of a prosperous economy. Individuals benefit from human capital investments because they are able to command higher salaries. The connection between human capital investments and productivity thus helps to explain differences in labor market earnings, with college graduates earning more than those without college degrees (Anderson & Keys, 2007; Mincer, 1958; Rupert et al., 1996). Accordingly, the policy implications of this theory are that individuals should make some contributions to their educational costs, but that public subsidy of higher education is justified on the basis of societal benefits associated with higher levels of educational attainment (McMahon, 2009).

Human capital theory has proven highly influential in US higher education policy and scholarship (Engberg & Allen, 2011; Leslie & Brinkman, 1988; McMahon, 2009; Perna, 2002, 2003; Thomas & Zhang, 2005; Toutkoushian & Hillman, 2012). In early iterations of human capital theory, both private (individual) and public (social) returns of higher education were emphasized, and human capital was seen as an economic development tool that benefited society and individuals (Leslie & Brinkman, 1988). In other words, state spending to develop human capital through higher education was an efficient use of public money because it was quickly converted into private-sector economic growth. Employers did not have to spend as much time and money training workers, and workers were more productive. Public investment thus could be high and tuition low because there was general confidence that many of these dollars would end up in the private economy, a process from which society as a whole would benefit.

Neoliberal economists, such as Friedman and Friedman (1990), depart substantially from the human capital tradition by arguing that government spending constrains individual choices because the citizenry must pay for this spending through taxes. Hence government investment can be too high, and tuition too low. Neoliberal economists acknowledge the positive externalities (e.g., better citizens, reduced health-care costs, and so forth) that investment in human capital produces but contend that the overall benefits are primarily private. These scholars argue that public benefits will spill over from private investment in human capital without government subsidy or intervention.

In the 1980s and 1990s, neoliberalism came to dominate many arenas of policy discourse (Harvey, 2005). Accordingly, although social returns to higher education had been a component of the human capital account, private or individual gain began to receive greater emphasis, and less was said about the social value of higher education (Labaree, 1997). Simon Marginson (2013) has wondered how best to reintroduce an element of the "public good" to an enterprise increasingly devoted to the pursuit of individual reward. With regard to undergraduate education, the Committee for Economic Development and the Carnegie Commission on Higher Education advocated for policies such as Pell grants, which essentially put vouchers in the hands of students. These policies rested on the assumption that encouraging colleges and universities to compete for resources would incentivize schools to provide the highest-quality educations at the lowest-possible prices (see Hearn & Longanecker, 1985). Economists in the human capital tradition countered that such competition did not occur in a market and so was unlikely to yield organization-level efficiency (Leslie & Brinkman, 1988; Leslie & Johnson 1974).

Despite these vigorous academic debates, nonprofit policy groups blended elements of human capital theory with the neoliberal marketization of higher education. This rhetoric often claimed that such market-like processes could create subsidies for needy students more effectively than could general subsidies to institutions. Such "high-tuition/high-aid" financing policies made the case that charging higher tuition, which middle- and upper-middle-class families were able to pay, would create surpluses that could yield substantial aid for disadvantaged students (Hearn & Longanecker, 1985; Heller, 1997). The logical consequence of this policy narrative was to increase tuition charges, as the neoliberal rationale assumed that the majority of higher education's benefits accrued to the individual in the form of lifetime earnings.

In addition to rationalizing tuition increases and deemphasizing the social benefits of higher education, the neoliberal narrative also privileges fields related to apparent workforce needs and economic growth. In his 2013 State of the Union address, for example, US President Barack Obama called for education policies that would "equip our citizens with the skills and training to fill those [manufacturing, energy, infrastructure, and housing] jobs." The president's justification for ongoing public investment in higher education, in other words, is that postsecondary education trains individuals for employment. Just so, the president's "completion agenda"—supported by a diffuse coalition of federal, state, and nonprofit entities that seek to increase the number of US citizens with postsecondary credentials (Humphreys, 2012; Walters, 2012)—stresses the importance of skill development for workers. This emphasis on useful areas has important consequences for fields, such as the humanities, whose contributions to economic growth are not necessarily apparent to casual observers. Moreover, its neoliberal approach stands at odds with McMahon's (2009) "modern human capital" approach, which values fields such as the humanities and social sciences for their contributions to civil society.

A complex intersection of neoliberal and human capital rationales also is apparent in federal research policy. Many policy groups supported research and development (R&D) that would stimulate economic development, including the Business Higher Education Forum (Slaughter, 1990; Slaughter & Rhoades 2005); the Carnegie Commission on Science, Technology, and Government (1993); the US Council on Competitiveness (1996); the Committee on Science, Engineering, and Public Policy (1993, 1995); Committee on Criteria for Federal Support for Research and Development (1995); the Brookings Institution; the American Enterprise Institute for Public Policy Research; and the Belfer Center for Science and International Affairs (Branscomb et al., 1997). Both academics and nonacademic professionals participated in these fully funded philanthropic endeavors, and university presidents often sat on their boards and blue-ribbon commissions. In other words, agenda-setting groups did not act on higher education only from the outside; many within higher education also participated. In ways that echo Ball's (2012) analysis, these policy groups comprised self-organizing networks that drew on elite—often private—sectors of academe, wealthy philanthropic (nonprofit) organizations, the business community, and state and federal governments. These networks collectively initiated neoliberal policies in academic research that paralleled those in student financial aid. They promoted more money for academic R&D in science, technology, engineering, and mathematics (STEM) fields so that discovery, (appropriable) technology development, and ensuing economic innovation would create jobs that would bring prosperity (Slaughter & Leslie, 1997; Slaughter & Rhoades, 1996, 2004, 2005).

President Obama frames higher education research policy in terms of discovery, technology development, economic innovation, and job growth, all aided by increased funding for faculty research and graduate students in STEM fields. His 2014 science and technology budget calls for "Strategic investments to boost research, fuel innovation, and grow the economy," emphasizing "significant, targeted investments in the U.S. research and development (R&D) enterprise and in science, technology, engineering, and mathematics (STEM) education—core elements of the Administration's strategy for ensuring continued economic expansion built on the foundation of a thriving middle class" (Office of Science and Technology Policy, 2013). The research budget seeks to prepare "the Nation's Future Innovators by providing $3.1 billion for STEM education to ensure the next generation is prepared for challenging 21st century careers" and proposes the greatest increases to the mission agencies most likely to contribute to economic growth (Office of Science and Technology Policy, 2013).

Given this powerful financial incentive, federal mission agencies too are establishing or preferring programs designed to promote economic growth while accomplishing agency goals. In response to legislative changes and federal policy initiatives in the late 1980s, federal agencies began to structure a greater share of their subsidies (e.g., research grants) to stimulate entrepreneurial research and economic innovation (Slaughter & Rhoades, 1996, 2004, 2005). By 2011, the director of the National Science Foundation (NSF) was unveiling the Innovation Corp, or I-Corp, to

> create a new national network of scientists, engineers, innovators, business leaders, and entrepreneurs. It will help strengthen our national innovation ecosystem. Innovation Corps awards will help to strategically identify nascent science and engineering discoveries, and will leverage NSF's investment in basic research for technology innovation. Universities and academic institutions will be key partners in the I-Corps national network. (Suresh, 2011)

Even though the NSF is the agency for basic science, it also is in the business of economic innovation and presumably has a strong interest in ensuring that the revenues for which universities compete are expended on the type of research it seeks to promote. Similarly, the National Institutes of Health (NIH), the largest university federal R&D funder, has played an important role in economic innovation. Between 1982 and 2006, one-third of all drugs and nearly 60% of promising new molecular entities approved by the US Food and Drug Administration cited either an NIH-funded publication or a patent based on NIH-funded research (NIH, 2011). The NIH also promoted "translational research" aimed at converting NIH-funded basic scientific discoveries into drugs and medical devices (Baskin, 2011).

US higher education policy is "steering" from a distance by promoting policies that incent universities and faculty to compete for external resources (Slaughter & Cantwell, 2012). As explained in Ball's (2012) account, the aim of these policies is to create entrepreneurial faculty who will self-organize into networks that link together academic, business, philanthropic, and government support in terms of policy and funds. Within these networks, the possession of human capital is essential. Whether the networks themselves serve to develop and deploy human capital effectively, however, is less clear.

Walter McMahon's (2009) "modern human capital" approach expresses notable skepticism about this relationship. McMahon explicitly critiques the blending of human capital theory with neoliberal policies that he argues reflect conceptual and methodological errors (pp. 288–89). In direct contrast to the neoliberal emphasis on limited public spending, McMahon calls for greater government investment in higher education, as did early human capital theorists. Even so, he acknowledges that such increased investment would likely take the form of increases in portable student financial aid as well as bolstered state support for higher education (pp. 288–89). Moreover, unlike early human capital theorists, McMahon acknowledges the enormous role of the federal government in academic R&D by calling for heavy investment in university-based research. These funds, McMahon contends, both support novel discoveries and allow this new knowledge to be "embodied in master's and PhD students as new human capital" (p. 258).

Stage 2: Ironies, Inconsistencies, and Unanticipated Consequences in Human Capital Narratives and Discourse

Despite widespread trumpeting of the benefits of human capital development as a means of stimulating economic growth, US higher education policy has not greatly increased funding for undergraduate education. Instead, colleges and universities compete for ever-scarcer public resources (Slaughter & Cantwell, 2012; Weisbrod, Ballou, & Asch, 2008), including research grants and contracts (Stephan, 2012), state funds allocated on the basis of organizational performance

(McLendon, Hearn, & Deaton, 2006; Volkwein & Tandberg, 2008), and students who are either able to pay the full sticker price or eligible to receive direct subsidies in the form of student financial aid (Doyle, 2006; Heller, 2006).

Notably, competition among colleges and universities lacks most of the salient features of an economic market because in most cases the state organizes and provides funds (federal student financial aid, whether in the form of grants or loans, and mission agency R&D funding), not free market competition (Leslie & Johnson, 1974; Marginson, 2013). Colleges and universities therefore compete in quasi-markets in which they vie for public funds to support educational activities (Le Grand & Bartlett, 1993). Quasi-markets stem from policy interventions, such as those affecting student financial aid and research policy, described above. Although policymakers issue statements that broadly support investment in higher education and human capital development, the specific quasi-markets that provide funding for undergraduate education and research may undermine broad goals—such as the development of human capital—that serve both individual students and the citizenry as a whole (Taylor et al., 2013).

Student financial aid is a familiar policy issue in which human capital goals and competition-based allocation devices may conflict with one another. This competition for students who receive targeted subsidies in the form of portable student financial aid has its roots in federal policies of the 1970s (Leslie & Johnson, 1974). In the early 1980s, the "Minnesota Model" brought this innovation to state-level policy, inaugurating the high-tuition/high-aid strategy in which students received direct support through need-based grants (Hearn & Griswold, 1994; Hearn, Griswold, & Marine, 1996; St. John, Daun-Barnett, & Moronski-Chapman, 2013). This tendency to award public funds directly to individuals assumes universities would become more effective at attracting and educating students in order to receive these state funds (Hearn & Longanecker, 1985). In other words, policymakers hoped quasi-market-style competition would incent colleges and universities to more efficiently develop students' human capital.

Instead of heightening their training efforts, however, institutions have geared themselves toward winning competitions for students. This tendency is particularly apparent among private four-year colleges (Taylor et al., 2013), but it increasingly characterizes public universities as well (Hillman, 2012; Rizzo & Ehrenberg, 2004). With the exception of individuals attending a few highly selective schools, students often make college choices on the basis of amenities and services (Jacob, McCall, & Stange, 2013). In other words, when students "vote with their feet," they appear to vote for facets of their education that are unlikely to net increases in their human capital. As McMahon (2009) worries, the competition-based allocation of funds through portable student financial aid may not serve the human capital model as well as contemporary policymakers anticipate.

President Obama's "completion agenda" may have similar consequences. Community colleges have appeared as integral nodes in raising completion rates (Mullin, 2011). This situation prompts Rhoades (2012) to wonder whether the completion agenda has narrowed postsecondary opportunity for a wide swatch of students who are pushed into vocational fields and two-year institutions. Rhoades's important critiques suggest a contradiction within the contemporary policy environment. While the human capital agenda rests upon decades of economic theory and research, most contemporary resource allocation mechanisms utilize competition rather than increased investment in postsecondary education and oversight with regard to outcomes (Ball, 2012; McMahon, 2009).

Federal support for academic research is a particularly large and influential quasi-market in US higher education (Slaughter & Cantwell, 2012; Taylor et al., 2013). The influence of this quasi-market over university operations results from two facets of academic research. First, the federal government invests heavily in university-based R&D. The federal government expended approximately $28.8 billion on academic research in 2009 (NSF, 2011), exceeding the approximately $27 billion spent on Pell grants in 2010 (US Department of Education, 2011). Second, federal contributions to academic R&D are concentrated in a few universities. The top one hundred recipients of federal science and engineering (S&E) support collected $26 billion of the $28.8 billion spent on academic research, with the top ten universities alone accounting for about $6 billion (NSF, 2011). While Pell grants are distributed broadly to a wide range of colleges and universities, competition for federal research support affects a relatively small number of institutions. As a result, these universities compete intensely for federal research support (Slaughter & Rhoades, 2004; Stephan, 2012; Weisbrod et al., 2008).

Discussions of academic R&D abound with anecdotes about breakthrough discoveries that benefited from federal support, such as the human genome project (Stephan, 2012). Perhaps not surprisingly, policymakers who call for greater investment in university-based research often rely heavily upon such accounts. Yet investment in academic research rests on the foundation of human capital theory at least as much as stories of previous breakthroughs. In this account, academic R&D allows highly skilled workers—often graduate students—to enhance their knowledge bases through practical work (McMahon, 2009; Stephan, 2012).

Despite this implicit human capital rationale for federal investment in academic R&D, federal support for research is increasingly allocated through competitive processes (Slaughter & Cantwell, 2012). Stephan (2012) terms this process a "tournament" because a great many faculty members apply for funding but only a few are rewarded. The combination of scarce resources and many applicants heightens competition (Weisbrod et al., 2008), so universities often change their operations in an effort to secure these funds (Taylor et al., 2013). These changes may represent subtle adaptations to shifting conditions. Alternately, they may also represent substantial changes undertaken in response to competitive pressures rather than the mandate of developing human capital (Slaughter & Leslie, 1997; Slaughter & Rhoades, 2004). The worst-case scenario is a bitter irony in which faculty at research universities focus most of their energy on tournament competitions, leaving little time for building the human capital of their students.

Stage 3: Human Capital and Market Strategies in Faculty Work Life

To explore the ways that market-like incentives shape faculty work and human capital development, the authors and an additional researcher conducted fieldwork at two public research universities in 2011 and 2012. We selected these universities, dubbed Flagship University (FU) and Arts and Sciences University (A&SU), because they compete vigorously for external R&D funding. In 2009, the last year in which institutional profile data were available for all categories for the universities in question, both institutions were in the top 10% of the nine hundred universities ranked on measures such as total federal obligations and total research expenditures (NSF, 2011). FU was in the top 5% on such measures, however, while A&SU fell between 7% and 9%. Both were the flagship university in their respective state.

We relied primarily on data from eighty-five semistructured interviews conducted with faculty members. We identified participants through a review of universities' websites and solicited participation via email. We divided these interviews into "high-resource" and "low-resource" academic units on the basis of external R&D support (as indicated in university documents). High-resource departments clustered in S&E fields but also included business, while low-resource departments included humanities disciplines such as English and history. We interviewed approximately equal numbers of faculty members in high- and low-resource units and across all ranks to provide a broad understanding of faculty experiences (see table 4.1).

Because women are historically underrepresented in S&E fields, we purposefully oversampled women in high-resource areas. Table 4.2 shows that sampled female participants are disproportionately concentrated in lower-ranking faculty positions, particularly those off of the tenure track, and assistant professor posi-

TABLE 4.1. Number of interview participants by case site, high- and low-resource departments, and rank

Rank	Flagship university		Arts and sciences university	
	High-resource	Low-resource	High-resource	Low-resource
Instructor / lecturer / research scientist	1	2	2	2
Adjunct	2	1	0	0
Assistant professor	3	2	4	6
Associate professor	1	6	5	5
Full professor	5	8	5	8
Endowed chair	0	1	2	4
Department head / dean / director	6	0	3	1
Total	18	20	21	26

Note: High- and low-resource departments are defined by their ability to generate external revenue through federal grants and contracts, industry funds, or consulting agreements. High-resource departments are primarily in STEM fields but also include business fields that have access to revenue through industry funds and consulting agreements. Low-resource departments were defined as departments with limited access to external revenue sources and included humanities fields, such as English and history.

tions in which they may face acute performance pressures. Conversely, women are notably outnumbered in associate and full professorships, and in endowed chair and academic administrator positions, suggesting that the neoliberal policy environment may have disproportionately disadvantaged women relative to men. We explore this possibility more extensively in other, related work.

Semistructured interviews drew from a protocol while providing participants the opportunity to discuss additional topics of importance (Roulston, 2010). Because the use of data from multiple sources can increase the trustworthiness of qualitative research, we also drew data from websites, institutional strategic plans, and figures reported to the National Center for Education Statistics (NCES) and NSF. In keeping with the principles of qualitative research, we developed, revised, and refined thematic codes throughout the research process (Merriam, 1998).

External Funding and Faculty Work

The 2010 Carnegie Classification of Institutions of Higher Education classified both FU and A&SU as belonging to the category "research university (very high activity)," suggesting federal R&D support represented an important resource stream at both campuses. External funding for research proved particularly wide-

TABLE 4.2. Number of interview participants by faculty rank and gender

Rank	Flagship university		Arts and sciences university	
	Female	Male	Female	Male
Instructor / lecturer / research scientist	1	2	3	1
Adjunct	2	1	—	—
Assistant professor	1	4	7	3
Associate professor	5	2	2	7
Full professor	4	10	4	11
Endowed chair	—	—	—	4
Department head / dean / director	2	4	1	4
Total	15	23	17	30

spread at FU. In 1986, FU received more than $6,000 in federal grants and contracts per full-time equivalent student (FTE).[1] This figure increased to around $10,000 per FTE by 2009. Research activity proved less extensive at A&SU, remaining relatively constant at $3,500 per FTE for the same twenty-one-year period. But because state appropriations per FTE declined at A&SU in constant dollars, federal grants and contracts proved of growing relative importance.

Faculty members at both A&SU and FU were acutely aware of the importance of external research funding. An assistant professor in a high-resource unit at A&SU told us that the university's administration was "sort of requiring that you get part of the funds yourself." An adjunct faculty member in a high-resource unit at FU concurred, stating, "If you want to do research, you have to bring in your own money." An associate professor in a high-resource unit at FU elaborated on these concerns by noting that pressures to secure extramural funding did not vanish with the awarding of tenure. "I'm not going to make full professor until I make some changes in the research stuff," she asserted. She noted the successful pursuit of external research funding as chief among these changes.

Perhaps because campus decision makers who can recover "indirect costs" from grant budgets view federal grants as being particularly important (Stephan, 2012), the pursuit of these funds consumed a great deal of participants' time. An assistant professor in a high-resource unit at A&SU indicated that the pursuit of funding detracted both from her private life and from other work-related tasks. "When I was really doing the grant writing and getting those submissions in, I was here all the time," she told us. "I just went home to sleep." Faculty members who were able to secure external funding then began to invest their time in post-award administration. "You've got to manage a budget, you've got to write grants, and you've got to manage people," said a contingent faculty member at A&SU. A full professor in a high-resource unit at A&SU phrased this concern more colorfully, stating, "I kind of wish I could go to business school" to learn to manage the operational details of his research projects.

Interview participants increasingly indicated that the desire to secure funds shaped faculty members' research agendas. This shift in faculty work reflected changes in the processes by which federal agencies solicited and reviewed grant proposals (Stephan, 2012). "They're wanting more and more things tailored toward their interests," said a director of a high-resource research center at FU. A full professor in a high-resource unit at A&SU reflected that, when he began his academic career, "several agencies had programs that would accept open submissions on pretty much any subject that related to environmental chemistry or hydrology." When interviewed in 2012, however, he said, "now there's almost no programs that support that kind of investigator driven interest." He concluded that researchers increasingly pursued "what's fundable." An assistant professor in a high-resource unit at A&SU agreed. "Our research is to a large degree driven by where we can get funds and how we can support the research," she stated. As a result, said an associate professor in another high-resource unit at A&SU, "Most of the people on the faculty have been recruited to primarily have a grant-driven research program," not on the basis of their knowledge, skills, teaching ability, or expertise.

Such hiring decisions, like the strategies individual faculty members used to pursue and administer grants, represented concessions to quasi-market allocation mechanisms. The faculty members and academic units we studied positioned themselves to prevail in these competitions. As interview participants ruefully acknowledged, however, this focus on securing funds often distracted them from the tasks of knowledge production and human capital development despite the fact that research grants were intended to support these tasks.

Variable Quality of Work Life

Although the aggressive pursuit of external support for R&D generally characterized faculty members at both A&SU and FU, it did not characterize all individuals equally. Some of these differences obtained between various high-resource fields, with the life sciences receiving more robust federal R&D support than other S&E fields from 1975 to 2009 (NSF, 2011). Despite some distinctions within high-resource fields, however, the greatest differences proved to be between high- and low-resource units. Where faculty members in high-resource units strategized about how best to secure resources in quasi-markets, faculty members in low-resource units faced the stark reality that such competitions were generally closed to them. This disparity led to deteriorating working conditions for faculty members in low-resource units. Some interview participants shared offices with other faculty members, and many noted declining support for travel and faculty development leave. Several others reported heightened scrutiny of student credit-hour production, which generated larger class sizes, alongside a contradictory tendency for campus administrators to reallocate tuition receipts away from the teaching-focused low-resource units that had generated them. As one associate professor at FU stated simply, "Our financial constraints do limit what we can do." A full professor and department chair at A&SU concurred, noting that the resources available to the humanities "will never be like they were 15 years ago when there was more money to do things, and there wasn't a sense of being basically poor. I feel poor." He anticipated no relief for this feeling of poverty. "I think that is going to be somewhat the new normal," he concluded.

Faculty members whom we interviewed indicated that stratification between high- and low-resource academic units undermined the sense that the university was a single organization engaged in complex but related activities. "Being a research department in a humanities or social sciences field is still always second rate compared to a research department in the sciences," according to a tenured faculty member in a low-resource unit at FU. A full professor in a low-resource unit at FU concurred. "I don't think that the jobs are the same at all, particularly between the sciences and the humanities," she stated. "Scientists are able to negotiate." This refrain, in which scientists and others in high-resource units enjoyed more favorable working conditions than their peers in low-resource units, proved common among interview participants. "The university is a very different institution for [S&E faculty] than it is for me," said a full professor in a low-resource unit at FU. A low-resource unit professor at A&SU concluded sarcastically, "We're lucky to be allowed to continue to hold a corner in the university."

In a particularly ironic turn from the human capital perspective, an emphasis on teaching became an emblem of the subordinate status of low-resource units. That is, where human capital theory stresses the importance of cultivating knowledge and skills through training, the reward structure of both A&SU and FU valued units that secured rewards in the quasi-market for research over those that engaged in instruction. An associate professor in a low-resource unit at FU acknowledged this state of affairs openly. "In general," she told us, "if you say the department is a teaching department, it carries a negative connotation, right? That they're kind of second rate. Maybe they're good at teaching, but their scholarship is not so strong." An adjunct faculty member in a low-resource unit at

A&SU agreed. "As resources grow more and more limited, I would say that administration expects more teaching from us," he said. While instructional work was a stated goal of the human capital model, quasi-market pressures created conditions in which it was subordinated to the pursuit of external financial support for research.

Deterioration of Traditional Meanings and Roles

As noted in the theory of academic capitalism, public policy that calls for heavy R&D investment privileges S&E fields and incents universities to build up expansive graduate departments with highly paid faculty to enable competition for these funds. Graduate education is thus favored over undergraduate education, as are S&E fields over the humanities and social sciences. By extension, undergraduate teaching—on which much of the human capital model rests—is devalued and often delegated to adjunct faculty. Nationally, the number of adjuncts increased from 35% in 1991 to 50% in 2011 (NCES, 2013), with particularly rapid growth in humanities, social science, and education departments and slow growth in engineering and natural sciences units (National Education Association, 2007). Given that adjuncts are paid at far lower rates than full-time professors, the use of contingent faculty members can create savings that research universities may invest in S&E research (Newfield, 2009).

Perhaps not surprisingly, then, both high- and low-resource units employed non-tenure-track faculty members to teach classes, primarily to undergraduate students. As a professor in a high-resource unit at FU noted, this division of labor allowed tenured and tenure-track faculty more time to pursue research funding. "We have members of the department [whose] primary focus is on teaching, and everyone recognizes the importance of that," he said. Conversely, he added, "others do spend most of their time on research and attracting funding." A lecturer in a low-resource unit at FU agreed. In his account, "the majority of work that's being done now is being done by people who are invisible in the traditional sense" because they are not on the tenure line. This use of contingent faculty to provide instruction represented a familiar and well-chronicled response to environmental pressures (Ehrenberg & Zhang, 2005; Schuster & Finkelstein, 2006) but also posed difficulties in the human capital model because it reduced the involvement of skilled individuals in teaching and training.

A second strategy that may be less familiar is the decline of the traditional "balanced portfolio" of teaching, research, and service for tenured faculty members who did not secure substantial external funds. "If you don't get [a big grant]," according to a chair of a high-resource department at FU, "you'll teach more classes." An associate professor in a high-resource department at A&SU reported that his unit employed a similar managerial orientation. "People who don't have grants" often "have been given other responsibilities to try and justify their existence," he told us. An associate professor in a high-resource unit at FU stated that her area also assigned heavy teaching loads to tenured faculty members who did not generate a large volume of external revenue. She worried that "if I don't get things cooking a little bit better, then I'll probably be tracked into one of those [teaching] slots."

This decline in traditional academic roles seemed to undermine the meaning individuals found in their work and, accordingly, the amount of themselves that they invested in their work. A number of interview participants explicitly related this sense of disconnection to competition for scarce resources. "There's a very strong felt sense of our being more adversaries than colleagues," a professor in a low-resource unit at FU told us. Faculty members whom we interviewed also asserted that patterns in resource allocation reflected quasi-market conditions, which were shaped by policy priorities rather than economic processes. An associate professor in a low-resource unit at FU stated, "I don't think there is not the money. I think choices have been made about how to disperse the money." An adjunct faculty member in a low-resource unit at A&SU agreed, reporting that there was "simply a greater societal and cultural valuing of the sciences."

As posited throughout this chapter, faculty members expressed a sense that these policy priorities—and the allocation mechanism of quasi-markets that reflected these priorities—distorted and distracted from higher education's purposes. In the terms of human capital theory, faculty members often expressed chagrin over what they perceived as the waste of skilled and knowledgeable workers. Reflecting on her unit's reliance on adjunct faculty, an associate professor in a low-resource unit at A&SU said, "The whole situation of hiring people because they're good at research and then offering them positions that do not allow them to do research is really grotesque." An endowed chair in a low-resource unit at A&SU likewise noted that, because of financial constraints, "we can't maximize the potential that we have." An assistant professor at A&SU found these conditions ironic. Where the human capital model frames higher education as a means of training skilled workers to fill jobs, this individual suggested that her department relied on graduate students to teach undergraduate classes as low-salaried teaching assistants, but harbored no expectations that they would become faculty members themselves. She asked rhetorically, "how can you keep admitting all these great grad students, which keeps us alive as a department, and then not be able to help them get jobs?"

The faculty in high-resource units, whether at A&SU or FU, seemed to accept the economization of their work lives willingly, sometimes eagerly. They strategized about how they and their colleagues could participate in large grant applications that depended on self-organizing networks of faculty who worked with similarly motivated faculty at other universities, representatives of federal funding agencies, and often in partnership with industry. A powerful example is a department at FU that voted to accept university pay only for a single semester in return for being able to act as semifree agents during the second semester. They are semifree rather than free because they have a negotiated wage cap. This maximum allows them to earn much more than a typical university salary—indeed, some are able to double their pay—but this freedom exists within prescribed limits. Although earnings are upward bounded, no safeguards exist on the lower extreme. Should any individual professor not be successful in competing for external funds in the second semester, that professor cannot turn to the university for pay.

The faculty in low-resource departments offered some critique of these arrangements, even going so far as to suggest that it may not be possible to think of the neoliberal university as a whole that encompasses STEM and business as well as the many low-resource fields. But their critique has not led them to any sort of obvious, organized challenge to these new conditions. Rather, faculty in low-resource fields, although unhappy, generally seemed resigned. As one faculty member in a low-resource department said when relating his initial reluctance to talk to us, "I don't want to pick over the corpse again."

Conclusion

Human capital theory has profoundly shaped US higher education policy. Yet, as noted in Ball's (2012) work and the theory of academic capitalism (Slaughter & Rhoades, 2004), the human capital rationale for investment in higher education coexists with the retreat of direct state support and the rise of market-like allocation mechanisms. Stage one of our analysis considers a range of contemporary policy documents that confirm the coexistence of the human capital model with market-like mechanisms, such as federal student financial aid and research funding. Stage two then suggests that this coexistence proves uneasy; where the human capital model would have higher education instill knowledge and skills in its students, neoliberal policies incent colleges and universities to focus instead on winning competitions. While such competitions are intended to promote efficiency (Hearn & Longanecker, 1985), research universities have suppressed neither total costs (Archibald & Feldman, 2011) nor tuition prices (Desrochers & Wellman, 2011), both of which have risen dramatically as direct state support has waned.

Stage three of our analysis indicates that tensions between the human capital model and market-like mechanisms profoundly shape faculty work. Training students is accorded little importance relative to securing research grants, and faculty members shape their research agendas to appeal to funding sources. Faculty in high-resource units, often located in the sciences and engineering, understand that they have to generate money to succeed in their careers. Unfunded science is not important, and neither is teaching science to undergraduates. Faculty in low-resource departments, often in the humanities and social sciences, understand that their disciplines are not regarded as producing valuable human capital. They fear that they are increasingly relegated to teaching, which does not generate research support and so is not valued.

Taken together, the three strains of our analysis indicate that the imperative of winning market-like competitions distorts the development and deployment of human capital. This tension between the human capital narrative and market-like mechanisms raises a crucial question for higher education scholars and policymakers. Can social policies that rely on competition yield widespread social benefits such as those envisioned in the human capital model? Both Ball (2012) and the theory of academic capitalism (Slaughter & Rhoades, 2004) stress that public policy, designed to benefit the citizenry as a whole, may be incommensurate with marketization. McMahon's (2009) articulation of a "modern human capital" approach proves rife with skepticism about market-like mechanisms that allow students to "vote with their feet." The policy solutions he proposes instead envision a more direct—and more expensive—role for the state in fostering human capital development and ultimately economic growth. Our analysis provides substantial confirmation for his position, indicating that market-like competitions do not efficiently deliver the benefits of higher education. Instead, as predicted by the theory of academic capitalism (Cantwell & Taylor, 2013; Slaughter & Cantwell, 2012), competition produces a few winners and a great many losers. Such a system underutilizes much of the human capital that it has produced.

On a final note, we acknowledge that many faculty members in low-resource units likely would find the human capital defense of higher education to be narrow and instrumental. After all, this account values higher education as a means to an end—such as higher lifetime wages, greater health outcomes, or economic growth—rather than as an intrinsically valuable activity. As such, the human capital narrative ignores other purposes of higher education; only the faint echo of what David Labaree (1997) termed the "democratic equality goal" remains in McMahon's (2009) assertion that improving human capital also improves voter turnout. We suggest, however, that the very narrowness of our approach constitutes its usefulness. If market-like allocation corrupts even the goal of human capital development, despite the fact that both narratives originate in economics, then the fate of higher education's broader purposes bears close scrutiny as policymakers rely ever more heavily on market-like mechanisms. Future theorizing and research must continue to attend to the effects of market-like competition in the United States lest the rationales that justify investment in higher education be lost.

ACKNOWLEDGMENT

We thank the Canadian Social Sciences and Humanities Research Council, which provided funding for Amy Metcalfe and Sheila Slaughter. Their grant "Gender and Academic Capitalism: Men and Women of the Entrepreneurial Academy, 2008–2011," supported this research.

NOTE

1. To protect the confidentiality of our case sites, all figures are approximations. All financial figures are adjusted for inflation using the Consumer Price Index.

REFERENCES

Anderson, G. A., & Keys, J. D. (2007). Building human capital through education. *Journal of Legal Economics, 14*(1), 49–74.

Archibald, R. N., & Feldman, D. H. (2011). *Why does college cost so much?* New York: Oxford University Press.

Ball, S. J. (2012). *Global education, Inc.: New policy networks and the neo-liberal imaginary.* New York: Routledge.

Baskin, P. (2011, February 23). NIH pushes ahead on research division to speed drug development, despite protests from scientists and others. *Chronicle of Higher Education.* Retrieved from http://chronicle.com/article/NIH-Pushes-Ahead-on-research/126500/.

Becker, G. S. (1962). Investment in human capital: A theoretical analysis. *Journal of Political Economy, 70,* 9–49.

Branscomb, L. M., Florida, R. L., Hart, D., Keller, J., & Boville, D. (1997). *Investing in innovation: Toward a consensus strategy for federal technology policy.* Washington, DC: Competitiveness Policy Council.

Cantwell, B., & Taylor, B. J. (2013). Global status, intra-institutional stratification and organizational segmentation: A time-dynamic Tobit analysis of ARWU position among US universities. *Minerva, 51*(2), 1–29.

Carnegie Commission on Science, Technology, and Government. (1993). *Science, technology, and government for a changing world.* New York: Author.

Committee on Criteria for Federal Support for Research and Development. (1995). *Allocating federal funds for science and technology.* Washington, DC: National Academies Press.

Committee on Science, Engineering, and Public Policy. (1993). *Science, technology, and the federal government: National goals for a new era.* Washington, DC: National Academies Press.

———. (1995). *Reshaping the graduate education of scientists and engineers.* Washington, DC: National Academies Press.

Desrochers, D. M., & Wellman, J. V. (2011). *Trends in college spending 1999-2009: Where does the money come from? Where does it go? What does it buy? A report of the Delta Cost Project.* Washington, DC: American Institutes for Research.

Donoghue, F. (2008). *The last professors: The corporate university and the fate of the humanities.* Bronx, NY: Fordham University Press.

Doyle, W. R. (2006). Adoption of merit-based student grant programs: An event history analysis. *Educational Evaluation and Policy Analysis, 28*(3), 259–85.

Ehrenberg, R. G., & Zhang, L. (2005). Do tenured and tenure-track faculty matter? *Journal of Human Resources, 40*(3), 647–59.

Engberg, M. E., & Allen, D. J. (2011). Uncontrolled destinies: Improving opportunity for low-income students in American higher education. *Research in Higher Education, 52*(8), 786–807.

Friedman, M., & Friedman, R. (1990). *Free to choose: A personal statement.* New York: Harcourt.

Harvey, D. (2005). *A brief history of neoliberalism.* New York: Oxford University Press.

Hearn, J. C., & Griswold, C. P. (1994). State-level centralization and policy innovation in US postsecondary education. *Educational evaluation and policy analysis, 16*(2), 161–90.

Hearn, J. C., Griswold, C. P., & Marine, G. M. (1996). Region, resources, and reason: A contextual analysis of state tuition and student aid policies. *Research in Higher Education, 37*(3), 141–78.

Hearn, J. C., & Longanecker, D. (1985). Enrollment effects of alternative postsecondary pricing policies. *Journal of Higher Education, 56*(6), 485–508.

Heller, D. E. (1997). Student price response in higher education: An update to Leslie and Brinkman. *Journal of Higher Education, 68*(6), 624–59.

———. (2006). The changing nature of public support for higher education in the United States. In P. N. Teixeira et al. (Eds.), *Cost sharing and accessibility in higher education: A fairer deal?* (pp. 133–58). Dordrecht: Springer.

Hillman, N. (2012). Tuition discounting for revenue management. *Research in Higher Education, 53*(3), 263–81.

Humphreys, D. (2012). What's wrong with the completion agenda—And what we can do about it. *Liberal Education, 98*(1), 8–17.

Jacob, B., McCall, B., & Stange, K. M. (2013). *College as country club: Do colleges cater to students' preferences for consumption?* Working Paper 18745. Cambridge, MA: National Bureau of Economic Research.

Johnstone, D. B. (2004). The economics and politics of cost sharing in higher education: Comparative perspectives. *Economics of Education Review, 23*(4), 403–10.

Kiker, B. F. (1966). The historical roots of the concept of human capital. *Journal of Political Economy, 74*(5), 481–99.

Labaree, D. F. (1997). Public goods, private goods: The American struggle over educational goals. *American Educational Research Journal, 34*(1), 39–81.

Le Grand, J., & Bartlett, W. (1993). *Quasi-markets and social policy: The way forward?* Basingstoke: Macmillan.

Leslie, L. L., & Brinkman, P. T. (1988). *The economic value of higher education.* New York: Macmillan.

Leslie, L. L., & Johnson, G. P. (1974). The market model and higher education. *Journal of Higher Education, 45*(1), 1–20.

Marginson, S. (2013). The impossibility of capitalist markets in higher education. *Journal of Education Policy, 28*(3), 353–70.

McDonough, P. M. (1994). Buying and selling higher education: The social construction of the college applicant. *Journal of Higher Education, 65*(4), 427–446.

McLendon, M. K., Hearn, J. C., & Deaton, R. (2006). Called to account: Analyzing the origins and spread of state performance-accountability policies for higher education. *Educational Evaluation and Policy Analysis, 28*(1), 1–24.

McMahon, W. W. (2009). *Higher learning, greater good: The private and social benefits of higher education.* Baltimore: Johns Hopkins University Press.

Merriam, S. B. (1998). *Qualitative research and case study applications in education.* San Francisco: Jossey-Bass.

Mincer, J. (1958). Investment in human capital and personal income distribution. *Journal of Political Economy, 66*(4), 281–302.

Mullin, C. M. (2011). *The road ahead: A look at trends in the educational attainment of community college students.* Washington, DC: American Association of Community Colleges.

National Education Association. (2007). Part-time faculty: A look at data and issues. *Higher Education Research Center Update, 11*(3). Retrieved from www.nea.org/assets/docs/HE/vol11no3.pdf.

NCES. National Center for Educational Statistics. (2013). *Characteristics of postsecondary faculty.* Washington, DC: Author. Retrieved from http://nces.ed.gov/programs/coe/indicator_cuf.asp.

Newfield, C. (2009). Ending the budget wars: Funding the humanities during a crisis in higher education. *Profession, 8*(1), 270–84.

NIH. National Institutes of Health. (2011). *NIH fact sheet.* Washington, DC: Author. Retrieved from www.aamc.org/research/adhocgp/081011.pdf.

NSF. National Science Foundation. (2011). *Institutional profiles.* Washington, DC: Author. Retrieved from http://webcaspar.nsf.gov/profiles/site?method=view&fice=1083.

———. (2012). *Science and engineering indicators.* Washington, DC: Author.

Office of Science and Technology Policy. (2013). *The FY 2014 science and technology R&D budget.* Washington, DC: Author. Retrieved from www.whitehouse.gov/sites/default/files/microsites/ostp/2014_R&Dbudget_Release.pdf.

Peck, J., & Tickell, A. (2002). Neoliberalizing space. *Antipode, 34*(3), 380–404.

Perna, L. W. (2002). Sex differences in the supplemental earnings of college and university faculty. *Research in Higher Education, 43*(1), 31–58.

———. (2003). The status of women and minorities among community college faculty. *Research in Higher Education, 44*(2), 205–40.

Rhoades, G. (2012). The incomplete completion agenda: Implications for academe and the academy. *Liberal Education, 98*(1), 18–25.

Rizzo, M., & Ehrenberg, R. G. (2004). Resident and nonresident tuition and enrollment at flagship state universities. In *College choices: The economics of where to go, when to go, and how to pay for it* (pp. 303–54). Chicago: University of Chicago Press.

Roulston, K. (2010). *Reflective interviewing: A guide to theory and practice.* Los Angeles: Sage.

Rupert, P., Schweitzer, M. E., Severance-Lossin, E., & Turner, E. (1996). Earnings, education, and experience. *Economic Review, 32*(4), 2–12.

Schultz, T. W. (1961). Investment in human capital. *American Economic Review, 51*(1), 1–17.

Schuster, J. H., & Finkelstein, M. J. (2006). *The American faculty: The restructuring of academic work and careers.* Baltimore: Johns Hopkins University Press.

Slaughter, S. (1990). *The higher learning and high technology: Dynamics of higher education policy formation.* Albany: State University of New York Press.

———. (forthcoming). Retheorizing academic capitalism: Actors, mechanisms, fields and networks. In B. Cantwell & I. Kauppinen (Eds.), *Academic Capitalism in an Era of Globalization.* Baltimore: Johns Hopkins University Press.

Slaughter, S., & Cantwell, B. (2012). Transatlantic moves to the market: The United States and the European Union. *Higher Education, 63*(5), 583–606.

Slaughter, S., & Leslie, L. L. (1997). *Academic capitalism: Politics, policies, and the entrepreneurial university.* Baltimore: Johns Hopkins University Press.

Slaughter, S., & Rhoades, G. (1996). The emergence of a competitiveness research and development policy coalition and the commercialization of academic science and technology. *Science, Technology, and Human Values, 21*(3), 303–39.

———. (2004). *Academic capitalism and the new economy: Markets, state, and higher education.* Baltimore: Johns Hopkins University Press.

———. (2005). From "endless frontier" to "basic science for use": Social contracts between science and society. *Science, Technology, and Human Values, 30*(4), 536–72.

———. (2011). Markets in higher education: Trends in academic capitalism. In P. G. Altbach, P. J. Gumport, & R. O. Berdahl (Eds.), *American higher education in the twenty-first century* (3rd ed., pp. 433–64). Baltimore: Johns Hopkins University Press.

Stephan, P. (2012). *How economics shapes science.* Cambridge, MA: Harvard University Press.

St. John, E. P., Daun-Barnett, N., & Moronski-Chapman, K. M. (2013) *Public policy and higher education.* New York: Routledge.

Suresh, S. (2011, July 28.) *Talking points on the national science foundation's innovation corps to strengthen the impact of scientific discoveries.* Washington, DC: National Science Foundation. Retrieved from www.nsf.gov/news/speeches/suresh/11/ss110728_icorps.jsp.

Taylor, B. J., Cantwell, B., & Slaughter, S. (2013). Quasi-markets in US higher education: Humanities emphasis and institutional revenues. *Journal of Higher Education*, *84*(5), 674–707.

Thomas, S. L., & Zhang, L. (2005). Post-baccalaureate wage growth within four years of graduation: The effects of college quality and college major. *Research in Higher Education*, *46*(4), 437–59.

Toutkoushian, R. K., & Hillman, N. W. (2012). The impact of state appropriations and grants on access to higher education and outmigration. *Review of Higher Education*, *36*(1), 51–90.

US Council on Competitiveness. (1996). *Endless frontier, limited resources: US R&D policy for competitiveness*. Washington, DC: Author.

US Department of Education. (2011). *Federal Pell grants: Fiscal year 2011 budget request*. Washington, DC: Author. Retrieved from www2.ed.gov/about/overview/budget/budget11/justifications/p-pell.pdf.

Volkwein, J. F., & Tandberg, D. A. (2008). Measuring up: Examining the connections among state structural characteristics, regulatory practices, and performance. *Research in Higher Education*, *49*(2), 180–97.

Walters, G. (2012). It's not so easy: The completion agenda and the states. *Liberal Education*, *98*(1), 34–39.

Weisbrod, B. A., Ballou, J. P., & Asch, E. D. (2008). *Mission and money*. New York: Cambridge University Press.

Zuckerman, H., & Ehrenberg, R. G. (2009). Recent trends in funding for the academic humanities and their implications. *Daedalus*, *138*(1), 124–46.

CHAPTER FIVE

The Ideas and Craft of the Critical Historian of Education

DERRICK P. ALRIDGE

What is critical history, and how has it influenced our understanding of education and schooling? These questions prompted me to think carefully about how the word "critical" is used among education scholars and exactly what it means to be critical as a historian of education. Seldom have I heard historians describe their own historical approach or perspective as being critical. When I consider the term within its historical milieu, however, the work of many historians comes to mind.

Critical historians dig beneath the surface of events and phenomena using critical theoretical interpretive frames to interrogate and challenge traditional canons. Critical historians of education ask, "What groups and individuals are advantaged and what groups and individuals are disadvantaged by particular historical educational plans and organizations?" (Villaverde, Helyar, & Kincheloe, 2006, p. 321). Critical historians of education also investigate how power relations shape education and schooling. Such historians use theory to consider alternative ways of thinking about questions and employ innovative methodological approaches to study the relationship of the past to the present.

In light of the recent and rapid changes occurring in K–12 and higher education, critical history of education is needed now more than ever before. The increasing implementation of neoliberal educational policies—along with rapid technological change, the privatization and corporatization of schools and colleges, and the increased standardization of curricula—are only a few of the issues radically changing education in the twenty-first century. Despite these fundamental changes, the insights of historians have largely been absent from recent discourse and debates on contemporary education. The absence of a historical perspective from this discourse is crippling to the conversation and to efforts to improve the US educational system. By understanding the historical context, educational historians provide vital insights into the complexities of contemporary education. Historians employing critical lenses and approaches to educational issues, I believe, contribute even greater depth to our understanding.

This chapter presents a personal examination of critical history and historiography. As a historian, I discuss the work of those critical historians who have most influenced my thinking about history and the study of education. The historians who have most influenced my conceptualization of the idea and craft of the critical historian have primarily written in the subfields of US intellectual history and African American history. As such, there are historians not covered in this essay who may be considered critical historians. Several key questions guide my inquiry: What is critical history? Who can be identified as a critical historian? What insights regarding issues of equity, equality, and democracy have critical historians offered to education and schooling? How might critical historians influence contemporary and future education?

What Is Critical History?

Critical history is defined differently by different people, but for most, critical history emerges from the foundation of critical theory. Critical theory is associated with a group of German intellectuals referred to as the Frankfurt School because of their connection with the Institute of Social Research, founded in 1923 at the University of Frankfurt. Observing the rise of Hitler and Nazism, the group relocated to New York and became affiliated with Columbia University. Some members of the Frankfurt School moved back to Germany in 1949, four years after the fall of the Third Reich. Despite the return to Germany, the group's influence on American thought was profound and long lasting (Storey, 2009).

The most prominent members of the Frankfurt School were Theodor Adorno, Walter Benjamin, Max Horkheimer, Leo Lowenthal, and Herbert Marcuse. Collectively, they were recognized for their eclectic mix of theory and penetrating analyses of society that challenged the status quo. They were also known for blending Marxism and psychoanalysis as a means of interpreting contemporary events, culture, media, and politics. The Frankfurt School's ideas became known as "critical theory," and their way of thinking about society influenced intellectual activists well into the 1960s, most notably 1960s radical and activist Angela Davis, who became a protégé of Marcuse (see Storey, 2009; Friedel, 2011).

While these scholars laid a philosophical foundation for the post-WWII generation, critical theory also began to permeate historical scholarship in the decades following the rise of the Frankfurt School. One of its young acolytes in the 1960s was literary scholar and historian Hayden White. In his influential essay "The Burden of History," published in 1968, White argued that historians had become irrelevant as a result of their obsession with positivistic history and their failure to use their knowledge of history to help inform the present. Because historians were overly concerned with gatekeeping the field of history, White noted, they would not allow history to inform contemporary society (White, 1968).

Moreover, White argued that historical training did not prepare historians to present analyses of pressing issues of the day, stating, "What is usually called the 'training' of the historian consists for the most part of study in a few languages, journeyman work in the archives, and the performance of a few set exercises to acquaint him with standard reference works and journals in his field" (White, 1968, p. 124). For White, historical training did not offer historians a broad intellectual view of the world, but instead produced overly specialized scholars who falsely claimed scientific authority. He further observed that "the historical past, therefore, is, like our various personal pasts, at best a myth, justifying our gamble on a specific future, and at worst a lie, a retrospective rationalization of what we have in fact become through our choices" (White, 1968, p. 123).

In *Metahistory: The Historical Imagination in Nineteenth-Century Europe,* White (1973) offered an illuminating treatise that supports the critical history project. He argued that history is not a set of facts waiting to be discovered, but rather disparate data that comprise a narrative based on a particular historian's emplotment of events. In other words, history is what we make it based on how we codify it. According to White, historians employ specific types of emplotment in writing history: romance, satire, comedy, and tragedy. His notion of emplotment reveals a key belief of critical historians: that all history has a particular interpretation that is influenced by the choices of the historian writing the history (White, 1973).

French philosopher Michel Foucault has also been a key influence on contemporary views of critical history. Foucault objected to the notion that history was stuck in the past and advocated writing history for the present. According to historian Paul Mazzocchi (2008), Foucault encourages us "to understand a present that is not a result of the past but a past that can only be understood in its sagittal relationship to the present" (p. 94).

In *The Archeology of Knowledge and the Discourse on Language,* Foucault (1972) elucidated his ideas about history. He argued that previous approaches to history that sought to link disparate events, identify causal succession between events, and establish continuity between events were outmoded. Instead, Foucault emphasized ruptures in established periodizations and argued that historical texts can be read in new ways if we jettison previously established periods and master narratives. In this way, history can offer fresh perspectives rather than merely rehashing the past (Foucault, 1972).

Disciplinary historians have disregarded Foucault's work for several reasons. First, because of the prominence of theory in his work, Foucault is often viewed as a philosopher rather than a historian. Second, Foucault did not adhere to the strict empiricism of citation used in traditional historical research, and the fact that he often used few citations placed him outside the methodological tradition of historians. Thus he was simply not viewed as a member of the historians' guild. Nonetheless, the academic world and historians today more readily engage Foucault's ideas of the past being one with the present (Megill, 1987).

The Frankfurt School, Hayden White, and Michel Foucault are perhaps the most significant theoretical contributors to critical history. But before and alongside the Frankfurt School, other historians were constructing radical counternarratives and proposing revisionist approaches to history that reflected a multiplicity of ideas and methods and challenged established canons and norms. The following discussion introduces several of these critical historians who have tremendously influenced my own work and that of many others in the field of critical history.

Of Du Bois, Hofstadter, Zinn, and Roediger

On December 30, 1909, the young historian W. E. B. Du Bois presented his paper "Reconstruction and Its Benefits" at the annual meeting of the American Historical Association. In the audience was historian William Dunning, a Southern sympathizer who argued that Reconstruction was a failure because of blacks' incompetence and the meddling of Northern whites in Southern affairs. Despite Dunning's pro-Southern views, he informed Du Bois's graduate school professor, Albert Bushnell Hart, that he was impressed with the young scholar's paper. Du Bois's presentation was later published in the July 1910 volume of *American Historical Review* (see Alridge, 2008; Butchart, 1988).

Du Bois's journey as a historian who challenged the field's traditions and canons began prior to his presentation at the American Historical Association. Trained in history and the social sciences at Harvard and the University of Berlin in the 1890s, Du Bois came to the study of history with great respect for empirical evidence. Historian Albert Hart's social scientific approach and philosopher William James's pragmatic philosophy tremendously influenced the young Du Bois's thinking about and approach to history. James's pragmatism encouraged Du Bois to challenge the canonical status quo by placing ideas under intense scrutiny. For the pragmatist, the search for truth is ongoing. Hart's emphasis on using robust data and empirical methods offered Du Bois a method to challenge the "Negro problem" with great authority and precision (Alridge, 2008; Du Bois, 1968).

Du Bois's training at the University of Berlin enhanced his ideas on pragmatism and provided a methodological approach. Studying with Heinrich von Treitschke and Gustav von Schmoller, Du Bois learned the importance of using research to provide insight and offer solutions to the problems of the present. Using the tools of history and empirical social science, Du Bois sought to challenge historical normativity and change the world in which he lived (Du Bois, 1968).

Du Bois's doctoral dissertation, *The Suppression of the African Slave-Trade to the United States of America, 1638–1870*, was a meticulously researched study that drew on government and congressional records and reports. Du Bois had little access to archival collections or papers, so he obtained many primary sources on his own, amassing an impressive collection of materials. Du Bois's methods were eclectic, and his approach was critical. In the final chapter of *Suppression of the African Slave Trade*, he takes his most critical stance by raising the issue of morality in the slave trade. By this point he had provided the meticulous documentation necessary to drive his progressive agenda. *Suppression* subsequently became the first volume in Harvard's Historical Studies series (see Du Bois, 1896/1969).

By the early 1900s, Du Bois became disenchanted with traditional historical and social scientific methods of attacking the "Negro problem." He felt that his work as a historian and social scientist needed to be more critical, propagandistic, and substantive in challenging the traditional and prevailing ideas about blacks. As a result, he published several works offering counternarratives to prevailing notions of history, including *John Brown* (1909), *The Negro* (1915/2002), and *The World and Africa* (1946/1965), among others.

After reading the flawed and racist analyses of Reconstruction of the day, historian Anna Julia Cooper called on Du Bois to respond, writing that Du Bois was "adequately, fully, ably, finally & again, it seems to me that Thou art the man" (Cooper, 1973/1997, p. 411). Du Bois heeded Cooper's call and renewed his challenge to the Dunning School, which he had begun decades earlier with his paper "Reconstruction and Its Benefits." This time, however, he would produce a fullblown critical history and historiography of Reconstruction. During the same period in which Du Bois was researching and writing his critical tome, the Frankfurt School was gaining popularity in Europe and New York (Alridge, 2008).

Du Bois's mammoth history *Black Reconstruction in America, 1860–1880* was timely and seemed to seize the zeitgeist of the day. Conceptually and methodologically, *Black Reconstruction* is a tour de force of critical history. Du Bois dismantled the widely accepted historiography of the time regarding Reconstruction, and his methodology was nontraditional. Limited to using many secondary sources and blocked from access to most primary sources because of discrimination he faced in the archives as a black historian, Du Bois turned historical methodology on its head by using some of the same sources the Dunning historians used, but to refute their thesis (Du Bois, 1935/1995).

Black Reconstruction was forthright as a piece of activist scholarship with an agenda. Du Bois embraced Marxism as a theoretical lens, but challenged even the Marxists by equally privileging race and class in his analysis. Finally, as Du Bois had done previously in *Suppression of the African Slave-Trade*, he offered his most critical analysis in the final chapter. In "The Propaganda of History," Du Bois harshly criticized contemporary educators and historians for developing a curriculum that gave students inaccurate and misleading information. Typical of many critical historians who would follow, Du Bois directly addressed issues of curriculum and pedagogy and suggested how historians could play an active role in curriculum and pedagogy in schools.

While Du Bois was writing *Black Reconstruction*, a young scholar of history was completing his doctoral studies at Columbia University. Richard Hofstadter studied with the prominent historian Merle Curti at Columbia from 1936 to 1942. Under Curti's influence, Hofstadter became immersed in the burgeoning field of intellectual history—a field Curti was instrumental in founding (Brown, 2006). Hofstadter was also knowledgeable about theory and methods in other fields. While at Columbia, he encountered the exciting new work of the Frankfurt School scholars, who were in New York at that time and who influenced Hofstadter both theoretically and methodologically. According to historian David Brown (2006), the Frankfurt School gave Hofstadter "social-psychological indexes"—including ethnicity, culture, and personality—to interpret politics and political behavior (p. 90). Hofstadter was influenced as well by Karl Mannheim's *Ideology and Utopia*, particularly Mannheim's idea that the desires of citizens and nations were hidden in fictions (ideologies) and wish-dreams (utopias). These ideas are reflected throughout Hofstadter's work in his approaches to codifying and making sense of ideas (Brown, 2006; Mannheim, 1936).

The result of Hofstadter's eclectic interests and interdisciplinary study was his ambitious *The American Political Tradition and the Men Who Made It*. This study of American political thought used the tropes of psychological dualism, paradox, and mythology to reveal the complexity and tensions among American thinkers and thought. Hofstadter was not interested in producing narrative or descriptive biographies of American politicians, but instead sought to present the complicated and oftentimes contradictory ideas of American politicians. At the heart of these paradoxes, Hofstadter argued, lay the complexity of American political thinking and life. Chapters titled "Thomas Jefferson: The Aristocrat as Democrat," "John C. Calhoun: The Marx of the Master Class," and "Theodore Roosevelt: The Conservative as Progressive" reveal the tropes of dialectics and paradox in Hofstadter's methodology. His nontraditional approach illuminates the complexity of American historical accounts and introduces alternative ways to read history (Hofstadter, 1948/1973).

Hofstadter himself called *American Political Tradition* "a young man's book," characterizing it as "a product of the social criticism of the 1930's, a book in which the American political tradition is being seen from a vantage point well to the left, and from the personal perspective of a young man who has only a limited capacity for identifying with those who exercise power" (Hofstadter, 1948/1973, p. xxv–xxvi). Using the trope of paradox, Hofstadter exposed elements of history that were often hidden in plain sight. Hofstadter's work embraced the critical historical tradition by illuminating uncomfortable truths about our heroes and cherished institutions.

Hofstadter's most enduring study was his Pulitzer Prize–winning book, *Anti-Intellectualism in American Life*. At the heart of *Anti-Intellectualism* was Hofstadter's argument that the United States had become increasingly hostile toward critical discourses and scholars on the left. But Hofstadter did not spare his compatriots on the political left from his criticism of anti-intellectualism. His chapters on American education harshly critiqued aspects of progressive education, for example, pointing out that the abandonment of liberal education in favor of experiential learning was an affront to intellectualism. In evaluating progressive education, Hofstadter criticized some of the ideas of the most prominent philosophical leader of the left during the first half of the twentieth century—John Dewey (see Hofstadter, 1963).

As the 1960s waned, Hofstadter saw his political views and scholarly approach become antiquated among the younger generation of historians. Whereas Hofstadter produced historical syntheses, this new group was strongly influenced by the "new history," which focused on producing specialized monographs of communities and historically oppressed groups. While the world may have been changing too fast for Hofstadter, however, he tried to maintain his critical persona and historical approach to thinking about the world. Thus, when asked by activist professor Paul Goodman of the University of California, Davis, to support Herbert Marcuse's former student and protégé Angela Davis after her firing from the University of California, Los Angeles, in 1969, Hofstadter quickly agreed (Brown, 2006). For although he did not favor the revolutionary upheaval occurring in academia and in the streets in the 1950s and 1960s, the core of his scholarship lay in his commitment to addressing the issues of his day. In 1960 he stated, "I know it is risky, but I still write history out of my engagement with the present" (quoted in Brown, 2006, p. 97).

While Hofstadter was in his prime, another historian-in-training at Columbia would become one of the best-known internationally recognized radical historians of the second half of the twentieth century. The young Howard Zinn, tremendously impressed by Hofstadter's *American Political Tradition*, would master Hofstadter's approach and go on to offer biting criticism of American traditional historical canons. Zinn accomplished his task by unearthing data that others overlooked, asking questions that others failed to ask, and employing theories that illuminated new historical questions and offered fresh answers to old questions.

Zinn would meld the role of the historian with political activism in a manner unprecedented in the twentieth century. When he became a professor of history at Spelman College in Atlanta in 1956, the civil rights movement was red hot. Zinn helped mobilize student protests and asked W. E. B. Du Bois to become involved in one of the Atlanta sit-ins in 1961 (because of illness, Du Bois was unable to accept). Zinn viewed Du Bois as an activist historian who connected his scholarship to the present—a tenet of critical history. Asking Du Bois to come to Atlanta for the sit-in, Zinn believed, was in the activist tradition of critical historians. Zinn and legendary civil rights activist Ella Baker met with a group of students in April 1960 at Shaw University in Raleigh, North Carolina, which founded the Student Nonviolent Coordinating Committee (SNCC). Zinn and Baker would become official advisors of the group (Alridge, 2008).

Zinn's activism and work with SNCC were intricately connected. In 1964, he published *SNCC: The New Abolitionists*. While not a history of SNCC, *New Abolitionists* was grounded in historical scholarship that employed ethnographic methods of observation and community engagement. The book is an excellent example of writing a history of the present—an idea that would become an important aspect of critical history. Of his methods, Zinn (1964/1985) wrote, "Much of my information is gained first-hand, from being where SNCC people work, watching them in action, talking to them. A good deal of the documentation comes from SNCC's extensive files in the Atlanta office" (p. ii). *SNCC: The New Abolitionists* is an insightful piece of scholarship that linked SNCC to the larger and longer history of the black freedom struggle, particularly the abolitionist movement. The study brings history to life and conveys the feel of the movement in real time while keeping the movement historically grounded. In this way, it not only provided a history of the present for students of the 1960s, but also became valuable historical data itself. Zinn's historical scholarship and teaching helped convey the revolutionary grassroots ideas of SNCC to the contemporary world.

Zinn's most well-known and influential critical work, *A People's History of the United States* (1980), forcefully challenged the traditional master narratives of American history. Unlike many histories of the United States, Zinn's book takes a bottom–up view, telling the stories of historically oppressed groups such as Native Americans, blacks, women, and the poor. Chapter titles such as "Columbus, the Indians, and Human Progress," "Slavery without Submission, Emancipation without Freedom," "The Empire and the People," "A People's War?," and "The Impossible Victory: Vietnam," among others, reveal Zinn's critical approach in interpreting American history. Instead of accepting traditional, top–down master narratives about American exceptionalism, Zinn presents the counternarrative to such views. *People's History* is one of the most influential works of historical scholarship ever published, as evidenced by the book's penetration into mainstream high school and university curricula. To date, the book has sold over two million copies and is required reading at many universities around the country (Cohen, 2013; Cohen and Morrow, 2013). All of Zinn's work is critical, challenging prevailing ideas and master narratives and uncovering significant but previously hidden histories. Zinn fused his activism and scholarship in a way that has made him one of the most important critical historians of our time. His work presents a history of the oppressed and unheard. It is truly a history of *the people*.

Another example of critical history in the Du Boisian tradition is David Roediger's *The Wages of Whiteness: Race and the Making of the American Working Class*. A student of Sterling Stuckey and George Fredrickson—"two of the most penetrating writers on race in the United States," according to Roediger (1991, p. vii)—Roediger would come to represent a new generation of critical historians whose work further pushed the boundaries of historical methodology and theory. Extending the notion of "the wages of whiteness" articulated by Du Bois in *Black Reconstruction*, Roediger (1991) demonstrated how capitalism provided fertile ground for solidifying whiteness in America and how the Irish American working class reified the concept of whiteness.

To set the stage for his critical study, Roediger (1991) opens with an innovative introductory chapter titled "On Autobiography and Theory," in which he situates himself as a historian and elucidates the theories and methods that guide his study. Such an approach is rare for a historical study, but it was clearly necessary for this work of critical history and reflects the innovative approach typical of the critical historian. Historians do not usually delineate their theory and methodology. Nor do they typically provide autobiography to help explain their approach. Roediger (1991) credits the writings of Frantz Fanon and Joel Kovel with influencing his work, as they "forcefully insist on the need for dialectical and materialist approaches within the psychoanalytic frame" (p. 14). Roediger provides an excellent example of how to use theory, interdisciplinary methods, and autobiography to reveal hidden history and how to write theoretically sophisticated and accessible history for professional historians and lay audiences.

Critical History and the Study of Education

One of the most prominent historians to study education was Carter G. Woodson. As an African American historian writing against white supremacist scholarship in the early twentieth century, Woodson intuitively developed a critical approach. In the field of history of education, his breakout work was *The Education of the Negro Prior to 1861* (1919/1992), a refutation of the belief in black inferiority that prevailed in early twentieth-century America. Woodson argued that blacks sought education even while enslaved and viewed education as a means of mental emancipation. Woodson's work, like that of Du Bois, challenged the views of William Dunning and other scholars of the period.

Woodson's research was critical and often viewed as biased, but the thoroughness of his methods was difficult to dispute. Of *Education of the Negro*, one reviewer wrote: "The author of this book exhibits what is coming of the modern scientific method with the bias of ancient prejudice. Thinking of slavery makes him angry . . . the value of the work, however, is not greatly injured by this, for the bias and flag waving are confined mainly to sweeping general statements, while the facts discovered are stated fairly and accurately" (W. L. F., 1916, p. 586).

The critique of Woodson's study as polemical was, from Woodson's perspective, not a slight. As a "race man," Woodson viewed it as his mission to produce such biased and critical historical work. It was his obligation, he believed, to write history that exposed inaccuracies about black Americans, addressed the present concerns of an oppressed people, and offered potential strategies for racial uplift. For Woodson, if this meant being polemical, so be it.

In addition, Woodson's *The Negro in Our History* (1922) was one of the most popular textbooks used in black schools for many years; along with his many other works, it provided critical interpretations of African American life and history. But his most enduring enterprise in critical history was the 1915 founding of the Association for the Study of Negro Life and History. Woodson created the organization to serve as a corrective force in American history. A year later he founded the *Journal of Negro History*, which disseminated knowledge for the organization. The *Journal of Negro History*, now the *Journal of African American History*, has been a venue for critical history for almost a century.

Woodson continued his critical historical work until his death in 1950. Perhaps his most enduring work was his historical polemic *The Mis-Education of the Negro*. In it, Woodson assessed the education of black people within the context of American history. He concluded that although institutional forces hindered "Negro" progress, blacks had also allowed those outside black communities to control their education. The book is thus a critique of both the American educational system and blacks' own misguided approach to education (Woodson, 1933/2005). While not a historical study, the book's critical impact is invaluable. It was a primer for civil rights activists and is among a pantheon of critical texts on the African American experience, including Du Bois's *Black Reconstruction*.

Alongside Du Bois and Woodson emerged another critical historian of education trained in both history and the social sciences. Horace Mann Bond received his PhD in the history of education from the University of Chicago. While at the university he was tremendously influenced by Robert Parks and the sociological work taking place there in the 1930s. Much of Bond's work emphasized the role of race, immigration, and assimilation on American society and culture, with a particular emphasis on the economic and psychological aspects of education (Urban, 1992).

Bond's first major published work, *The Education of the Negro in the American Social Order*, placed him front and center in contesting the traditional belief that US schools create equality for all. This thesis represented a major challenge to the traditional celebratory history of education scholarship, particularly that of famed educator and historian Ellwood Cubberley. Bond (1934/1966) opined, "Strictly speaking, the school has never built a new social order; it has been the product and interpreter of the existing system, sustaining and being sustained by the social complex" (p. 13).

In 1939, Bond followed up with his classic monograph, *Negro Education in Alabama: A Study in Cotton and Steel*. The book was a reworking of his award-winning doctoral dissertation, which examined economics and race as influential factors in educational policy toward blacks in Alabama. Bond saw his work as the antithesis of that of Edgar W. Knight, a former student of William Dunning, who viewed Reconstruction as a failure. Bond argued that although Alabama's Reconstruction government was not perfect, it was nevertheless instrumental in establishing common schools in Alabama (Bond, 1939/1969; Urban, 1987).

During the 1940s and 1950s, few historians of education adopted or expanded Bond's argument that schools reinforced rather than undermined the oppression of blacks and other marginalized groups. But the 1960s would see Bond's thesis revisited by a new generation of historians. With the counterculture and civil rights movements challenging prevailing notions of race, gender, and sexuality, the new history had a strong influence on historians of the time. Within this context, historians of education began to investigate the motives and power of educational institutions in relation to race, class, and ethnicity (Bond, 1939/1969; Urban, 1987).

Echoing some of Bond's ideas regarding American schooling, Michael Katz's *The Irony of Early School Reform: Educational Innovation in Mid-Nineteenth Century Massachusetts* (1968) presented a well-researched study and polemic on school reform during the common school period. Katz challenged the notion of schools as purveyors of enlightenment, arguing that the elite constructed schools to protect their self-interest. Employing social scientific methods and quantitative analysis, Katz's work reflected a thesis and approach similar to those of Horace Mann Bond's *Education of the Negro*. Katz's study, however, was more forthrightly critical and polemical, identifying him as a member of the radical revisionist school of educational historians (Cohen, 1999; Katz, 1968).

The radical revisionists were critical historians whose work sought to explain the problems of American education and schooling in their time. The focus of their work was narrating the social histories of marginalized groups—including the poor, blacks, women, Native Americans, and Latinos—whose social stratification was influenced by political and economic institutions and structures. In studying the oppressed, the radical revisionists sought to debunk educational myths to produce better and more contextualized educational reform and policies (see Donato & Lazerson, 2000).

The same year Katz published *Irony of Early School Reform*, historian Henry Perkinson published his critical historical work *The Imperfect Panacea: American Faith in Education, 1865–1965*. In his study, Perkinson revisited an argument proposed by Horace Mann Bond that schools were not the panaceas idealized in the American consciousness. He acknowledged his indebtedness to critical historians like Merle Curti, Richard Hofstadter, C. Vann Woodward, and Rush Welter, among others. Perkinson's chronological and thematic approach was emblematic of intellectual history, and the book's themes reveal his engagement with the issues of the day: racial inequality, economic opportunity, and urbanization. For Perkinson (1968/1991), "the school failed to solve the multiple problems generated by urbanization, industrialization, emancipation, and nationalization" (p. 220). He argued further that schools reinforced segregation.

One of the most prominent of the radical revisionists was Clarence Karier, who in 1967 published *Man, Society, and Education: A History of American Educational Ideas* (reissued in 1986 as *The Individual, Society, and Education: A History of American Educational Ideas*). At a time when the history of ideas seemed to be fading from the field of history, Karier embraced it with a vengeance to illustrate how ideas had shaped American education. For example, Karier argues that ideas and ideologies such as the Enlightenment, pragmatism, humanism, Fascism and Communism, and the Cold War shaped how schools were conceptualized and operated. Karier's critical approach is summed up best in his own words: "History is not the story of man's past but rather that which certain men have come to think of as their past" (Karier, 1967/1986, p. xvii).

Decontextualized interpretations of the history of education and schooling, Karier believed, could lead to faulty understandings of education in the present. *Individual, Society, and Education* attempted to foreground ideological and intellectual currents in history to better explain American education and schooling. The book provides robust interpretations of history and education, which established Karier as a highly respected critical historian of education.

Karier (1986) took a similar approach with his collection of lectures titled *Scientists of the Mind: Intellectual Founders of Modern Psychology*. The book was a reworking of lectures that Karier delivered at the University of Rochester in the 1960s and the University of Illinois in the 1970s. *Scientists of the Mind* dissected the writing of Western intellectuals such as John Dewey, Sigmund Freud, William James, and Karl Marx, among others. Karier was concerned with excavating the religious and philosophical assumptions that undergirded psychology. The book's relevance for education lay in the close connection between the study of psychology and the field of educational thought, and in Karier's belief that a careful explication of the work of certain influential thinkers could provide an understanding of contemporary education. Karier's premise was not unlike that of his friend and mentor Merle Curti, who also studied individual educators as a means of illuminating the educational ideas of the day. It is perhaps not surprising that Curti read early drafts of *Scientists of the Mind* (see Karier, 1986).

While Karier insisted that ideas must be examined within their historical milieu, he focused his studies on individuals and educational thought instead of larger forces, such as the economy or educational bureaucracies. According to James Anderson (2001), Karier believed "that human beings have a considerable amount of freedom to construct their own conceptions of human nature and society and are not mere reflections for understanding economic and political contradictions" (p. 142).

Several years later, historian Joel Spring published *Education and the Rise of the Corporate State* (1972). Spring anticipated the ascendency and possible take-over of education by corporations and through collaborations between the state and business interests. Philosopher Ivan Illich explicates the book's critical approach early in his foreword, noting, "In [Spring's] perspective the history of schooling turns out to be the account of the increasing sophistication, hypocrisy, and futility of the social controls wearing the mask of preparation for democratic participation" (Spring, 1972, p. ix).

Over four decades, Spring has had a significant influence on educators through his work *The American School, A Global Context: From the Puritans to the Obama Administration* (2013), now in its ninth edition. Widely used in schools of education, *The American School* employs Marxist and critical approaches. At its core, the work foregrounds the experiences of historically oppressed groups. Spring's critical approach, like Zinn's, undertakes a bottom–up examination of education and schooling, presenting education through the eyes of those who experience it. Spring also brings a critical frame of reference to his work by illuminating racism. His work provides a critical multicultural history of American education that shows the interrelationship of civil rights and other social justice movements in the United States.

Another recent critical historical survey of American education appears in John Rury's *Education and Social Change: Contours in the History of American Schooling*. Rury's balanced critical synthesis of American education is grounded in both the past and present. His approach is clear: "This is a history book, one that addresses a broad and complicated topic. Its purpose is both analytic and descriptive, relating what has transpired and explaining why events have taken a particular path" (p. ix). While the text offers a detailed account of the history of education, it also provides much more. Early on, Rury discusses the relationship between history and social theory, examining the history of education in the context of the issues of the day. The critical "contours" of the book may be observed in the chapter titles, such as "Colonial America: Religion, Inequality, and Revolution"; "Education, Equity, and Social Policy: Postwar America through the 1970s"; and "Globalization and Human Capital: From 'A Nation at Risk' to Neo-Liberal Reform." Rury's textbook—as well as those of his predecessors Carter G. Woodson and Joel Spring—provide excellent examples of critical history written for the masses.

Some of the most critical work in the history of education has come from scholars examining issues of race and gender. Historians of African American education have tended to follow the critical tradition of predecessors such as Bond, Du Bois, and Woodson. Signaling the continuation of this tradition in the post–civil rights era was V. P. Franklin and James D. Anderson's *New Perspectives on Black Educational History* (1978). Clearly influenced by the black nationalist energy of the late 1960s and the rise of black studies during the 1970s, *New Perspectives* represented the most significant of the insurrectionary histories that did not privilege integration as the panacea for African American education.

In 1979, V. P. Franklin published *The Education of Black Philadelphia: A Social and Educational History of a Minority Community, 1900–1950,* which reflected the critical vigor of Du Bois's penetrating *The Philadelphia Negro: A Social Study* published in 1899. In his influential study, Franklin also builds on Bond's thesis, undermining the belief in schools as a panacea for blacks. Using Philadelphia as a case study, Franklin argues that the status of blacks did not improve between 1900 and 1950. This perspective was antithetical to the integrationist perspective dominant among historians and the left at the time (Franklin, 1979).

James Anderson's (1988) *The Education of Blacks in the South, 1860–1935,* was published during a period in which historians began to write more forcefully about black self-determination. Anderson argues that blacks have always actively sought to acquire an education, often founding and running their own schools. The book continues to serve as an exemplar of critical history in the tradition of Bond, Du Bois, Woodson, and Anderson's doctoral advisor, Clarence Karier (see Anderson, 1988). Thoroughly researched, well argued, and theoretically sound, Anderson's tome is arguably one of the most significant histories of the African American experience ever published.

Vanessa Siddle Walker further challenged the conventional wisdom of school desegregation and the notion of inferior black schools in her work *Their Highest Potential: An African American School Community in the Segregated South* (1996). Walker's meticulously researched book provides a case study of the Caswell County Training School in rural North Carolina, reflecting the pride and agency of many black schools and educators. A methodological note in the book's appendix reveals that Walker's exemplary study is critical in its interpretation and methodology. Transcending the traditional archival approach, she masterfully weaves ethnography and oral history to create a rich historical tapestry (Walker, 1996).

Historians such as Joan Burstyn (1980), Linda Eisenmann (2006), Lynn Gordon (1990), and Linda Perkins (1987), among others, have made their mark in the field of women's history and higher education. Linda Perkins's *Fanny Jackson Coppin and the Institute for Colored Youth, 1837–1902,* published in 1987, arrived amidst the culture wars of the 1980s and 1990s, when conservatives touted the pervasiveness of the black "welfare queen." Perkins's study countered this master narrative by presenting a black woman, Fanny Coppin, who personified the "race woman." Coppin sensed that a special type of education was needed to prepare black women for leadership in the decades to come. Perkins illustrated black women's self-determination through Coppin's establishment of a school for black girls. This study, along with Perkins's other work, has been influential in illuminating the role of the black educator (Perkins, 1987).

Over the past decade and a half, historian and policy scholar Catherine Lugg has produced critical analyses of US educational policy. Her first book, *For God and Country: Conservatism and American School Policy* (1996), provides an excellent example of theoretical and methodological critical analysis. Lugg argues that contemporary manifestations of educational policy are usually the result of how successfully politicians have promoted their policies through public relations, a phenomenon she calls PRolicy. Lugg employs an interdisciplinary approach to the study of education policy, which is inherently critical in that she forthrightly acknowledges her attempt to uncover meaning in symbols in American educational reform (Lugg, 1996).

Lugg has produced a corpus of critical scholarship that draws on political and intellectual history and tackles lesbian, gay, bisexual, transsexual, and queer (or LGBTQ) issues as well as issues of education and religion. Her historical and political analysis of education, *Kitsch: From Education to Public Policy*, borrows its key concept from Murray Edelman's (1995) *From Art to Politics: How Artistic Creations Shape Political Conceptions*. Lugg (1999) defines Kitsch as "art that engages the emotions and deliberately ignores the intellect, and as such, is a form of cultural anesthesia. It is this ability to build and exploit cultural myths—and to easily manipulate conflicted history—that makes Kitsch a powerful political construction" (p. 4). For Lugg, political Kitsch is "a type of propaganda that incorporates familiar and easily understood art forms (Kitsch) to shape the direction of public policy" (p. 3). Within American educational policy, Lugg argues, politicians and policymakers have promoted "Kitsched mythology." Through this belief system, a Judeo-Christian heritage grounded in ideas of civility, consensus, and rationality has shaped our ideal of the public school and thus influenced policy (p. 84). As a critical analysis of education, much can be learned from Lugg's use of Kitsch and symbolism in exploring the manifestations of educational reform and policy.

The work of William Pencak (2002) and Joe Kincheloe has clearly influenced Lugg's work. Lugg and I were both Kincheloe's students at Penn State University in the mid-1990s. While not engaged with the field of history of education in the decade before his death in 2008, Kincheloe wrote invaluable essays on historical methodology and theory that influenced numerous historians of education. In

"Educational Historiographical Meta-Analysis: Rethinking Methodology in the 1990s," Kincheloe (1991) offers a radical reconceptualization of the history of education that reflects the critical historical tradition. Like Hayden White, Kincheloe argues that prevailing methods of training historians of education are antithetical to the critical tradition and fail to teach novice historians about the role of ideology and theory in historical research. The result, he argues, is a decontextualized history parading as objectivity and truth. Kincheloe (1991) advocates that historians adopt a methodology of meta-analysis "to uncover ideological assumptions implicit in historical interpretations and historical methodologies" (p. 232).

A recent groundbreaking work in critical history is Karen Graves's *And They Were Wonderful Teachers: Florida's Purge of Gay and Lesbian Teachers* (2009). Graves, a student of Clarence Karier, consistently addresses the education of the oppressed in her work. In *They Were Wonderful Teachers*, Graves masterfully brings to fore the discrimination gay and lesbian teachers have faced in American education. Her case study of Florida seeks to uncover the broader dynamics of the treatment of gays and lesbians in American education and schooling (Graves, 2009).

The field of history of higher education has produced several works that have influenced my thinking on critical history, offering insights into critical historical approaches. In 1990, Clyde W. Barrow made a critical interpretation of higher education in *Universities and the Capitalist State: Corporate Liberalism and the Reconstruction of American Higher Education, 1894–1928*. In the introduction, Barrow (1990) forthrightly notes, "This book is firmly situated in a critical American genre that traces its origins to Thorstein Veblen" (p. 10). Similar to arguments made by Joel Spring two decades earlier, Barrow applies his critical approach to the study of higher education (Barrow, 1990). As part of the University of Wisconsin's History of American Thought and Culture Book series, Barrow's study astutely engages higher education within the constellation of American and European thought, ideas, and ideology. As such, issues such as the American political economy, the military industrial complex, "the proletarianized professional," and corporate idealism are used to frame Barrow's critical analysis of higher education in the United States. This book remains one of the most critical historical analyses of higher education to date.

In 2004, John Thelin's *A History of American Higher Education* offered a much-needed update to the literature in the history of higher education. Thelin's critical sensibilities are apparent early in the text when he proposes to "gently upset some conventional notions about how colleges and universities have developed." In so doing, Thelin considers the economic, political, and social contexts within which institutions evolved, and he utilizes a horizontal rather than vertical historical approach to unearth hidden history. While vertical history is a top–down approach of examining the most prominent colleges and universities as representatives of the whole, horizontal history examines institutions across "the higher-education landscape," thus providing a more realistic view of colleges and universities and what I believe are more accurate and critical interpretations.

In 2010, historian Marybeth Gasman published an edited volume titled *The History of U.S. Higher Education: Methods for Understanding the Past*. In addition to Gasman's thoughtful introductory essay, the book contains work from both established and a new generation of historians who push the field of history of higher education to be more critical both theoretically and methodologically. Gasman (2010) sets the critical tone, saying: "this volume focuses on themes that are often ignored, such as race, class, gender, and sexuality" (p. 1). She further hopes that the volume will bring about "a rich appreciation of the craft of history and the importance of having a critical understanding of higher education's past" (p. 2). Collectively, the authors in the volume encourage the recognition of socio-economic status, horizontal theory, race and ethnicity, and geography as useful frames of reference. Gasman's volume also promotes oral history, life history, institutional history, and critical historiography as approaches that need to be further utilized in the field of higher education history (Gasman, 2010). The volume is poised to become a major conceptual and methodological primer in the history of higher education and among critical historians of education.

While all the essays in Gasman's volume are informative, several resonated with me as a critical historian of education. Linda Eisenmann's essay, "The Literature Review as Scholarship: Using Critical Reviews and Historiography," is extremely useful in several ways. Eisenmann's delineation of the differences between a historiography and literature review has been helpful when I teach courses composed of the work of both historians and social scientists of education. Eisenmann states that historiography is an analysis of a "body of work focused on a particular topic, traced over time," whereas literature reviews provide categorizes of scholarship on a topic, revealing where a scholar may contribute to the topic. Historiographies and literature reviews, she stresses, are serious forms of scholarship that should challenge canons, provide nuance to existing norms, and find holes in the scholarship on a particular a topic. What came to mind as I read Eisenmann's description of historiography and critical reviews as scholarship was historian Ronald Butchart's (1988) "Outthinking and Outflanking the Owners of the World: A Historiography of the African American Struggle for

Education," a historiography that is an excellent example of the type of critical review that helps expose the types of master narratives and canons that critical historians seek to interrogate. Eisenmann's essay provides a rationale for critical and noncritical historians alike to use historiography and the literature reviews as methods in critical historical work.

Of particular relevance in Gasman's volume is the last section, titled "Critical Examinations of Special Issues." Essays by Philo Hutcheson, Sharon Lee, Jana Nidiffer, Christopher Tudico, and Amy E. Wells-Dolan explain their critical approaches to studying pressing contemporary issues. As a historian of education born and raised in the South, Wells-Dolan's chapter "The Challenge of Writing the South" particularly resonated with me. In it, she explains her autobiographical approach to studying higher education in the South. Like many critical historians who do critical work, Wells-Dolan explicates how she engages ideals, symbols, and tradition in exploring the phenomenon of higher education in the South. She also discusses a fascinating methodological approach that she calls "collective memory studies."

Drawing on the historical approaches of historians who study the memory of history, collective memory is the way that people remember certain things without actually experiencing them. As I understand it, collective memories are formulated and sustained through traditions, symbols, ideas, and ideals. Wells-Dolan's approach is squarely within the critical tradition and will be influential among critical historians studying K–12 or higher education.

Another influential recent work in higher education that reflects critical approaches is Christopher Loss's *Between Citizens and the State: The Politics of American Higher Education in the 20th Century*, a treatise that makes a significant contribution to critical historiography. Loss's (2012) exhaustively researched and richly theorized synthesis challenges traditional notions of higher education as a phenomenon that arose primarily in tandem with "the rise of the professions and the growth of the federal-academic research matrix" (p. 1). Arguing that higher education played a significant role in American political development, Loss employs a novel approach that seems as much sociological as historical. In this way, his study is reminiscent of the social scientific approach of historians like Horace Mann Bond.

In addition to the historians of higher education mentioned above, other scholars who have influenced my thinking include Dyer (1980), Urban (1992), Wagoner (2004), and Williamson (2003). Each of these scholars has contributed to my thinking as an educational historian doing intellectual and critical history.

Collectively, their work in the areas of intellectual history and biography—as well as the history of ideas—can be useful to the critical historian of education.

Let me now turn to my own scholarship as a critical historian and discuss how others have influenced my work. Historian Sol Cohen, who wrote *Challenging Orthodoxies: Toward a New Cultural History of Education* in 1999 in the Counterpoints: Studies in Postmodern Studies of Education Series, edited by Joe Kincheloe and Shirley Steinberg, has contributed much to the advancement of critical history and historiography over the past forty years. An intellectual historian, Cohen (1999) proposes a new direction for historians of education that he calls a "new cultural history of education." This history draws on methods and approaches in intellectual and social history. It "assumes that all historians must be concerned with problems of meaning and interpretation of 'text,' inclusively defined." It also expands "our repertoire of writing, reading, and interpretative methodologies" (p. x). Drawing on the ideas of anthropologist Clifford Geertz, Cohen argues that the new cultural history approaches encourage the use of interpreting history through cultural artifacts such as texts and language. These artifacts have historical meaning. Cohen's ideas have been liberating for a scholar like myself who is fascinated with the juxtaposition of "texts" and material cultural artifacts with more traditional archival sources.

Challenging Orthodoxies is a collection of previously published essays, but all have been substantively revised, and the book includes a new essay as the epilogue. The chapter that has most influenced me is "Representations of History in the Linguistic Turn." In it, Cohen argues that texts are revealing primary sources that may be read in many different ways. As a result, texts can offer multiple interpretations and versions of history. Being cognizant of the ideas of the "linguistic turn" is essential to understanding the history around us. Cohen thus encourages historians of education to become versed in literary theory as a means of becoming astute of alternative readings of texts (Cohen, 1999). Likewise, Cohen believes that film is an important cultural artifact and primary source. He does not place film above written sources but argues that they are complimentary sources of data that can provide a fuller picture of a historical moment. He notes that "films can potentially carry ideas and information with more power than the written word, and more effectively than the written word" (p. 147). Cohen's ideas encourage penetrating analyses of film and video as a means of exploring alternative and complimentary approaches to reading and writing history. Cohen's ideas have profoundly influenced a current project examining hip-hop as an intellectual phenomenon and form of pedagogy in which I use films, videos, rap lyrics, and material artifacts, along with traditional primary sources, to gain insight about ideas in generated in hip-hop (see Alridge, 2005). *Challenging Orthodoxies* is now back in print, and I encourage all historians interested in critical history to locate and include a copy of the book in their libraries.

Like most historians trained in schools of education, scholars from various disciplines have influenced me. But it was the field of Africana studies that provided the foundation of my critical approach to the history of education. Evolving out of the black freedom struggle of the 1960s, Africana studies was formulated as an interdisciplinary field grounded in the struggle of historically oppressed people—people of African descent. Africana studies traces its long history to the ideas of Du Bois and Woodson and seeks to uncover the hidden and marginalized history of the oppressed (the poor, blacks, women, and others). In particular, the work of Africana studies scholars Gresson (2004), Hilliard (1998), and Stewart (2004) has been influential in my development and evolution as a critical historian. Each of these scholars prompted me to acknowledge the relationship between the present and the past. They have challenged me to consider what we can learn from the thought of black educators of the past to inform us about the education of black people in the present. They have also encouraged me to use culturally and socially relevant theories and methods in excavating and uncovering the history of African American education.

African American intellectual history has also helped frame much of my work as a historian. My 2007 article "Of Victorianism, Civilizationism, and Progressivism: The Educational Ideas of Anna Julia Cooper and W. E. B. Du Bois, 1892–1940," for instance, explicates the educational ideas of Cooper and Du Bois within three intellectual currents of early twentieth-century American history. Drawing on the concept of the African American intellectual tradition elucidated by V. P. Franklin (1995) and the ideas of creative conflict discussed by Wilson Moses (2004), the essay explores the seeming contradictions in Cooper's and Du Bois's use of contemporary white supremacists' language to advocate for black racial uplift. It further identifies Cooper and Du Bois as two of the many educators comprising the African American intellectual tradition.

In other works I have drawn on intellectual history to explore ideas and their influence on contemporary educational practices (see Alridge, 2005, 2006). Likewise, *The Educational Thought of W. E. B. Du Bois: An Intellectual History* (2008) challenged the traditional binary of vocational versus classical education symbolized by the "great debates" between Booker T. Washington and Du Bois. In it I question traditional ideas about African American thought. My work in Africana studies provides a political agenda that often accompanies critical scholarship: to promote recognition of Du Bois and his ideas on education as part of a larger African American intellectual tradition. I also wanted to make a political statement, giving Du Bois his rightful place within the pantheon of American educational theorists and thinkers of the twentieth century, in response to a long tradition of scholars of education privileging the ideas of John Dewey and William James without acknowledging Du Bois's contributions.

A decade ago, in an essay titled "The Dilemmas, Challenges, and Duality of an African-American Educational Historian" (2003), I explained my work as an African American historian and laid out my theoretical and methodological approaches. Greatly influenced by Anderson, Du Bois, V. P. Franklin, Kincheloe, Walker, White, and Woodson, among others, I discussed the challenges I faced regarding questions of objectivity, presentism, and voice and agency in my scholarship. My thesis was that as historians of education we inevitably bring our subjectivities to our work and thus cannot attain absolute objectivity; we are creatures of the time in which we live, and therefore our work will always be influenced by our context (Alridge, 2003). The significance of my argument was to show that historians can adhere to traditional notions of objectivity, but those notions do not limit them. In fact, as I see it, acknowledging one's subjectivities and place in history is one of many forms of rigor used by the critical historian.

Conclusion

As we move further into the twenty-first century, historians will continue to confront a multiplicity of social changes that will transform society and therefore influence their work. Historians of the critical tradition have often been at the forefront of responding to such changes and must continue to take the lead in the decades to come. We must continue to break new ground and offer penetrating critical analyses of educational issues related to race, ethnicity, gender, sexuality, and religion, and we must do so by attending to new theories and approaches that accurately reflect the groups and communities we study. Some exciting work has already emerged in these areas, but much more needs to be done.

Several policy issues of vital importance are currently on the horizon:

1. For decades, standardization and testing have dominated the discourse on school reform. As we move ahead with such reform, how will historians reexamine the origins of these movements, which began over a hundred years ago and continued throughout the twentieth century? Historian Diane Ravitch (2013) is producing critical commentary and analysis of

standardized testing. Her recent work provides an exemplar of the kind of public critique of educational policy in which I hope historians of education will actively engage during the years to come.

2. Technological advancement has made the world much smaller, greatly accelerating the dissemination of knowledge in secondary school and college classrooms and in society at large. How will historians write about and critique these changes? What historical events can inform policymakers and reformers today, enabling us to examine this phenomenon in new and more enlightening ways?

3. Corporations play a greater role than ever in influencing school curricula. Reform and privatization have introduced countless corporate educational entities that offer "accredited" knowledge to students. What will be historians' role in interpreting this phenomenon for the general public?

4. The culture wars of the 1980s and 1990s appear to have been reborn with the election of President Obama in 2008. Since that time, various ethnic groups have demanded a place in the curriculum. How can historians reinterpret the culture wars of today? How are they similar to and different from previous culture wars? How can historians help inform curriculum development in light of these debates? Historian Jonathan Zimmerman (2002) has laid excellent groundwork for studying the new culture wars.

5. "Public intellectuals" are increasingly debating educational policy. What role can critical historians of education play in the public sphere? How should historians disseminate their ideas to the wider public and among policymakers?

The long view of historians of education, particularly those with a critical perspective, can provide valuable insight into such phenomena. It is my hope that the new generation of educational historians will continue the critical tradition of challenging dominant historical narratives, offering alternative narratives, producing history that speaks forthrightly about contemporary political and social issues, connecting scholarship to activism, and engaging theory to tease out hidden history. At the same time, I call on them to consider history in new ways and to seek new methods, theories, and topics that may not yet be visible. This approach, I believe, is the responsibility of the critical historian.

REFERENCES

Alridge, D. P. (2003). The dilemmas, challenges, and duality of an African-American educational historian. *Educational Researcher, 32*(25), 25–33.

———. (2005). From civil rights to hip-hop: Toward a nexus of ideas. *Journal of African American History, 90*(3), 226–52.

———. (2006). The limits of master narratives in history textbooks: An analysis of representations of Martin Luther King, Jr. *Teachers College Record, 108*(4), 662–86.

———. (2007). Of Victorianism, civilizationism, and progressivism: The educational ideas of Anna Julia Cooper and W. E. B. Du Bois, 1892–1940. *History of Education Quarterly, 47*(4), 416–46.

———. (2008). *The educational thought of W. E. B. Du Bois: An intellectual history.* New York: Teachers College Press.

Anderson, J. D. (1988). *The education of blacks in the South, 1860–1935.* Chapel Hill: University of North Carolina Press.

———. (2001). Democratic agitations: Transformation of a critical historian. In K. Graves, T. Gladner, & C. Shea (Eds.), *Inexcusable omissions: Clarence Karier and the critical tradition in history of education scholarship* (pp. 139–54). New York: Peter Lang.

Barrow, C. W. (1990). *Universities and the capitalist state: Corporate liberalism and the reconstruction of American higher education, 1894–1928.* Madison: University of Wisconsin Press.

Bond, H. M. (1966). *The education of the Negro in the American social order.* New York: Octagon. (Original work published 1934).

———. (1969). *Negro education in Alabama: A study in cotton and steel.* New York: Atheneum. (Original work published 1939).

Brown, D. S. (2006). *Richard Hofstadter: An intellectual biography.* Chicago: University of Chicago Press.

Burstyn, J. (1980). *Victorian education and the ideal of womanhood.* London: Croom Helm.

Butchart, R. (1988). "Outthinking and outflanking the owners of the world": A historiography of the African American struggle for education. *History of Education Quarterly, 28*(3), 333–66.

Cohen, R., & Morrow, S. (2013, August 5). Who's afraid of radical history? Mitch Daniels's covert war on Howard Zinn's A People's History of the United States. *The Nation.* Retrieved from www.thenation.com/article/175592/whos-afraid-radical-history.

Cohen, S. (1999). *Challenging orthodoxies: Toward a new cultural history of education.* New York: Peter Lang.

———. (2013, January 7). When assessing Zinn, listen to the voices of teachers and students. *History News Network.* Retrieved from http://hnn.us/article/149974.

Cooper, A. J. (1997). In H. Aptheker (Ed.), *The Correspondence of W. E. B. Du Bois: Selections, 1877–1934* (p. 141). Amherst: University of Massachusetts Press. (Original work published 1973.)

Du Bois, W. E. B. (1909). *John Brown.* Philadelphia: G. W. Jacobs.

———. (1965). *The world and Africa: An inquiry into the past which Africa has played in world history.* New York: International. (Original work published 1946).

———. (1968). *The autobiography of W. E. B. Du Bois: A soliloquy on viewing my life from the last decade of its first century.* New York: International.

——. (1969). *The suppression of the African slave-trade to the United States of America, 1638–1870.* Baton Rouge: Louisiana State University Press. (Original work published 1896)

——. (1995). *Black Reconstruction in America, 1860–1880.* New York: Touchstone. (Original work published 1935).

——. (1996). *The Philadelphia Negro: A social study.* Philadelphia: University of Pennsylvania Press. (Original work published 1899).

——. (2002). *The Negro.* New York: Humanity Books. (Original work published 1915).

Dyer, T. G. (1980). *Theodore Roosevelt and the idea of race.* Baton Rouge: Louisiana State University Press.

Edelman, M. (1995) *From art to politics: How artistic creations shape political conceptions.* Chicago: University of Chicago Press.

Eisenmann, L. (2006). *Higher education for women in postwar America, 1945–1965.* Baltimore: Johns Hopkins University Press.

Foucault, M. (1972). *The archaeology of knowledge and the discourse on language.* New York: Pantheon.

Franklin, V. P. (1979). *The education of black Philadelphia: The social and educational history of a minority community, 1900–1950.* Philadelphia: University of Pennsylvania Press.

——. (1995). *Living our stories, telling our truths: Autobiography and the making of the African-American intellectual tradition.* New York: Oxford University Press.

Franklin, V. P., & Anderson, J. D. (Eds.). (1978). *New perspectives on black educational history.* Boston: G. K. Hall.

Friedel, J. (2011, October 28). Marcuse Society hosts 1960s political activist Angela Davis. *Daily Pennsylvanian.* Retrieved from www.thedp.com/article/2011/10/mar cuse_society_hosts_1960s_political_activist_angela_davis.

Gasman, M. (Ed.). (2010). *The history of U.S. higher education: Methods for understanding the past.* New York: Routledge.

Gordon, L. D. (1990). *Gender and higher education in the progressive era.* New Haven, CT: Yale University Press.

Graves, K. (2009). *And they were wonderful teachers: Florida's purge of gay and lesbian teachers.* Urbana: University of Illinois Press.

Graves, K., Gladner, T., & Shea, C. (Eds.). (2001). *Clarence Karier and the critical tradition in history of education scholarship.* New York: Peter Lang.

Gresson, A. D., III. (2004). *America's atonement: Racial pain, recovery rhetoric, and the pedagogy of healing.* New York: Peter Lang.

Hilliard, A. G., III. (1998). *SBA: The reawakening of the African mind.* Gainesville, FL: Makare.

Hofstadter, R. (1963). *Anti-intellectualism in American life.* New York: Vintage.

——. (1973). *The American political tradition and the men who made it.* New York: Vintage. (Original work published 1948)

Jay, M. (1996). *The dialectical imagination: A history of the Frankfurt School and the Institute of Social Research, 1923–1950.* Berkeley: University of California Press.

Karier, C. J. (1986). *The individual, education, and society: A history of American educational ideas.* Urbana-Champaign: University of Illinois Press. (Original work published 1967)

———. (1986). *Scientists of the mind: Intellectual founders of modern psychology.* Urbana: University of Illinois Press.

Katz, M. B. (1968). *The irony of early school reform: Educational innovation in mid-nineteenth century Massachusetts.* Cambridge, MA: Harvard University Press.

Kincheloe, J. L. (1991). Educational historiographical meta-analysis: Rethinking methodology in the 1990s. *International Journal of Qualitative Studies in Education,* 4(3), 231–45.

Loss, C. P. (2012). *Between citizens and the state: The politics of American higher education in the 20th century.* Princeton, NJ: Princeton University Press.

Lugg, C. A. (1996). *For God and country: Conservatism and American school policy.* New York: Peter Lang.

———. (1999). *Kitsch: From education to public policy.* New York: Falmer.

Mannheim, K. (1936). *Ideology and Utopia: An introduction to the sociology of knowledge.* San Diego: Harvest.

Mazzocchi, P. (2008). Foucault, Benjamin, and the burden of history. *Critical Studies in History,* 1, 91–109.

Megill, A. (1987). The reception of Foucault by historians. *Journal of the History of Ideas,* 48(1), 117–41.

Moses, W. J. (2004). *Creative conflict in African American thought: Frederick Douglass, Alexander Crummell, Booker T. Washington, W. E. B. Du Bois, and Marcus Garvey.* New York: Cambridge University Press.

Pencak, W. (2002). *The films of Derek Jarman.* New York: McFarland.

Perkins, L. (1987). *Fanny Jackson Coppin and the Institute for Colored Youth, 1837–1902.* New York: Garland.

Perkinson, H. J. (1991). *The imperfect panacea: American faith in education, 1865–1965* (3rd ed.). New York: McGraw-Hill. (Original work published 1968).

Ravitch, D. (2013). *Reign of error: The hoax of the privatization movement and the danger to America's public schools.* New York: Alfred A. Knopf.

Roediger, D. R. (1991). *The wages of whiteness: Race and the making of the American working class.* London: Verso.

Rury, J. L. (2013). *Education and social change: Contours in the history of American schooling* (4th ed.). New York: Routledge.

Spring, J. H. (1972). *Education and the rise of the corporate state.* Boston: Beacon Press.

———. (2013). *The American School, A global context: From the puritans to the Obama Administration* (9th ed.). Boston: McGraw Hill.

Stewart, J. B. (2004). *Flight: In search of vision.* Trenton, NJ: African World Press.

Storey, J. (2009). *Cultural theory and popular culture: An introduction.* Harlow, UK: Pearson Longman.

Thelin, J. R. (2004). *A history of American higher education.* Baltimore: Johns Hopkins University Press.

Urban, W. (1992). *Black scholar: Horace Mann Bond, 1904–1972*. Athens: University of Georgia Press.

Villaverde, L., Helyar, F., & Kincheloe, J. L. (2006). Historical research in education. In K. Tobin & J. Kincheloe (Eds.), *Doing educational research: A handbook*. Dordrecht: Sense.

Wagoner, J., Jr. (2004). *Jefferson and education*. Charlottesville: University of Virginia Press.

Walker, V. S. (1996). *Their highest potential: An African American school community in the segregated South*. Chapel Hill: University of North Carolina Press.

White, H. (1968). The burden of history. *History and Theory, 5*(1), 111–34.

———. (1973). *Metahistory: The historical imagination in nineteenth-century Europe*. Baltimore: Johns Hopkins University Press.

Williamson, J. A. (2003). *Black Power on campus: The University of Illinois, 1965–75*. Urbana: University of Illinois Press.

W. L. F. (1916, March). Review of *The Education of the Negro Prior to 1861*. *Mississippi Valley Historical Review, 2*(4), 586–89.

Woodson, C. G. (1922). *The Negro in our history*. Washington, DC: Associated Publishers.

———. (1992). *The education of the Negro prior to 1861: A history of the education of the Colored people of the United States from the beginning of slavery to the Civil War*. New York: A&B. (Original work published 1919).

———. (2005). *The mis-education of the Negro*. Washington, DC: ASALH Press. (Original work published 1933).

Zimmerman, J. (2002). *Whose America? Culture wars in the public schools*. Cambridge, MA: Harvard University Press.

Zinn, H. (1980). *A people's history of the United States, 1492–present*. New York: Harper & Row.

———. (1985). *SNCC: The new abolitionists*. Westport, CT: Greenwood. (Original published 1964).

CHAPTER SIX

The State and Contest
in Higher Education in the Globalized Era

Critical Perspectives

IMANOL ORDORIKA AND MARION LLOYD

Since their emergence in twelfth-century Europe, higher education institutions have been the sites of political conflict and contest. Once controlled by church or crown, universities today function as key political institutions of the state. As such, they serve as a staging ground for conflicting societal demands, ranging from capitalist accumulation and the reproduction of existing class structures on the one hand to upward mobility and social equality on the other (Ordorika, 2003).

In spite of historical evidence, theoretical perspectives that focus on issues of power and political interactions within higher education—as well as those occurring between universities and the state—are still scarce. In recent decades, few scholars have conducted studies of higher education that are theoretically grounded and focus on political perspectives. This approach, which fills a key void in the field of contemporary higher education research, incorporates theories of the state and political economy into a broader analysis of the combined impact of the decline of the welfare state and the advent of globalization on higher education institutions. In particular, it challenges mainstream notions that universities are largely apolitical and autonomous institutions, and that academe is somehow a privileged space exempt from external pressures (Marginson, 2007; Pusser, 2006).

In this chapter, we seek to contribute to those theoretical perspectives by focusing on the role universities play in the struggle for hegemony in the globalized era. We begin by providing a brief overview of the history of political contests within universities, from their origins in Italy and France in the twelfth century to the present day. We then review the dominant theories of authority relations in higher education since the 1970s, with emphasis on the limitations of those models and analytical perspectives, in particular, the lack of explicit theories of the state and higher education. Next, we describe the main tenets of globalization and the conflicting theories regarding its impact on the nation-state. We follow with a discussion of the utility of critical theories for analyzing the effects of changing power relations in higher education. Finally, we propose a hegemonic model for the study of politics, governance, and change in higher education that builds on emerging critical theories of the state and contest in higher education.

The struggle for economic, political, and cultural hegemony has intensified as a result of the shifting power dynamics of globalization. We recognize that globalization is not a monolithic process. Instead, its impact varies significantly from country to country, as well as among regions. But there are many similarities in the ways governments and other institutional actors respond to the new demands. Among fundamental transformations affecting higher education institutions are the commodification of education and the decline of the public sphere in general (Boggs, 1997; Pusser, 2011), which has been replaced with notions of individual responsibility and market competition. Other changes include a new emphasis on accountability, flexibility, and quality control; major reductions in government funding; closer ties to industry; and demand for skilled workers for the global knowledge economy.

These changes, which are fueled by the hegemonic market-oriented logic of governance, have triggered resistance from both dominant and subaltern groups (Jessop, 2000), where subaltern is defined as fragmented, subordinate, and subject to the hegemony of the dominant ruling classes (Gramsci, 1971). The resulting conflict can be viewed as a sign of the repoliticization of higher education. Among new spheres of political contest are the dispute over affirmative action policies in the United States and Brazil; the protests against skyrocketing student-loan debt in Chile, Colombia, the United Kingdom, and the United States; and the backlash against the international university rankings paradigm in Latin America and elsewhere. This conflict is not restricted to public institutions, as both public and private universities are subject to state oversight, in many cases rely on state funding, and carry out broader state goals (Pusser, 2008; Pusser & Marginson, 2012). As institutions of the state, universities play a crucial role in adapting to market and societal demands. Change in higher education is largely the result of internal and external power dynamics, however, with implications that extend far beyond university walls. In sum, postsecondary change is the result of power and politics within—and external to—higher education.

One of the main proponents of studying higher education through the lens of political dynamics is Sheila Slaughter. Her work focuses on power and the relationship between institutions and the state, which Slaughter (1988) views as subject to similar internal and external pressures: "It may be necessary to conceive of the state and higher education as engaged in multiple and sometimes conflicting functions simultaneously. For example, the state and higher education are both the subject and object of struggle. They are arenas of conflict in which various groups try to win ideological hegemony, yet at the same time they are resources for members of contending groups intent on political mobilization in external arenas" (p. 245).

Brian Pusser (2004) has argued that the university should be understood as "an institution with both symbolic and instrumental political value in broader contests for state power and authority" (p. 3). We argue that universities are not only engaged in political conflict with the state, but also are themselves political institutions of the state. As such, they play a fundamental role in hegemonic contest (Ordorika, 2003, 2004; Ordorika Sacristán, 2001). These conflicts have acquired renewed intensity in the globalized era. Along similar lines, Pusser and Marginson (2012) state that, in the context of international university rankings, "postsecondary organizations in the United States (and elsewhere) are usefully conceptualized as political institutions of the state, where the state is understood as encompassing political institutions, laws, rules and regulations, judicial systems, and formal systems of power including law enforcement and military organizations, as well as a variety of other formal organizations that serve to shape collective activity and protect individual rights" (pp. 91–92).

This emphasis on the political nature of higher education represents a departure from mainstream approaches in the field. Apart from a brief period in the late 1960s and early 1970s, when student movements throughout the world focused attention on political conflict within universities, political-theoretical perspectives have largely been absent from the study of higher education (Ordorika, 2003; Pusser, 2008). Instead, research since the early 1970s has tended to utilize structural approaches that downplay the role of the state and other sources of institutional power in fueling change within higher education institutions.

Mainstream theories tend to view the state either as a source of funding or as an intrusive entity interfering with the development of professional and scientific expertise (Slaughter, 1988). At the same time, they adopt an implicit view of the state as a pluralist institution that represents the interests of society at large, rather than certain elite sectors (Rhoades, 1992). A powerful myth about the apolitical nature of education undergirds that perspective (Wirt & Kirst, 1972), portraying higher education institutions as politically neutral and autonomous organizations rooted in professional competence and rational behavior (as opposed to the politically driven, irrational state; Ordorika, 2004; Rhoades, 1992). "This myth or modern narrative of the university (Bonavecchio, 1991) was based on the idealization of the German model of free and autonomous academic communities that produced universal culture and knowledge" (Ordorika, 2004, p. 9). In consequence, political conflicts within universities are viewed as an aberration from the harmonious, disinterested, and pluralistic status quo, rather than a fundamental part of university life (Pusser, 2004).

Whether intentionally or not, these theories have served to reproduce existing power relations in higher education. As Ordorika Sacristán and López González (2007) note, "The denial of politics is essential discourse for the exercise of power and the legitimation of dominant groups, as well as a basic element of the political nature of the university" (p. 478). In moments of open conflict, this tradition of apoliticism is frequently invoked to disqualify and dismiss actors and social movements involved in the university conflict. Such was the case of conflicts in the 1970s between administrators and unions at the National Autonomous University of Mexico, when members of the latter group were denounced as "politicians" and "university outsiders" (Ordorika Sacristán & López González, 2007, p. 478).

Prevailing theories of the impact of globalization, which present a weakening or dissolution of the state and its role in dictating policy (Rosecrance, 1999), such as at the university level, may have recently strengthened the widespread tendency to disregard the state's role. Mainstream studies tend to view structural changes underway in higher education as the natural outcome of globalization, without taking into account the political nature of the drastic reduction in public funding for higher education and the new evaluation culture, among related trends. Nor do they acknowledge the conflicts generated by those policies, particularly between dominant and subaltern social groups.

We argue that these perspectives oversimplify the changing power dynamics wrought by globalization, in which the role of the nation-state is increasingly transformed but not necessarily diminished. In that context, we view political approaches as providing a particularly essential framework for understanding the multiple ways in which globalization has affected higher education. Perhaps more than ever, higher education institutions play a critical role in broader state efforts to compete in the global knowledge economy, as well as in meeting industry demands for a globalized workforce. But that relationship is complicated by the state's diminishing financial support for higher education in many national contexts and the resulting pressure on institutions and academics to secure alternative forms of funding (Ordorika, 2004; Pusser et al., 2012).

According to Slaughter (1990), conflict in higher education is expressed around "major policy issues" such as access, social uses of knowledge (career preparation as well as research and service), and the allocation of resources (p. 30), all of which are deeply political in nature. Pusser (2008), in revisiting Burton Clark's

(1983) triangle of coordination, found that the dynamics of a contemporary legislative contest over university restructuring placed the state, the market, and the institutional estate in "an orbit of contest and negotiation" (p. 133), one in which these forces are politically interdependent and in competitive tension.

Universities and Conflict in Historical Perspective

From their origins in twelfth-century Europe, universities have occupied a privileged place in society. But their potential to shape cultural and economic processes has also made them the sites of political contest. The term *universitates* originally referred to communities, technical associations, or publicly constituted corporations that emerged in Europe (Rashdall, 1936) through a process that mirrored the guild system (Le Goff, 1980). Students approached renowned professionals—called doctors—in order to learn a trade, leading to the creation of a new category of scholar-apprentices. Teaching evolved slowly into a distinct way of life, through which scholars attempted to create their own special corporate arrangement vis-à-vis the Catholic Church, secular authorities, and the rest of society (Le Goff, 1980).

The first universities were founded in Italy and France in the twelfth century, and though they quickly became powerful, they were not completely autonomous from the Church or state. The University of Bologna, a largely student-led initiative, acquired extensive privileges and jurisdiction as a result of the confrontation between the pope and the emperor (Luna Díaz, 1987b). The University of Paris, meanwhile, grew out of the cathedral schools of Notre Dame and was strongly tied to the Church, although professors wielded considerable control (Le Goff, 1993; Wences Reza, 1984).

In spite of their differences, both institutions enjoyed a large degree of autonomy owing to the absence of a unique centralized source of power in medieval societies (Luna Díaz, 1987a). But university demands for academic and administrative freedom—as well as efforts by the Church, the crown, and local authorities to exercise external control over the institutions—led to frequent conflicts (Le Goff, 1993; Luna Díaz, 1987b).

One such conflict triggered a two-year strike at the University of Paris in 1229. The university's prolonged closure in turn prompted the mass migration of faculty and students, a period known as the Great Dispersion, to a second wave of European universities (Brunner, 1990; Young, 2014). These institutions included the new universities in Vicenza (1204) and Padua (1220), both of which were heavily influenced by the lay and student-centered university model of Bologna (Perkin, 1984). The Italian model eventually succumbed to external controls by the pope and the commune, but it gave birth to a strong tradition of student participation (Perkin, 1997). The Church-centered model of Paris, meanwhile, inspired the creation of universities in Spain and Portugal, including Alcalá, Barcelona, Lisbon, and Salamanca (Brunner, 1990), as well as Oxford (1167) and Cambridge (1209) in England. Eventually, the Paris model was to give birth to the still-dominant university tradition in which scholars oversee students and the learning process (Perkin, 1984).

The university as an institution grew rapidly throughout the continent, where it played a key role in fueling political and social change. But the process was not without conflict. Tensions between university traditions and state needs permeated higher education institutions during the Enlightenment and the Industrial Revolution, leading to the eventual shift of control over higher education from the Church to the state (Perkin, 1984, 1997).

In Latin America, where the first universities were established during the sixteenth century, institutions were frequently caught in the crossfire of Church-state conflicts (Brunner, 1989; González-Polo y Acosta, 1983; Lanning & Heliodoro Valle, 1946), disputes that continued through the early years of independence. Among the most relevant of those conflicts was the 1918 university autonomy movement in Córdoba, Argentina, which inspired subsequent battles for institutional autonomy in no fewer than eighteen countries in the region (Marsiske Schulte, 2004; Portantiero, 1978).

Fueled in part by the rapid growth in enrollments in the post-WWII era, political conflicts in higher education erupted again during the 1960s with the emergence of student movements throughout the world. Those conflicts, exemplified by the student revolts in France, Germany, and Mexico—as well as at Columbia, Kent State, and UC Berkeley in the United States—prompted scholars in the social sciences to begin to address the political nature of higher education over the next decade (Ehrenreich & Ehrenreich, 1969; Lipset & Altbach, 1969). That focus gave way to a new emphasis on the managerial aspects of university governance starting in the 1970s—a focus that remains dominant today.

Mainstream Theories of Governance and Change in Higher Education

Despite eight centuries of conflict within universities, contemporary approaches to authority relations tend to downplay political factors. Instead, they either focus exclusively on structures or view decision-making processes as deterministic, causal relations between social actors. These functionalist approaches can be divided into two broad perspectives,[1] both of which provide helpful, but incomplete, analyses of the dynamics fueling patterns of governance, politics, and change in higher education (Ordorika, 2003; Pusser & Marginson, 2012).

The most common perspectives are concerned primarily with the management functions of a university and decision-making processes (Ordorika Sacristán, 2001), positing that universities change through rational responses to internal inefficiencies, organizational growth, and increased complexity (Clark, 1983). A few studies also suggest that internal politics and interest dynamics drive change within higher education institutions, where administrative leaders weigh various interests in making decisions (Baldridge, 1971). In most cases, however, these theories tend to overstate internal homogeneity—and harmony. More notably they fail to acknowledge the impact of external requirements upon universities as well as the contested nature of internal and external demands. In reality, universities' organizational development often responds to dynamics that contradict the internal rationality of bureaucratic or collegial arrangements.

Other perspectives contrast with organizational perspectives in that they present change as being imposed from the outside. They view university dynamics as a function of the internal strategies adopted by institutions to adapt or minimize the influence of largely hostile or disruptive external surroundings, such as in the case of organizational responses to market dynamics (Massy, 1992). Resource dependency theories, meanwhile, argue that universities change in order to increase their odds of surviving in an environment where resources are scarce (Pfeffer & Salancik, 1978; Slaughter & Leslie, 1997).

There is no doubt that markets and resources are extremely relevant in the transformation of higher education, particularly in the globalized era. While these theories usefully turn attention to the need for resources, however, they offer little insight into the ways in which universities define key resources or the choices they make in pursuit of resources. These theories are further limited in their ability to explain why many universities resist or remain unresponsive to labor and economic market demands, maintain unique forms of organization and governance, and remain highly subsidized (Ordorika, 2003). They also fail to explain situations in which universities make decisions that limit their access to financial resources.

Yet another group of theories emphasizes the importance of culture and meaning in determining organizational dynamics. These approaches focus more on processes than on structures, and highlight the relationship between the subject and object of study. Institutional theorists, for example, explain change in higher education as a response to social and cultural demands for conformance to prevailing sets of shared beliefs (Clark, 1983; Meyer & Rowan, 1978). They have focused on symbolic as well as substantive interactions, and argue that myths and belief systems are essential parts of organizational legitimacy (Meyer & Rowan, 1978; Weick, 1976).

Together, institutional perspectives have brought a much-needed cultural dimension into the study of higher education. But like other approaches, they pay insufficient attention to areas of conflict and contest both within and outside organizations. There is no recognition that institutional myths and cultural perceptions shape and are in turn shaped by political contests at the organizational and societal levels. Pusser and Marginson (2012) note that "there is unrecognized conflict between those in power and the larger interests of social society" (p. 96). That conflict is reproduced within higher education organizations, and those tensions have acquired renewed relevance in the globalized era. In that context, political theories provide a more effective lens through which to examine the multiple changes underway in universities today, in part given the evolving role of the state and its institutions due to globalization.

The Globalization Debate

In analyzing the impact of globalization on higher education institutions, we begin by outlining the basic characteristics that define this latest phase of capitalist development. In the discourse of everyday life and in the social sciences, globalization has become an all-encompassing notion that attempts to be inclusive and at the same time obscures a broad set of processes, ideas, policies, and structures. Like the notion of industrialization, globalization broadly depicts a historical period characterized by distinct dynamics, ideologies, forms, and institutions.

The vagueness and ambiguity of the concept itself account for the multiplicity of definitions, perspectives, and debates about and over globalization (Altbach & Balán, 2007; Carnoy & Rhoten, 2002; Castells, 1996; Marginson, Murphy, & Peters, 2010; Putzel, 2005; Sen, 2002; Stiglitz, 2002). Most notable among these exchanges are arguments over the degree to which this contemporary phenomenon is truly unique in light of historical instances of economic and cultural internationalization (Lechner & Boli, 2000); discussions about the extent to which capital accumulation has transcended nation-states to become supranational or transnational in essence (Carnoy, 1993); or debates over the role and power of nation-states in the face of globalization (Evans 1997; Jessop, 2000; Marginson et al., 2010; Rosecrance, 1999; Stiglitz, 2002, 2006).

In general, most authors agree that the essence of this phase of capitalist development lies in the fact that economic processes, social interactions, politics, culture, and even individual relationships transcend national borders (Muñoz

García, 2011). These exchanges take place in a world made smaller and at a virtually instantaneous pace by information technologies, digital communications, and modern transportation. Interactions occurring in real time and on a planetary scale redefine space and time (Castells, 1996).

At the same time, the scholarship of globalization rarely accounts for the multiple dimensions of globalization. Manuel Castells (1996, 1997, 1998) identifies at least three significant spheres: economy, society, and culture. For many authors, globalization is essentially a new economic order (Castells, 1996), a "force that is reorganizing the world's economy" (Carnoy & Rhoten, 2002, p. 1). The reorganization of core economic processes is based on the use of information and communication technologies, which are knowledge intensive (Carnoy, 1999; Castells, 2012). Knowledge, information, and symbolic communication have consequently become the most important sources of productivity and profit (Appadurai, 1996).

Among many aspects, this discourse addresses material transformations at the level of economic production (Castells, 1996; Krugman, 2004); the future of the nation-state (Castells, 1997; Evans, Rueschemeyer, & Skocpol, 1985; Rosecrance, 1999); changes in the nature and speed of communications (Carnoy, 2000); incredibly fast exchanges in the financial and commercial realms; the preeminence of market and business practices and discourse in many spheres of societal interaction (Santos, 2006; Sen, 1999; Touraine, 2000); the economization of social life (Wolin, 1981); and the emergence of a hegemonic discourse based on deification of the free market (Ball, 2012; Touraine, 2000). These changes emerged from new conservative coalitions in the United Kingdom and United States that transformed the economic and ideological foundations of the welfare state in the 1970s and 1980s. A new approach to the political economy emerged—neoliberalism—that endeavored to redirect state purposes and in turn propelled the hegemony of a new discourse, a new public philosophy of a state focused on privileging markets and private benefits through public action (Harvey, 2005; Wolin, 1981).

Despite common definitions of globalization, there is little consensus on its impact on the state—in particular, whether the nation-state is destined to disappear or give way to a global unified state. In Rosecrance's (1999) view, the "virtual nation"—defined as "based on mobile capital, labor, and information" (p. 3)—has essentially replaced the traditional nation-state. "Nations are shrinking—in function if not in geographic size" (p. 3). That view implies a diminished role of the state in guiding domestic policy, including in the realm of higher education, which is seen as being at the mercy of market demands (Pusser et al., 2012). "Although post-secondary education initially remained relatively autonomous relative to lower levels, it has subsequently lost control of its pact with the devil in opening itself to commercialization in the name of public responsibility" (Morrow, 2005, p. xvii).

Such changes do not imply the absence of the state, however, but rather its shifting role on a global scale. Under globalization, the state continues to promote capitalist and other societal interests, albeit in a more multifaceted manner. The privileged group is no longer a solely domestic industry; it has expanded to include multinational corporations and institutions, such as the Organisation for Economic Co-operation and Development (OECD) and the World Bank, under the guiding principle of promoting competitiveness on a global scale. Building on Poulantzas's prescient analysis of the shifting economic paradigms of the 1970s, Jessop (2000) describes the post-Fordist era as one in which the state promotes "flexibility and permanent innovation in open economies by intervening on the supply-side and tries to strengthen as far as possible the competitiveness of the relevant economic spaces" (p. 11). Under what Jessop terms the new "Schumpeterian workfare post-national regime" (p. 10), competitiveness depends more on "penetrating the micro-social level in the interests of valorization" (p. 11).

Higher education institutions play a dual role in this process: creating knowledge and providing technical capacity for the global marketplace. But decisions about the types and uses of knowledge, as well as the ideal profile of workers, are largely determined from abroad and later internalized through domestic and institutional policies (Rhoads & Torres, 2006). Among external actors influencing university policy are international organizations such as the OECD, UNESCO, and the World Bank; national and international industries; and of course the state. The latter exerts its influence through instrumental means as well as through cultural processes and hegemony building.

Nonetheless, while the role of universities in stimulating economic growth and development has perhaps never been greater, higher education institutions in general receive diminishing financial support from the state. Underscoring that apparent contradiction is the hegemonic "neoliberal core message: that higher education is a competitive market in the economic sense, that it primarily generates private benefits rather than common benefits, and that higher education organizations, which must resource themselves, are primarily focused on their own interests" (Pusser & Marginson, 2012, p. 104).

These trends do not signify that the state is no longer necessary, but rather that its priorities have changed in conformance with the hegemonic model. The state "is not only an important actor in many individual governance mechanisms but also retains responsibility for the oversight in light of the overall balance of class forces and the maintenance of social cohesion" (Jessop, 2000, p. 13).

We share Jessop's view of the shifting, rather than diminished, role of the state in the post-Fordist era. Rather than a pluralistic or cohesive entity, however, we view the state as serving privileged capitalist interests over subaltern ones, particularly in contexts such as Latin America (Ordorika, 2003; Santos, 2006). It is also the site of struggle between competing groups and agendas. In the case of higher education, the state plays a key role in promoting hegemonic values and in shaping policies designed to bring institutions in line with the dictates of the global marketplace, but those efforts are not without resistance. For example, students in Canada, Chile, Colombia, the United Kingdom, and the United States (among other countries) have staged mass protests over the past few years in opposition to government funding policies for higher education that have resulted in crippling levels of student-loan debt. Governments in all those countries have implicitly defined higher education as a private—rather than public—good, shifting the financial burden of paying college tuition from the state to students and their families.

Slaughter and Leslie (1997) identify two distinct processes through which globalization manifests itself in higher education: the reduction of public money for higher education institutions and the emergence of new markets and market connections for higher education products and institutions. The adoption of market-oriented and market-like behavior in colleges and universities is among the most relevant features of contemporary higher education (Slaughter & Leslie, 1997). At the same time, governments exert pressure to expand knowledge production and skilled-labor training in order to attract foreign capital. In the process, the university is expected to play a leading role in producing knowledge goods and highly skilled graduates for a knowledge- and global-based economy (Altbach, 2003; Morrow & Torres, 1995). "Governments have realized that science and technology are essential to international competitiveness, at the same time that a new global market has emerged for knowledge and its applications" (Muñoz García, 2011, p. 24).

Among manifestations of globalization is the rise of for-profit higher education providers, which are typically operated by US-based corporations. The for-profit sector now accounts for half of all higher education enrollment in Brazil (Lloyd, 2013) and an increasing share in other countries, in large part because of the acquiescence or promotion on the part of the state as well as the legal backing of institutions such as the World Trade Organization. But the overtly commercial nature of the for-profit model, as well as its aggressive business model, has sparked heated controversy in many countries, including in the United States and Chile. Recent studies commissioned by the US Senate and the US Department of Education concluded that for-profit universities have adopted questionable recruitment tactics in their efforts to increase enrollment (Lloyd, 2012). Meanwhile, in Chile, an early 2012 government investigation determined that a number of universities were illegally operating as for-profits—a frequent allegation of the student protest movement (Gibney, 2012).

International university rankings are another essential site of contest. Having first gained prominence with the introduction of the Shanghai Jiao Tong University ranking in 2003, a variety of rankings have expanded to become among the dominant measures of institutional performance on a global level. Despite their questionable methodologies (Lloyd, Ordorika Sacristán, & Rodríguez Gómez-Guerra, 2011; Marginson, 2012; Ordorika & Lloyd, 2013), governments throughout the world have increasingly adopted these hierarchical classification systems to justify sweeping higher education reforms in countries such as Denmark, France, Malaysia, and Russia. Those changes have in turn sparked resistance from students, scholars, and administrators in many countries in yet another sign of the repoliticization of higher education.

The popularity of rankings reflects the increasingly pervasive "culture of accountability" in policy agendas as well as societal demands for access to information in both the public and private spheres (Pusser and Marginson, 2013). Supporters of rankings argue for the need to reestablish the principle of academic hierarchy, which the massification and indiscriminate dissemination of knowledge via the Internet have undermined (Ordorika & Lloyd, 2013; Ordorika Sacristán et al., 2008). The methodology responds to demands, established from a market perspective, to classify institutions for the benefit of potential consumers of knowledge, research, and status credentialing. The rankings also reflect the evolving contest on a global level for control over the flow of knowledge (Marginson & Ordorika, 2011).

Even so, there is a growing backlash against the international university rankings among academics in many countries. Critics view the tables as imposing a single Anglo-centric model of higher education at the expense of local and national development priorities (Ordorika Sacristán et al., 2009). Others warn that institutions are being forced to compete in an increasingly costly and high-stakes "academic arms race" (Dill, 2006; Ehrenberg, 2004) to the detriment of more pressing local or national development priorities. In Latin America, for instance, critics cite the rankings' failure to take into account their institutions' broader contributions to society as "state-building universities" (Ordorika & Pusser, 2007), a regional tradition that has no equivalent in the English-speaking world (Muñoz García, 2009). The debate signals the growing resistance within institutions to models imposed from abroad, a central contest over higher education policy in the globalized era.

Critical Theories of the State and Contest in Higher Education

None of these developments in higher education can be explained without taking into account the role of internal and external power dynamics, a phenomenon we believe is best explained by theories of the state. In developing a conceptual frame for studying higher education, we draw from critical theories of the role of the state, and higher education in particular. Many of these perspectives view the state as representing, in some way or another, the interests of the economic ruling class.

These perspectives vary essentially in two areas: the degree of autonomy or "capture" of the state by the capitalist class and the weight of the economic structure versus the superstructure in the process of domination (Ordorika, 2003). In this analysis we adopt the concept of hegemony and the state as a site of conflict as expressed by Gramsci (1971) and Poulantzas (1978). Their perspectives provide an understanding of the capitalist state as a dynamic institution, the product of historically evolving relations between competing classes in society. They also emphasize the importance of the development of dominant (hegemonic) ideologies and provide a theory of social change as a product of the confrontation between dominant and subaltern sectors of society. Finally, and critically, they situate higher education in a broader context as a state institution.

As in many societal conflicts, the contested nature of higher education is largely the result of competing demands for capital accumulation and demands for equalization. But political disputes within universities take a different form than in the case of other state institutions (such as courts or political parties). In higher education, the objects of the contest involve access to knowledge and its social uses, the distribution of resources necessary for the production and distribution of knowledge, and the participation of university actors in decision making. In addition, universities serve as the "critical conscience of the nation" and participate in diverse social and political processes (Ordorika & López González, 2007, p. 479).

Of the various contested terrains in higher education, access is perhaps the most contentious and politically charged. It is shaped by conflicting goals—on the part of the government and industry, of regulating the reproduction of skilled labor, and social demands for higher education as a mechanism for upward social mobility (Labaree, 1997). The regulation of access is typically based on a meritocratic ideology, which is in turn based on the principles of social Darwinism. The certification process, meanwhile, rewards "skills and attitudes possessed in abundance by the middle class—cultural literacy, numeracy, perseverance, self-confidence, appropriate assertiveness, and social agreeable manners—and not found as frequently among immigrants, the working class, or the working poor" (Slaughter, 1990, p. 31).

Another area in which higher education reproduces existing class structures is in the hierarchical structure, both among and within disciplines and professions. In Mexico and many other countries, for example, a disproportionate share of working-class students become teachers, a profession that ranks low in terms of status and economic remuneration (Vaillant, 2004, p. 12). Meanwhile, wealthier students tend to migrate toward more competitive professions, such as law and business, where both tuition and potential earnings are considerably higher (Osa Edoh & Alutu, 2011). Affordability and the related patterns of resource allocation—the sources of the funding and the share of the burden resting on individuals and their families—are other sources of contest.

Other areas of conflict involve the evolving labor divisions between academic, administrative, and clerical hierarchies (the latter group ranks the lowest). Managerial requirements are producing changes in the autonomous and self-regulated components of faculty work (Rhoades, 1992). The new "evaluation culture" (Ordorika Sacristán, 2001) is replacing collegiality with competition while giving birth to a new, highly influential class of higher education bureaucrats whose primary job it is to secure government or private grants for research and other high-priority activities (Acosta Silva, 2010).

A final area of contest involves students. Academic organizations have traditionally been viewed as "people-processing" or "student-centered" institutions. Individuals—in this case students—with specific needs come into the organization from the environment, the organization acts upon them, and they are returned to society (Ordorika, 2003). But the nature of student participation—once a fundamental part of university power dynamics—has changed dramatically in the globalized era. In most countries, students are expected to shoulder an increasing financial burden but are largely excluded from institutional decision making. This is particularly true in the case of online degree programs, in which students have little contact with their professors and even less with university administrators. The resulting exclusion of students from university reform processes has fueled protests in Canada, Europe, and Latin America, where students are demanding a return to free public higher education.

At the heart of many of the conflicts are demands for rapid changes in the role and nature of higher education institutions in the globalized era. At the internal level, faculty and students react against perceptions about the role of the institution and challenge established rights and practices, while at the external level the state and international organizations pressure students and institutions to conform to new economic and cultural priorities. Taken together, these distinct sites of conflict demonstrate the complex power that dynamics present in the university as both the staging ground and instrument of contest.

A Hegemonic Analytical Perspective

We have identified what we view as deficiencies in historical and contemporary frameworks for the study of change and governance in higher education. The most important is the lack of an explicitly analyzed theory of the state, through which power relationships can be viewed (Pusser, 2008; Rhoades, 1992). Another is the tendency to assume a pluralistic state, even in studying higher education in contexts such as Latin America and other regions, in which democracies are either fragile or nonexistent. A third weakness is the tendency to make distinctions between governance, management, and leadership, thereby implicitly confining the locus of power to a restricted notion of governance as decision making (Ordorika, 2003). This distinction is based on the assumption that the university is essentially a technical institution. Finally, few theories define universities as political institutions of the state (Pusser, 2004), instead portraying political struggle as anomalous and generally counterproductive.

The absence of an understanding about the state and the position of postsecondary organizations within society, as well as an insufficient accounting of theories of change, manifests in the limited success of postsecondary scholars' attempts to grasp the complex relationship between "internal" and "external" processes in higher education. There is a need to incorporate broader issues of political economy and power relations within higher education organizations and beyond in order to understand power and change in higher education.

Central to that framework is the following assumption: as an institution of the state, higher education is a key site of struggle for cultural and economic hegemony. That struggle typically manifests through competing reform projects, particularly during periods of profound and rapid change, such as in the current globalized era. But just as higher education has the potential to reproduce existing inequalities, it can also be a site of equalization and democratization (Carnoy & Levin, 1985). The development of a political theory of conflict in higher education is based on the analysis of power struggles, understood as the potential capacity of different groups to determine outcomes (Hardy, 1990). Central to this process is the effort to understand the forces from which cultural hegemony derives—the conformation and incorporation of perceptions, cognitions, and preferences into a dominant ideology (Gramsci, 1971; Lukes, 1974). The outcome depends on the resolution of demands generated both internally and externally.

This conceptual approach, as it turns attention to four key elements, enhances our understanding of the process of governance and change in higher education. It provides the foundations for a political theory of governance by

1. framing political contest in education as a confrontation over ideology and resource allocation;
2. enabling the understanding of decision-making structures and processes in education as a historical product of power struggles between dominant and subaltern groups in education and the broader state;
3. explaining the dynamics of educational reform as a consequence of competing demands for the reproduction and production of ideology and skills on the one hand and struggles for social transformation and equality on the other; and
4. establishing the linkages between political contest at the internal and external levels as central to understanding new sites of educational contest and reform.

Together, these analytical perspectives enhance our understanding of the complex relationship between internal and external forces in higher education, and between the state and the institutions themselves. Yet the specific nature of the political system in question also shapes power dynamics within higher education institutions. In order to place governance and policy making in context, four central characteristics should be taken into account: (1) the scope and limits of political contest; (2) the nature of the dominant ideology; (3) the degrees of political struggle or citizen participation; and (4) the characteristics of political leadership, that is, the role of political parties and other formal state institutions (Ordorika Sacristán, 2001). These elements have a major impact on power relations within state institutions, including higher education. Acknowledging the complex interplay between the broader state and its institutions is key to understanding the forces behind change and governance in higher education.

Conclusion

In this chapter, we have presented the principal limitations of mainstream theories of higher education governance and proposed critical alternatives to enrich our understanding of the internal and external dynamics affecting institutions in the context of globalization. We have argued that the study of higher education requires alternative theoretical approaches that focus on political processes, from the origins of the idea of the university to its current forms in the twenty-first century. Among key trends affecting postsecondary institutions are the new emphasis on accountability and efficiency, the evaluation culture, dwindling public support for higher education as part of a broader degradation of the public sphere, the commodification of higher education, and a new emphasis on training workers for the global knowledge economy.

Hegemonic models of higher education fuel those trends, dividing universities into two starkly unequal groups: "the autonomous and elite research university focused on knowledge and prestige," of which Harvard is the premier example, and "the heteronomous mass training institutions focused on economic volumes and revenues" (Marginson & Ordorika, 2011, p. 106), exemplified by the new for-profit model of higher education. "The Bourdieuian binary logic of the global sector . . . is the divide between knowledge power and the commodity economy in higher education, and the ultimate divide between inclusion and exclusion" (p. 110).

Such extremes are characteristic of the growing socioeconomic inequalities present on a global scale—the legacy of several decades of neoliberal policies and the dynamics of globalization. Universities play a key role in both advancing the agenda of the economic elites and resisting it through the opposition of subaltern groups. Thus there is a need to repoliticize the study of higher education by acknowledging the role of universities within the broader state apparatus. By defining universities as political institutions of the state, we are highlighting their role in the struggle for cultural hegemony on a global level.

This theoretical perspective integrates distinct levels of analysis and processes, from the most general level of the state to the more particular spaces of higher education organizations. The integration of these levels of analysis with critical theoretical standpoints constitutes a powerful tool for a holistic understanding of the complex arrangement of actors, norms, agendas, and cultural views upon which domination within higher education institutions is founded. Only by reclaiming a critical model of postsecondary politics and conflict can we fully grasp the evolving power relations shaping higher education under globalization.

NOTE

1. Ordorika (1999) divides these approaches into two broad schools: organizational-functional and societal-functional. The first school, which dominated research

on higher education for decades, includes "the *bureaucratic model* (Stroup, 1966), its variation the *professional bureaucracy model* (Mintzberg, 1991), and the *collegial model* (Millett, 1962), all of which are perceived as natural outcomes of rational processes" (p. 12). The second school, which emphasizes the impact of outside forces on institutional dynamics, is common in mainstream literature dealing with issues of university autonomy and in studies about State involvement in higher education.

REFERENCES

Acosta Silva, A. (2010). *Príncipes, burócratas y gerentes: La educación superior en México*. Mexico City: ANUIES.

Altbach, P. G. (2003). Globalization and the university: Myths and realities in an unequal world. *Current Issues in Catholic Higher Education, 23*, 5–25.

Altbach, P. G., & J. Balán (Eds.) (2007). *World class worldwide: Transforming research universities in Asia and Latin America*. Baltimore: Johns Hopkins University Press.

Appadurai, A. (1996). *Cultural dimensions of globalization*. Minneapolis: University of Minnesota Press.

Baldridge, J. V. (1971). *Power and conflict in the university: Research in the sociology of complex organizations*. New York: Wiley.

Ball, S. J. (2012). *Global Education Inc.: New policy networks and the neo-liberal imagery*. New York: Routledge.

Boggs, C. (1997). The great retreat: Decline of the public sphere in late twentieth-century America. *Theory and Society, 26*(6), 741–80.

Bonavecchio, C. (1991). *El mito de la universidad*. Mexico City: Siglo XXI.

Brunner, J. J. (1989). *Educación superior y cultura en América Latina: Función y organización*. Santiago: FLACSO.

———. (1990). Gobierno universitario: Elementos históricos, mitos distorsionadores y experiencia internacional. In C. Cox (Ed.), *Formas de gobierno en la educación superior: Nuevas perspectivas* (pp. 29–50). Santiago: FLACSO.

Carnoy, M. (1993). Multinationals in a changing world economy: Whither the nation-state? In M. Carnoy (Ed.), *The new global economy in the information age: Reflections on our changing world* (pp. 45–96). University Park: Pennsylvania State University Press.

———. (1999). *Globalization and educational reform: What planners need to know*. Paris: UNESCO International Institute for Educational Planning.

———. (2000). *Globalization and educational restructuring*. Paris: UNESCO International Institute of Educational Planning.

Carnoy, M., & Levin, H. M. (1985). *Schooling and work in the democratic state*. Stanford, CA: Stanford University Press.

Carnoy, M., & Rhoten, D. (2002). What does globalization mean for educational change? A comparative approach. *Comparative Education Review, 46*(1), 1–9.

Castells, M. (1996). *The rise of the network society*. Malden, MA: Blackwell.

———. (1997). *The power of identity*. Malden, MA: Blackwell.

———. (1998). *End of millennium*. Malden, MA: Blackwell.

———. (2012). *Networks of outrage and hope: Social movements in the Internet age.* Cambridge: Polity Press.

Clark, B. R. (1983). *The higher education system: Academic organization in cross-national perspective.* Berkeley: University of California Press.

Dill, D. D. (2006, September 9). *Convergence and diversity: The role and influence of university rankings.* Keynote address at the Consortium of Higher Education Researchers 19th Annual Research Conference, University of Kassel, Germany.

Ehrenberg, R. G. (2004). Econometric studies of higher education. *Journal of Econometrics, 121,* 19–37.

Ehrenreich, B., & Ehrenreich, J. (1969). *Long March, short spring: The student uprising at home and abroad.* New York: Monthly Review Press.

Evans, P. B. (1997). The eclipse of the state? Reflections on stateness in an era of globalization. *World Politics, 50*(1), 62–87.

Evans, P. B., Rueschemeyer, D., & Skocpol, T. (1985). *Bringing the state back in.* Cambridge: Cambridge University Press.

Gibney, E. (2012, August 30). The mañana project. *Times Higher Education.* Retrieved from www.timeshighereducation.co.uk/features/the-maana-project/420981.article.

González-Polo y Acosta, I. F. (1983). La Nueva España y sus motines estudiantiles. In G. Guevara Niebla (Comp.), *Las luchas estudiantiles en México* (pp. 65–80). Mexico City: Editorial Línea / Universidad Autónoma de Guerrero / Universidad Autónoma de Zacatecas.

Gramsci, A. (1971). *Selections from the prison notebooks of Antonio Gramsci* (Q. Hoare & G. N. Smith, Ed. & Transl.). London: Lawrence & Wishart.

Hardy, C. (1990). Putting power into university governance. In J. C. Smart (Ed.), *Higher education: Handbook of theory and research* (Vol. 6, pp. 393–426). New York: Agathon Press.

Harvey, D. (2005). *A brief history of neoliberalism.* New York: Oxford University Press.

Jessop, B. (2000). *Globalization and the national state* (19 pp.). Lancaster: Department of Sociology, Lancaster University.

Krugman, P. (2004). *The great unraveling: Losing our way in the new century.* New York: W. W. Norton.

Labaree, D. F. (1997). Public goods, private goods: The American struggle over educational goals. *American Educational Research Journal, 34,* 39–81.

Lanning, J. T., & Heliodoro Valle, R. (1946). *Reales cédulas de la Real y Pontificia Universidad de México de 1551 a 1816.* Mexico City: Imprenta Universitaria.

Lechner, F., & Boli, J. (2000). *The globalization reader.* Malden, MA: Blackwell.

Le Goff, J. (1980). *Time, work & culture in the Middle Ages.* Chicago: University of Chicago Press.

———. (1993). *Intellectuals in the Middle Ages.* Cambridge, MA: Blackwell.

Lipset, S. M., & Altbach, P. G. (1969). *Students in revolt.* Boston: Houghton Mifflin.

Lloyd, M. (2012, August 9). El senado de EU arremete contra universidades con fines de lucro. *Campus Milenio, 473.* Retrieved from www.ses.unam.mx/publicaciones/articulos.php?proceso=visualiza&idart=1645.

————. (2013). *Las políticas de fomento a la ciencia y tecnología en México y Brasil: Un estudio de caso de la Universidad Autónoma Nacional de México y la Universidad de São Paulo* (master's thesis). National Autonomous University of Mexico, Mexico City. Retrieved from http://132.248.9.195/ptd2013/febrero/510451136/Index.html.

Lloyd, M. W., Ordorika Sacristán, I., & Rodríguez Gómez-Guerra, R. (2011). *Los rankings internacionales de universidades, su impacto, metodología y evolución.* Mexico City: DGEI-UNAM.

Lukes, S. (1974). *Power: A radical view.* New York: Macmillan.

Luna Díaz, L. M. (1987a). El desarrollo de la conciencia corporativa universitaria y la política eclesiástica en Nueva España. In L. M. Luna Díaz (Ed.), *Historia de la universidad colonial* (Avances de investigación: La Real Universidad de México, estudios y textos) (pp. 105–15). Mexico City: CESU/UNAM.

————. (1987b). El surgimiento de la organización corporativa en la universidad medieval. In L. M. Luna Díaz (Ed.), *Historia de la universidad* colonial (Avances de investigación: La Real Universidad de México, estudios y textos) (pp. 13–28). Mexico City: CESU/UNAM.

————. (2007). The new higher education landscape: Public and private goods, in global/national/local settings. In S. Marginson (Ed.), *Prospects of higher education: Globalization, market competition, public goods and the future of the university* (pp. 29–77). Rotterdam: Sense.

————. (2012, June 10). Improving Latin American universities' global ranking. *World University News*, 225. Retrieved from www.universityworldnews.com/article.php ?story=20120606174803978.

Marginson, S., Murphy, P., & Peters, M. A. (2010). *Global creation: space, mobility and synchrony in the age of the knowledge economy.* New York: Peter Lang.

Marginson, S., & Ordorika, I. (2011). "El central volumen de la fuerza": Global hegemony in higher education and research. In D. Rhoten & C. Calhoun (Eds.), *Knowledge matters: The public mission of the research university* (pp. 67–129). New York: Columbia University Press.

Marsiske Schulte, R. (2004). Historia de la autonomía universitaria en America Latina. *Perfiles Educativos, 26*(105–6), 160–67.

Massy, W. F. (1992). *Measuring performance: How colleges and universities can set meaningful goals and be accountable.* Stanford, CA: Stanford Institute for Higher Education Research.

Meyer, J. W., & Rowan, B. (1978). The structure of educational organizations. In M. W. Meyer (Ed.), *Environments and organizations* (pp. 78–109). San Francisco: Jossey-Bass.

Millett, J. D. (1962). *The academic community: An essay on organization.* New York: McGraw-Hill.

Mintzberg, H. (1991). The professional bureaucracy. In M. W. Peterson (Ed.), *Organization and governance in higher education* (4th ed., pp. 53–75). Needham Heights, MA: Simon & Schuster.

Morrow, R. (2005). Foreword—Critical theory, globalization and higher education: Political economy and the cul-de-sac of the postmodernist cultural turn. In

R. A. Rhoads & C. A. Torres (Eds.), *The university, state, and market: The political economy of globalization in the Americas* (pp. 321–52). Stanford, CA: Stanford University Press.

Morrow, R., & Torres, C. A. (1995). *Social theory and education: A critique of theories of social and cultural reproduction.* Albany: State University of New York Press.

Muñoz García, H. (2003). *Power and politics in university governance: Organization and change at the Universidad Nacional Autónoma de México.* New York: RoutledgeFalmer.

———. (2004). Ajedrez político de la academia. In I. Ordorika (Coord.), *La academia en jaque: Perspectivas políticas sobre la evaluación de la educación superior en México* (pp. 9–23). Mexico City: CRIM/UNAM.

———. (2009). Introducción. In H. Muñoz García (Coord.), *La universidad pública en México* (pp. 5–22). Mexico City: Seminario de Educación Superior / Miguel Ángel Porrúa.

———. (2011). La universidad mexicana en el escenario global. *Perfiles Educativos, 333,* 21–33.

Ordorika, I., & Lloyd, M. (2013). A decade of international university rankings: A critical perspective from Latin America. In P. T. M. Marope, P. J. Wells, & E. Hazelkorn (Eds.), *Rankings and accountability in higher education: Uses and misuses* (pp. 211–31). Paris: UNESCO.

Ordorika, I., & Pusser, B. (2007). La máxima casa de estudios: Universidad Nacional Autónoma de México as a state-building university. In P. G. Altbach & J. Balán (Eds.), *World class worldwide: Transforming research universities in Asia and Latin America* (pp. 189–215). Baltimore: Johns Hopkins University Press.

Ordorika Sacristán, I. (2001). Aproximaciones teóricas para un análisis del conflicto y el poder en la educación superior. *Perfiles Educativos, 23*(1), 77–96.

Ordorika Sacristán, I., & López González, R. (2007). *Política azul y oro: Historias orales, relaciones de poder y disputa universitaria.* Mexico City: UNAM-Seminario de Educación Superior, Plaza y Valdés.

Ordorika Sacristán, I., et al. (2008). Comentarios al Academic Ranking of World Universities 2008. *Cuadernos de Trabajo de la Dirección General de Evaluación Institucional, 1*(1).

Ordorika Sacristán, I., et al. (2009). *Las revistas de investigación de la UNAM: Un panorama general,* 1(4).

Osa Edoh, G. I., & Alutu, A. N. G. (2011). Parents' socio-economic status and its effect in students' educational values and vocational choices. *European Journal of Education Studies, 3*(1), 11–21.

Perkin, H. (1984). The historical perspective. In B. R. Clark (Ed.), *Perspectives on higher education: Eight disciplinary and comparative views* (pp. 17–55). Berkeley: University of California Press.

———. (1997). History of universities. In L. F. Goodchild & H. S. Wechsler (Eds.), *ASHE reader on the history of higher education.* Needham Heights, MA: Simon & Schuster.

Pfeffer, J., & G. R. Salancik (1978). *The external control of organizations: A resource dependence perspective.* New York: Harper & Row.

Portantiero, J. C. (1978). *Estudiantes y política en América Latina: El proceso de la reforma universitaria (1918–1938).* Mexico City: Siglo XXI.

Poulantzas, N. A. (1978). *State, power, socialism.* London: NLB.

Pusser, B. (2004). *Burning down the house: Politics, governance and affirmative action at the University of California.* Albany: State University of New York Press.

———. (2006). Reconsidering higher education and the public good: The role of public spheres. In W. Tierney (Ed.), *Governance and the public good* (pp. 11–28). Albany: State University of New York Press.

———. (2008). The state, the market and the institutional estate: Revisiting contemporary authority relations in higher education. In J. C. Smart (Ed.), *Higher education: Handbook of theory and research* (Vol. 23, pp. 105–39). New York: Agathon Press.

———. (2011). Power and authority in the creation of a public sphere through higher education. In B. Pusser et al. (Eds.), *Universities and the public sphere: Knowledge creation and state building in the era of globalization.* New York: Routledge.

Pusser, B., Kempner, K., Marginson, S., & Ordorika, I. (2012). Introduction and overview of the book. In B. Pusser et al. (Eds.), *Universities and the public sphere: Knowledge creation and state building in the era of globalization.* New York: Routledge.

Pusser, B., & Marginson, S. (2012). The elephant in the room: Power, global rankings and the study of higher education organization. In M. N. Bastedo (Ed.), *The organization of higher education: Managing colleges for a new era* (pp. 86–117). Baltimore: Johns Hopkins University Press.

———. (2013). University rankings in critical perspective. *Journal of Higher Education, 84*(4), 544–68.

Putzel, J. (2005). Globalization, liberalization and prospects for the state. *International Political Science Review, 26*(1), 5–16.

Rashdall, H. (1936). *Universities of Europe in the Middle Ages* (Vol. 1, F. M. Powicke & A. B. Emden, Eds.). Oxford: Oxford University Press.

Rhoades, G. L. (1992). Beyond "the state": Interorganizational relations and state apparatus in post-secondary education. In J. C. Smart (Ed.), *Higher education: Handbook of theory and research* (Vol. 8). New York: Agathon.

Rhoads, R. A., & C. A. Torres (Eds.). (2006). The global economy, the state, social movements, and the university: Concluding remarks and an agenda for action. In R. A. Rhoads & C. A. Torres (Eds.), *The university, state, and market: The political economy of globalization in the Americas* (pp. 321–52). Stanford, CA: Stanford University Press.

Rosecrance, R. (1999). *The rise of the virtual State: Wealth and power in the coming century.* New York: Basic Books.

Santos, B. D. S. (2006). The university in the 21st century: Toward a democratic and emancipatory university reform. In R. A. Rhoads & C. A. Torres (Eds.), *The uni-*

versity, state, and market: The political economy of globalization in the Americas (pp. 60–100). Stanford, CA: Stanford University Press.

Sen, A. (1999). *Development as freedom.* Oxford: Oxford University Press.

———. (2002, January 4). How to judge globalization? *American Prospect.* Retrieved from http://prospect.org/article/how-judge-globalism.

Slaughter, S. (1988). Academic freedom and the state: Reflections on the uses of knowledge. *Journal of Higher Education, 59,* 241–62.

———. (1990). *The higher learning and high technology: Dynamics of higher education policy formation.* Albany: State University of New York Press.

Slaughter, S., & Leslie, L. L. (1997). *Academic capitalism: Politics, policies, and the entrepreneurial university.* Baltimore: Johns Hopkins University Press.

Stiglitz, J. E. (2002). *Globalization and its discontents.* New York: W. W. Norton.

———. (2006). *Making globalization work.* New York: W. W. Norton.

Stroup, H. H. (1966). *Bureaucracy in higher education.* New York: Free Press.

Touraine, A. (2000). *Can we live together? Equal and different.* Stanford, CA: Stanford University Press.

Vaillant, D. (2004). *Construcción de la profesión docente en América Latina. Tendencias, temas y debates.* PREAL Document 31. Santiago: Programa de Promoción de la Reforma Educativa en América Latina y el Caribe. Retrieved from www.oei.es/docentes/articulos/construccion_profesion_docente_AL_vaillant.pdf.

Weick, K. E. (1976). Educational organizations as loosely coupled systems. *Administrative Science Quarterly, 21,* 1–19.

Wences Reza, R. (1984). *La universidad en la historia de México.* Mexico City: Línea / Universidad Autónoma de Guerrero / Universidad Autónoma de Zacatecas.

Wirt, F. M., & M. W. Kirst (1972). *The political web of American schools.* Boston: Little, Brown.

Wolin, S. S. (1981). The new public philosophy. *Democracy: A Journal of Political Renewal and Radical Change, 1,* 23–36.

Young, S. E. (2014). *Scholarly community at the early University of Paris: Theologians, education and society, 1215–1248.* New York: Cambridge University Press.

CHAPTER SEVEN

Critical Policy Analysis, the Craft of Qualitative Research, and Analysis of Data on the Texas Top 10% Law

ANNA NEUMANN AND AARON M. PALLAS

This essay presents an approach to teaching some key "moves" in the critical analysis of qualitative data bearing on higher education policy. We discuss the use of evidence-based methods of induction; the generation of trustworthy claims; and attentiveness to the social, political, and human features of research. We assert that researchers who, at key points, infuse critical social theory (conceptual frameworks) into their studies heighten the likelihood that their work will address matters of social and educational equity. To produce critical research, we suggest, researchers must be attuned to criticality as a frame of mind and to research as craft—with the two blended. Criticality—including equity-mindedness as its anchoring frame—can be applied to many education-based practices: research, reading, writing, speaking and discussing, teaching, mentoring, and so on (Bensimon, 2007).[1] Research as craft—as systematic, purposeful, driven by theory, and anchored in evidence—is more focused. We propose that to understand and engage in critical research, one must understand criticality broadly, and research, as practice, deeply, thus positioning researchers to infuse critical views strategically and sensibly into their work.

Given the complexity of both criticality and research, we limit ourselves to discussion of two critical perspectives—policy values (Stone, 2001) and rhetorics of reaction (Hirschman, 1991)—both of which we consider through a single phase of research (data analysis) on a single case of policy implementation (the Texas Top 10% law). Because such information is of value, especially to newcomers to critical higher education research, we draw heavily on our own experiences as researchers and as teachers of research to doctoral students, and most recently through preparation and delivery of a three-day seminar on critical policy research sponsored by the Association for the Study of Higher Education (ASHE) Institutes on Equity and Critical Policy Analysis. This approach positions us to emphasize aspects of critical qualitative data analysis from a critical pedagogical perspective.

The ASHE Institutes as a Context for Learning

For two summers, we met with a group of junior scholars—most with doctorate in hand and several in advanced dissertation stages—to share with them an approach for analyzing qualitative data. We sought to cultivate craft knowledge of qualitative analysis. Learning a craft involves surfacing what one knows (or assumes), moment by moment, about an object of inquiry, holding that lightly and reshaping tentatively what one knows, sees, and believes as one repeatedly practices the craft (Heaton & Lampert, 1993).

A potter (as craftsperson) must know her clay (the substance with which she works); she must have deep predictive understanding of how the clay she molds on any given day will respond to different forms of touch and pressure and under varying conditions (temperature, humidity, tools, etc.). (For related insights on how scholars and artists interact with their subjects of study and performance, see Neumann [2009]). This view of craft, in pottery and art broadly, provides a useful starting point for thinking about craft in qualitative data analysis.

The Institute's Design and Underlying Principles

Several principles underpinned the form, content, and pedagogies of the institute:

PRINCIPLE 1: Expert researchers know how to read a research report in multiple ways, one of which speaks to the "insides" of the research process that novices are expected to master—as a narrative of the researcher's investigation inasmuch as about the topic investigated.

Learning to read in this way gives novices a glimpse of the nature and scope of their forthcoming learning. From within a "narrative of investigation" perspective, the novice researcher learns to read a research report with two aims: to learn what the author-researcher found, but also to *follow, learn from,* and *evaluate* the act of finding it. To do this, a researcher must be able, first, to discern the very process of such "finding." Learning to read like a researcher involves identification of what the researcher came to know content-wise and also how the researcher came to know it and to conceptualize it, hence grasping the researcher's narrative of investigation.

We sought to sensitize fellows to this second approach to reading research—as a narrative of investigation—viewing it as a small but important step toward their coming to think about research as crafted inquiry characterized by focused research questions; study designs strategized to support meaningful analytic strategies; data collection that is faithful to the plan of study yet attentive (and responsive) to study site realities; and data analysis attuned to production of full, trustworthy, and useable knowledge claims. A reader who views a research report in this way—as a report of content and also as a narrative of investigation—positions herself to engage in the craft of research: she is learning to think about research as "doing research" and as requiring strategic planfulness, foresight, flexibility, and judgment, all linked to knowledge and skill.

We enacted Principle 1 by having fellows read Prudence Carter's *Keepin' It Real: School Success beyond Black and White* (2005), an ethnography that examines cultural capital in the school and neighborhood lives of sixty-eight black and Hispanic youth in Yonkers, New York, and the methodological appendix to Annette Lareau's renowned book *Home Advantage* (2000), a sociological analysis of social-class differences in parent involvement in their children's elementary school that also originated as a doctoral dissertation. Carter's book highlighted a researcher struggling through complex decision making and as making solid progress, whereas Lareau's appendix featured a researcher struggling to get to decisions about what to do in the field or in the name of data analysis, or making poor choices and then struggling to correct them. Both texts highlight realities of research, including how researchers work through and experience them. Both provide insights to which beginning researchers, and many readers of research, are not usually privy.

PRINCIPLE 2: Learning research as a craft requires direct, face-to-face, open, and authentic engagement with researchers about research. In so doing, the expert researcher publicly identifies the novice researcher as being on a trajectory toward becoming a researcher, while the novice researcher identifies the expert as vulnerable, as still growing and becoming, as apt to err just as the novice is. Substantive learning about research goes on amid this kind of identity building.

As Principle 2 shows, learning to read for the researcher's thinking through the conduct of research (e.g., how the researcher made decisions, addressed unanticipated problems, corrected them or adjusted, coped with uncertainty, all as part of the narrative of investigation) can help orient early career scholars to the practice of research, including its unseen but essential "back stage." But reading by itself cannot produce a competent practitioner of research any more than reading about teaching can make one a competent teacher. Nothing beats learning research—or learning any professional practice—while doing it, hands on, under the guidance of experts. But before that, it may be instructive to spend some sustained time talking—in open, grounded, and human ways—with "live researchers" about "what the doing of research" is like for them, and about their successes and failures in the field. Doing that can accomplish several things. It paints the expert researcher as a human being who at one time was a novice and who, despite her achieved expertise, must remain open to learning. It portrays research as malleable and in part unpredictable, though definable and subject to planning. It positions research—certainly in education—as social, political, and human.

For this phase, Anna Neumann, one of the ASHE Institute leaders, talked with the fellows about the process of her study of the learning of newly tenured professors in five universities, including how their relationship to their own experiences of inquiry changed through the courses of their careers. In addition to presenting her findings, Anna described some of the challenges she encountered over time: needs to make unanticipated decisions or to adjust prior plans and decisions, encounters with researcher error, efforts to correct mistakes, pleasant and unpleasant surprises. This kind of engagement, just prior to their entering a hands-on research opportunity, brought them still closer to the kind of engagement we were edging toward.

PRINCIPLE 3: The practice of qualitative research may be viewed as an amalgamation of distinct but interrelated strands of thought and action that must be considered singly and in relation to one another.

To understand research, a researcher must grasp research as a complex of multiple processes that, though distinct, bear on each other. We list these strands below, recognizing that, despite our efforts to the contrary, this arrangement communicates a linearity to the research process that obscures their interrelatedness within any given research project.

· Identifying one or more questions that can be addressed through research (research questions).
· Building an initial conceptual framework to guide the inquiry.
· Designing a study that will enable the researcher to gather data from which claims may be derived so as to respond to research questions.
· Collecting data.
· Cleaning and otherwise processing, archiving, and readying data for analysis.
· Analyzing data by reducing their complexity and searching for credible and meaningful patterns.
· Reporting what the researcher learned, and how that bears on a community's collective understandings of the phenomenon under study.

We positioned fellows to take notice of all phases of the research process, asking them to consider a set of diagnostic questions that guided our discussions of Prudence Carter's *Keepin' It Real,* and Neumann's *Professing to Learn*, surfacing technical terms (e.g., research questions, conceptual framework, design, etc.), and using them as lenses for reflecting on what the researchers did in each study and why. In other words, we addressed Principle 3 in the course of addressing Principles 1 and 2.

PRINCIPLE 4: Qualitative data analysis, one of the strands of research, is itself composed of multiple threads.

Much like the research process overall, any linear sequence of the threads comprising data analysis would do violence to the view of data analysis that we espouse. But the threads of data analysis include familiarizing oneself with and reflecting on the data that the researcher has collected, comparing bits of content embedded in different data elements, searching for resonances in meaning across data elements and critiquing one's own claims about them, linking resonant data into claims, testing these claims against data that did not generate them, examining discrepancies between claims and data, and so on. These within-analysis threads intertwine, often in unpredictable ways. Principle 4 exemplifies an important feature of research overall: the craft of research may be viewed as a set of interrelated practices, each of which embeds still other interrelated practices.

The remainder of this chapter discusses qualitative data analysis, and how we introduced fellows to a single core analytic "move"—the creation and use of analytic questions in deriving evidence-based claims. We see the creation and use of analytic questions as a critical entry point to qualitative data analysis, largely because of their power to guide researchers flexibly but directly. Analytic questions allow researchers not only to search directly for responses to research questions, but also to consider potentially relevant surrounding content without crossing undue bounds. They also position researchers to critique and revise their original research questions while remaining true to one's original research intent.

At the institute we sought to teach about analytic questions in light of the four principles above, with a particular focus on Principle 4. This concentration compelled us to provide fellows with a hands-on opportunity to write analytic questions, assemble and review pertinent data, articulate initial claims, test and retest as well as write and rewrite the claims, search for disconfirming data, retest, and finalize defensible data-grounded claims. Holding true to the institute's focus on critical policy analysis as a source of research topics, perspectives and frames, and challenges, we specified, in advance, two framing theories and a prepared but limited body of data.

Drawing on research by Stone (2001) and others, we introduced fellows to some of the major values embedded in discourse about education policy. We hoped this approach would sensitize fellows, as future researchers, to view policy as framed in light of policymakers' personal, social, and political values, and thus as subject to critique in light of still others' potentially competing values. We also hoped to suggest that values need not compete with each other, but rather could be viewed as complementary, as when equity and quality—or equity and efficiency—are paired as analytic lenses. Second, we devoted institute time to watching a news documentary of a policy—the Texas Top 10% policy broadcast on the CBS television newsmagazine *60 Minutes* in October 2004—that we deemed ripe for critical policy analysis; we would use this case, including publicly available data about it, for the fellows' hands-on analytic experience. Finally, we introduced fellows to Albert Hirschman's (1991) classic theory, the rhetoric of reaction, as a framework for launching the Top 10% data analysis, given its power to conceptualize public policy and the politics of response.

Policy Values

Because the suite of institutes sponsored by ASHE was devoted to equity as a base value of critical policy analysis, we viewed it important (1) to surface the power of values to contravene leaders' policy choices and (2) to juxtapose equity against other values as justifications for government action. Policy discourse often pits one value against another, arguing that some outcomes are more important or reasonable than others. Understanding the structure of policy arguments is a necessary precursor to critiquing them. Our intent was not to introduce particular political philosophies, such as liberalism or populism, but rather to discuss specific policy values, the kinds of issues they can bring out in a specific case, and values underpinning responses to public policy.

We drew attention to five values applicable to policy and response: equity, efficiency or effectiveness, liberty or freedom, security, and community or solidarity (see Stone, 2001). These values are not exhaustive, and different analysts divide the political territory in varying ways. In presenting each value, we sought to persuade fellows that abstract statements of values can mask substantial disagreements about their meaning, and what would count as empirical evidence of movement toward or away from a particular value. In this sense, identification, comparison, and assessment of the values underlying a policy, as solutions to a social or educational problem, can help to scaffold analysis of policy intentions, desired effects, and the framing of response. What does a particular policy seek to do? And what does it accomplish relative to intent? Whose intent counts?

Equity, as a policy value, can be defined broadly as a fair distribution of resources. But that definition immediately invokes questions about definitions of fairness. Does fairness mean giving equal amounts of a valued resource to everyone? Amounts proportional to needs? A minimum threshold below which no one can fall? Equal chances but unequal amounts? All of these have, in one setting or another, been defined as "fair" ways to distribute resources. Or is fairness primarily about the *process* by which the distribution of a resource is determined, rather than the amount that each individual receives? Additional questions can be posed regarding which resources count, who is eligible for them or to distribute them, and who is not.

Efficiency and its sibling *effectiveness* refer to maximizing the output for a given array of inputs: getting the biggest bang for the buck. But even that tired phrase raises thorny questions. Is the desired output a big bang, rather than a big flash of light? What counts as an output, and who decides? Some outputs might benefit everyone in a community, whereas others may be of value to some individuals but not others. Does it matter who benefits? Who decides? What counts as an input, and who bears the costs—direct or indirect—of those inputs? All of these questions make clear that efficiency, a term that is presented as value neutral, is in fact value laden.

Liberty or *freedom*, oft-heard policy values, pertain to freedom of action unless the actions harm others. What counts as a "harm" is often contested, and there can be disagreements over what types of harms society should prevent, either because of the consequences for individuals or for society at large. A recent example drawn from the headlines is the effort by former New York City Mayor Michael Bloomberg to ban the retail sale of sugary soft drinks larger than sixteen ounces on the grounds that consuming such drinks contributes to obesity and diabetes for individuals and increased public health costs for the city. The court ruled against the ban on narrow grounds, but the policy debates framed it as an incursion on the freedoms of consumers to purchase such beverages, and of store-owners to sell them (Grynbaum, 2013).

As a policy value, *security* refers to the satisfaction of basic human needs such as food, shelter, and clothing. Even this abbreviated list invites the question of what counts as a basic human need. Should adequate health be a basic need? Education? Self-determination? Is security absolute or relative? Do the quantity and quality of education needed to be a productive member of society vary by the geographic context, or are they uniform across time and place? Security as a policy value might apply to the needs of individuals, the needs of a social group, or both.

The final policy value, *community* or *solidarity*, pertains to the collective responsibility of a social group to maintain the well-being of the group itself. This value invokes thorny questions about group boundaries, and who determines who lies inside boundaries and who is an outsider. Collective responsibility also varies in meaning, prompting considerations of when it is appropriate for some group members to bear more responsibility for the well-being of the group than others.

Our objective in presenting these five policy values, including some of the questions and challenges they imply, was twofold. First, we sought to sensitize fellows to the reality that statements of policy values often fail to take account of the interests of subordinated groups who are, ironically, the targets of public policy. This presentation was designed to inspire fellows to discern and articulate tacit assumptions undergirding particular policy issues and debates in higher education (and public policy generally), to critique those values from the standpoint of equity as an overriding value, and to imagine equity-anchored alternatives. Second, we used this presentation as a bridge to the specific case to which we would turn in the final phase of the institute, when we planned to engage fellows in authentic data analysis: policy discourse about the Texas Top 10% law. Policy values gave us an initial frame for making sense of the Texas ruling, its seen and likely unseen effects, and possible responses and alternatives.

A Case in Point: The Texas Top 10% Law

In addressing the Texas Top 10% case in 2009 and 2010 through the institute, we focused first on the debates taking place in the Texas legislature regarding possible repeal or revision of the law. Our colleague Shaun Harper brought to our attention a segment about the case that had aired on *60 Minutes* in October 2004. The report, titled "Top Ten %," was narrated by correspondent Lesley Stahl and described the consequences of a Texas law, passed in 1997, that guaranteed admission to any public postsecondary institution in the state to students graduating in the top 10% of their high school class (see Leung, 2009 for a transcript). In her introduction to the segment, Stahl states that the legislature passed the law "in an effort to promote ethnic diversity."

"How has the law worked?" she asks rhetorically. "At the University of Texas in Austin—UT," Stahl continues, "it appears to have worked *too well*." Her language is striking, and as we will see the segment fails to rise above this ignominious start. A law designed to promote ethnic diversity has worked "too well"? Is the implication that there are *too many* ethnic minority students attending UT? Has the law been so efficient and effective in doing its work that it could now be repealed?

The segment pits two students against one another: Laura Torres, a Latina living in public housing in San Antonio who was admitted to UT under the Top 10% rule, and Elizabeth Aicklen, a white woman who attended a wealthy, competitive high school in Austin and hoped to join family members as UT alumni. The piece weaves in the voices of just two other people: state Senator Jeff Wentworth, who at the time was seeking to repeal the law, and Larry Faulkner, the president of UT, who sought to cap the number of students admitted under the Top 10% law to no more than 50% of the entering class. Wentworth states that the Top 10% law was enacted in response to the 1996 *Hopwood v. Texas* decision by the Fifth Circuit Court of Appeals, which outlawed the use of race as a criterion in Texas admissions. In 2003, the Supreme Court's ruling in *Grutter v. Bollinger* trumped the *Hopwood* decision, once again permitting use of a "narrowly tailored" definition of race in college admissions to further a compelling state interest in the benefits arising from a diverse student body.

In the segment, Senator Wentworth argues that because affirmative action was once again legal, "we don't need the Top 10% rule anymore." Regrettably, Lesley Stahl does not interrogate Wentworth on this point. She might have posed an effectiveness question, such as asking how successful the University of Texas had been in enrolling Latino/a and black students when affirmative action was the official policy of the university. (Answer: not very. Enrollment rates of Latino/a and black students were considerably higher under the Top 10% rule than during the earlier period, when affirmative action was university policy.) And she could have probed why he thought that affirmative action would work better in 2004 than it did in 1996.

Although the segment acknowledges that Texas high schools are separate and unequal, that fact is presented in a taken-for-granted way. "So many schools are essentially segregated. Take Laura's high school," Stahl states. "It's almost entirely Hispanic. So most of its top 10% are Hispanic." But Laura's school is also described as "inferior" and nonrigorous, conflating school quality and student quality. Stahl describes the consequences of the law for UT as being "almost out of control" and "forced" to accept an increasing number of Top Ten percenters— about two-thirds of the entering class in 2004.

And Senator Wentworth piles on: "You can have a young man who is an Eagle Scout, who's president of his student council, and captain of his football team, but because he's in the top *twelve* percent, he's not automatically admitted. But somebody else who's in the top *ten* percent, who didn't even take the recommended curriculum for college work, who took the minimum curriculum, automatically goes to the University of Texas at Austin, and that's not fair."

"Goes to" is slippery language in that only a small fraction of the students in the state who are guaranteed admission to public colleges and universities apply to and enroll at UT. And the students who are admitted under the law are quite successful at the university, suggesting that they were adequately prepared for college. But only, Stahl intimates, if students get special help: "Did you get tutoring?" she asks Laura Torres. (Yes, Laura did.) Stahl's setup is unmistakable: the law is unfair to the legions of (mostly white) students and their families, who played by what they thought were the rules and yet were denied admittance. Elizabeth Aicklen grew up in Austin, and attending UT was a lifelong dream. "Did you do anything *extra* in high school to make sure you got in?" Stahl asks. Elizabeth took a number of advanced placement (AP) classes at Westlake High School, which Stahl tells us is "filled with overachievers from upscale families." "You were competing with the brainiest kids at one of the best schools in the whole state," she says, eliciting that Elizabeth, like many others at her school, was obsessed with her class rank and had a grade point average (GPA) of 3.9 out of 4.0. (Stahl does not mention that GPAs at Westlake are weighted, so that an A in an AP class equals a 4.6, and an A in a pre-AP or honors course equals a 4.2.) "And you still didn't make the top ten in the school?" Stahl marvels.

In contrast, at Fox Tech, Laura Torres's high school, there were "fewer challenging courses, less competition, most of the kids from poor families," Stahl tells us. She asks Laura about her high school GPA, which was around 3.4 or 3.5. "Did you take a lot of tough courses?" she asks. Laura responds that she did not take any AP courses, just "regular" courses. The difference could not be clearer. "If Laura had gone to Westlake, she'd barely have made the top *fifty* percent," Stahl states. "If Elizabeth had gone to Fox Tech, she might have been the *valedictorian*." And the comparison cannot conclude without noting that Elizabeth scored "hundreds of points" higher on the SATs than did Laura.

The penultimate phase of the segment seeks to further personalize what is obviously a structural problem. Stahl describes each woman to the other, and asks if the outcome is fair. Laura went to a high school that was "inferior" and yet was admitted to UT.

"You get hurt—someone else gets a benefit," Stahl says to Elizabeth. "Can you see that?"

"Yes," Elizabeth replies, "but I felt like I didn't get what I deserved." The clip then cuts to Stahl describing Elizabeth to Laura.

"She had a 3.9 average."

"3.9?" Laura reacts with wonder.

"So she feels that the playing field wasn't level," Stahl tells Laura. "She feels that there's an unfairness. An imbalance." There is a pause, and then Lesley Stahl says something quite extraordinary. "I can see in your mind, you know, you're even thinking maybe she's right! Are you?"

"Now I feel really bad," Laura eventually replies.

"Really?" asks Stahl.

"Yeah, I do."

Not surprisingly, the *60 Minutes* piece provoked a great deal of discussion among the fellows, who were appalled by Stahl's interviewing style and framing of the law's consequences. While fellows voiced surprise, indignation, and anger at Stahl's superficial treatment of a policy problem at the heart of American higher education, we sought to have them think it through also as a large-scale value tradeoff: desires for efficiency up against commitments to equity, and the multiple ways of operationalizing equity (Stone, 2001). In the face of Stahl's grossly oversimplified representation, aired in millions of American living rooms on a Sunday evening, and upon realizing too the conflict of values at its core, fellows redoubled in their determination to tell a deeper and truer story, one more mindful than Stahl's, of the social and political realities undergirding education in the state of Texas. Our next step, however, was to identify a conceptual framework for considering, still more deeply than the values analysis permits, the rhetorical responses to the Texas Top 10% law. In laying that out, the fellows would be prepared to analyze political debate from its multiple sides and in light of overall effects.

The Rhetoric of Reaction as a Conceptual Framework for Critical Analysis

We advocate that a conceptual framework, typically identified early in a study (see Principle 3), should be "held lightly" and thus considered provisional and subject to review and revision as the research process unfolds. And early on at the institute, we presented cases of research studies in which scholars revised their conceptual frameworks midstream (Lareau, 2000; Neumann, 2009). We thereby sought to portray frameworks as subject to change through the process of research. In so doing, we positioned fellows to understand that researchers need to move fluidly among their initial conceptual frameworks, the data, insights emerging during data analysis, and the broader scholarly context of the research; sometimes they add in new frames late in their research (Lareau, 2000). We did not identify this reconstruction of the conceptual framework as a distinct phase because it does not appear to happen in all qualitative research.

We acknowledge that our introduction of a conceptual framework in support of data analysis was perhaps one of the more artificial features of the institute, as the compressed time led us to propose one rather than allowing fellows the time to identify framing theories consistent with their intellectual identities. Adopting a conceptual framework for one's research involves an assertion both of what one believes in and finds useful and what one views as unhelpful and as needing to be discarded (Lareau, 2000). A deep understanding of the theories and concepts that are useful to one's understanding of the social world is built up over years of immersion in the relevant scholarly literatures and ideas, and no one researcher will be immersed to the same literatures and ideas, nor in the same way, as others.

For the data analysis portion of the workshop, we knew that fellows would bring to bear the scholarly worldviews they had constructed through their own graduate studies and engagement with the literature in higher education. To provide a common platform from which all could start—and to emphasize the need to be in touch with theoretical literatures to make the most out of any analysis— we introduced Hirschman's (1991) ideas about the rhetoric of reaction. Hirschman, a towering figure in twentieth-century social science, grew interested in the nature of policy discourse characterizing reactions—in his words, "ideological counterthrusts"—to "progressive" government reforms in the nineteenth and twentieth centuries. His analysis led to three common arguments posed by those challenging progressive reforms, which he labeled the rhetoric of reaction: the perversity thesis, the futility thesis, and the jeopardy thesis. Each thesis is nominally sympathetic to the goals of the reform but conjures a distinctive argument about why the reform cannot realize those goals.

The perversity thesis argues that efforts to address an objective will through unanticipated mechanisms have the perverse consequence of making things worse than they were prior to the onset of reform. Hirschman's most vivid example is the neoliberal arguments against the expansion of the welfare state— state-sponsored social programs designed to protect the most vulnerable citizens through cash benefits and in-kind welfare services. If the welfare state is intended to increase personal autonomy among the disadvantaged and promote the building of strong families, the perversity thesis argues, it will have the opposite effect, increasing their dependence on the state and further destabilizing the family and other social institutions. A contemporary case is the argument posed by former New York City Mayor Michael Bloomberg against then–mayoral candidate Bill de Blasio's proposal to fund universal pre-kindergarten in New York City by raising taxes on the wealthiest New Yorkers. Bloomberg predicted that implementing such a tax would cause the city's richest citizens to flee, thereby reducing city tax revenues (Sledge, 2013). More broadly, the perversity thesis takes a familiar form: efforts to reduce social and educational inequality will have the unanticipated consequence of increasing inequality; policies designed to increase social efficiency will reduce efficiency; and reforms intended to increase freedom and liberty will backfire, resulting in less freedom of action.

Hirschman's futility thesis stipulates that some problems are so large and intractable that any efforts to address them are simply futile. In this view, the "natural order" of things is so powerful that attempts at social engineering to stop them, or perhaps even to slow them down, are doomed to failure. It is irrational, the futility thesis argues, for societies to direct precious resources toward insoluble problems. The French aphorism *plus ça change, plus c'est la même chose*—the more things change, the more they stay the same—sums up well the futility thesis. Opponents of efforts to stem global warming embrace the futility thesis, arguing that the natural world evolves in ways that are indifferent to human intervention. Conversely, economists might argue that efforts to eliminate poverty are a fool's errand, as there is a "natural" rate below which unemployment cannot fall in a long-run equilibrium economy.

Finally, Hirschman's multidimensional jeopardy thesis is arguably more complex than either the perversity thesis or the (simple-minded) futility thesis. The jeopardy thesis argues that any effort to implement progressive policies to address a particular social problem will jeopardize valuable progress already made on other social problems. Because this risk is so high, reform critics say, such reforms should not be undertaken. Handgun registration, for example, while arguably enhancing public safety, threatens hard-won progress on individual liberties. The social cost to compromising individual freedoms, the jeopardy thesis might argue, exceeds the social benefits of public safety. The late political scientist Samuel Huntington offered another version of the jeopardy thesis by claiming that US immigration policy, while expanding opportunities for the disadvantaged, jeopardized a coherent national identity and culture (Huntington, 2004).

Our aim in presenting Hirschman's framework was to offer fellows entry points to considering arguments and counterarguments around the Texas Top 10% law (and especially its effects). To envision the possibility of an alternative to a stated view—like Wentworth's or Stahl's—invites questions, then critiques, of its content, and possibly responsive alternative stances.

Engaging Fellows in Critical Policy Analysis of Rhetoric

To better understand the various streams of public reaction to the Texas Top 10% law and the possibility of its discontinuance, we sought to engage fellows in a brief but authentic evidence-driven analysis of the "talk" around the law. In March 2009, the Texas Senate and House of Representatives held hearings on a bill to modify the Top 10% law. The hearings were videotaped and archived on the Texas legislature website. Prior to the institute, we downloaded and transcribed portions of the testimony, and compiled biographical information of about fifteen speakers and legislators commenting on the law and proposed changes. The fellows analyzed approximately ten single-spaced pages of testimony and a similar volume of data on the speakers and organizations they represented.

Divided into small groups, the fellows had two tasks: (1) to formulate an analytic question as an outgrowth of the original research question (they might use Hirschman's theses to stimulate their thinking) and (2) to develop at least one claim in response to the analytic question along with supporting data. Both tasks were challenging to carry out under the institute's timetable. In the summer 2009 institute, we asked the groups to post the memos describing their work within a few weeks of the institute's conclusion, and we read and responded to them. In the 2010 institute, fellows presented their claims in a closing session, and we along with the fellows' peers verbally commented on them.

Our approach to analysis relies on addressing what we have come to term *analytic questions*. Faced with an expanse of data and one or more broad research questions, a researcher might easily be overwhelmed, paralyzed by the absence of a clear pathway to addressing the research questions. Research questions are generally a guide to research design and data collection, much more so than to data analysis. In qualitative research, moreover, data are drawn from multiple instances of the phenomenon under study—interviews with a number of research participants, or field notes describing human interaction in different places and times. How does one know where to begin analysis?

We recommend formulation of analytic questions that are responsive both to the research questions and to the features of the data that the research has gathered. A good analytic question should contribute to answering a research question, and be possible to address with the data in hand. Thus analytic questions link research questions and data. A simile that has proven useful is that an analytic question is like a small shovel, shaped (and iteratively reshaped) to enable the researcher to "scoop" out of the data a subset that can respond to a question of interest. At the outset, analytic questions may be a bit of a fishing expedition:

one may not know as analysis begins which questions are the most important to address en route to answering the research questions, or just phrasing a question so that data can respond to them. Over time, as researchers engage with their data and tack back and forth between the data and the original research questions, these analytic questions may become more refined.

We used a metaphor to explain the power of analytic questions: creating an analytic question is akin to coming up with questions that allow one person to move, systematically and carefully, through a probing conversation with another person narrating a complicated experience, one that may be incomplete and difficult to summarize or express. Identifying a good way to phrase the question is key. For example, Anna might ask Aaron, who has just had a fast-paced, challenging day, "How are you doing?" Once the initial formalities are concluded— "okay" or "not too bad"—Aaron may continue to respond in general terms, but from time to time he may "mark" (Weiss, 1994) for Anna's attention aspects of his situation that she realizes might bear closer examination. "Colleague problems?" Anna might ask. "What do you mean?" Or "can you tell me more about that?" These are the same types of probes that students learn to use in semistructured interviews.

And so Anna might again ask "How are you doing?" but this time with different words that direct Aaron to the segment of his response that she had heard as marked. She could continue in this process, successively reaching deeper and deeper into Aaron's experience, pulling out more and more, until she is able to hear many specifics around the particular conditions that Aaron has faced as well as his experience of them. Perhaps she will learn that "colleague problems" refers to bad behavior by a colleague that the institution does not monitor or regulate. If so, the next time that Aaron or another colleague refers to colleague problems, Anna will know to ask if the problems are linked to institutional structures or to their absence. She will frame an analytic question directed more pointedly at understanding the nature of the colleague problems and their institutional sources as the speaker understands them.

There is, then, a bit of trial and error as well as induction involved in the formulation of analytic questions in that they are designed to emerge from the original research questions and the data collected simultaneously. For this reason it is critical that data analysis be viewed as iterative, with analytic questions—and even research questions!—being subject to revision over time. Much as in a conversation, a researcher must iteratively rephrase her questions so that the data she has just collected can respond to them. This is, of course, impossible to do at the point that research questions are asked.

A researcher can also ask an analytic question at different "levels" of analysis, each contributing to a different objective. At ground level, an analytic question such as "What do the data about this particular instance of the phenomenon [a transcript of an interview or fieldnotes describing a particular observation] tell us about X?" draws on a single transcript or field note and is used to scoop data out of that transcript or field note that respond to the question. An intermediate analytic question takes the form "What do the data from all cases in my sample say about X?" This intermediate analytic question draws on all data in the sample that are responsive to the question, and these data are used to build categories and to formulate patterns observed in the sample. The third, most abstract, analytic question is "What might all cases, beyond just those in my sample, tell us about X?" This question draws on the entire corpus of data considered in the intermediate analytic question but looks especially for discrepancies, inconsistencies, and boundaries around the phenomenon of interest; it searches for variance in the data, cases of exception.

The objective of an analytic question of this type is to generate claims about the phenomenon at issue supported by the data, and possibly generalizable beyond the specific cases studied. Such claims are typically phrased as propositions, carefully crafted so as to communicate possibility, though framed in light of a researcher's uncertainty and stated in forthcoming ways. There is an inherent leap of faith in drawing such generalizations—or statements of the findings' general value—as they involve extrapolation from a sample to a larger population of interest, and this extrapolation typically cannot be justified on large-sample statistical grounds (Lucas, 2012). But what is "found" by way of qualitative data analysis is less about the population sampled (though that must be acknowledged) than about the nature of the phenomenon studied (what is it and how is it manifest?), possibly reflected in the larger population, a portion of it, or beyond it. Emergent propositions must therefore speak to both the nature of the phenomenon of study and more traditional concerns about the likelihood of its appearance in the population sampled. Hence the claims that are formulated as responses to the most abstract form of the analytic question (propositions) must inevitably address the researcher's uncertainty about validity. Another way to view this is to say that the findings of any one study serve as a stepping-off point for where, substantively and conceptually, a new study in another site can begin. One of the aims of that study would be to verify the findings of the first study, revise misrepresentations or state their inconclusiveness, extend earlier findings, and open up new ground. Generalization in qualitative research carries a different meaning than in statistical studies (Maxwell, 2005; Yin, 2009).

To illustrate the use of analytic questions, Anna drew on an account of her research on professors' learning and scholarly identity development in the early posttenure career, a project culminating in publication of *Professing to Learn* (Neumann, 2009). She noted that there were two research questions motivating her study. (1) How do newly tenured professors learn and develop in their scholarly identities, and what is it about these professors' lives, careers, and environments that supports (but also thwarts) such learning and development? (2) What contexts—of life and work—appear to matter most in newly tenured professors' scholarly identity development and learning, both for better and for worse? What makes them matter?

Anna invited fellows to imagine her interviewing a research participant, an astronomer with the pseudonym David Mora, in the first year of her study. The conversation yielded a forty-page single-spaced transcript. She conducted interviews with the other thirty-nine research participants, using the same interview guide, with each yielding a transcript varying from roughly forty to sixty pages in length—approximately two thousand single-spaced pages of data for the first year of a two-year study. What now?

As Anna repeatedly combed through her data upon returning from the field, she realized a few things. First, for analytic purposes, she would have to treat separately the concepts of *scholarly learning* and *scholarly identity development*, perhaps with the same data or in overlapping ways (though she might later relink them). The data spoke directly to learning, but not as directly to scholarly identity and its development. Taking professors' learning, then, as her analytic starting point, she found herself posing an analytic question resonant with one that researchers of learning often ask of students in classrooms: Professors learning *what* exactly? Reviewing her data, Anna enumerated many things that the professors in her study indicated learning on the job posttenure. She coded the data for the various things they indicated learning, whether asked directly about them or more indirectly offering information while talking about other matters.

Anna came to realize that even this seemingly foundational analytic question— the professors learning *what* exactly?—could be probed further. Realizing that the professors participating in her study were learning about their favored topics of study, she gleaned that they were doing so in many facets of their work, not just in research. More analytic questions emerged from her dual engagement with the data and with the existing literatures. In research on the professoriate, for example, there is often a tripartite distinction drawn among research, teaching, and service—common categories for describing faculty work, although shot through with ambiguities and overlaps. This finding led to some analytic questions re-

garding what professors might learn about their subjects in each of these domains. What can professors learn about their favored subjects as they teach? As
they carry out service responsibilities? As they engage in research or creative
scholarly endeavors?

Such questions can be refined further. Teaching, for example, is complex: professors prepare to teach, engage in substantive interaction with students, and may
then reflect on the experience, and each of these teaching activities may serve as
a site for learning about subject matter. Similarly, professors in different fields
might think in different ways about their subjects of study, or they might use
different terms to describe their thinking, leading to another analytic question:
How do professors describe the processes of thought in which they engage as
they work on their subjects of study?

With this example as a guide, we asked the fellows to write a single analytic
question with which to analyze the ten pages of data on diverse constituents' reactions to the Texas Top 10% law that we had provided them and then to respond
to it, drawing explicitly on the data in hand. As noted, we hoped that our extended interim discussion—with conceptual framing of policy values from Stone
(2001) and rhetoric of reaction from Hirschman (1991)—would encourage socially astute and critical analytic questions. Though we would have liked fellows
to find their own critical theories, our doing so for them modeled a key way to
infuse criticality into research: Find yourself a guiding critical theory. We explained carefully that the final product that fellows would present to us and to
each other—an iteratively revised analytic question and alongside it a provisional
response with data from the case to back it up (i.e., a claim)—was not an end. It
was only a beginning; we expected that in due time they would revise that claim,
identify additional analytic questions to pursue, and derive more claims, some of
which might coalesce with others. Through the institute we stayed purposefully
close to the ground, drawing in theory (e.g., Stone, Hirschman) and referring
to examples from earlier parts of the institute (Neumann, Carter, and Lareau) to
broaden and enrich our views.

More than three years have passed since we conducted the institute. We have
remained in contact with many fellows and have elaborated our teaching about
analytic questions and research claims in our classes and in guidance of dissertation students. Three of the fellows extended the institute exercise, applying critical
race theory to a more elaborate corpus of data transcribed from the legislative
hearings on the Texas Top 10% law, culminating in an article now in print (Winkle-
Wagner, Thandi Sule, & Maramba, 2014). Looking back on our own experience

of teaching in the institute, we continue to ask how we might better merge crafts of academic research with theory and with topical substance while retaining a critical edge to questions about social and educational equity that are anything but academic or theoretical, being grounded in the pragmatics and pains of real persons' everyday existence in inherently inequitable social structures. How can we frame and teach about research on poignantly personal topics—experiences of discrimination and inequity—while turning that research into tools for advancing the social good, possibly rebuilding its meanings? We have no clear response other than we hope that the institute fellows—as well as students in our classes today—will be better poised to address these questions than we are.

Conclusion

As is often the case in public policy, especially education policies formulated in an era dominated by concerns for social mobility (Labaree, 1997), revisions to the Top 10% law adopted by the Texas legislature in 2009 were unpalatable to some stakeholders and deeply unsatisfying to others. The new law continued to provide automatic admission to eligible students in the top 10% of their high school class applying for admission to the fall 2010 class. For admissions in 2011 through 2017, however, the law stipulated that 75% of the spaces in the freshman class allotted for Texas residents must be made available through the automatic admissions process.

Capping the number of admissions slots meant that not everyone in the top 10% of their high school class would be automatically admitted, as that number exceeded the number of available seats in the class. The law's revisions charged the university with determining what class rank would guarantee admission and notifying Texas school officials, students, and their families of the cutoff two years in advance. Thus the University of Texas at Austin announced in September 2009 that students applying for admission in the fall of 2011 would be automatically admitted if they were in the top 8% of their high school class. The figure rose to 9% for the class entering in the fall of 2012, and then returned to 8% for the class entering in the fall of 2013. For the upcoming admissions for fall 2014 and 2015, the university has announced that students in the top 7% of their high school class will be automatically admitted (Planas, 2012). The class rank for automatic admission in the fall of 2016 remains to be determined.

ACKNOWLEDGMENT

We acknowledge with gratitude dedicated research and teaching support provided by Milagros Castillo-Montoya and assistance from Jolie Harris Woodson.

NOTE

1. Referring to college and university actors in practitioner roles (instructors, advisors, administrators, policymakers), Bensimon (2007) defines equity-mindedness as efforts to "bring into the open [practitioners'] sense-making about inequalities, increasing awareness of perspectives that make inequality appear natural, and taking responsibility for the educational outcomes of minority students" (458). This view positions equity-mindedness as driven by practitioners' (college instructors, administrators, staff, etc.) cognition and values, including equity. We view research as a practice too and researchers as its practitioners (Neumann, Pallas, & Peterson, 1999) who, like instructors and administrators, can be guided in their work by values of equity-mindedness.

REFERENCES

Bensimon, E. M. (2007). The underestimated significance of practitioner knowledge in the scholarship on student success. *Review of Higher Education, 30*(4), 441–69.
Carter, P. L. (2005). *Keepin' it real: School success beyond black and white.* New York: Oxford University Press.
Grynbaum, M. (2013, October 17). New York soda ban to go before state's top court. *New York Times.* Retrieved from www.nytimes.com/2013/10/18/nyregion/new-york-soda-ban-to-go-before-states-top-court.html.
Heaton, R. M., & Lampert, M. (1993). Learning to hear voices: Inventing a new pedagogy of teacher education. In D. K. Cohen, M. W. McLaughlin, & J. E. Talbert (Eds.), *Teaching for understanding: Challenges for policy and practice* (pp. 43–83). San Francisco: Jossey-Bass.
Hirschman, A. O. (1991). *The rhetoric of reaction: Perversity, futility, jeopardy.* Cambridge, MA: Belknap Press of Harvard University Press.
Huntington, S. P. (2004). *Who are we? The challenges to America's national identity.* New York: Simon & Schuster.
Labaree, D. F. (1997). *How to succeed in school without really learning: The credentials race in American education.* New Haven, CT: Yale University Press.
Lareau, A. (2000). *Home advantage: Social class and parental intervention in elementary education* (2nd ed.). Boulder, CO: Rowman & Littlefield.
Leung, R. (Correspondent), & Stahl, L. (Reporter). (2009). Is the "Top 10" plan unfair?" *60 Minutes.* Retrieved from www.cbsnews.com/8301-18560_162-649704.html.
Lucas, S. R. (2012). Beyond the existence proof: Ontological conditions, epistemological implications, and in-depth interview research. *Quality and Quantity, 48*(1), 387–408. Retrieved from www.springerlink.com/content/u272h22kx2124037/.
Maxwell, J. A. (2005). *Qualitative research design: An interactive approach* (2nd ed.). Thousand Oaks, CA: Sage.
Neumann, A. (2009). *Professing to learn: Creating tenured lives and careers in the American research university.* Baltimore: Johns Hopkins University Press.
Neumann, A., Pallas, A. M., & Peterson, P. L. (1999). Preparing education practi-

tioners to practice education research. In E. Condliffe Lagemann & L. S. Shulman (Eds.), *Commission for Improving Educational Research, National Academy of Education Issues in Education Research: Problems and possibilities* (pp. 247–88). San Francisco: Jossey-Bass.

Planas, R. (2012, November 2). Top 10 Percent admissions reduced at UT-Austin, least likely to affect Latinos. *Huffington Post*. Retrieved from www.huffingtonpost. com/2012/11/02/top-10-percent-ut-austin_n_2064055.html.

Sledge, M. (2013, October 21). Bill de Blasio on "transcendent moment" that exposes income inequality's wrongs. *Huffington Post*. www.huffingtonpost.com/2013/10/18/bill-de-blasio-income-inequality_n_4125555.html.

Stone, D. (2001). *Policy paradox: The art of political decision making* (3rd ed.). New York: W. W. Norton.

Weiss, R. S. (1994). *Learning from strangers: The art and method of qualitative interview studies*. New York: Free Press.

Winkle-Wagner, R., Thandi Sule, V., & Maramba, D. C. (2014). When race disappears: College admissions policy discourse in the state of Texas. *Educational Policy, 28*(4), 516–46. doi:10.1177/0895904812465114.

Yin, R. K. (2009). *Case study research: Design and methods*. Los Angeles: Sage.

CHAPTER EIGHT

Critical Action Research on Race and Equity in Higher Education

ALICIA C. DOWD, ROBIN M. BISHOP,
AND ESTELA MARA BENSIMON

Like the other contributors to this book, we are interested in conducting research that "makes a difference" (Bensimon et al., 2004) to produce knowledge, promote actions, and bring about social relations that will constitute a more just society. In our case, the goal is to involve higher education practitioners in action research for the purpose of studying the ways in which taken-for-granted administrative and educational practices enable (or prevent) equity in educational outcomes for racial and ethnic groups whose educational and societal experience is marked by inequality, from kindergarten to higher education.

To contribute to the development of a critical action research methodology for postsecondary education in the United States (where it is not well established), in this chapter we concentrate on the potential of critical action research to bring about transformative social change. Action research "aims to solve pertinent problems in a given context through democratic inquiry in which professional researchers collaborate with local stakeholders to seek and enact solutions to problems of major importance to the stakeholders" (Greenwood & Levin, 2005, p. 54). Action research is "critical" when its purpose is to expose and dismantle power asymmetries, institutionalized inequalities that perpetuate discriminatory practices, and the systematic reproduction of privilege, wealth, and status. Critical action research investigates the enactment of values that are seemingly democratic or principled, such as merit and equal opportunity, yet are functioning to produce inequities. Critical action research in education is a research methodology intended to "uncover those aspects of the dominant social order which undermine . . . emancipatory goals" (Kincheloe, 1995, p. 74).

In this chapter, we describe the methods we have developed to pursue critical aims by producing knowledge in collaboration with college and university practitioners engaging in reflective practice ("inquiry") using the Equity Scorecard, a set of action research tools and processes that we and our colleagues at the Center for Urban Education (CUE) have developed. Critical action researchers aim to take on issues of inequality by empowering practitioners to make change and to articulate the need for more socially just educational practices and policies. The methods we use are practical, grounded in educational practice, and carried out in collaboration with practitioners in their settings of practice.

The first section of this chapter introduces the action research design principles underlying CUE's Equity Scorecard (see Bensimon & Malcom, 2012, for more in-depth discussion). The second section presents a case analysis focused on the experiences of two Equity Scorecard team leaders. The choice to focus on two individuals at a single institutional site is appropriate for gaining a deeper understanding of the practice of action research,[1] which is "obstinate about its focus on changing particular practitioners' particular practices . . . in 'the here and now'" (Kemmis & McTaggart, 2005, p. 564). In conclusion, we offer reflections on the conditions necessary to support the practice of critical action research in postsecondary settings in the United States.

Engaging in Critical Action Research through the Equity Scorecard

A group of practitioners who form an evidence team carry out their inquiry using CUE's action research tools. The evidence team typically has about ten members from a range of professional roles (administrators, faculty, and student affairs professionals). Two members typically serve as co–team leaders. Our objective in convening the Equity Scorecard evidence team is to bring together a cross-functional and racially diverse group of practitioners who will engage in a learning process on behalf of their college or university (Huber, 1991). The Equity Scorecard process is designed to introduce cultural artifacts into the inquiry process to prompt critical, self-reflective awareness of "contradictions" between espoused values (the values by which we believe we enact our work) and our actual practices (Seo & Creed, 2002). For instance, we may believe that we work in racially equitable ways, yet if we avoid speaking of race and assume (without questioning) that all policies at our institution are equitable, we may unintentionally perpetuate existing inequities.

As action researchers acting with critical goals, we introduce language that is new to the participants. "Equity mindedness," "equity gap," and "equity goals" act as technical terms to structure the completion of the Equity Scorecard process, but more fundamentally they are language tools. We provide these tools to practitioners to assist them in unlearning, through dialogue and new cognitive framing, previously unexamined "deficit-minded" cultural assumptions that, for example, blame student and family characteristics as the causes of persistent racially based inequities in student participation and outcomes (Bensimon, 2005a,b, 2007; Bensimon & Malcom, 2012).

We introduce and support the use of the language of the Equity Scorecard by practitioners in their own settings, using approaches that are familiar and acceptable within professional norms. For example, CUE gives leadership training in professional development workshops and "leadership institutes" for Equity Scorecard evidence team leaders. The workshops provide team leaders with protocols (such as "ground rules" and "meeting agendas") for leading conversations about racial inequities, particularly as they are observed in institutional data. Data tools, such as cross-sectional "snapshot" data presented in the Scorecard's "vital signs" and longitudinal cohort data presented in the Benchmarking Equity and Student Success Tool (BESST), provide easy-to-interpret data displays that become the subject of team talk about racial equity gaps.

The Blackstone University Case

In the case analysis presented below, which features evidence team leaders Kim and Lee at Blackstone University (all pseudonyms[2]), the focus is on racial inequity in admissions, particularly as it affects African Americans. At Blackstone, when the Equity Scorecard evidence team conducted an inquiry using the Scorecard's BESST data tool, the data showed that the admissions rate for Caucasians was 80% and for African Americans it was 40%. The case illustrates how the team leaders learned about this equity gap in admissions and how their willingness to use or modify the "social media" of their educational practices, to use Kemmis and McTaggart's (2005, p. 565) terms, grew as they acquired knowledge of the equity gap and of admissions procedures. It also illustrates how the "activity system" and "artifacts" introduced to the team leaders through the action research design process of the Equity Scorecard enabled them to reconfigure their sense of purpose (the "object" of their actions in cultural activity theoretical terms) as well as the perceived norms of behavior, community, and division of labor for faculty members in relation to admissions personnel and African American student applicants (Engeström 2001, 2008, 2010).

Blackstone University is located in a nonurban area of a state with a high degree of racial segregation. African Americans in the state tend to be heavily concentrated in a small number of urban areas. Latinos and Southeast Asian Americans and other immigrant families are located primarily in cities, but a growing number are settling in exurban and rural areas. The small but historically significant and culturally distinct American Indian population is located primarily on land owned by the tribal authority.

In the data analyzed below, Blackstone University evidence team leaders Kim and Lee, who are both faculty members, confront the low numbers of African Americans attending their university. Like most faculty members, they had not previously been involved in reviewing undergraduate admissions practices at their university, but their growing attention to the lack of African Americans in their classrooms and on their campus illustrates the changes in beliefs and practices that action inquiry can bring about.

The case examines how the use of Equity Scorecard data disaggregated by the racial and ethnic groups attending Blackstone University acted as a remediating artifact, moving equity in admissions into the scope of Kim and Lee's educational practice. We present the narrative case we have constructed from observational field notes by a CUE researcher in the role of participant-observer and subsequent individual interviews with the two team leaders using the present tense and italic text.[3] The text also draws on direct interpretations (Stake, 1995) recorded by the participant-observer at the time the observational data were collected. Data replicated from field notes appear in quotation marks, and a longer passage is indented. We give our interpretive commentary in plain text.

The focus of the narrative is on interactions between Kim and Lee and the institute presenters, who include Estela M. Bensimon (EMB), a CUE professional staff member (referred to as the "project specialist"), and a representative of the university system office. Other team leaders participated in the workshop, but they and their institutional context are not represented here simply to delimit the scope of the analysis.

The Leadership Institute

The two team leaders for the Blackstone University Equity Scorecard evidence team, Kim and Lee, settle at their table. Their demeanor is serious, quiet, and professional. The meeting is not underway for long before it is apparent that they are concerned about how much time implementing the Equity Scorecard will take and how all the work to lead the team will fit into their existing responsibilities. At the first opportunity, they point out that the scheduling of the kickoff meeting for evidence team members conflicts with other important dates on their university calendar. Some evidence team members may miss out on the orientation. Those who miss out, Kim and Lee worry, may never really buy in to the process. This concern appears to be heightened when Andy, a former team leader from another university who presents to the group through videoconferencing, emphasizes how important it is to involve faculty. Faculty "are the toughest sell," Andy says, because they already have their own areas of expertise. They discuss but ultimately reject the idea of changing the kickoff date because it would create "even more work." This concern explains why the two team leaders "may seem a little discouraged" about the prospects of getting off on the right foot, Lee explains.

Concerns also quickly emerge about whether the outcomes of the Equity Scorecard process will be worth all the effort. The team leaders were not involved in choosing the team members and do not know most of them. CUE has the provost invite faculty and administrators to participate on the team using a team selection template, which is intended to communicate to evidence team members that the Scorecard effort has the support of the executive leadership. Nevertheless, Kim and Lee express concerns that the Equity Scorecard will lack leadership support. Kim comments that the campus has a history of reporting for the sake of reporting, and then nothing comes of it; policies do not change. Lee indicates that diversity is essentially a "nonconversation" on the campus. The team leaders sense that they will need to start a conversation with people who may not be all that interested in getting involved.

Despite these apprehensions, Kim and Lee are attentive during welcoming remarks and initial segments of the meeting, and a CUE project specialist explains the contents of a binder full of information about the Equity Scorecard. They laugh when the system office leader jokes about the overwhelming number of diversity and institutional improvement initiatives going on. The overwhelming situation is real—yes, they are being asked to take on yet another project—yet they acknowledge it with good humor and seem to appreciate the system leader's recognition that the campuses are being asked to take on more even at a time when resources are strained and tensions are high because of budget cuts.

The reactions from Kim and Lee reveal aspects of the organizational culture of their work world, including the division of labor, community, and implicit rules governing faculty work. The division of labor is hierarchical—it is up to the provost to provide leadership—and horizontal—they do not have any particular authority over other Equity Scorecard evidence team members. The rules are to exhibit a professional demeanor and to interact in collegial ways. Time is highly valued and scarce, and most community members are busy—facts that appear to be important to acknowledge. Although most professionals have some discretion over their time use, faculty members, whose identities as professors are often defined by their expertise and their authority to define what counts as quality work, are particularly busy.

Kim and Lee have reactions suggesting that they have been asked to take on something new, and they feel uncomfortable because they do not know the rules of this new activity. In the following segment of the narrative, they become more engaged as CUE's project specialist describes the inquiry tools that CUE is introducing through the Scorecard process. The narrative refers to the project specialist diagramming the time commitments for the project on a large poster pad displayed on an easel. Using an easel and markers to present time commitments for completing the Equity Scorecard is intentional, as written words can quickly be modified or elaborated on in response to participants' questions or concerns. This process shows respect for the rule that faculty and many college administrators have authority over the prioritization of their time. The "project specialist" provides a predetermined scheduling method to the team leaders as a resource for time and process management. Throughout the eighteen-month Scorecard process, the project specialist will also hold monthly meetings with the team leaders and help scaffold the month-by-month inquiry activities that lead to the development of the Equity Scorecard. These aspects of the Scorecard process reveal its underlying cultural activity theoretical design. As action researchers, we are introducing new tools and resources to remediate practice, community, norms, professional roles, and division of labor.

> The CUE project specialist diagrams the time commitments and steps of the Equity Scorecard using markers, a pad, and easel. She is well prepared to address concerns about time because other team leaders and team members have expressed similar worries. Kim and Lee nod to indicate they are following along with the presentation and write notes for their own planning purposes.
>
> CUE's participant-observer notes that "participants are eager to know this part. They appear relieved to get this information, as it helps them concretize their responsibilities." Despite Lee and Kim's tentative start, "By the afternoon, they seemed intent on 'mastering' what was being presented (as evidenced by their forming many active questions and taking notes)."

Their demeanor indicates that they are actively engaged in learning about group leadership techniques; they want to be able to draw on the team and time management tools CUE is providing.

After listening to Andy, the former team leader, describe how the Scorecard data had influenced a change in admission practices at his university, Lee reacts by saying that he wants to "go back to my college and find out" how it uses advanced placement, SAT, and ACT scores. So even though Lee has expressed skepticism about his ability to lead the Scorecard team, he is becoming engaged by a specific action to find out how standardized test scores are used in admissions. It appears this engagement arises from Lee's perception that knowledge of the test data might afford the opportunity to influence policies that affect diversity and equity.

The interest in "hands-on" data is also evident when the CUE co-director (EMB) previews the Scorecard data analysis process by showing a data table. Kim jumps right in, asking multiple questions about the data, details that EMB intended to leave until later on. The CUE participant-observer notes, "Kim and Lee seem to want to become better equipped with the tools to do this job, which they may not feel confident about yet." Luckily, the agenda for the day includes time planned for a brief "hands-on" data analysis. The data motivate attention and engagement in the learning process. "Members' interest was piqued once they saw it; they wanted to begin to understand it rather than wait. Although still making assumptions without realizing that they are assumptions, Kim is actively engaged with the tool in a process of sense-making." One of these assumptions is that African American students are at college mainly to play basketball and participate in other athletics. This is a recurring assumption among Equity Scorecard evidence team members. EMB uses it to introduce the concept of "hunches," a language tool designed to point out, without shutting down the conversation, that a speaker is making stereotyped assumptions that can be examined by obtaining "fine-grained" data. The leadership training is designed to encourage subsequent data-based inquiry, and the field notes indicate some initial success: "Lee is working to master the concept of fine-grained questions . . . using the data examples tool to practice this new skill . . . Both Kim and Lee begin interpreting the data, posing 'hunches,' and also asking 'How can we find out?' "

The preceding segment of the narrative features a number of CUE's action research tools, including data tools and the introduction of tools for reframing the discourse, such as hunches and fine-grained questions. These are used to challenge and change discourse that exhibits unconscious acceptance of "deficit-minded" assumptions (Bensimon & Malcom, 2012) about the reasons for the lack of representation of students of color on campus (or in graduating classes or certain fields of study, such as in science, technology, engineering, and mathematics). Labeling an assumption a hunch is a way of expanding the range of explanations and making clear that some explanations lack evidence. Language tools are easily portable and can be introduced to peers in other settings. Further, language is powerful because it is part of the social media that constitute social structures. The action research field notes call attention to the active effort on the part of Kim and Lee to learn the meaning of the new terms that were introduced as part of the Scorecard process.

The data tools are also central in the narrative because knowledge claims can be constructed from data. Acting with expertise is a rule for faculty behavior. Gaining skill with the data tools is a way to gain knowledge and expertise as a foundation for the role of team leader. Lee's immediate interest in learning more about the use of SAT/ACT scores in admissions at Blackstone University reflects an intuitive or perhaps culturally inculcated awareness that data-supported ideas are respected within the institution and among faculty.

Lee and Kim's interactions with the data tools are rewarding to us as action researchers because our role as tool designers is to make data accessible as a way to empower practitioner participants in inquiry as knowledge producers about racial inequities. The language and data tools are designed to act in tandem as artifacts that mediate equity-minded thought and action. To say "that sounds like a hunch" is to use the language tool of hunches in an activity system where the subsequent action of inquiry is an appropriate professional behavior. A practitioner enabled by inquiry tools can learn more about the evidence in support of or in opposition to an assumption, for example, the common (in our experience) assumption that African American students do not want to study in rural areas (unless they are there to play sports), which is why so few apply or accept offers of admission.

Permission for "Race Talk"

The following narrative was constructed from individual interviews conducted with Kim and Lee one year after the leadership institute, approximately midway through the eighteen-month Scorecard process. Kim recalls a frank comment made by a person of color as the two of them were talking in between sessions at Blackstone's evidence team kickoff meeting. The other team member took advantage of the Scorecard setting, which values and emphasizes the need to call attention to racialized patterns of interaction, to point out that Kim was acting from a position of "white privilege." As Kim related the exchange in the interview:

> I was just blathering on with her about, "Geez, I just don't know if I have enough room on my plate, I'm already doing this and that for this population and that population . . . I'm working on [so many things] . . . Now I also have to help the minority students?" And she said, "Well . . . that really shows your white privilege . . . because you *can* choose to deal with this. Whereas, when you're born in skin that isn't white, it's not a choice. It's just something you have to do every day whether you feel like it or not." And I was like "Oh, crap . . . you have to point out to me when I am exhibiting some sort of attitude of white privilege. Because obviously, there's a lot I don't know."

The instructional and collaborative aspects of the Equity Scorecard design are evident in this exchange, where Kim explicitly asks the participant of color for help seeing white privilege in everyday actions and beliefs, as in this case regarding choices about one's use of time. Although Kim's statement "you have to help me" might be experienced by the woman of color as an oppressive form of "cultural taxation" (Padilla, 1994) in a dominant-culture institution, Kim's reflections indicate that Kim was engaging in the "unlearning" of white privilege that is necessary to dismantle institutional racism (Howard, 2006).

Kim became more aware of racialized patterns of participation at Blackstone University. Despite having noticed the near-absence of students of color in her own department for quite some time, Kim had avoided reflecting on it too intently, not concluding that it was a university problem and instead rationalizing that the students might be elsewhere on campus. Faced with the Scorecard data, it was no longer possible to rationalize the problem away.

> I think the thing that still takes my breath away is the fact that in [the year being examined] we only managed to enroll five African American students. That was just, like, "Five?" You know, the fact that you could count them on one hand was just painful . . . I knew that in *my* sphere it seemed really, really white . . . but then seeing the numbers made me see that it wasn't an illusion, as if all the racially underrepresented kids were over in the sciences or psychology or something. It was like, "No, they really aren't here. *They really are not here.*"

Seeing the data using the Scorecard data tools, broken down in a simple way and disaggregated by racial/ethnic groups, Kim could no longer avoid the reality that Blackstone University only enrolled a handful of African American students each year. In the interview, Kim said that Blackstone needed to do a better job of recruiting African American students. Kim's statement that seeing the data "still takes my breath away" reveals the emotional impact of the data, which motivates attention to what is happening in a broader social context.

Similarly, by acting as a leader on the Equity Scorecard evidence team, Lee became more conscious of the fact that over a decade not a single African American student had ever been in his classroom. In an interview toward the end of the Scorecard process, Lee reflected,

> I think that when you see a pattern like that that has persisted over time, you start thinking to yourself, "Why? There must be an underlying reason that things are the way they are and this constancy has remained as strongly as it has, and you want to do something to change it."

The power of simple numbers to provoke reflection is evident when Lee independently references the same data point as Kim had about the handful of African Americans on campus:

> So the one [data point] that we stumbled on very early last January was about the African American population, where 140 African American students started the application process, and through the steps of the process, only five of them ended up on our campus in the fall . . . And there were questions about why we do so poorly with African American and Latino populations? About how students and applicants have financial concerns; and the communication issues that we have on our campus; and the question of how do we build the community for the underrepresented minority students at our institution?

These comments indicate that Lee's sense of the university community is changing to include African American and Latino students who are absent from the campus, students who applied but did not enroll, even among those who were accepted. The division of labor between a faculty member's role and the roles of admission professionals shifts slightly but discernibly as Lee considers a variety of factors that might be keeping African American and Latino students from enrolling (whether lack of financial aid, unappealing recruitment communications, or a negative sense of the racialized campus climate). This shift is also evident in the following quotation when Lee describes a conversation with colleagues about the Scorecard data:

> I tell people about the Scorecard meetings, and I say, "We're looking at data. For example, [only five African Americans]" and they're like, "Wow!" The example

seems to hit home with them, and to help them understand why eleven people on this team are working on tasks to help understand why the data are what they are.

The artifacts Kim and Lee plan to use to remediate the practices of their peers around equity issues are not the same artifacts we created as action researchers. They plan to tap into existing structures for faculty development. Kim's description indicates the intention to use accepted discourse about a faculty member's service responsibilities and personal philosophies of teaching and service to invite other faculty into the equity agenda:

> part of what Lee and I have been talking about was presenting about the Scorecard on this panel for the faculty development conference . . . about making your university service fit with your own personal philosophy, so that it feels more like work that you would want to do.

This strategy is attentive to the rules of faculty life. Lee and Kim are sensitive to the issue of time as they begin to reach out to others on their campus to ask them to get involved. Kim was aware that her colleagues would not receive information about the low numbers of African American students on campus with the same emotional sense of contradiction between mission and reality that had struck the evidence team members in the Equity Scorecard meetings, where discussions took place in a setting in which the rules of social interaction permitted discussion of racism. Kim anticipated that others would be hesitant to embrace what they might perceive as additional work, just as the two team leaders themselves had begun the Scorecard process with a strong concern for their time—a concern that Kim only came to view through the lens of racial privilege through her interaction with a person of color on the Scorecard team.

> I think what's going to be important for us is just keeping our spirits up as we take our work out and start to experience apathy and complacency and the notion that change is gonna require someone to do extra work . . . I think people feel really stretched thin.

Kim does not view the Blackstone evidence team as a group with collective agency for organizing and advocacy. Sizing up the potential of an individual actor to bring about change on a larger scale, Kim is willing to take satisfaction in small changes. Recalling a conversation with two admissions representatives who responded enthusiastically to a number of ideas about how to more effectively recruit students of color, Kim said, "I feel like just the fact that we sat down to establish a common goal to improve things . . . if that's all that comes out of the Equity Scorecard process for me, I will feel like it was a success."

Producing Knowledge through Inquiry Using Disaggregated Data

As noted in introducing the case, the Blackstone University evidence team conducted inquiry using CUE's BESST depicting cohort progression data. The BESST made it easy for the team members to see how students of different racial and ethnic groups fared in the milestones of the admissions pipeline. The data show the loss of African American students from the point of a student's initial application, to submission of all required application materials ("application completion"), to acceptance by the university, and finally to enrollment as part of the university's "yield." The data showed that only 40% of African Americans completed the application process after initiating it. This number compared with an 80% application completion rate for students overall. Using the language tools of the Scorecard, the Blackstone University evidence team designated this "equity gap" in the applications of African American students as a "focal effort" for inquiry and action to close equity gaps. In addition to digging deeper into the data after asking fine-grained questions, team members conducted peer interviews with admissions staff at their university and reviewed admissions documents.

This proved to be a powerful knowledge-producing activity. Kim and Lee and the Blackstone University team members learned that of the approximately one hundred African Americans who initiated an application to the university, 54% did not submit an application fee, 50% did not submit test scores, and 30% did not submit high school transcripts. This level of specificity moved beyond hunches to explain why African Americans do not complete their applications. The data revealed specific aspects of the application process that were acting as barriers to African American student enrollment. The data enabled the team to make specific recommendations to Blackstone University leaders that had potential to close the equity gap in admission completion.

For example, the evidence team recommended that the admissions office monitor disaggregated application data on a weekly basis to monitor a student's progress toward a complete application (e.g., submitting transcripts and test scores and paying admission fees). Building on action research principles of inquiry and data use as strategies for organizational change, the team recommended that this information be communicated as a weekly report to the provost from the admissions office. They recommended that admissions staff contact African American students and offer to help the students complete their applications, for example, by providing a high school transcript fee waiver. The team also suggested that the admissions office purchase test score data and use it to contact academically eligible African American students rather than relying on students to realize they were eligible for admission to Blackstone.

Using CUE's document analysis inquiry tool to review admissions information on the website, evidence team members found that the university advised students with "special circumstances" to declare such circumstances during the application process. By treating this routine admissions language as data in the inquiry process, the evidence team was able to point out that such self-evident, "normal" language might seem strange to students unfamiliar with the admissions process. What are special circumstances, and how does one describe them? What counts as special? What happens when a student identifies herself as special? Will it make her stand out (stigmatize her) in some way?

After asking these questions and taking the perspective of a young African American applicant, the team recommended that examples of special circumstances be posted along with stories from successful alumni who had identified themselves as facing special circumstances when they applied. The objective was to create models for applicants to follow. In activity system theoretical terms, the Blackstone University evidence team recommended the invention and use of new admissions artifacts—the special circumstances examples and success stories—that they believed would help promote equity.

In addition to using the Equity Scorecard tools to inform their own learning, Lee and Kim appropriated them as cultural artifacts for communicating with their colleagues. Lee engaged in "data talk" with colleagues in casual conversations in the office in order to explain why the activities of the Equity Scorecard team were important. Kim was looking for ways to incorporate discussions about the inequities revealed through the data into a campus professional development conference. Their sense of the "rules" for their professional activities had changed somewhat, including responsibility to pay attention to racial inequities. Their sense of community had expanded to include both the handful of African Americans enrolled on their campus as well as those African Americans who had initiated an application but did not complete it. Both team leaders became aware of the absence of African Americans in their classrooms and began to question the underlying causes of their absence. They took some steps, albeit modest ones, to influence admissions practices and policies as well as retention and completion.

As a result of their participation in the Equity Scorecard, Kim and Lee, faculty members who held a variety of leadership roles in university-wide committees and chaired their respective departments, began to pay more attention to racial and ethnic representation in the student body. They may have become more likely to ask the "race" question when it is absent from institutional reports on student success, or when their colleagues discuss student outcomes in the aggregate without recognizing or giving importance to interracial differences.

Developing awareness of racial/ethnic inequities, learning to view them as a problem of institutional effectiveness, and establishing equity goals to increase the representation of racial/ethnic groups in outcomes that symbolize student success provide evidence of important individual and institutional changes that came about as a result of the action research process. These changes may lead to improved outcomes for African American students, the target group that was the focus of Blackstone's Equity Scorecard and the group that, in our experience at institutions that implement the Scorecard, often face the largest equity gaps. But it is not apparent that the Equity Scorecard assisted Kim and Lee in developing the critical perspective necessary to remediate the cultural practices and organizational routines of a seemingly meritocratic and culturally neutral university that are systematically producing racial inequities.

The Limitations of Individual Agency in Postsecondary Settings

The Blackstone University evidence team, under Kim and Lee's leadership, used the Equity Scorecard data to set goals to improve equity in the admissions yield, aiming to convert admitted African Americans applicants into enrolled Blackstone University students. Yet, despite the fact that the admissions rate for African Americans was disturbingly low relative to other racial/ethnic groups, the evidence team did not set equity goals to increase the percentage of African Americans who were being admitted to Blackstone. Unlike the task of improving the admissions yield, which can be viewed as a technical matter that can be addressed through better communications and marketing, changing admissions criteria or who is involved in the admissions review processes is an idea that challenges beliefs about merit and who deserves to get a college education. The Equity Scorecard process was effective in motivating attention to technocratic change, but it did not spur a deeper critique or willingness to interrogate the meritocratic ideology underlying the admissions criteria.

By the conclusion of the project, the university response to the recommendations[4] of the Blackstone University evidence team was ambiguous. At a concluding "retreat" for the evidence team members, including admissions officers and campus leadership, the steps needed to establish the process for monitoring incomplete applications and producing a report for the provost was described as being "in progress." The recommendation to contact African American students with qualifying SAT or ACT scores was deemed impractical owing to limitations of access to the necessary data. Finally, several months after the retreat, no additional information had been added to the Blackstone University website to clarify or make less stigmatizing the term "special circumstances." On the other hand, the website now includes a new page with all institutional data disaggregated by race and ethnicity, a practice that developed as a result of the college's participation in the Equity Scorecard. Another indication of change is that many more African Americans have submitted applications; however, the rate of admissions continues to be much lower than for white students.

While some recommended changes may have been enacted but are not represented in our data, and others might yet be enacted with the passage of time, we note that these recommendations concerning admissions were not enacted despite being within the scope of the authority of institutional actors. In our experience, this is often a stopping point for Scorecard participants at institutions where the leadership is ambivalent about addressing equity issues. This stopping point often highlights tensions between equity as a value and goal and other values, which are often expressed in democratic terms such as attending to the success of "all" students rather than focusing on the outcomes of specific racial/ethnic groups. At times, institutional leaders feel impotent to take actions in ways that may appear to go against institutional norms in their sector. In the case of Blackstone University, which was experiencing enrollment declines, priority was given to recruitment activities that would increase enrollment numbers overall, not necessarily the enrollment of students of color.

When institutional leaders seem ambivalent about addressing inequities because they do not want to invite complaints about racial preference and reverse racism, we at CUE struggle with taking a position and making direct recommendations to advocate for stronger equity oriented goals. At Blackstone the most glaring inequity was its admissions rates. But the team decided not to set a goal to increase the rate of African American admissions to that of whites, even though it would have meant admitting only nineteen additional African American students. Institutional leaders perceived that increasing the admittance rate of black students would face strong objections. Additionally, several members of the evidence team were ideologically against making changes in the admissions criteria or review process. The equity gap between Caucasians and African Americans was so large that we felt we could not be silent about it. Therefore, to highlight those gaps beyond the documentation provided by the team's Equity Scorecard report, we wrote a report with our own recommendations to close equity gaps, separate from those of the team, and sent it to the provost and chancellor as well as to Kim and Lee.

Although our report was well received, we do not know whether Blackstone University implemented the specific actions intended to monitor the admission process and its impact on African Americans. The time frame of our involvement in this setting, and in most of the settings in which the Equity Scorecard is implemented, was not long enough for us to continue in the action researcher's role of facilitating data use and advocating for equity-enhancing changes. Whether such changes will emerge in the future as a result of the individual or collective agency of team members remains to be seen.

The Blackstone University case illustrates that, as critical action researchers, we act by introducing remediating artifacts, tools, instruments, and resources such as project specialists into the existing organizational routines. In our experience, beliefs are formed more powerfully through constructing knowledge and doing than through the receipt of information. When shown to be relevant and productive in shaping discourse, artifacts introduced through action research can lead to the use of new social media in the activity system, because artifacts act on subjects to mediate the purpose, or meaning, that actors ascribe to their actions (Engeström, 2001, 2008). Further, even partial or hesitant action can expose practitioners to contradictions in their mode of work and work role. These contradictions may motivate attention at a deeper level of commitment under certain conditions of action research. But the Blackstone University case illustrates some of the challenges to the implementation of critical action research methodology in postsecondary settings.

Conclusion

We believe that higher education practitioners and institutions are contributing to racial and ethnic inequities in education and in society. Therefore it is incumbent on us to pursue a critical research agenda and for practitioners to engage in critical assessment of their practices. If we do so ineffectively from the outset, our experience suggests that our agenda will immediately hit a dead end. Our critical stance is therefore consciously softened by pragmatic considerations.

We often enter settings where the Equity Scorecard has been adopted or introduced (by us or by others) using language emphasizing the technocratic, problem-solving aspects of practitioner inquiry. Such implementation makes the tools accessible to professionals who are in effect adult learners, and who enter the pedagogical setting with a wide range of prior knowledge, experiences, and attitudes. The discourse of the Scorecard, as represented by the orientation and marketing materials we produce and make available to new and potential participants, bridges the discourse of bureaucratic accountability (represented in terms such as effectiveness, outcomes, and student success) and practitioner agency (represented in terms such as knowledge, expertise, and the development of the capacities of a change agent). We introduce the Scorecard to evidence team members as a tool for inquiry at both a process-oriented, step-by-step level and as a tool for critical reflective practice.

We conduct action research in a way that attempts to combine a pragmatic bureaucratic accountability orientation and a critical action orientation. In the ideal conception, those who undertake critical action research would likely need to acknowledge from the outset that "racism" is endemic in practice and outcomes. The explicit purpose of an action research project in any setting would be to uncover racism in how things are done, what is valued, what is questioned, what is noticed. Our approach is critical in that it is motivated by the recognition that racism is an inherent aspect of higher education, that differences in higher education access and outcomes will be impossible to eliminate under conditions of race muteness.

Yet engaging campus practitioners in a project to uncover and dismantle racism requires that they take an initial interest or at least are sufficiently open to the possibility that racism is a characteristic of higher education—a condition that is not found on many college campuses today. If we were to arrive at places like the case study site and exclaim loudly and insistently that institutionalized racism is ubiquitous and persistent, there is a good chance we would be denied entry. Therefore the political aspect of our critical action research is muted, and as a consequence its potential to empower participants in a political and emancipatory sense depends on the receptivity of participants like Kim and Lee to critical perspectives about the causes of racial inequity as well as the willingness of leaders to use the power and authority of their offices to take actions to change the status quo. Clearly, much more time would need to be allocated within our work in dialogue among all the action research participants and powerful stakeholders to face critical perspectives on higher education's role in perpetuating racial inequities and oppressive social structures.

At the same time, critical action research can contribute to the unwinding of norms of privatization, inequality, and stratification that have taken root in national and institutional policy over the past four decades (Marginson, 2007, 2011). Neoliberal discourse is displacing deeper attention to higher education's role as a knowledge producer and incubator of the public good. In fact, as colleges and universities are being called on to forge closer ties to private consumer and research markets (Slaughter & Rhoades, 2004; see also chap. 4, this volume, by Sheila Slaughter, Barrett J. Taylor, and Kelly O. Rosinger), those institutional characteristics that are "quasi-public" are becoming more pronounced, while those that situate institutions as part of the "public sphere" are being diminished (Pusser, 2006, 2011). From the outset, prevailing constructions of meritocracy and the normalization of a "separate and unequal" higher education system constrain the action researcher's ability to emphasize a critical perspective (Carnevale & Strohl, 2013).

Therefore, to achieve the aims of critical research, action research must have the capacity for egalitarian discourse and knowledge creation as well as an orientation to social and institutional justice through organization and education. It is questionable whether such work can occur without the explicit endorsement, from broader segments of the political economy, of higher education's role in creating a public sphere. Transformational action through action research can succeed where it promotes an egalitarian, generative discourse with the purpose of promoting the public good through higher education.

NOTES

1. Because of our primary focus in this chapter on action research methods, we do not attempt to present a full case study with comprehensive, rich detail of the case sufficient to enable naturalistic generalizations.

2. We have elected to mask the identities of the two team leaders (except to reveal that neither is a person of color) in order to protect their anonymity.

3. Portions of the interview data appeared previously in a conference paper presented by Robin Bishop at the annual meeting of the Association for the Study of Higher Education (held in Las Vegas in 2012), titled "Developing a Shared Campus Narrative about Racial (In)Equity."

4. The recommendations highlighted here are only a sample; many more were included in the final report that the evidence team submitted to the provost.

REFERENCES

Bensimon, E. M. (2005a). Closing the achievement gap in higher education: An organizational learning perspective. In A. Kezar (Ed.), *Organizational learning in higher education* (Vol. 131, pp. 99–111). San Francisco: Jossey-Bass.

———. (2005b). *Equality as a fact, equality as a result: A matter of institutional accountability*. Washington, DC: American Council on Education.

———. (2007). The underestimated significance of practitioner knowledge in the scholarship of student success. *Review of Higher Education, 30*(4), 441–69.

Bensimon, E. M., & Malcom, L. E. (2012). *Confronting equity issues on campus: Implementing the Equity Scorecard in theory and practice*. Sterling, VA: Stylus.

Bensimon, E. M., Polkinghorne, D., Bauman, G., & Vallejo, E. (2004). Doing research that makes a difference. *Journal of Higher Education, 75*(1), 104–26.

Carnevale, A., & Strohl, J. (2013). *Separate and unequal: How higher education reinforces the intergenerational reproduction of white racial privilege.* Washington, DC: Center on Education and the Workforce, Georgetown University.

Engeström, Y. (2001). Expansive learning at work: Toward an activity theoretical reconceptualization. *Journal of Education and Work, 14*(1), 133–56.

———. (2008). *From teams to knots: Activity-theoretical studies of collaboration and learning at work.* Cambridge: Cambridge University Press.

———. (2010). Activity theory and learning at work. In M. Malloch (Ed.), *The Sage handbook of workplace learning* (pp. 86–104). Thousand Oaks, CA: Sage.

Greenwood, D. J., & Levin, M. (2005). Reform of the social sciences and of universities through action research. In N. K. Denzin & Y. S. Lincoln (Eds.), *The Sage handbook of qualitative research* (3rd ed.). Thousand Oaks, CA: Sage.

Howard, G. R. (2006). *We can't teach what we don't know: White teachers, multiracial schools.* New York: Teachers College Press.

Huber, G. P. (1991). Organizational learning: The contributing processes and the literatures. *Organization Science, 2*(1), 88–114.

Kemmis, S., & McTaggart, R. (2005). Participatory action research. In N. K. Denzin & Y. S. Lincoln (Eds.). *The Sage handbook of qualitative research* (2nd ed.). Thousand Oaks, CA: Sage.

Kincheloe, J. (1995). Meet me behind the curtain: The struggle for a critical postmodern action research. In P. L. McLaren and J. M. Giarelli (Eds.), *Critical theory and educational research* (pp. 71–89). Albany: State University of New York Press.

Marginson, S. (2007). The new higher education landscape: Public and private goods, in global/national/local settings. In S. Marginson (Ed.), *Prospects of higher education: Globalization, market competition, public goods and the future of the university* (pp. 29–77). Rotterdam: Sense.

———. (2011). The "public" contribution of universities in an increasingly global world. In B. Pusser et al. (Eds.), *Universities and the public sphere: Knowledge creation and state building in the era of globalization.* New York: Routledge.

Padilla, A. M. (1994). Ethnic minority scholars, research, and mentoring: Current and future issues. *Educational Researcher, 23,* 24–27.

Pusser, B. (2006). Reconsidering higher education and the public good: The role of public spheres. In W. G. Tierney (Ed.), *Governance and the public good.* Albany: State University of New York Press.

———. (2011). Power and authority in the creation of a public sphere through higher education. In B. Pusser et al. (Eds.), *Universities and the public sphere: Knowledge creation and state building in the era of globalization.* New York: Routledge.

Seo, M. G., & Creed, W. E. D. (2002). Institutional contradictions, praxis, and institutional change: A dialectical perspective. *Academy of Management Review, 27*(2), 222–47.

Slaughter, S., & Rhoades, G. (2004). *Academic capitalism and the new economy.* Baltimore: Johns Hopkins University Press.

Stake, R. E. (1995). *The art of case study research.* Thousand Oaks, CA: Sage.

CHAPTER NINE

Using Critical Race Theory to (Re)Interpret Widely Studied Topics Related to Students in US Higher Education

LORI D. PATTON, SHAUN R. HARPER,
AND JESSICA HARRIS

In her 1998 article "Just What Is Critical Race Theory and What's It Doing in a Nice Field Like Education," Gloria Ladson-Billings describes the emergence of an epistemological lens that had been recently imported from other fields (viz., legal studies) to critically examine race and racism in education. Critical race theory (CRT) had not yet been widely employed in the study of schools, education policy, and pedagogical practices at that time. In fact, she and William F. Tate IV had just introduced a critical race theory of education, in which they argued that race had essentially remained untheorized and that, because of this lack of theorization, it became increasingly difficult for educators, policymakers, and communities to grasp the full nature of educational inequality and to articulate its connection to racism (Ladson-Billings & Tate, 1995). They stated, "By arguing that race remains untheorized, we are not suggesting that other scholars have not looked carefully at race as a powerful tool for explaining social inequity, but that the intellectual salience of this theorizing has not been systematically employed in the analysis of educational inequality" (p. 50).

Since the publication of this article, CRT has garnered the attention of education scholars who have used the framework to analyze a range of issues related to racism, racial inequities, and the experiences of minoritized[1] persons at all levels of education (Dixson & Rousseau, 2005; Lynn & Parker, 2006). Despite its proven utility elsewhere, Harper (2012) observed that CRT was used in only five articles published over a ten-year period in seven major higher education, student affairs, and community college journals, suggesting that CRT has not assumed a firm intellectual space in higher education scholarship. Patton et al. (2007) also highlighted several problems associated with what they characterized as "raceless" theories and frameworks commonly used in higher education research.

Although CRT has a presence in higher education scholarship, it has not yet reached its fullest potential. Any substantive examination of educational literature would reveal that the bulk of CRT research and scholarship has been concentrated in the K–12 sector, focusing on teacher education, school policy, inequitable funding, and substandard treatment of children from racially minoritized backgrounds (Patton et al., 2014). In this chapter, we examine educational research and scholarship but focus specifically on popular topics related to college students. Our goal is to illustrate how higher education research has been devoid of in-depth examinations of racism and white supremacy. We also shed light on the possibilities that exist when researchers make conscious choices to purposefully engage issues of racism and white supremacy in their scholarship. Using the tenets of CRT, we discuss three widely studied topics concerning undergraduate students: (1) college access and admission, (2) theories of college student development, and (3) college student engagement. Ultimately, we aim to show how CRT as an analytic lens could be used to advance a more complicated understanding of the structures that determine inequity and the experiential realities of students of color in postsecondary institutional contexts. We apply tenets of CRT to each topic and offer new research questions that necessarily complicate racism and power structures in higher education research.

Critical Race Theory

A host of scholars have used CRT to examine racial injustice and white supremacy as it exists in and beyond higher education. Consistent throughout critical race scholarship is an effort to unveil the insidious nature of racism and its disproportionate impact on communities of color. Also consistent is the goal of disrupting racist knowledges (e.g., presumed intellectual inferiority of people of color, postracial ideologies that minimize the existence and impact of racism, race-neutral ideologies that rely solely on merit without accounting for societal racism and its impact—the conventional paradigm under which understandings of race operate). In this chapter, CRT is a beneficial framework for critiquing current higher education research, not simply at face value but for understanding how the research collectively operates to maintain systems of racial oppression.

CRT has its roots in the field of law and serves as a framework and a movement of scholars, educators, researchers, and community activists committed to confronting the complexities of race, racism, and power as they exist in various social systems. CRT dates to the 1970s with the work of Derrick Bell, Alan Freeman, and a host of scholars who were dissatisfied with legal reform following the civil rights movement (CRM; Lawrence et al., 1993). While many had hoped that federal legislation stemming from the CRM would address rampant racial discrimination and inequality, it became abundantly clear that the intended racial reforms were at best inadequate for dealing with overt racism, and at worst incapable of tackling more covert operations of racism. In addition, legal scholars of color, many of whom were heavily involved with the critical legal studies (CLS) movement, were disenchanted by the CLS movement's failure to meaningfully acknowledge the inherent racism in the law (Delgado, 1995b; Delgado & Stefancic, 2001; Lawrence et al., 1993; Lynn & Parker, 2006). These scholars sought to push a different agenda in which the law might be reinterpreted to account for deeply ingrained racism in legal jurisprudence.

Matsuda et al. (1993) were among the earliest to offer a set of tenets through which CRT might be understood. While their emphasis was on the performance of these tenets in a legal context, we introduce these tenets by providing examples grounded in higher education recognizing that both contexts are mutually influential. According to Matsuda et al., CRT acknowledges the endemic nature of racism in America and how it permeates every social system in this country whether political, legal, or educational. The normalized existence of racism is linked to the history of the United States, particularly the dual construction of the law and racial categories to determine one's societal standing. Race, racism, and racist laws constructed by white male colonizers, for example, dictated who was or was not white (Lopez, 2006), who could own property and whose bodies were treated as property (Harris, 1993), and whose rights would be protected in colonizing and conquering occupied land (Brayboy, 2005). These historical constructions have virtually shaped or in some way influenced present-day contexts, understandings, and operations of race and racism.

CRT scholars argue that racism naturally extends to all systems, including higher education. Racism is pervasive in both hidden and obvious forms on college campuses. Discernable forms of racism can be seen when examining white fraternity and sorority parties in which members dress in costumes that denigrate other racial groups and reduce their existence to stereotypical images (see Khouri, 2012; Manapsal, 2007; Quan, 2013). Covert forms of racism are more deeply rooted and difficult to recognize, particularly by those least affected by its consequences. For example, a campus search committee may begin their selection process with the premise that they are only interested in hiring the most qualified applicants, yet they do not realize that the criteria for hiring and their own biases may lead them to a primarily white subset of candidates. Similarly, an admissions counselor may choose to travel to only the "best" schools, which are typically characterized as predominantly white, suburban, and resource rich. As a result, talented and equally qualified students from racially minoritized groups go unnoticed with fewer opportunities.

The endemic nature of racism is closely tied to Matsuda et al.'s (1993) point that CRT challenges and is highly skeptical of claims rooted in neutrality, colorblindness, meritocracy, and objectivity. This particular tenet upsets the ideal of equality of opportunity in higher education and the belief that all people have a fair chance to attend college if they simply "work hard." Such arguments aim to deracialize any attempts made to remedy historical injustices that have consistently ensured postsecondary access to a majority white population while depriving those who represent racially minoritized groups of the same opportunities. The majority of colleges and universities are predominantly white with either minimal to no significant representation of racial diversity. CRT scholars would argue that this lack of representation is not merely accidental but instead by design; institutions, states, federal policies, and policymakers—most of whom are white—all play a role in who gains access to higher education and who is afforded prime opportunities to thrive in these environments. Given the preponderance of postracial rhetoric, higher education as an entity has been complicit in submitting to the ideals of colorblindness and race neutrality. For example, Morfin et al. (2006) examined enrollment patterns of racially minoritized students following the *Gratz v. Bollinger* and *Grutter v. Bollinger* US Supreme Court rulings in which race could be considered as a "compelling interest" for institutions to diversify their student body. Their analysis indicated that while the importance of diversity was upheld, colleges and universities failed to take bold steps, instead opting for a racially neutral stance. They noted the *Grutter* decision should have effectively prompted institutions to enhance racial demographics on campus toward greater diversity, particularly through their admissions decisions. Instead, most institutions focused on the *Gratz* decision, which ruled the use of quotas and points to be unlawful in admissions decisions. While there was some noticeable progress in terms of an increase in enrollment among racially minoritized students, Morfin et al. (2006) concluded that, "despite these tremendous increases, students of color remain significantly behind their White peers in enrollment and completion across the postsecondary landscape. To be blunt, Whites remain overrepresented in elite institutions of higher education. Asian Americans have been given tentative honorary White status in the admissions process as long as it does not result in majority Asian American students on these campuses" (258). In sum, this example reflects the ongoing dialectic between race, law, and higher education. Institutions were granted tremendous leeway toward increasing their diversity efforts. Most of them, because of increased institutional reliance on legal opinion from in-house counsel, used the rulings to appear more law abiding (code word: race neutral) rather than as transformative spaces where issues of race and racism are acknowledged and addressed.

The fact that higher education has been less than transformative in its efforts toward racial diversity and equity are rooted in its racist past. Matsuda et al. (1993) noted that CRT challenges ahistoricism and insists on a contextual/historical analysis of structures. Those who utilize CRT as a framework are aware that history is often shaped and misreported to celebrate the oppressor (Haynes Writer, 2002). These histories center on majoritarian perspectives that leave little to no room for reinterpretation. The Morrill Land Grant Act of 1890, for example, is lauded as critical legislation that led to the creation of many black land grant colleges. The establishment of institutions to serve recently emancipated and freed blacks was certainly admirable. But three points are worth noting for engaging a deeper comprehension of this act and its impact. First, it required states to either admit blacks or create separate institutions. Most states chose the latter, which ultimately furthered racial segregation in higher education and fueled the idea of black intellectual inferiority (Anderson, 1988; Davis, 1998; Harper, Patton, & Wooden, 2009). Second, the act focused primarily on agricultural and mechanical trades instead of liberal arts and disciplines that at the time would have contributed to Du Bois's hope of a talented tenth or black educated class to provide leadership and direction for black people (Anderson, 1988; Davis, 1998; Harper et al., 2009). Third, funding was sorely inequitable and at times nonexistent for these institutions owing to the states' unwillingness to provide the necessary money and outright neglect. Jenkins (1991) described how this situation actualized in Alabama: "state funding for Alabama's black land-grant institution remained constant at $4,000 annually. Unlike its white counter-part, whose state funding averaged $65,000 yearly between 1900 and 1916" (p. 66). Such information is reminiscent of the present-day underfunding of historically black colleges and universities (HBCUs) in comparison to their white counterparts (Bowman, 2010; Sav, 2010).

Matsuda et al. (1993) also contend that CRT insists on recognizing the experiential knowledge of people of color. Such recognition is filtered through counterstorytelling, narrative, biographies, and life histories. When the experiences and knowledges of people of color are shared, the process allows for a more authentic and unique understanding of how they experience racist, oppressive structures. Sharing also provides a sense of liberation and "psychic preservation" for those who attempt to tell their experiences in the midst of dominant narratives that dismiss everyday acts of racism (Ladson-Billings & Tate, 1995; Tate, 1997). There is a range of dominant narratives, situated in white racial ideologies that surface and maintain themselves on college campuses. There exists a claim that when students of color gather in campus spaces, such as the dining hall or the campus cultural center, they are not only noticed but also presumed to be engaging in self-segregation, a practice that will not serve them well if they are to function successfully in a diverse campus environment. Moreover, these students are seen as contributing to racial balkanization and fueling separatism and division between racial groups on campus (antonio, 2001; Harper & Hurtado, 2007; Patton, 2011; Villalpando, 2003).

Villalpando (2003) upsets this dominant narrative, arguing that white students who congregate are hardly ever noticed, nor are they perceived to be separating themselves. His research in this area revealed that when students of color come together, their cultures and identities are reaffirmed and their connections have a positive impact on their retention and ability to navigate institutional racism. In her research on campus cultural centers, Patton (2006a,b) debunks the accusation of separatism that often plagues cultural centers where many students of color convene. From her research, she learned that cultural centers promoted greater involvement and leadership for students, particularly serving as a springboard for involvement in larger campus organizations and activities. These centers likewise served as spaces in which students learned about their history, which was not present in the larger institutional curriculum, and students perceived centers as the one place they could go to feel as if they mattered.

According to Matsuda et al. (1993), CRT has an interdisciplinary aim that not only situates it in the legal field but also in sociology, philosophy, ethnic studies, and a host of other academic fields that scrutinize race and racism. Thus CRT has emerged not simply as a form of race scholarship, but also a movement committed to dismantling, sexism, classism and poverty, gender discrimination, and heterosexism, to name a few. As CRT has developed over time, its lexicon has grown equally as fast. There are three key concepts that buttress CRT and strengthen it as an analytical framework: (1) intersectionality, (2) whiteness as property, and (3) interest convergence. Intersectionality, coined by Kimberlé Crenshaw (1989, 1991), refers to the operation of identity politics, particularly how overarching systems of oppression and domination collude and create uniquely disenfranchising experiences for individuals who are situated at the crux of multiple marginalized identities. Crenshaw (1989) argues that intersectionality is about the centering of experiences that get "theoretically erased" when identity dimensions are treated as "mutually exclusive categories of experience and analysis" (p. 139). Crenshaw (1991) describes structural, political, and representational intersectionality and their implications for women of color. Structural intersectionality refers to the ineffective structures that undergird the law and policy, making it extremely difficult to support and provide resources to women of color who occupy multiple spaces of oppression. Crenshaw defines political intersectionality as a predicament that forces women of color and other multiply marginalized individuals to choose political alliances, often between groups (antiracists vs. feminists) that clash or have divergent stances on critical issues. Women of color must not only make a choice about alliances, but they are also often disempowered and caught between conflicting ideologies that are incapable of fully expressing the complexities of their lives. Representational intersectionality includes "both the ways in which [cultural] images are produced through a confluence of prevalent narratives of race and gender, as well as a recognition of how contemporary critiques of racist and sexist representation marginalize women of color" (Crenshaw, 1991, p. 1283). Overall, she argues that any intersectional analysis must acknowledge diverse forms of oppression and their mutually shaping nature on identity politics. Intersectionality is not simply about categories of identity but is concerned with "social hierarchies" and how power is situated to buttress certain categories, while stripping the humanity and agency of others toward further subordination. Furthermore, intersectional identities should be viewed as opportunities for coalition building and must be addressed simultaneously in order to be most effective (Crenshaw, 1991).

In her discussion of whiteness as property, Harris (1993) expounds on the intricate linkages between constructions of property and racial identity in the United States. She explains, "Whiteness shares the critical characteristics of property . . . In particular, whiteness and property share a common premise—a conceptual nucleus—of a right to exclude . . . white identity became the basis of racialized privilege that was ratified and legitimated in law as a type of status property" (p. 1714). Harris (1993) describes four property functions of whiteness: (1) rights of disposition, (2) the right to use and enjoyment, (3) reputation and status property, and (4) the absolute right to exclude. Rights of disposition describe how the law allows for property to be transferred. Whiteness as a personal characteristic would not typically be deemed legal property. The manner in which whiteness operates, however, allows it to maintain its inalienability yet also be transferred through a range of means (e.g., birth of a child to a white couple, inherited wealth of a white family bestowed upon an heir or generational wealth, legacy admission into an elite, predominantly white college, etc.). In sum, the values embedded in whiteness can actually be shared and transferred to other white people. The right to use and enjoyment references the capacity of whiteness to "both be experienced and deployed as a resource" (p. 1734). In other words, white people can physically experience what it means to be white, take advantage of white privilege, and use their whiteness to exercise power over others. Historically, it was lawful for whites to control anyone who was not deemed white. In present contexts, such control has been abolished, but it is much a part of the systemic legacy of whiteness that permeates the interpretation and enactment of the law.

Reputation and status property locate white racial identity as an outward manifestation that acts as a resource to define who is worthy of personhood. In essence, being considered white confers individuals with benefits, namely, being perceived as fully human, capable of maintaining one's status in racial hierarchy, and garnering the trust and respect of others without having to prove anything other than one's own status as white. The absolute right to exclude involves the power to decide and the process of determining not only who is white but also, more importantly, who is not white. In property terms, whiteness is a valuable commodity. To be white is to suggest the existence of a pure racial identity, and as a result the value and exclusivity of whiteness increase.

Croom and Patton (2012) used intersectionality as part of a critical race feminism framework to analyze the raced and gendered experiences of black women full professors in higher education. Their analysis highlighted how issues of racism and sexism, coupled with power, have ensured the paucity of black women faculty at the highest faculty ranks. They also relied on whiteness as property to explain that the full professor rank has been historically reserved for white men and is treated as a form of property, whereby full professors create barriers and double standards to exclude advancement for people of color (intentionally and unintentionally). Stated differently, the highest faculty status is situated as property, which whites should rightfully possess, enjoying its benefits and privileges, and maintaining the status quo of a predominantly white and male group.

Interest convergence, coined by the late Derrick Bell, is perhaps one of the most popular concepts within CRT. Bell argued that racial advancement for people of color was inextricably linked to serving white interests. In other words, white people will tolerate advancements for people of color only when white interests are ultimately served. Bell (2004) used this principle to explain the political processes that govern the law and disproportionately affect racially minoritized groups to the benefit of white interests. In their policy analysis of black progress in higher education, Harper et al. (2009) maintain that any movement toward racial progress for racially minoritized groups should be viewed with skepticism because they likely promote "three steps forward and two steps backward" (p. 410). The present landscape of affirmative action in higher education is perhaps the most salient example of how seemingly positive strides toward advancement are often subject to dismantling, particularly because they are erroneously perceived to disenfranchise white people. In the following sections, we provide readers with an opportunity to examine through a CRT lens commonly studied topics in the field of higher education as they relate to students.

College Access and Admission

Over the past two decades, researchers have produced important scholarship on student access to US higher education. Much of this literature highlights racial and socioeconomic gaps in the formation of college aspirations, students' behaviors in the college search and choice process, and the number of students who enroll and the types of institutions they attend. Black, Latino, and Native American students, for example, particularly those from lower-income families, are less likely than whites to apply to college generally (McDonough, 1997) or enroll at highly selective colleges specifically (Bowen & Bok, 1998; Harper & Griffin, 2011; Hurtado et al., 1997). Given this fact, scholars have examined how the following factors differently structure college opportunities for minoritized students: school resources and curricular offerings (McDonough, 1997; Perna, 2005); college counseling and the availability of information about the college admission process (Bell, Rowan-Kenyon, & Perna, 2009; McDonough, 1997; McDonough, Korn, & Yamasaki, 1997; Perna, 2006); parents' educational attainment and income levels (Bowen, Kurzweil, & Tobin, 2005; Hossler, Schmit, & Vesper, 1999); financial aid (Long & Riley, 2007; Perna, 2000, 2006); and public policies (Flores, 2010; Moses, 2001; Perna & Thomas, 2009; Perna & Titus, 2004; St. John, 2003). Several CRT tenets and concepts would prove useful in advancing research on college access by more explicitly exploring how racist norms and assumptions affect how access is determined and who is deemed worthy of admission.

The historical condition of access for minoritized student populations has received significantly less attention than the aforementioned topics. Access scholars often write about inequities without acknowledging how higher education's racist history has manufactured and sustained them over time. The CRT tenet that challenges ahistoricism demands tracing contemporary access barriers to the colonial colleges, a foundation built for white elites while Native Americans and Africans were being slaughtered in the name of nation building. Few scholars (e.g., Harper et al., 2009; Yosso et al., 2004) have used CRT to analyze the durability of racist policies that undermined espoused commitments to expanding access to higher education. The CRT permanence of racism thesis (Bell, 1991) is also useful in illustrating the long-standing exclusion of people of color from predominantly white institutions. Trends and practices that have persisted for centuries, or at least the residual effects of them, are likely to be everlasting. Researchers concerned about access should therefore aim to better understand how policies could be revised and more effectively designed in institutional contexts that have struggled to make access equitable.

College admission is supposedly about merit. Grade point averages, academic transcripts, SAT and ACT scores, essays, and letters of recommendation distinguish some students from others in competitive applicant pools. Articles published over the years in the *Journal of College Admission* and elsewhere have focused on getting more students from diverse backgrounds to apply to a range of postsecondary institutions, and narrowing gaps between who is deemed college ready and admissible. Not explored are the characteristics, predispositions, and racial socialization of those who set the parameters of access to an institution. One CRT tenet suggests that merit is elusive and that colorblindness in an admission process is unlikely and perhaps impossible. The American Association of Collegiate Registrars and Admissions Officers (AACRAO) reports that blacks, Latinos, Native Americans, and Asian Americans constituted 9% of its membership in 2013 (AACRAO, 2013). If these demographics are reflective of the composition of the profession, then it is clear that whites overwhelmingly create and enact admissions policies that determine what merit is, which applicants are qualified, and which thresholds are good enough to signify a commitment to diversity.

Concerning the third point, table 9.1 shows undergraduate student enrollments at the eight Ivy League institutions in 2012. Here is an important question for access researchers: Who determined that 6%–8% of black undergraduates and an average of 15% of Pell Grant–eligible students was enough? Who these decision makers are, and how their prior racial socialization and colorblind ideologies influenced their consideration of applicants from minoritized backgrounds deemed worthy of admission, are other questions that may reveal problematic insights into sluggish diversity trends in college access. Harris's (1993) whiteness as property concept could be useful in crafting additional research questions pertaining to whites as architects, owners, and gatekeepers of racially consequential college admission policies and practices.

The interdisciplinarity of CRT would also complicate commonly pursued questions in the college access literature. Researchers who document racial differences in enrollments, for example, should situate their findings in larger, multidimensional frameworks that are raced. The availability of rigorous curricula, sufficient numbers of guidance counselors, and abundant information about postsecondary education will undoubtedly produce *some* gains in college-going rates among black and Latino students who attend low-resource high schools. But matriculation patterns will continue to lag if police routinely profile and harass these students during their daily commute home from school, if students'

TABLE 9.1. Undergraduate student enrollments at Ivy League institutions, fall 2012

Institution	Black (%)	Latino (%)	White (%)	Pell Grant recipients (%)
Brown University	6	10	45	15
Columbia University	8	14	40	16
Cornell University	6	10	44	17
Dartmouth College	7	8	47	13
Harvard University	6	9	48	18
University of Pennsylvania	7	9	46	17
Princeton University	7	7	48	12
Yale University	7	10	47	12

Source: US Department of Education, Integrated Postsecondary Education Data System.

families do not have access to high-quality and affordable health care, if college guidance counselors are racist, if college admission officers refuse to visit the perceivably hopeless public high schools in which they are disproportionately enrolled, and if students see few faculty and students of color during their campus visits to postsecondary institutions. This complex matrix of factors might also negatively affect students' performance in high school, college aspirations, and subsequent college search and choice behaviors. Yet the college choice literature has largely failed to acknowledge racism and racist institutional practices and environments as being potentially influential.

Researchers most often place emphasis on exploring barriers instead of facilitators of college opportunity for minoritized student populations (Harper & Griffin, 2011; Harper et al., 2012; St. John, Hu, & Fisher, 2011). Components of Yosso's (2005) model of community cultural wealth—specifically aspirational capital, navigational capital, resistant capital, and familial capital—could be useful in moving access researchers beyond depressing, deficit-oriented questions concerning minoritized students. For instance, Hossler et al. (1999) found that "about 19% of the students whose parents' income was below $15,000 attended a four-year school, whereas more than 58% of the students whose parents' income was more than $45,000 attended a four-year school" (p. 106). The underrepresentation of students from lower-income families (which tends to be disproportionately people of color) at four-year colleges and universities is a serious issue. But what about students who somehow saw beyond their present circumstances and applied to college? How did those whose parents earned less than $15,000 a year manage to navigate their ways to higher education generally and four-year institutions in particular? What sacrifices did their parents make, how did their parents acquire information about college, and in what ways were parents helpful during the college search and choice processes?

College Student Development

The social, psychological, and identity development of 18- to 24-year-old college students is one of the longest-standing and widely researched topics in US higher education. The *Journal of College Student Development*, a peer-reviewed academic journal, is one of many venues in which studies about how students develop and the effects of campus environments, practices, and cultures on student change are published. McEwen and Talbot (1998) noted that "the concept of student development and the related student development theories represent one of the hallmarks of the student affairs profession" (p. 133). Understanding student development and the contexts that shape it is critical in research that endeavors to understand what enables and undermines undergraduate student success, learning, and growth. Even so, methods, theories, and frameworks in the student development literature have not been appropriately critical of whiteness or the universal application of dominant epistemologies in studies of minoritized students in college contexts.

Teaching and learning about student development are commonplace in graduate programs that prepare higher education professionals. Over 50% of higher education and student affairs graduate programs offer a student development theory course (Kuk & Cuyjet, 2009; Patton & Harper, 2009). As such, students who take these courses are primarily exposed to theories that are rooted overwhelmingly in the experiences of white students. Bloland, Stamatakos, and Rogers (1994) suggested that student development is a necessary foundation in the field of higher education but acts as a master narrative that remains unchallenged. The study of college student development is incomplete and in desperate need of more diverse perspectives. The underutilization of racial lenses to deconstruct and evaluate theories has far-reaching implications, as the way students learn about these lenses (through colorblind frames) is likely to influence how they utilize them when they become practitioners.

A great deal of the literature and research on college student development is devoid of any substantive consideration of race and racism. Early theories emerged from studies in which white people, especially men, comprised the participant samples (e.g., Chickering, 1969; Chickering & Reisser, 1993; Erikson, 1968, 1959/1980; Josselson, 1987; Marcia, 1966; Perry, 1968). Thus theories of cognitive and psychosocial development mirror much of the early social science research in that findings were based upon the experiences of white men. Consequently, theoretical frameworks on college student development are inherently situated within racist assumptions, one of which is the notion that the experiences of white students are general and broad enough to capture all students' experiences regardless of race.

Some scholars have attempted to challenge "traditional" student development theories and account for the experiences of students of color. These theories play a major role in filling theoretical gaps left from previous theories that did not address race as a salient aspect of identity. McEwen et al. (1990) argued for the inclusion of black students in theories of psychosocial development. Similarly, Kodama et al. (2001, 2002) offered a perspective on the psychosocial identity of Asian American college students. These scholars contended that the development of racially minoritized college students involved nuances that were neither fully nor clearly addressed in existing student development literature. Torres, Howard-Hamilton, and Cooper (2003) summarized a range of theories from the social science and counseling psychology literature that could be used to frame college student development in relation to racial identity. They highlighted the work of Cross (1971, 1991), who is credited with presenting one of the earliest theories on black identity development, as well as Helms (1990, 1995), who wrote about the identity development of people of color and whites. Were it not for scholars such as Cross and Helms, the race-neutral assumptions undergirding much of the student development literature would remain intact. This is not to say that these assumptions have been dispelled, but rather indicates that the introduction of more perspectives on racial identity development helped, if only minimally, to upset the dominant narrative that white students' experiences sufficiently capture all student experiences.

For the past twenty-five years, new theories have emerged from research on multiracial students (e.g., Kerwin & Ponterotto, 1995; Kich, 1992; Renn, 2004), Latino students (Ferdman & Gallegos, 2001; Torres, 1999, 2003), Asian American students (Ibrahim, Ohnishi, & Sandhu, 1997; Kawaguchi, 2003; Kim, 2001), and Native American students (Choney, Berryhill-Paake, & Robbins, 1995; Garrett, 1996; Horse, 2001). Each of these theoretical perspectives, grounded in research, has contributed to an enhanced understanding of how college students develop their identities, particularly in the racialized contexts of college campuses. In addition to these perspectives, theories have emerged that offer a more integrated viewpoint. For example, Abes, Jones, and McEwen's (2007) reconceptualized model of multiple dimensions of identity is credited with offering a more integrated perspective because it acknowledges that individuals' identities are shaped and influenced on the basis of how that identity is situated within systems of power and privilege. The emphasis in this theory is not on one identity in isolation but how various aspects of identity are less or more salient in the context of a society that privileges and oppresses particular identities.

Patton et al. (2007) offered this critique of college student development theories: "What has been lacking in the knowledge and use of theory by higher education and student affairs professionals is critical examination of theories: the research base, the perspective of the theorists, the research generated, and how theories evolve" (p. 41). Their critique provided examples of racial omissions in theoretical research that has been popularized in the literature, yet lacks an examination of race or racism's impact. For instance, Kohlberg's (1975, 1981) theory of moral development focuses on the ideals of justice and autonomy in determining levels of morality. Yet the authors contend that Kohlberg missed a prime opportunity to critique the racist histories undergirding societal laws and policies, to explain how these laws are often (mis)interpreted to promote differential racialization between whites and people of color, and to understand that notions of what is moral and right are too frequently understood through a Eurocentric paradigm (Patton et al. 2007).

When considering college student development as an area of research and a movement, critical race theory is most helpful in gleaning how a seemingly forceful movement and clearly popular line of research has fueled racist ideologies. First, the normative acceptance of white students' experiences as an unquestioned standard for understanding the experiences of all students is not only problematic but also reflective of CRT's contention that racism is endemic. This erroneous assumption is deeply embedded in the college student development literature and has cultivated families of theories rooted in whiteness. Put differently, white perspectives, ways of knowing, and the largely white student samples on which most theories are based are treated as the norm.

The language in which many college student development theories are framed substantiates how whiteness is situated in that they are labeled as "traditional" or "foundational." This framing helps ensure that the only method through which future theories would be validated and perceived as credible is by referencing older theories, despite their inherent flaws. Delgado (1984, 1992) calls this the practice of "imperial scholarship," which allows a small contingency of scholars to essentially dictate the discourses surrounding a body of knowledge, discourses that rarely account for the perspectives and experiential knowledges of communities of color. He shared, "It does not matter where one enters this universe; one comes to the same result: an inner circle of about a dozen white, male writers who comment on, take polite issue with, extol, criticize, and expand on each other's ideas. It is something like an elaborate minuet" (Delgado, 1984, p. 563).

The study of college student development is also reflective of whiteness as property, particularly the absolute right to exclude. In other words, scholars may freely continue to produce theories of college student development, as they currently do, while maintaining a majority white pool of participants without fear of repercussion or criticism. In fact, the more popular the scholar, the more likely it is that this individual will be excused for not having more diverse participants, because their reputation imbues a certain status upon them, providing them with a pass or status property. Even when white scholars of developmental theories acknowledge the limitations of their scholarship (e.g., Baxter Magolda, 1992), oftentimes their work is still used to generalize diverse populations of students despite the lack of diversity among study participants.

In a sense, college student development theories on the whole are colorblind because they fail to deal with issues of racism and other forms of oppression. The research on racial identity is the only format in which issues of race and racism are likely to emerge. Unfortunately, racial identity theories are generally perceived as being too narrow and relevant to only one racial group. Thus the experiences of individuals highlighted within racial identity theories presumably apply to that group only. The underlying assumption is that there is nothing relevant about the racial identity of people of color that could be useful for understanding development on a broader scale. This assumption relates directly to normative beliefs about white people, and what remains is an unchecked assumption about people of color as anything but normal.

When examining which scholars produce research focused specifically on college student development, most of them are white, raising several questions. Whose epistemological perspectives are being privileged? How are such perspectives subsequently transmitted through publication and into course curricula? How do these perspectives emerge in translation of theory to practice? Given that white faculty are overrepresented in higher education, questions regarding "who" generates theory are not surprising and neither is the resulting outcome; that is, fewer voices from researchers of color are present within the discourses surrounding college student development theory research.

College Student Engagement

Postsecondary educators and administrators are deeply concerned about what students do inside and outside the classroom, as well as the extent of their participation in activities, experiences, and practices that have been shown to produce particular educational outcomes. Wolf-Wendel, Ward, and Kinzie (2009) highlight some conceptual similarities among the terms "involvement" (Astin, 1984), "integration" (Tinto, 1993), and "engagement" (Kuh et al., 2005), all of which concern student effort. In their book *Student Engagement in Higher Education*, Harper and Quaye (2009) note that Alexander Astin's theory of student involvement is one of the most frequently cited theories in the field. Astin (1984) argued, "The extent to which students can achieve particular developmental goals is a direct function of the time and effort they devote to activities designed to produce these gains" (p. 301). In their synthesis of the published evidence on student engagement, Pascarella and Terenzini (2005) similarly concluded, "The impact of college is largely determined by individual effort and involvement in the academic, interpersonal, and extracurricular offerings on a campus" (p. 602). Concerning one specific outcome, Tinto (2000) posited that being integrated into the academic and social domains of a campus is the single most significant predictor of an undergraduate student's inclination to persist through baccalaureate degree completion. Many who drop out of college do so because they do not establish substantive relationships or a firm sense of membership at the institution, Tinto added.

Given its proven effects on student outcomes and persistence, various institutional stakeholders and scholars have spent the past thirty years routinely assessing student engagement inside and outside the classroom. Questions that measure how many hours students do particular things (e.g., study or attend social programs on campus), the number of clubs and organizations in which they hold membership, and how often they take advantage of particular opportunities (e.g., interacting with someone from a different religious background, collaborating with peers on group assignments in their courses, or attending a professor's office hours) have appeared on Cooperative Institutional Research Program surveys, the National Survey of Student Engagement, the College Student Experiences Questionnaire, and assorted instruments developed by Noel-Levitz and other consulting firms that provide retention-related data and services to institutions. At this point, more than three decades of scholarship can be easily leveraged to convince anyone in higher education of the importance of how college students spend their time.

Kuh (2008) deemed study-abroad programs, service learning opportunities, undergraduate research programs, summer internships, and senior-year capstone projects "high-impact educational practices." Accordingly, these activities require students to interact in educationally purposeful ways with professors and peers, including those who are different from themselves, often over extended time periods. They also allow students to receive feedback on their performance while becoming more skillful at synthesizing and applying what they learn in one setting (e.g., a community service site) to another environment or situation (e.g., an internship or the classroom). Hence getting more undergraduates connected to high-impact practices has emerged as a priority on many campuses and as an area of interest for the Association of American Colleges and Universities.

In at least three ways, CRT is useful in deconstructing and rethinking the topic of college student engagement. First is the racelessness with which scholars and practitioners have approached the assessment of student effort. The CRT tenet on the experiential realities of people of color could raise some important questions about why some students may find engagement in some experiences to be unappealing. Not captured on surveys are students' interactions with classroom environments in which they are the lone representatives of their racial/ethnic groups, where the professor either commits or permits racial microaggressions, where the threat of confirming racist stereotypes about them is high, and where all the authors of class assignments are white. Also not asked are questions about students' inclination to get involved in campus activities that appeal exclusively to white cultural interests or organizations in which white interests are protected through elections, investments, and agenda setting. It is plausible that a Latina student who is the only person of color on her residence hall floor will consider the engagement opportunities in the building to be unappealing. How these racialized experiences undermine engagement has not been studied, but they are commonplace for so many students of color on predominantly white campuses (Harper, 2013; Solórzano, Ceja, & Yosso, 2000; Yosso et al., 2009).

Also related to the same CRT tenet is a second set of questions, among them asking what is deemed to be "high impact." While many researchers have repeatedly posed similar questions about how students spend their time, less attention has been devoted to exploring their engagement in a different set of experiences that may have a higher impact on their learning, sense of belonging, persistence, and rates of degree completion. Being called a "nigger," "wetback," or "alien," for example, is undoubtedly a high-impact experience. It is also arguably educational, as it teaches black and Latino students about the realities of race on campus and in our larger society. Racial battle fatigue—feelings of exhaustion that ensue among those who are constantly confronted with racism, racist stereotypes, and racial underrepresentation (Smith, Allen, & Danley, 2007)—may affect students of color in more consequential ways than completing a senior-year capstone project, for example. Experiencing the tenure denial and subsequent departure of the lone professor of color in one's department may have significantly large effects on a minoritized student's outcomes.

Lastly, CRT's whiteness as property concept (Harris, 1993) raises the question of who gets to determine what is "educationally purposeful," a term that student engagement researchers often use. The most cited student engagement pioneers are all white; they decided which experiences and activities add value to a student's college experience. They are unlikely familiar with particular activities and practices in which minoritized students are engaged that bolster their sense of belonging and keep them (and their same-race peers) engaged and retained. One example is what Harper (2013) termed "peer pedagogies"—students of color teaching other students of color about the realities of race on campus and the skills necessary to survive racist institutional settings. Peer pedagogies are educationally purposeful in that the students who employ them often do so with an explicit purpose of retaining their peers. This form of engagement also confers unto student teachers a sense of importance because they recognize how the collective success of their community depends on them. Notwithstanding, student engagement surveys do not measure peer pedagogies. Researchers also have not considered how the burden of this work, as well as how minoritized students being constantly thrust into the position of having to teach their white peers about race, detracts from their ability to engage in other high-impact and educationally purposeful activities on campus.

Conclusion

The scholarship related to college students helps illustrate the utility of CRT as a framework for disrupting the dominant ideologies so deeply embedded in higher education research. Our analysis reveals that research in higher education, while important and certainly necessary, would translate differently if framed by a CRT lens that centers race and racism. CRT, when properly used in higher education research, exposes issues of race neutrality and racelessness that are representative of many topics in education literature. CRT also uncovers the dominant narratives that often shape higher education research, allowing for more accurate, diverse, and visible perspectives to emerge from research. Moreover, CRT is useful in disrupting the language that shapes the daily discourses of research and ensures that critical meanings and interpretations that recognize the experiences of racially minoritized people replace the dominant paradigms within scholarship. Finally, a CRT lens reminds readers that racism and white supremacy are realities within the academy and that, regardless of efforts toward greater equity in higher education through research, white people will more than likely be the major or sole beneficiaries of those efforts. Despite this reality, we encourage higher education scholars to engage in strategies that produce quality, critical research in which issues of race, racism, and power are at the center. CRT should be used as a primary tool to guide how researchers frame their research questions, generate their study design, and engage in the interpretation and presentation of findings.

Croom and Patton (2012) discuss the relevance of a critical race research agenda and its implications for studying the faculty pipeline. Below we offer nine tenets that can help guide the creation and implementation of a critical race research agenda for the broader landscape of higher education research.

1. A critical race research agenda explicitly commits to examining the confluence of racism, white supremacy, and power as they emerge in every aspect of the research process.

2. A critical race research agenda is framed by critical questions that foreground the experiences of people of color and consider these populations as diverse with multiple knowledges and experiences rather than as a monolithic group.

3. A critical race research agenda encourages researchers to purposefully explore the racialized histories that shape present-day issues and problems in higher education.

4. A critical race research agenda acknowledges that, while racism may be centered, it exists and operates in combination with other forms of oppression, ultimately contributing to the differential racialization of various groups and social identities

5. A critical race research agenda asserts that there is no such thing as objective or neutral research, and contends that the researcher's experiences within systems of oppression and privilege ostensibly shape every aspect of the research process.

6. A critical race research agenda addresses the implications for research findings and their interpretation in relation to institutional, state, and federal educational policies.

7. A critical race research agenda is committed to action for social justice. Research is viewed as a form of activism rather than research for research's sake, and researchers are committed to using their work to positively influence the creation and implementation of equitable educational outcomes for all people. A critical race research agenda is not simply about studying research problems; it also identifies crucial solutions for real-world applications.

8. A critical race research agenda is not only situated in the researcher's field of study but also expands to incorporate interdisciplinary perspectives that contribute to a richer and more robust context for examining the research questions.

9. A critical race research agenda disrupts dominant paradigms within research by engaging in an explicit reinterpretation of those ideas to provide audiences with a new perspective for examining a given research question.

Our belief in the value of a critical race research agenda is closely linked to a desire to see higher education research expand in a way that explicitly addresses racism and other structural inequities that reproduce unjust policies, behaviors, and climates in postsecondary contexts. While the emphasis of our analysis in this chapter was on research related to college students, similar analyses could be applied to examine research related to faculty, institutional governance and leadership, policy, and administrative and staff-related challenges. The tenets of a critical race research agenda can help effectively frame research on the aforementioned areas and many more. Each of the tenets, whether applied singularly or in combination, can position scholars to approach educational research with a CRT lens while emphasizing efforts to destabilize white supremacy and other structures in the academy. Furthermore, the tenets can serve as useful framing for scholars wishing to reinterpret dominant notions of higher education research that have permeated the discourse with little to no attention on issues of racism in the academy.

NOTE

1. We use "minoritized" (Gillborn, 2010) instead of "minority" throughout this article to signify the social construction of underrepresentation and subordination in US social institutions, including colleges and universities. Persons are not born into a minority status nor are they minoritized in every social context (e.g., their families, social fraternities, and churches). Instead, they are rendered minorities in particular situations and institutional environments that sustain an overrepresentation of whiteness.

REFERENCES

AACRAO. American Association of Collegiate Registrars and Admissions Officers. (2013, September 1). *2013 membership demographics.* Retrieved from www.aacrao .org/About-AACRAO/demographics/2013demographics.aspx#.UiNPyrwpc18.

Abes, E. S., Jones, S. R., & McEwen, M. K. (2007). Reconceptualizing the model of multiple dimensions of identity: The role of meaning-making capacity in the construction of multiple identities. *Journal of College Student Development, 48,* 1–22.

Anderson, J. D. (1988). *The education of blacks in the south, 1860–1935*. Chapel Hill: University of North Carolina Press.

antonio, a. l. (2001). Diversity and the influence of friendship groups in college. *Review of Higher Education, 25*(1), 63–89.

Astin, A. W. (1984). Student involvement: A developmental theory for higher education. *Journal of College Student Personnel, 25*(2), 297–308.

Baxter Magolda, M. B. (1992). *Knowing and reasoning in college: Gender-related patterns in students' intellectual development*. San Francisco: Jossey-Bass.

Bell, A. D., Rowan-Kenyon, H. T., & Perna, L. W. (2009). College knowledge of 9th and 11th grade students: Variation by school and state context. *Journal of Higher Education, 80*(6), 663–85.

Bell, D. A. (1991). Racism is here to stay—Now what? *Howard Law Journal, 35*(1), 79–93.

———. (2004). *Silent covenants:* Brown v. Board of Education *and the unfulfilled hopes for racial reform*. New York: Oxford University Press.

Bloland, P. A., Stamatakos, L. C., & Rogers, R. R. (1994). *Reform in student affairs: A critique of student development*. Greensboro, NC: ERIC Counseling and Student Services Clearinghouse.

Bowen, W. G., & Bok, D. (1998). *The shape of the river: Long-term consequences of considering race in college and university admissions*. Princeton, NJ: Princeton University Press.

Bowen, W. G., Kurzweil, M. A., & Tobin, E. M. (2005). *Equity and excellence in American higher education*. Charlottesville: University of Virginia Press.

Bowman, N., III. (2010). Fundraising during an economic downturn within the historically black college and university environment. *International Journal of Educational Advancement, 9*, 266–72.

Brayboy, B. M. J. (2005). Toward a tribal critical race theory in education. *Urban Review, 37*(5), 425–46.

Chickering, A. W. (1969). *Education and identity*. San Francisco: Jossey-Bass.

Chickering, A. W., & Reisser, L. (1993). *Education and identity* (2nd ed.). San Francisco: Jossey-Bass.

Choney, S. K., Berryhill-Paake, E., & Robbins, R. R. (1995). The acculturation of American Indians: Developing frameworks for research and practice. In J. G. Ponterotto et al. (Eds.), *Handbook of multicultural counseling* (pp. 73–92). Thousand Oaks, CA: Sage.

Crenshaw, K. (1989). Demarginalizing the intersection of race and sex: A black feminist critique of antidiscrimination doctrine, feminist theory, and antiracist politics. *University of Chicago Legal Forum, 140*, 139–67.

———. (1991). Mapping the margins: Intersectionality, identity politics and violence against women in color. *Stanford Law Review, 43*(6), 1241–99.

Croom, N., & Patton, L. (2012). The miner's canary: A critical race perspective on the representation of black women full professors. *Negro Educational Review, 62*(1), 13–39.

Cross, W. E., Jr. (1971). Toward a psychology of black liberation: The Negro-to-black conversion experience. *Black World, 20*(9), 13–27.

———. (1991). *Shades of black: Diversity in African American identity.* Philadelphia: Temple University Press.

Davis, J. E. (1998). Cultural capital and the role of historically black colleges and universities in educational reproduction. In K. Freeman (Ed.), *African American culture and heritage in higher education research and practice* (pp. 143–53). Westport, CT: Praeger.

Delgado, R. (1984). The imperial scholar: Reflections on a review of civil rights literature. *University of Pennsylvania Law Review, 132*(3), 561–78.

———. (1992). The imperial scholar revisited: How to marginalize outsider writing— Ten years later. *University of Pennsylvania Law Review, 140*(4), 1349–72.

———. (1995a). Rodrigo's tenth chronicle: Merit and affirmative action. *Georgetown Law Journal, 83*(4), 1711–48.

———. (1995b). *Critical race theory: The cutting edge.* Philadelphia: Temple University Press.

Delgado, R., & Stefancic, J. (2001). *Critical race theory: An introduction.* New York: New York University Press.

Dixson, A. D., & Rousseau, C. K. (2005). And we are still not saved: Critical race theory in education 10 years later. *Race Ethnicity and Education, 8*(1), 7–27.

Erikson, E. H. (1968). *Identity: Youth and crisis.* New York: Norton.

———. (1980). *Identity and the life cycle.* New York: Norton. (Original work published 1959).

Ferdman, B. M., & Gallegos, P. I. (2001). Racial identity development and Latinos in the United States. In C. L. Wijeyesinghe & B. W. Jackson III (Eds.), *New perspectives on racial identity development: A theoretical and practical anthology* (pp. 32–66). New York: New York University Press.

Flores, S. M. (2010). State "Dream Acts": The effect of in-state resident tuition policies on the college enrollment of undocumented Latino students in the United States. *Review of Higher Education, 33*(2), 239–83.

Garrett, M. T. (1996). "Two people": An American Indian narrative of bicultural identity. *Journal of American Indian Education, 36*(1), 1–21.

Gillborn, D. (2010). The colour of numbers: Surveys, statistics and deficit-thinking about race and class. *Journal of Education Policy, 25*(2), 253–76.

Harper, S. R. (2012). Race without racism: How higher education researchers minimize racist institutional norms. *Review of Higher Education, 36*(1), 9–29.

———. (2013). Am I my brother's teacher? Black undergraduates, peer pedagogies, and racial socialization in predominantly white postsecondary contexts. *Review of Research in Education, 37*(1), 183–211.

Harper, S. R., & Griffin, K. A. (2011). Opportunity beyond affirmative action: How low-income and working class black male achievers access highly selective, high-cost colleges and universities. *Harvard Journal of African American Public Policy, 17*(1), 43–60.

Harper, S. R., & Hurtado, S. (2007). Nine themes in campus racial climates and implications for institutional transformation. In S. R. Harper & L. D. Patton (Eds.),
Responding to the realities of race. (New Directions for Student Services No. 120;
pp. 7–23). San Francisco: Jossey-Bass.

Harper, S. R., Patton, L. D., & Wooden, O. S. (2009). Access and equity for African
American students in higher education: A critical race historical analysis of policy
efforts. *Journal of Higher Education, 80*(4), 389–414.

Harper, S. R., & Quaye, S. J. (Eds.). (2009). *Student engagement in higher education:
Theoretical perspectives and practical approaches for diverse populations* (1st ed.).
New York: Routledge.

Harper, S. R., Williams, C. D., Jr., Pérez, D., II, & Morgan, D. L. (2012). His experience: Toward a phenomenological understanding of academic capital formation
among black and Latino male students. *Readings on Equal Education, 26*(1), 65–87.

Harris, C. I. (1993). Whiteness as property. *Harvard Law Review, 106*(8), 1709–91.

Haynes Writer, J. (2002). Terrorism in Native America: Interrogating the past, examining the present and constructing a liberatory future. *Anthropology and Education Quarterly, 33*(3), 317–30.

Helms, J. E. (1990). *Black and white racial identity: Theory, research, and practice*.
Westport, CT: Greenwood Press.

———. (1995). An update of Helms's white and people of color racial identity models.
In J. G. Ponterotto et al. (Eds.), *Handbook of multicultural counseling* (pp. 181–98).
Thousand Oaks, CA: Sage.

Horse, P. G. (2001). Reflections on American Indian identity. In C. L. Wijeyesinghe
& B. W. Jackson III (Eds.), *New perspectives on racial identity development: A the-
oretical and practical anthology* (pp. 91–107). New York: New York University
Press.

Hossler, D., Schmit, J., & Vesper, N. (1999). *Going to college: How social, economic, and
educational factors influence the decisions students make*. Baltimore: Johns Hopkins University Press.

Hurtado, S., Inkelas, K. K., Briggs, C., & Rhee, B. (1997). Differences in college access
and choice among racial/ethnic groups: Identifying continuing barriers. *Research
in Higher Education, 38*(1), 43–75.

Ibrahim, F., Ohnishi, H., & Sandhu, D. S. (1997). Asian American identity development: A culture specific model for South Asian Americans. *Journal of Multicultural Counseling and Development, 25*, 34–50.

Jenkins, R. L. (1991). The black land-grant colleges in their formative years, 1890–
1920. *Agricultural History, 65*(2), 63–72.

Josselson, R. E. (1987). *Finding herself: Pathways to identity development in women*.
San Francisco: Jossey-Bass.

Kawaguchi, S. (2003). Ethnic identity development and collegiate experience of Asian
Pacific American students: Implications for practice. *Journal of Student Affairs
Research and Practice, 40*(3), 13–29.

Kerwin, C., & Ponterotto, J. G. (1995). Biracial identity development: Theory and research. In J. G. Ponterotto et al. (Eds.), *Handbook of multicultural counseling* (pp. 199–217). Thousand Oaks, CA: Sage.

Khouri, A. (2012, December 6). Penn State sorority put on probation over Mexican-themed party. *Los Angeles Times.* Retrieved from http://articles.latimes.com/2012/dec/06/nation/la-na-nn-penn-state-sorority-racist-photo-20121206.

Kich, G. K. (1992). The developmental process of asserting a biracial, bicultural identity. In M. P. P. Root (Ed.), *Racially mixed people in America* (pp. 304–17). Thousand Oaks, CA: Sage.

Kim, J. (2001). Asian American identity development theory. In C. L. Wijeyesinghe & B. W. Jackson III (Eds.), *New perspectives on racial identity development: A theoretical and practical anthology* (pp. 67–90). New York: New York University Press.

Kodama, C. M., McEwen, M. K., Liang, C., & Lee, S. (2001). A theoretical examination of psychosocial issues for Asian Pacific American students. *Journal of Student Affairs Research and Practice, 38,* 411–37.

———. (2002). An Asian American perspective on psychosocial student development theory. In M. K. McEwen et al. (Eds.), *Working with Asian American college students* (New Directions for Student Services No. 97; pp. 45–59). San Francisco: Jossey-Bass.

Kohlberg, L. (1975). The cognitive-developmental approach to moral education. *Phi Delta Kappan, 56,* 670–77.

———. (1981). *Essays on moral development* (Vol. 1). *The philosophy of moral development.* San Francisco: Harper & Row.

Kuh, G. D. (2008). *High-impact educational practices: What they are, who has access to them, and why they matter.* Washington, DC: Association of American Colleges and Universities.

Kuh, G. D., Kinzie, J., Schuh, J. H., Whitt, E. J., & Associates (2005). *Student success in college: Creating conditions that matter.* San Francisco: Jossey-Bass.

Kuk, L., & Cuyjet, M. (2009). Graduate preparation programs: The first step in socialization. In A. Tull, J. B. Hirt, & S. A. Saunders (Eds.), *Becoming socialized in student affairs administration: A guide for new professionals and their supervisors* (pp. 89–108). Sterling, VA: Stylus.

Ladson-Billings, G. (1998). Just what is critical race theory and what's it doing in a nice field like education? *International Journal of Qualitative Studies in Education, 11*(1), 7–24.

Ladson-Billings, G., & Tate, W. G. (1995). Toward a critical race theory of education. *Teachers College Record, 97*(1), 47–68.

Lawrence, C. R., III, Matsuda, M. J., Delgado, R., & Crenshaw, K. W. (1993). Introduction. In M. J. Matsuda et al. (Eds.), *Words that wound: Critical race theory, assaultive speech, and the first amendment* (pp. 1–16). Boulder, CO: Westview Press.

Long, B. T., & Riley, E. (2007). Financial aid: A broken bridge to college access. *Harvard Educational Review, 77*(1), 39–63.

Lopez, I. H. (2006). *White by law* (2nd ed.). New York: New York University Press.

Lynn, M., & Parker, L. (2006). Critical race studies in education: Examining a decade of research on U.S. schools. *Urban Review, 38*(4), 257–90.

Manapsal, E. (2007, April 3). Students protest fraternity parties. *Cornell Daily Sun.* Retrieved from http://cornellsun.com/node/22467.

Marcia, J. E. (1966). Development and validation of ego-identity status. *Journal of Personality and Social Psychology, 3,* 551–58.

Matsuda, M. J., Lawrence, C. R., III, Delgado, R., & Crenshaw, K. (Eds.). (1993). *Words that wound: Critical race theory, assaultive speech, and the first amendment.* Boulder, CO: Westview Press.

McDonough, P. M. (1997). *Choosing colleges: How social class and schools structure opportunity.* Albany: State University of New York Press.

McDonough, P. M., Korn, J. S., & Yamasaki, E. (1997). Access, equity, and the privatization of college counseling. *Review of Higher Education, 20*(3), 297–317.

McEwen, M. K., Roper, L., Bryant, D., & Langa, M. (1990). Incorporating the development of African American students into psychosocial theories of student development. *Journal of College Student Development, 31,* 429–36.

McEwen, M. K., & Talbot, D. M. (1998). Designing the student affairs curriculum. In N. J. Evans & C. E. Phelps Tobin (Eds.), *The state of the art of preparation and practice in student affairs: Another look* (pp. 125–56). Lanham, MD: University Press of America.

Morfin, O. J., Perez, V. H., Parker, L., Lynn, M., & Arrona, J. (2006). Hiding the politically obvious: A critical race theory preview of diversity as racial neutrality in higher education. *Educational Policy, 20*(1), 249–70.

Moses, M. S. (2001). Affirmative action and the creation of more favorable contexts of choice. *American Educational Research Journal, 38*(1), 3–36.

Pascarella, E. T., & Terenzini, P. T. (2005). *How college affects students* (Vol. 2). *A third decade of research.* San Francisco: Jossey-Bass.

Patton, L. D. (2006a). Black culture centers: Still central to student learning. *About Campus, 11*(2), 2–8.

———. (2006b). The voice of reason: A qualitative examination of black student perceptions of black culture centers. *Journal of College Student Development, 47,* 628–46.

———. (2011). Promoting critical conversations about identity centers. In P. M. Magolda & M. B. Magolda (Eds.), *Contested issues within student affairs* (pp. 255–60). Sterling, VA: Stylus.Patton, L. D., & Catching, C. (2009). Teaching while black: Narratives of African American student affairs faculty. *International Journal of Qualitative Studies in Education, 22*(6), 713–28.

Patton, L. D., & Harper, S. R. (2009). Using reflection to reframe theory-to-practice in student affairs. In G. McClellan & J. Stringer (Eds.), *The handbook for student affairs administration* (3rd ed.; pp. 147–65). San Francisco: Jossey-Bass.

Patton, L. D., Haynes, C. M., Harris, J. C., & Ivery, S. M. (2014). Perhaps the field of education isn't so nice after all: A review essay and examination of critical race research in postsecondary contexts. *NASAP Journal, 15*(2), 135–48.

Patton, L. D., McEwen, M., Rendón, L., & Howard-Hamilton, M. F. (2007). Critical race perspectives on theory in student affairs. In S. R. Harper & L. D. Patton (Eds.), *Responding to the realities of race* (New Directions for Student Services No. 120; pp. 39–54). San Francisco: Jossey-Bass.

Perna, L. W. (2000). Differences in the decision to attend college among African Americans, Hispanics, and whites. *Journal of Higher Education, 71*(2), 117–41.

———. (2005). The key to college access: Rigorous academic preparation. In W. G. Tierney, Z. B. Corwin, & J. E. Colyar (Eds.), *Preparing for college: Nine elements of effective outreach* (pp. 113–34). Albany: State University of New York Press.

———. (2006). Understanding the relationship between information about college costs and financial aid and students' college-related behaviors. *American Behavioral Scientist, 49*(12), 1620–35.

Perna, L. W., & Thomas, S. L. (2009). Barriers to college opportunity: The unintended consequences of state-mandated testing. *Educational Policy, 23*(3), 451–79.

Perna, L. W., & Titus, M. A. (2004). Understanding differences in the choice of college attended: The role of state public policies. *Review of Higher Education, 27*(4), 501–25.

Perry, W. G., Jr. (1968). *Forms of intellectual and ethical development in the college years: A scheme.* New York: Holt.

Quan, K. (2013, February 7). Duke University fraternity suspended over Asian-themed "racist rager." *Time.* Retrieved from http://newsfeed.time.com/2013/02/07/duke -university-fraternity-suspended-over-asian-themed-racist-rager/#ixzz2djt1piCB.

Renn, K. A. (2004). *Mixed race students in college: The ecology of race, identity, and community on campus.* Albany: State University of New York Press.

Sav, G. T. (2010). Funding historically black colleges and universities: Progress toward equality? *Journal of Education Finance, 35*(3), 295–307.

Smith, W. A., Allen, W. R., & Danley, L. L. (2007). Assume the position . . . you fit the description: Psychosocial experiences and racial battle fatigue among African American male college students. *American Behavioral Scientist, 51*(4), 551–78.

Solórzano, D. G., Ceja, M., & Yosso, T. J. (2000). Critical race theory, racial microaggressions, and campus racial climate: The experiences of African American college students. *Journal of Negro Education, 69*(1), 60–73.

St. John, E. P. (2003). *Refinancing the college dream: Access, equal opportunity, and justice for taxpayers.* Baltimore: Johns Hopkins University Press.

St. John, E. P., Hu, S., & Fisher, A. S. (2011). *Breaking through the access barrier: How academic capital formation can improve policy in higher education.* New York: Routledge.

Tate, W. F. (1997) Critical race theory and education: history, theory and implications. *Review of Research in Education, 22*(1), 195–247.

Tinto, V. (1993). *Leaving college: Rethinking the causes and cures of student attrition* (2nd ed.). Chicago: University of Chicago Press.

———. (1999). Validation of a bicultural orientation model for Hispanic college students. *Journal of College Student Development, 40*, 285–98.

———. (2000). Taking retention seriously: Rethinking the first year of college. *NACADA Journal, 19*(2), 5–10.

Torres, V. (2003). Influences on ethnic identity development of Latino college students in the first two years of college. *Journal of College Student Development, 44*, 532–47.

Torres, V., Howard-Hamilton, M. F., & Cooper, D. L. (2003). *Identity development of diverse populations: Implications for teaching and administration in higher education.* San Francisco: Jossey-Bass.

Villalpando, O. (2003). Self-segregation or self-preservation? A critical race theory and Latina/o critical theory analysis of a study of Chicana/o college students. *International Journal of Qualitative Studies in Education, 16*(5), 619–46.

Wolf-Wendel, L., Ward, K., & Kinzie, J. (2005). Whose culture has capital? A critical race theory discussion of community cultural wealth. *Race Ethnicity and Education, 8*(1), 69–91.

———. (2009). A tangled web of terms: The overlap and unique contribution of involvement, engagement, and integration to understanding college student success. *Journal of College Student Development, 50*(4), 407–28.

Yosso, T. J., Parker, L. J., Solórzano, D. G., & Lynn, M. (2004). From Jim Crow to affirmative action and back again: A critical race discussion of racialized rationales and access to higher education. *Review of Research in Education, 28*(1), 1–25.

Yosso, T. J., Smith, W. A., Ceja, M., & Solórzano, D. G. (2009). Critical race theory, racial microaggressions, and campus racial climate for Latina/o undergraduates. *Harvard Educational Review, 79*(4), 659–90.

CHAPTER TEN

Whose Structure, Whose Function?

(Feminist) Poststructural Approaches in Higher Education Policy Research

AMY SCOTT METCALFE

In his essay "Thinking Critically about the 'Critical': Quantitative Research as Social Critique," Benjamin Baez (2007) stated, "As critics of society, researchers must also be critical of their role in society. That is, critical researchers must be attentive to the privilege and authority that such a role carries, and to its potential to exert its own kind of oppression" (p. 20). As contributors to this volume on critical approaches to the study of higher education, we are each undoubtedly aware of our social roles and responsibilities, even if we might debate what constitutes a "critical approach." Baez challenged us to consider "how research in higher education is or can be *critically transformative*—that is, to what extent educational research can offer critiques of our world that allow us to transform it" (p. 18, italics in original). After mapping the move from Marxism to critical theory, Baez offered the opportunity for us to reflect upon not only the goals of our research but also our position within the research process, stating, "given their importance in shaping the course of our lives, all researchers and scholars must be self-critical" (p. 21). For my part, I strive to answer Baez's challenge by viewing my present and future work as "postcritical," foregrounding what Patti Lather called the "lack of innocence" in my position as an educational researcher (Lather, 1995, p. 168).

Becoming postcritical is the heretical transgression of noting the sedimentation of some forms of critical theory while rejecting the master narratives that continually reassert themselves in dominant, disciplinary discourses. For example, postcriticality permits us to ponder the simultaneous rise of neoliberalism and the movement of women into the global workforce, as suggested by Fraser (2009). Postcriticality offers the position from which to recognize that our academic performance review systems and commensurate individualistic rewards sit upon a foundation of imperialistic intellectual and economic capital, the capture of which was made possible through women's unpaid labor and which is also imbued with the false profits derived from genocide and the cultural appropriation of indigenous knowledge (Harding, 2007; Morgensen, 2012; Smith, 1999). Postcriticality also gives us pause to reflect upon the multiple marginalizations that occur through the implementation of "gender equity" policies (Bryson & De Castell, 1993).

In this chapter I first position myself as a nomadic (Deleuze & Guattari, 1987) researcher working within a genderized (Braidotti, 2012) academy. From this position I view the possibilities of postcriticality and poststructuralism in higher education policy studies (Lather, 1995; Peters & Burbules, 2004; Polanyi, 1962). Toward a postcritical reading of higher education policy research, I note how multiple definitions of *structure* and *function* complicate our work, leading to the questions asked in the title of this chapter: Whose structure? Whose function? These interrelated queries are meant to challenge conventional notions of the object of higher education research and the audiences for which it is intended. With these potentialities in mind, I consider the development of feminist critical policy analysis (Bensimon & Marshall, 1997) and feminist poststructural policy analysis (Allan, Iverson, & Ropers-Huilman, 2010) as significant methodological developments useful to the work of deterritorializing (Braidotti, 1994, 2012) the academy. Finally, a (feminist) poststructural policy approach is used to analyze parental leave policy in the academy. Poststructural analysis permits the deconstruction of dominant narratives within this policy environment, along the way highlighting the missing voices and implications of these absences. While at first glance it may appear that the potential benefits of parental leave policy are reserved for academic parents and therefore the study of such a policy may have limited appeal in the broad field of higher education, I suggest that a postcritical, poststructural examination permits us to see it as a set of codified values and practices regarding academic labor, providing an opportunity for wider scholarly reflection upon normative constructions of the ideal academic.

Becoming Postcritical

Repositioning the role of policy studies to that of interpretation and interrogation instead of consultation provides researchers with a new voice with which to speak to policymakers. In our present era of public sector accountability, nonpositivist methods may serve as a source of constituent-based counternarratives that are potentially influential to the policy process. Scholar-activists (Apple, 2009) who resist the increasing strictures of the quality/excellence movement (Rizvi & Lingard, 2011) may find that feminist and poststructural methods are particularly "useful" in their challenges to dominant narratives of utility. Further, narrative approaches to policy analysis hold the potential to insert new stories and voices into the sound bite *gestalt* of our media-saturated contemporary policy environment. We might, for example, "put Foucault to work" (Lather, 2006) as part of a postcritical interrogation of higher education policy.

By postcritical I mean the act of undertaking a critique of the hierarchies and stratifications that Critical Theory[1] and its proponents have ignored or perpetuated (see Kincheloe & McLaren, 2002; Kincheloe, McLaren, & Steinberg, 2011). Becoming postcritical is an ontological positioning that acknowledges the privileges and legacies derived from several decades of critical thought. Just as the institutions in which we work unwittingly shoulder the visage of imperialism, slavery, the annihilation of indigenous peoples, and misogyny (which are evident in the ivy-covered walls of our neoclassical, Gothic, Georgian, and federal-style edifices that serve as material evidence of academia's historical role as an apparatus of dominance), we have become so accustomed to the emancipatory goals of Criticality that we often fail to acknowledge our implicit collusion with the elitist agenda as members of the academy.

I work as a foreign-born, white, female, tenured professor at a medical/doctoral research institution that is located in the western Canadian province of British Columbia on the unceded territory of the Musqueam First Nation (Clapperton, 2010; Pleshakov, 2010; Valverde, 2012). My employing institution's English Gothic buildings and institutional crest evoke the remains of the British Empire in the colonized lands of the white, settler nation of Canada (Razack, 2002). Arriving to work every day is an opportunity to come to terms with the unearned privilege and imperial legacy I bear as a member of this academic community, situated as it is on contested ground. In addition, I am politicized as an American, betrayed by my Yankee physicality and affectations, attempting to navigate the "progressive" waters of the Canadian professoriate while calling into question national assumptions that have been carefully held under the surface (see Bow [2008] for a discussion of anti-Americanism in Canada). Becoming is itself a theoretical, desirous act (Braidotti, 2002); becoming postcritical is a theoretical and material embodiment by which I try to take responsibility for what I have not earned, even as I question the possibilities presented by "working from the center" of elite privilege (Braidotti, 2012).

But taking a critical, or postcritical, position is not to be done lightly. As Lincoln (2010) stated,

> Paradigms and metaphysics do matter. They matter because they tell us something important about *researcher standpoint*. They tell us something about the

researcher's proposed *relationship to the Other(s)*. They tell us something about what the researcher thinks *counts as knowledge,* and *who can deliver the most valuable slice of this knowledge.* They tell us how the researcher intends to *take account of multiple conflicting and contradictory values* she will encounter. (p. 7, italics in original)

It may be that the challenges presented to the subject positions of the researchers who employ these methods hamper the uptake of particular critical and postcritical approaches. For some scholar-activists, postcriticality is confrontational, but not just to dominant narratives; this work may alter or call into question one's raisons d'être.

Whose Structure?

An initial step toward postcriticality in higher education research is to question concepts and assumptions that potentially constrain our work. Structuralism is one such concept. The common usage of the term in higher education research stems from the concept of social structures, as in the macrosocial theory of structural-functionalism described by Talcott Parsons in 1940. For example, Kezar (2011) stated, "an underlying premise of structuralism is to understand the broader hidden or obscured practices and policies (called structures) that become practiced norms that create barriers for certain classes to advance. The focus is on the larger structure or system as determining and shaping human behavior, rather than seeing class distinctions as only a result of individual actions or behavior" (p. 10). In their review of contemporary research on higher education policy change, Saarinen and Ursin (2012) found that a structural approach is the most common. They defined a structure as a "socially constructed entity in which similar patterns and relationships interact" (p. 3). The primary role of structural policy research, they stated, is to support decision making, but they critique this orientation for its macro level, statist approach: "While the structural approach is analytical and understandable for wider audiences, it nonetheless is descriptive rather than explanatory, heuristic rather than theory-laden. This approach stresses the role of nation states and comprehends them as descriptive frameworks, thereby emphasising that higher education is closely associated with the goals of national level policy making" (p. 4). While many higher education scholars, including Kezar, would likely agree that the structural approach to higher education research is limiting if not oppressive, the scholarly reaction should not be understood as "poststructural," a term known throughout the social sciences as pertaining to the linguistic structures and meaning-making "regimes of truth" that preoccupied theorists such as Butler, Derrida, Foucault, and others who have been categorized as poststructuralists.

Rather than seeing poststructuralism as a response to entrenched social structures, Lather (1992) views it as a policy studies methodology that operates at the level of language and discourse, challenging the Saussurean, structural understanding that language is a closed set of signs and signifiers where meaning resides, and moving toward the notion that language is a key to reading policy contextually and subjectively, with consideration of historical and collectively constructed dimensions. According to Lather (1992), "Structuralism is premised on efforts to scientize language, to posit it as systematizable. Post-structuralism's focus is on the remainder, all that is left over after the systematic categorizations have been made" (p. 90). Social structures do matter, but in the sense that society is constituted by and through discourse. As Simons, Olssen, and Peters (2009) stated, "An important assumption [of post-structuralism] is that the social order is at once a discursive order, and that this order is not to be analysed in structural or binary (linguistic or materialistic) models and neither is it to be analysed in relation to an objectivity or given outside" (p. 58). Further, they explain that (1) a focus on language, (2) a recognition of assemblages and regimes of power that are mutable over time rather than structural (static) forms of power, and (3) a creative approach to the use and development of social theory characterize poststructuralism, particularly that associated with educational policy analysis (pp. 57–58). While not exclusive or exhaustive, I hold on to this definition as a touchstone for my understandings of the scope and potential of poststructural research. The above-listed characteristics of poststructuralism are the antithesis of much of our higher education research to date, which largely fails to recognize the role of language in policy matters, underestimates regimes of power on nearly every level, and dismisses creative approaches to social theory. There are a few exceptions, thankfully, which I describe in the following sections.

Whose Function?

In her two-volume edited collection *Feminist Critical Policy Analysis*, Catherine Marshall (1997a,b) presented the international and interdisciplinary work of feminist educational policy researchers. In the second volume, subtitled *A Perspective from Post-Secondary Education*, she and Estela Mara Bensimon outlined what feminist critical policy analysis (FCPA) means in terms of higher education research. They began their introduction with a series of rhetorical questions, stating that "our purpose in this chapter is to answer two questions we anticipate will be in the minds of readers: 1) How do you read policy studies from a feminist perspective? and 2) How do you conduct feminist policy studies?" (Bensimon & Marshall, 1997, p. 3).

Early in the introductory chapter for the second volume, Bensimon and Marshall contended that "conventional policy studies in postsecondary education assume that academic structures, processes and practices are gender blind" (p. 2). By this they meant that gender and sex are not explicitly mentioned as variables or conceptual constructs, further stating, "the project of feminist policy analysis in education is to disable patriarchy primarily through the research strategy of gendering everyday practices and traditions through which academic culture is created and recreated" (p. 14).

In a review of the book, Anderson (2003) critiqued FCPA for its rejection of conventional tools for policy analysis and its disregard for traditional audiences of such scholarship. Anderson contended that "the role of the policy analyst . . . is to conduct research to help *managers* make decisions about how to organize, regulate, and police the internal order of an institution defined, in part, by genuine conflicts of interest" (pp. 327–28, italics in original). She went on to say that the goal of policy analysts "is to persuade politicians—those who have the power to determine what policy objectives will be followed" (p. 329). In a published response titled "Like It or Not, Feminist Critical Policy Analysis Matters," Bensimon and Marshall (2003) argued that Anderson "believes policy analysts must serve those leaders, [and] must take as a given the questions as framed by them" (p. 346). Although situated in the issues and questions of contemporary feminism, the exchange generally centered on the intent and audience of policy studies in higher education. Whose definition of function should serve as the basis of policy research?

In reasserting their position in response to Anderson's review, Bensimon and Marshall simplified the tenets of FCPA as being policy research where "gender is a fundamental category" and that its goal "is to transform institutions and not simply 'add' women" (Bensimon & Marshall, 2003, pp. 338–39). They provided sample research questions that contrasted how one might approach gender if it were an analytical category rather than a mere variable. For example, rather than asking "Why do women faculty earn less than male faculty?" one should ask "In what ways is 'gender' embedded in definitions of merit?" (p. 345). Reframing policy-related questions so that gender is an analytic category entails rethinking women's work and women's location solely in relation to men. It requires rethinking the "male standard" and instead views gender as a category inclusive of both men and women, male and female. Bensimon and Marshall concluded their reply to Anderson by saying, "too many 'inheritor' women academics today think the problems are solved, that their fellowships, invitations to conferences, and publications demonstrate that sexism is gone. Don't they notice that their salaries are lower than those of their male colleagues? Don't they notice that their tenure review files have to be more perfect than those of their male counterparts? Don't they notice that if they do not act as men think women should act they are shunned?" (p. 348).

In their introduction to the second volume of *Feminist Critical Policy Analysis*, Bensimon and Marshall noted, "Ultimately, we need to construct a feminist theory of the state to explain the maintenance of gender regimes in the academy and other institutions" (Bensimon & Marshall, 1997, p. 17). More than a decade later, third-wave feminists have reframed the agenda of gender work to also consider the ways in which discursive regimes position subjects, academic and otherwise, rather than raging against the machines of patriarchy (Petersen, 2009).

Feminist Poststructuralism

The influence of Bensimon and Marshall's work in the late 1990s can be seen in Allan, Iverson, and Ropers-Huilman's *Reconstructing Policy in Higher Education: Feminist Poststructural Perspectives* (2010). Allan et al. introduce feminist poststructuralism (FPS) as a framework that provides "a focus on the relationship between discourse and subjectivity—providing a theory for understanding how language and meaning produce dynamic and contradictory subject positions" (p. 5). In an introductory chapter, Allan (2010) defines poststructuralism as "a loosely connected group of theories predicated upon a critique of structuralist approaches to the investigation of language" (p. 12). Allan then outlines the premises and implications of three methodologies associated with FPS: Derridian deconstruction, Foucauldian genealogy, and policy discourse analysis. This introduction is useful and provides examples of educational policy scholarship employing these techniques.

The contributors to *Reconstructing Policy in Higher Education* focus on the constitutive aspects of power relations. In contrast with the notion of elite power understood from the vantage point of critical theory, the authors employ a feminist poststructural lens that aligns with the work of Foucault in seeing power as certainly productive but uncertainly directed. According to Foucault (1999), for example, "it is both a methodological and a historical error to consider power as an essentially negative mechanism of repression whose principal function is to protect, preserve, or reproduce the relations of production" (p. 50). As such, power is understood to be polyvalent and mutable, not just associated with governments, institutions, or dominant groups.

In an earlier work, Allan (2008) explained that "instead of analyzing policy by beginning with a focus on implementation and effectiveness in achieving intended outcomes, a post-structural approach typically begins by examining assumptions embedded in the naming of the policy problem and hence the unintended consequences of policy solutions" (pp. 7–8). In *Reconstructing Policy in Higher Education*, however, the reference to reconstruction in the title does not mean offering policy solutions so much as emphasizing the productive aspects of policy discourses, as Allan (2010) clarifies: "FPS approaches to policy call for researcher reflexivity to consider how our subjectivity enters and shapes policy analysis and to work toward interrupting and destabilizing the modernist impulse to produce fixed truths or conclusions as a result of our analyses" (p. 31).

Feminist scholars have made considerable contributions to the possibility of poststructuralism by opening a space within scientific discourse for ontological and epistemological questions that are now commonplace (Lincoln, 2010). In my view, educational scholars need not commit to the language and position of making policy recommendations (reconstruction), especially if we are able to illuminate the "discontinuities, compromises, omissions and exceptions" (Ball, 1990, p. 3) that are also part of the policy process. Reconstruction, while valuable, can be separate from the theories and methods of exposure, disturbance, and "[making] the familiar strange" (Biesta, Allan, & Edwards, 2011, p. 226).

My interest in exploring the co-constructed discourses of power relative to higher education policy necessitate that I bracket the emancipatory and reconstructive goals of feminism to indicate my rejection of usual suspects and my assertion that patriarchy need not be the default unit of analysis. I refer to this approach as (feminist) poststructural policy analysis. The act of acknowledging the unintended consequences and false property of academic Feminism, informed by the challenges posed by antiracist feminism (Calliste, Sefa Dei, & Aguiar, 2000), does not negate my interest in gender work nor does it preclude my participation in the debates surrounding feminist topics of study. Rather, using feminism as a placeholder instead of a platform permits me to reclaim the power of the intellectual and political schism that it once signified.

While my previous work could be characterized as explicitly Critical in a neo- or post-Marxist sense, in becoming postcritical and working toward a (feminist) poststructural policy analysis, I now see higher education policy through a different lens. Peters and Burbules (2004) stated that poststructuralists question the construction of the subject, including the "Cartesian-Kantian subject, the questioning of the Hegelian and phenomenological subject, the questioning of the subject of existentialism, [and] the questioning of the Marxian collective subject"

(p. 21). They also noted that poststructuralism is "an anti- or post-epistemological standpoint, and is fiercely anti-foundationalist. It also adopts an anti-realist position, at least when it comes to questions of meaning and reference, rejecting the established picture of knowledge as an accurate representation. In particular, poststructuralism tends to eschew the traditional account of truth corresponding to reality, emphasizing the idea that language functions as a *differential system*" (p. 4, italics in original). In this sense, poststructuralism can be considered counterproductive, in both a social and economic sense, perhaps toward what Peters (2003) has described as "post-structural Marxisms" in relation to "knowledge capitalism."

These considerations have challenged the Critical basis of my training and previous research. Perhaps not coincidentally, becoming a "mother while academic" in the shared space of becoming postcritical has influenced the scope of my awareness. This reflective period has been developmentally ideal for (feminist) poststructural policy analysis as I consider the tensions produced by parental leave policy in higher education contexts.

Parental Leave and Technologies of Power

I presently embody the constrictions of Canada's "generous" "family-friendly" policy apparatus (Prentice & Pankratz, 2003; Tremblay, 2010) and the stultifying effects of my institution's parental leave "benefits." Parental leave policies ostensibly permit time away from campus duties to promote child welfare and maternal health, but the policies also demarcate a particular period of time in such a way as to constitute the only recognizable or legitimate accommodation for academic parenthood that one might ever receive (Waters & Bardoel, 2006). Further, time spent on parental leave is literally inscribed on the chronological life course (noted in deed or absence on the curriculum vitae) and thus constitutes an amortized "time-out" that is commensurate with the number of days spent off the clock. The period of leave is compartmentalized and shuttered for bureaucratic purposes, with no accountability or support for the persistence and maintenance of academic and intellectual activities undertaken while "away." Considering (feminist) poststructuralism while on official parental leave has been ironically generative in its difficulty. It is in this space, a space within which I was explicitly not paid to not think, that I came to understand and embrace what it is to be a nomadic subject, in between and mindful of alternative, figurative, potentialities (Braidotti, 2012).

I see parental leave policies as intertwined with the desires of academic Feminism. As Hart (2008) has noted, Feminist academics formed coalitions at various American institutions to help establish frameworks for the successful integration of women into the professoriate, resulting in so-called family-friendly policies such as tenure clock stoppage and parental leave (Quinn, 2010). National-level social reforms such as Canada's Unemployment Insurance Act (1971) and the United States' Pregnancy Discrimination Act (1978) and Family and Medical Leave Act (1993) undergirded these policies. (See Trzcinski and Alpert [1994] for a comparison of US and Canadian legal precedents for parental leave legislation.)

Most higher education institutions in North America now have parental leave policies. As written, these policies provide a parent the opportunity to take a leave of absence from regular work duties for the purpose of caring for a child. Yet many policies fall short of addressing the role-stress endemic to academe and the actual needs of new parents. Redefinition of parenting has contributed to the successes and also to the limitations of these policies, as more academics are finding that institutions do not recognize their parental responsibilities (Comer & Stites-Doe, 2006).

Research within the field of higher education has shown that academic men and women are largely hesitant to avail themselves of parental leave benefits because of performance pressures, and that gendering still occurs (Lester, 2013; Lester & Sallee, 2009; Sallee, 2008; Ward &Wolf-Wendel, 2012). The degree of participation in such benefits by men, for example, has been seen as essential to ensure a shift in workplace culture at colleges and universities (Philipsen & Bostic, 2010; Sallee, 2013). Some believe that the more "gender neutral" the policy, the more likely change will occur. These latter arguments stem from an equity stance that seeks to "even the playing field" of academia to enhance occupational outcomes for women (Probert, 2005; Sanders, Willemsen, & Millar, 2009). But some also believe that increased male participation in the absence of female participation might further expand the gender inequities that exist among parenting professors (Hollenshead et al., 2005).

While coalitions of academic women and allied men have successfully established parental leave and other family-friendly policies, Feminism's theoretical and political stances operate through these policy mechanisms as one of many discursive power relations that discipline academic bodies (Pillow, 2003). It is through these policies that we read the academic subject position and the valuation of academic labor(ing). Approaching these policies from a (feminist) poststructural stance attunes us to ways that parental leave makes evident the nature of preferred academic bodies and the sex-specific valuation schemata that are applied to academic work.

Foucault's concept of biopower is useful to understand how policy is thusly embodied. In the first volume of *History of Sexuality* (1978), Foucault discussed the historical emergence of two forms of a sovereign's dominance: over the body as a means of production (laborer, economic actor, etc.) and over the body as means of reproduction (sexual being, propagator/progeny, etc.). The social institutions that had developed by the seventeenth century, including schools and universities, were subsequently redirected to the regulatory control of the productive and reproductive functions of the body, and therefore the lives of the citizenry. Universities, as instruments of the state, were developed as technologies of power, with enduring disciplinary effects both in terms of academic subject positions and academic subject matter. Techniques of disciplining the body through academia evolved into academic disciplines with techniques, as the sovereign's need and support for demography invented sociology, the militaristic regimentation of health care coalesced into academic medicine, and so forth.

From this perspective we might see the development of the modern university as a process of becoming part of the apparatus of biopower, using the techniques of what Foucault (1978) termed "segregation and social hierarchization" (p. 141) to promote/curtail an entire population's production and reproduction in specific ways. Foucault stated that "bio-power was without question an indispensible element in the development of capitalism; the latter would not have been possible without the controlled insertion of bodies into the machinery of production and the adjustment of the phenomena of population to economic processes" (p. 141). But it was not enough to maintain biopower through institutions; the techniques of power extended to definitions of family and vitality (including the life of the mind). Through the mechanisms of governmentality, there is no need for an actual sovereign because the logic of the sovereign's techniques are embedded within one's self-constructions. Here we begin to see how the discursive power of gender relations has reinforced particular notions of the ideal worker, the ideal academic, the ideal family, and the ideal society. Foucault noted that "for millennia, man remained what he was for Aristotle: a living animal with the additional capacity for a political existence; modern man is an animal whose politics places his existence as a living being in question" (p. 143). For the marginalized, the (re)assertion of one's existence as a living being puts her political existence in question. As such, the academic arena shapes and is shaped by elite, racialized, sexualized, and gendered forms of segregated production that are inscribed in the academic body politic. Who we are and who we might become are bounded by normalization and ascription though the simultaneous forces of professional socialization and governmentality.

It is for this reason that I utilize biopower from a (feminist) poststructural approach to read policy as one of several technologies of power that operate through academic institutions. In other words, biopower frames the inherent contradictions embedded within parental leave policy such that we might see how the discourses of equity play out when one's reproductive capacities are perceived to disrupt one's productivity as an employee. From the liberal Feminist position, parental leave policy is deemed necessary as an insertion into the previously male production cycle to create "equal opportunity" for female employees. As the Feminist equity discourse unfolds, men are called upon to desire this benefit "equally," to desegregate and flatten the hierarchies of production/reproduction. But the expansion of parental leave eligibility through reframing reproduction to encompass a larger population of individuals (parents and not just mothers) does not negate the phallocentric assumptions of the academy and its capitalist, imperialist complicities. Rather, the insertion of such policies into the previously sex-segregated production cycle, regardless of the expansion of eligibility, emphasizes the need for sex-specific or gendered exceptions in the face of normative productivity expectations and as such does not provide protection so much as it puts people in harm's way. Perhaps inadvertently, the Feminist equity project has reinscribed the (re)productive binaries of academic work, as the (neo)liberalized policy stance assumes that one is either on parental leave or not, capable of absorbing the career consequences of this choice. Parenthood is only recognized within *parental leave* policy or tenure clock *stoppage*: there is no *parental arrival* policy, for example, that might address the pressures of academia that affect working parents who are *always on*.

It has not been widely recognized in the higher education literature that parental leave is not merely gendered, but also elite and racialized, in that high-status white faculty members (men and women) have less to lose in making work/life tradeoffs than low-status whites or minoritized faculty members. In addition, there is limited research on the policy gaps for contingent faculty who might not be eligible for benefits afforded only to full-time or tenure-track employees (Nikunen, 2014). Furthermore, there is little to no attention being paid to the social implications of childcare arrangements after parental leave is over, except perhaps in countries like Canada, where a nationalized immigration policy for domestic caregivers is debated even while it is firmly institutionalized and supportive of elite (white) reproduction in many forms (Calder, 2003; Catarino, Kontos, & Shinozaki, 2013). As Rhee (2013) stated, "the imperative of biopower in the age of neoliberalism requires governing the formerly colonized in different ways"

(p. 566). When employment benefits are extended to "equalize the playing field" in the gendered academic landscape, we should ask who is still paying a higher price to play and who is not even in the game.

In many of its manifestations around the globe (but not necessarily in the United States, where there is little to no paid time off for family formation), parental leave means leaving: leaving campus, leaving students, leaving colleagues, and leaving the globalized intellectual community. Stone and Hernandez (2013) call this the "all-or-nothing workplace." Yet in practice the tasks associated with the academic profession are difficult to leave behind or aside entirely, even for a brief period of time. Graduate student supervision, the cycle of grant applications and awards, ongoing research, and scholarly collaboration are a few aspects of academic work that are challenging or impossible to ignore while on parental leave. Variation in parental leave policies worldwide, both in terms of salary benefits (paid or unpaid) and the length of possible leave periods that range from a few weeks to several years, provide analytic challenges but demonstrate on the whole that there is a global preference for granting a period of employment leave for parenting, around the time of childbirth or family formation, in order to attract and retain women in the workforce. But it may be that the more historically sex-segregated the occupation, the more impossible leaving work becomes. In the case of academia, the implementation of nationalized (and occupationally generic) parental leave policies does not necessarily provide adequate recognition of the role-stress experienced by academic parents. Perhaps it is not that the academy fails to fully understand the needs of academic parents, but that the corporate world's accommodations for family care assume a different organizational culture than what currently exists in academia. Academic parenthood must become a hybridized existence, as the productive self is so essential to the academic enterprise that it cannot be abandoned even for a short while. When women (or men) stop out, they are penalized, resulting in sex segregation and gendered salary stratification (Coltrane et al., 2013; Rudman & Mescher, 2013).

While not pertaining exclusively to academic employment, the Organisation for Economic Co-operation and Development (OECD) provides statistics on paid parental leave in member states as part of its Family Database, outlined in a report titled "Key Characteristics of Parental Leave Systems" (OECD, 2014). In the OECD report, the general set of family care policies associated with "employment-protected leaves of absence" is described under the heading of "parental leave," but three types of leave are defined: maternal, paternal, and parental. We learn that the average paid maternity leave for OECD countries is eighteen weeks, with paid paternity leave being "considerably shorter" or absent (p. 2). The third type of leave—parental—is described as supplemental to the leaves that are "exclusive to mothers or fathers." The report states, "With regards to parental leave entitlements, most OECD countries allow parents to decide amongst themselves as to who takes leave and claims income support, and in practice this generally means that the parent on lower earning[s], most often the mother, takes the leave" (p. 2). The OECD data set and statistical report provide evidence of two assumptions that are embedded within many parental leave policies: parental sex binaries and gendered earning differentials. A biological sex binary undergirds parental leave policies in OECD countries. In this official and dominant discourse, families are composed of (presumably female) mothers who give birth and (presumably male) fathers who do not. The OECD's description of "parental" does not recognize that two mothers or two fathers also lead families, and that these couples might share employment-related leave for childbirth or family formation. Single parents are not mentioned in the summary, nor are adoptive parents. Some countries listed in the OECD report do recognize these family categories in their parental leave structures, but such exceptions did not warrant attention in the OECD's multi-country summary.

While generic, the assumptive sex roles categorized in the OECD report affect how parental leave is enacted in the academic workspace through the construction and reinscription of master narratives regarding sex roles, elite (white) exceptionalism, and heteronormativity. Parental leave is modeled onto and after the female body and offered as the policy answer to this anatomical difference as measured against the male ideal. Analyzed through the lens of biopower, we see that the anatomic preferences of academia's innovation mechanisms reward capitalism's ideal academic worker: transient, unfettered, and perpetually inchoate. The reproductive academic body cannot be fully realized because of the threat it poses to academic production capacities, creating the necessity of the "all-or-nothing workplace" (Stone & Hernandez, 2013) and policy solutions such as tenure clock stoppage and parental leave (Pribbenow et al., 2010). In places like the United States, where paid parental leave is not federally guaranteed, reproduction is pathologized and shuttered, leading to the "May baby" phenomenon in an attempt to synchronize biological clocks, tenure clocks, and academic calendars (Armenti, 2004a). This also occurs in Canada, where parental leave is not mandatory, and in fields where the career costs of stop-outs for reproduction are high (Armenti, 2004b).

The OECD data set and report demonstrate that the biologically female activity of childbirth is not the only reason for countries to provide the female worker with more paid weeks of leave than her partner. If the mother is, generally speaking, the one who earns less in the family partnership, an economically rational family would opt for the mother to step out of the workforce to take parental leave rather than the higher-earning co-parent. Given that many paid parental leaves are capped at a minimum wage or a low-income threshold (e.g., Canada's paid leave rate is 55% of average earnings, with a maximum of about $25,220 per year of taxable income), the lower-earning mother will have her annual wage reduced by at least half while she takes paid parental leave. A mother's benefit probably amounts to less than what a male partner's benefit would be at half of his salary were he to take the leave, saving the public purse the expense of compensating male wage-earning potential. At the lower end of the income scale, a heterosexual female taking parental leave likely costs the state less. At the higher end of the income scale, where some workplaces "top up" a person's parental leave benefit salary, it may still be more desirable from an employer's standpoint for a heterosexual mother to take parental leave to avoid losing the father's productivity while also paying his higher compensatory wages. In this view, the "benefit" of parental leave is understood within the gendered state and gendered workplace, such that the entity making the payments (government or employer) demonstrates preference for the lower-earning member of a dual-career couple as a way to reduce expenditures.

In the socially progressive space of the academy, we might expect more equity, more fairness. Indeed, because of the "successes" of gender equity discourse, the promotion of equal uptake of the parental leave policy construct across all categories of academic parenthood and parenting relationships must erase (sex) difference. Yet the normative, ideal academic worker is nonreproductive—whether male or female, single or partnered, gay or straight—as the historic absence and invisibility of fathering in the industrialized academy and its monastic antecedents suggest. It is for this reason that academic parents, whether availing themselves of family-friendly policy constructs or not, must come against the nonfamilial production values of the academy and be measured accordingly.

How a parental leave stop-out, underpayment, or unpaid labor might cumulatively affect one's income over time has yet to be fully understood, but may be related to the persistence of sex segregation and salary gaps in the academy (Cha, 2013; Crowley & Kolenikov, 2014; Lips, 2013). In other sectors, this is known as the "family gap" or the "motherhood penalty"—the difference between the salaries of women with children as compared to women without children (Budig, Misra, & Boeckmann, 2012; Waldfogel, 1998), which may also extend to nonmothering parents who take parental leave. Yet if the gender equity project and its fixation on wage gaps were abandoned or put aside for a moment, without failing to acknowledge that the historical undervaluing of women's labors (maternal and otherwise) is insidiously embedded in academic production, a reevaluation of academic labor could take its place. Furthermore, if we decenter gender equity, we might also realize its whiteness and the alibi needed to maintain it (Leonardo & Zembylas, 2013).

Approaching parental leave policies through (feminist) poststructural policy analysis calls into question the very nature of who we are and what we might become as academics. The lens of biopower aids in our understanding of the academy as part and parcel of a capitalist enterprise that is infused with the historic legacies of sex segregation / exploitation, gendering, and colonization. A (feminist) poststructural reading of parental leave departs from the question of productivity in multiple directions that might encourage nomadic, transitive possibilities (Braidotti, 2012; Delueze & Guattari, 1987).

Conclusion

In this chapter, I have outlined a movement of thought that has personal ontological and epistemological resonance. This process of becoming (Braidotti, 2002) has concerned academic productivity on many levels, and the policies by which productivity is defined and produced. Poststructuralism has provided an opportunity for grasping the subtle changes in normative associations within the academy relative to neoliberalism and fluctuating gender relations. As Ball (1994) put it, "Post-structuralism offers very different ways of looking at and beyond the obvious and puts different sorts of questions on the agenda for change" (p. 2). I continue to draw inspiration from Lather (1992), who said that "the goal of deconstruction is to keep things in process, to disrupt, to keep the system in play, to set up procedures to continuously demystify the realities we create, to fight the tendency for our categories to congeal" (p. 96). Claiming a postcritical, (feminist) poststructuralist position means necessarily letting go of the multiple readings that might be taken of the work, to be satisfied with disturbance rather than reform. It also entails acceptance of the consequences of heresy, and the vulnerability of being branded a (sex/race/class) traitor (Preston & Chadderton, 2012). As Humes and Bryce (2003) cautioned, "Researchers have to learn to live with the confusions, ambiguities and value conflicts of the postmodern world as best they can: the notion of the intellectual as a detached enquirer after truth, operating outside the forces of power, has been shown to be a self-deceiving (and, in many cases, a self-serving) illusion" (p. 185).

Shrugging off the comforting mantle of structural functionalism, or the Critical standpoint taken to mend it, may seem particularly difficult for higher education researchers, and perhaps also for those who pursue educational policy studies more broadly. Yet, as Vidovich (2007) noted, "some of the most productive theoretical development is located around the cusp between modernist and post-modernist/post-structuralist perspectives" (p. 286). This is not research *of* or *for* policy, but research *in spite of* policy. We might then eventually find delight in saying that (feminist) poststructural policy analysis is an exercise in (f)utility. In the spirit of that troubled space, I end this chapter where it started, with two interrelated questions that pertain to future interrogations from a (feminist) post-structural approach in higher education: Whose policy? Whose analysis?

NOTE

1. A note on capitalization: The words "critical" and "feminism" are used through-out in two different ways. When capitalized, the words reference entrenched or dom-inating discursive regimes in academia.

REFERENCES

Allan, E. J. (2008). *Policy discourses, gender, and education: Constructing women's sta-tus.* New York: Routledge.

———. (2010). Feminist poststructuralism meets policy analysis: An overview. In E. J. Allan, S. Iverson, & R. Ropers-Huilman (Eds.), *Reconstructing policy in higher ed-ucation: Feminist poststructural perspectives* (pp. 11–39). New York: Routledge.

Allan, E. J., Iverson, S., & Ropers-Huilman, R. (Eds.). (2010). *Reconstructing policy in higher education: Feminist poststructural perspectives.* New York: Routledge.

Anderson, H. (2003). As if gender mattered: Feminism and change in higher educa-tion. *Journal of Higher Education, 74*(3), 321–36.

Apple, M. W. (2009). Can critical education interrupt the right? *Discourse: Studies in the Cultural Politics of Education, 30*(3), 239–51.

Armenti, C. (2004a). May babies and posttenure babies: Maternal decisions of women professors. *Review of Higher Education, 27*(2), 211–31.

———. (2004b). Gender as a barrier for women with children in academe. *Canadian Journal of Higher Education, 34*(1), 1–26.

Baez, B. (2007). Thinking critically about the "critical": Quantitative research as social critique. *New Directions for Institutional Research, 2007*(133), 17–23.

Ball, S. J. (1990). *Politics and policy making in education: Explorations in policy sociol-ogy.* New York: Routledge.

———. (1994). *Education reform: A critical and post-structural approach.* Bucking-ham: Open University Press.

Bensimon, E. M., & Marshall, C. (1997). Policy analysis for postsecondary education: Feminist and critical perspectives. In C. Marshall (Ed.), *Feminist critical policy analysis* (Vol. 2). *A perspective from post-secondary education* (pp. 1–21). London: Falmer Press.

———. (2003). Like it or not: Feminist critical policy analysis matters. *Journal of Higher Education, 74*(3), 337–49.

Biesta, G., Allan, J., & Edwards, R. (2011). The theory question in research capacity building in education: Towards an agenda for research and practice. *British Journal of Educational Studies, 59*(3), 225–39.

Bow, B. (2008). Anti-Americanism in Canada, before and after Iraq. *American Review of Canadian Studies, 38*(3), 341–59.

Braidotti, R. (1994). *Nomadic subjects: Embodiment and sexual difference in contemporary feminist theory*. New York: Columbia University Press.

———. (2002). *Metamorphoses: Towards a materialist theory of becoming*. Cambridge: Polity Press.

———. (2012). *Nomadic theory: The portable Rosi Braidotti*. New York: Columbia University Press.

Bryson, M., & De Castell, S. (1993). En/gendering equity: On some paradoxical consequences of institutionalized programs of emancipation. *Educational Theory, 43*(3), 341–55.

Budig, M. J., Misra, J., & Boeckmann, I. (2012). The motherhood penalty in cross-national perspective: The importance of work–family policies and cultural attitudes. *Social Politics: International Studies in Gender, State and Society, 19*(2), 163–93.

Calder, G. (2003). Recent changes to the maternity and parental leave benefits regime as a case study: The impact of globalization on the delivery of social programs in Canada. *Canadian Journal of Women and the Law, 15*, 342.

Calliste, A. M., Sefa Dei, G. J., & Aguiar, M. (2000). *Anti-racist feminism: Critical race and gender studies*. Halifax: Fernwood.

Catarino, C., Kontos, M., & Shinozaki, K. (2013). Family matters: Migrant domestic and care work and the issue of recognition. In F. Anthias (Ed.), *Paradoxes of integration: Female migrants in Europe* (pp. 133–52). New York: Springer.

Cha, Y. (2013). Overwork and the persistence of gender segregation in occupations. *Gender and Society, 27*(2), 158–84.

Clapperton, J. A. (2010). Contested spaces, shared places: The Museum of Anthropology at UBC, aboriginal peoples, and postcolonial criticism. *BC Studies: The British Columbian Quarterly, 165*, 7–30.

Coltrane, S., Miller, E. C., DeHaan, T., & Stewart, L. (2013). Fathers and the flexibility stigma. *Journal of Social Issues, 69*(2), 279–302.

Comer, D. R., and S. Stites-Doe. (2006). Antecedents and consequences of faculty women's academic–parental role balancing. *Journal of Family and Economic Issues, 27*(3), 495–512.

Crowley, J. E., & Kolenikov, S. (2014). Flexible work options and mothers' perceptions of career harm. *Sociological Quarterly, 55*(1), 168–95.

Deleuze, G., & Guattari, P. F. (1987). *Thousand plateaus: capitalism and schizophrenia*. Minneapolis: University of Minnesota Press.

Foucault, M. (1978). *The history of sexuality: An introduction* (Vol. 1). New York: Vintage.

———. (1999). *Abnormal: Lectures at the Collège de France, 1974–1975* (G. Burchell, Trans.; V. Marchetti and A. Salomoni, Eds.). New York: Picador.

Fraser, N. (2009). Feminism, capitalism, and the cunning of history. *New Left Review, 56*, 97–117.

Harding, S. (2007). Evaluation policies for academics. In B. J. Bank (Ed.), *Gender and higher education* (pp. 367–73). Baltimore, MD: Johns Hopkins University Press.

Hart, J. (2008). Mobilization among women academics: The interplay between feminism and professionalization. *NWSA Journal, 20*(1), 184–208.

Hollenshead, C. S., Sullivan, B., Smith, G. C., August, L., & Hamilton, S. (2005). Work/family policies in higher education: Survey data and case studies of policy implementation. *New Directions for Higher Education, 2005*(130), 41–65.

Humes, W., & Bryce, T. (2003). Post-structuralism and policy research in education. *Journal of Education Policy, 18*(2), 175–87.

Kezar, A. (Ed.). (2011). *Recognizing and serving low-income students in higher education: An examination of institutional policies, practices, and culture.* New York: Routledge.

Kincheloe, J. L., & McLaren, P. (2002). Rethinking critical theory and qualitative research. In Y. Zou & E. T. Trueba (Eds.), *Ethnography and schools: Qualitative approaches to the study of education* (pp. 87–138). Lanham, MD: Rowman & Littlefield.

Kincheloe, J. L., McLaren, P., & Steinberg, S. R. (2011). Critical pedagogy and qualitative research. In N. K. Denzin & Y. S. Lincoln (Eds.), *The Sage handbook of qualitative research* (pp. 163–77). Thousand Oaks, CA: Sage.

Lather, P. (1992). Critical frames in educational research: Feminist and post-structural perspectives. *Theory into Practice, 31*(2), 87–99.

———. (1995). Post-critical pedagogies: A feminist reading. In P. McLaren (Ed.), *Postmodernism, postcolonialism and pedagogy* (pp. 167–86). James Nicholas.

———. (2006). Foucauldian scientificity: Rethinking the nexus of qualitative research and educational policy analysis. *International Journal of Qualitative Studies in Education, 19*(6), 783–91.

Leonardo, Z., and Zembylas, M. (2013). Whiteness as technology of affect: Implications for educational praxis. *Equity and Excellence in Education, 46*(1), 150–65.

Lester, J. (2013). Work-life balance and cultural change: A narrative of eligibility. *Review of Higher Education, 36*(4), 463–88.

Lester, J., and Sallee, M. (Eds.). (2009). *Establishing the family-friendly campus: Models for effective practice.* Sterling, VA: Stylus.

Lincoln, Y. S. (2010). "What a long, strange trip it's been . . . ": Twenty-five years of qualitative and new paradigm research. *Qualitative Inquiry, 16*(1), 3–9.

Lips, H. M. (2013). The gender pay gap: Challenging the rationalizations. Perceived equity, discrimination, and the limits of human capital models. *Sex Roles, 68*(3–4), 169–85.

Marshall, C. (Ed.). (1997a). *Feminist critical policy analysis* (Vol. 1). *A perspective from primary and secondary schooling.* New York: Routledge.

———. (1997b). *Feminist critical policy analysis* (Vol. 2). *A perspective from post-sec-ondary education.* London: Falmer Press.

Morgensen, S. L. (2012). Destabilizing the settler academy: The decolonial effects of indigenous methodologies. *American Quarterly, 64*(4), 805–8.

Nikunen, M. (2014). The "entrepreneurial university," family and gender: Changes and demands faced by fixed-term workers. *Gender and Education, 26*(2), 119–34.

OECD. Organisation for Economic Co-operation and Development. (2014). OECD Family Database. Paris: Author. Retrieved from www.oecd.org/social/family/database.

Parsons, T. (1940). An analytical approach to the theory of social stratification. *American Journal of Sociology, 45*, 841–62.

Peters, M. (2003). Post-structuralism and Marxism: Education as knowledge capital-ism. *Journal of Education Policy, 18*(2), 115–29.

Peters, M. A., & Burbules, N. C. (2004). *Poststructuralism and educational research.* Lanham, MD: Rowman & Littlefield.

Petersen, E. B. (2009). Resistance and enrolment in the enterprise university: An eth-no-drama in three acts, with appended reading. *Journal of Education Policy, 24*(4), 409–22.

Philipsen, M. I., & Bostic, T. B. (2003). "Bodies are dangerous": Using feminist gene-alogy as policy studies methodology. *Journal of Education Policy, 18*(2), 145–59.

———. (2010). *Helping faculty find work-life balance: The path toward family-friendly institutions.* San Francisco: Jossey-Bass.

Pleshakov, A. S. (2010). *"We do not talk about our history here": The Department of Indian Affairs, Musqueam-settler relations, and memory in a Vancouver neighbour-hood* (Unpublished master's thesis). University of British Columbia, Vancouver.

Polanyi, M. (1962). *Personal knowledge: Towards a post-critical philosophy.* Chicago: University of Chicago Press.

Prentice, S., and Pankratz, C. J. (2003). When academics become parents: An over-view of family leave policies at Canadian universities. *Canadian Journal of Higher Education, 33*(2), 1–26.

Preston, J., & Chadderton, C. (2012). Rediscovering "race traitor": Towards a critical race theory informed public pedagogy. *Race Ethnicity and Education, 15*(1), 85–100.

Pribbenow, C. M., Sheridan, J., Winchell, J., Benting, D., Handelsman, J., & Carnes, M. (2010). The tenure process and extending the tenure clock: The experience of faculty at one university. *Higher Education Policy, 23*(1), 17–38.

Probert, B. (2005). "I just couldn't fit it in": Gender and unequal outcomes in aca-demic careers. *Gender, Work and Organization, 12*(1), 50–72.

Quinn, K. (2010). Tenure clock extension policies: Who uses them and to what effect? *NASPA Journal about Women in Higher Education, 3*(1), 185–209.

Razack, S. (2002). *Race, space, and the law: Unmapping a white settler society.* Toronto: Between the Lines.

Rhee, J. E. (2013). The Neoliberal Racial Project: The tiger mother and governmen-tality. *Educational Theory, 63*(6), 561–80.

Rizvi, F., & Lingard, B. (2011). Social equity and the assemblage of values in Australian higher education. *Cambridge Journal of Education, 41*(1), 5–22.

Rudman, L. A., & Mescher, K. (2013). Penalizing men who request a family leave: Is flexibility stigma a femininity stigma? *Journal of Social Issues, 69*(2), 322–40.

Saarinen, T., & Ursin, J. (2012). Dominant and emerging approaches in the study of higher education policy change. *Studies in Higher Education, 37*(2), 143–56.

Sallee, M. W. (2008). A feminist perspective on parental leave policies. *Innovative Higher Education, 32*(4), 181–94.

———. (2013). Gender norms and institutional culture: The family-friendly versus the father-friendly university. *Journal of Higher Education, 84*(3), 363–96.

Sanders, K., Willemsen, T. M., & Millar, C. C. J. M. (2009). Views from above the glass ceiling: Does the academic environment influence women professors' careers and experiences? *Sex Roles, 60*(5–6), 301–12.

Simons, M., Olssen, M., & Peters, M. A. (2009). *Re-reading education policies: A handbook studying the policy agenda of the 21st century.* Rotterdam: Sense.

Smith, L. T. (1999). *Decolonizing methodologies: Research and indigenous peoples.* London: Zed Books.

Stone, P., & Hernandez, L. A. (2013). The all-or-nothing workplace: Flexibility stigma and "opting out" among professional-managerial women. *Journal of Social Issues, 69*(2), 235–56.

Tremblay, D.-G. (2010). Paid parental leave: An employee right or still an ideal? An analysis of the situation in Québec in comparison with North America. *Employee Responsibilities and Rights Journal, 22*(2), 83–100.

Trzcinski, E., & Alpert, W. T. (1994). Pregnancy and parental leave benefits in the United States and Canada: Judicial decisions and legislation. *Journal of Human Resources, 29*(2), 535–54.

Valverde, M. (2012). The Crown in a multicultural age: The changing epistemology of (post) colonial sovereignty. *Social and Legal Studies, 21*(1), 3–21.

Vidovich, L. (2007). Removing policy from its pedestal: Some theoretical framings and practical possibilities. *Educational Review, 59*(3), 285–98.

Waldfogel, J. (1998). Understanding the "family gap" in pay for women with children. *Journal of Economic Perspectives, 12*(1), 137–56.

Ward, K., & Wolf-Wendel, L. (2012). *Academic motherhood: How faculty manage work and family.* New Brunswick, NJ: Rutgers University Press.

Waters, M. A., & Bardoel, E. A. (2006). Work–family policies in the context of higher education: Useful or symbolic? *Asia Pacific Journal of Human Resources, 44*(1), 67–82.

CHAPTER ELEVEN

A Critical Examination of the College Completion Agenda

Advancing Equity in Higher Education

ROBERT T. TERANISHI AND ANNIE W. BEZBATCHENKO

In his first State of the Union address in 2009, President Barack Obama proclaimed, "In a global economy where the most valuable skill you can sell is your knowledge, a good education is no longer just a pathway to opportunity—it is a prerequisite." Aligning with large-scale investments by foundations, new efforts by higher education policy centers, and burgeoning state-based initiatives, President Obama set as a national priority the following goal: "By 2020, America will once again have the highest proportion of college graduates in the world." This broad-based higher education reform movement, called the college completion agenda, set into motion large-scale efforts to create new policies that incentivize degree completion, improve the efficiency of degree production, and broadly define institutional performance as degree attainment.

While the college completion agenda has been lauded as a critically important paradigm shift in higher education, it has also faced criticism for its narrow focus, which omits other important aspects of the role and function of higher education. In this chapter, we offer a lens through which to critically examine the college completion agenda relative to race, equity, and the stubborn and persistent inequality of American higher education. Specifically, through an exploration of the college completion agenda with an equity-minded lens, this chapter focuses on the role of critical inquiry as a tool with which national priorities in higher education can help expand opportunity and mitigate inequality. This perspective affords scholars, policymakers, and practitioners the ability to see beyond normative frameworks that currently shape the higher education arena, and allows for the development of powerful approaches to policy making, philanthropy, and broader reform efforts. The chapter concludes with examples of efforts to target investments that may help to close the equity gap, and discusses how and why these strategies are important for reshaping policy and practice.

Critical Policy Analysis

Public policy plays a critical role in American higher education and figures in a significant body of scholarly work in the field of higher education. Historically, policy analysis has been rooted in rational econometric approaches—conceptual lenses that treat the process of creating or analyzing policy by utilizing "facts" that emerge from value-neutral research processes (Allan, Iverson, & Ropers-Huilman, 2010). Assumptions of objectivity whereby scholars can analyze policy decisions and outcomes through a process of weighing costs and benefits have also driven traditional policy studies. These approaches have been criticized for overlooking social and cultural contexts (Sabatier & Jenkins-Smith, 1988) and the extent to which the differential impact of policy has consequences for the experiences and outcomes of marginalized and vulnerable student and community groups (Chase et al., 2012; Harper, 2012; Iverson, 2007).

In response to the traditional framework of policy analysis, critical policy analysis provides a lens through which policy research—questions, data sources, and analyses—can centrally position stratification and inequality within the study of policy decisions, processes, and outcomes. Critical policy analysis has been utilized to examine both overt forms of discriminatory policies and covert aspects of policy with consequences that emerge through what is absent in policy (Chase et al., 2012). Central to critical policy analysis is a process through which researchers can pursue generative questions within the context of power, social stratification, and inequality, all of which are endemic in US society (Anderson, 2012; Iverson, 2007; Pusser & Marginson, 2012). For example, critical policy analysis has been used to effectively reframe issues such as student learning assessment in policies like No Child Left Behind. Within these studies are efforts to identify deficit approaches to defining problems and solutions, the collection and use of data, and language used in portraying the causes and consequences of inequality.

By better understanding the texture of intricate issues such as the college completion agenda through a critical lens, we can develop better educational policy that effectively addresses forms of inequality that are creating disparate educational outcomes by race and class. Critical policy analysis can challenge normative approaches to higher education policy by utilizing perspectives that bring inequality and its consequences to the fore. In this chapter, we utilize a critical policy lens to examine a key tenet of the national higher education arena—the college completion agenda—to understand how and why equity is positioned as a relevant, timely, and central goal. Our primary focus is on the extent to which equity is explicitly or implicitly stated in the goals, strategies, and desired outcomes of the college completion agenda.

The College Completion Agenda

The college completion agenda is an attempt to improve the degree attainment rates in the United States, which have been stagnant at approximately 39% over the last four decades (Lumina Foundation for Education, 2009). The Lumina Foundation's "Big Goal" is to increase the proportion of Americans with high-quality degrees and credentials to 60% by the year 2025. In absolute numbers, such goals represent a significant challenge for American higher education. The National Center for Higher Education Management Systems (NCHEMS) prepared a report in 2010 stating that, adjusting for population growth and educational attainment, the United States would need an additional eight million college degree holders to close the attainment gap for young adults aged 25 to 34.

The argument is often made that the consequences of a flat attainment rate in the United States have already begun to materialize, as statistics show a trend toward being out-educated by other developed nations. More specifically, as the United States is increasingly engaged in an interconnected global economy, concerns exist about its ability to compete with other developed nations, which have been experiencing an increase in educational attainment rates (Lumina Foundation for Education, 2009). Therefore a central focus of the college completion agenda is to increase attainment rates as a way to enhance the workforce and economic output for the United States relative to other developed nations. Over the last four decades, while college degree attainment rates in the United States have remained stagnant, other developed countries have experienced an increase in attainment rates, with as high as 50% of young adults holding college degrees (Lumina Foundation for Education, 2009). According to data from the Organisation for Economic Co-operation and Development (OECD), while the United States previously boasted the highest percentage of young adults with college degrees in the world, it has since experienced a precipitous drop in the rankings (NCHEMS, 2010).

In addition to concerns about being out-educated by other nations, there are concerns about how the stagnation in degree attainment affects the US workforce. For example, the United States will experience a shortfall of an estimated three million workers with a postsecondary degree by 2018 (Carnevale, Smith, & Strohl, 2010). Policymakers also point to the need for a more educated workforce by discussing a significant decline in the number of low-skilled jobs that traditionally did not require a postsecondary degree (Business Roundtable, 2009). In their place are jobs are requiring at least some postsecondary education, which are estimated to increase to 63% of the total pool in the United States over the next decade (Carnevale et al., 2010).

To summarize, within this college completion context are the following realities: (1) globalization is challenging the long-term competitiveness of American workers in the global workplace, making degree production critical to sustaining the US economy; (2) as the nation's economy has shifted from a basis in industry to one in knowledge, a college-educated workforce is becoming increasingly essential (Carnevale, 2008); and (3) low-skilled jobs that traditionally did not require a postsecondary degree are disappearing, being replaced by jobs requiring some postsecondary education (Carnevale et al., 2010). These realities put college completion on the forefront of the higher education policy agenda, and thus on the agenda of those who care about equity in higher education.

Echoes of the Equity and Excellence Debate

Given that college completion is a priority on the higher education policy agenda, a critical analysis of it is both necessary and instructive. Our critical analysis begins by unpacking tensions and debates within in the agenda: strains between the public and private good of higher education and the echoes of this tension on debates surrounding excellence and equity.

The Public and Private Purposes of Higher Education

Embedded in the completion agenda is the tension between the public purpose of higher education (i.e., civic reasons to train and educate) and the private purpose of higher education (i.e., economic reasons to train and educate). Historically speaking, the public purpose of higher education has been a pillar of the American university's mission (e.g., King & Mayhew, 2004; Zemsky, Wegner, & Massy, 2005). As Kerr (2001) articulates, "As society goes, so goes the university; but also, as the university goes, so goes society" (p. 194). Kerr's statement suggests an obligation on the behalf of the higher education community to carefully heed the national public dialogue in order to examine it, but also that institutions play a critical role in leading change.

Today, most college and university mission statements, while not always reflective of campus practices, include some language about preparation for citizenship or service to society. And in terms of outcomes, students who participate in college vote more and are incarcerated less (Perna, 2005). Yet these public outcomes are often pitted against the private purposes discussed above (i.e., economic reasons to train and educate) when they need not be. Both the US democracy and economy rely on a significant increase in the number and diversity of people finishing college with a high-quality degree or credential (College Board, 2008). Pitting public and private purposes against each other therefore creates an unnecessary and false dichotomy in the college completion agenda.

One place where this tension exists is within the framing of college completion in the context of the labor market. The college completion agenda is, in part, concerned with the ways in which the global work environment continues to evolve and workplace demand for postsecondary education increases. In President Obama's 2009 speech at Macomb Community College announcing the American Graduation Initiative, a plan that focuses on having an additional five million Americans earn degrees and certificates over ten years, the rhetoric centered on education for short-term outcomes. In particular, he spoke of training for specific jobs, with little mention of quality or longer-term outcomes, such as contributions to our democracy or an education that would prepare students for multiple jobs over a lifetime. For instance, Obama praised a Michigan program that is geared toward "training to become a medical technician, or a health IT worker, or a lab specialist, or a nurse" (White House Press Office, 2009).

A critical analysis of Obama's speech suggests that "college completion" is framed broadly to include both degrees and certificates, but the examples given focus more on certificates rather than degrees. While certificates do provide training for a job immediately following the program, these graduates—who are disproportionately students of color—often need to be retrained for the next job within a matter of years. During the 2007–8 academic year, for example, the share of black and Hispanic students earning certificates in short-term certificate programs (less than one year) and long-term certificate programs (one to four years) was 34.9% and 35.6%, respectively. This was a higher representation than was the case for blacks and Hispanics earning associate (23.5%) and bachelor degrees (17.3%; Bosworth, 2010). Meanwhile, the degree holders—who are disproportionately white, especially among bachelor degree recipients—are trained for a lifetime of jobs in a rapidly evolving economy. A critical analysis suggests that an unintended consequence of such an approach may be a further stratification of society.

The Rise in Institutional Differentiation

Related to the tension between the public and private purposes of higher education is the debate around the quality of higher education. A focus on completion tends to emphasize the finish line as measured by the number of students completing college, but it is less mindful of the importance of broad access and a responsibility to help all students obtain a degree or credential. In other words, there are ways in which the nation can experience a rise in the proportion of Americans with a college degree while also increasing the gaps in attainment between groups. A critical lens begs the questions: Where are students attending college? In which programs are they enrolling? Who is lost along the way? Attention must be paid to the entire pipeline and the range and quality of higher education institutions that are accessible for students who vary by race, class, and gender.

To this point, quality of learning varies widely within the US system of higher education, yet much of the focus on excellence relates to colleges and universities, while the focus on access, especially for low-income students of color, relates to community colleges. While American higher education has significantly expanded enrollment to meet the increased demand for college over the past sixty years, the rise in access to higher education has not necessarily been matched with equal access to a high-quality experience (Orfield & Miller, 1998). Colleges and universities and the academic programs within them have become increasingly differentiated with regard to content and quality. Marginalized groups are concentrated at the lower ranks of the postsecondary education system in programs with low quality of student learning and poor records of student completion, and the credentials from these places offer little value in the labor market (Carnevale & Stohl, 2013). As a result, while greater proportions of young people from all groups are entering college, large proportions of students who are attending low-quality programs fail to complete college.

There is a need for a more thoughtful dialogue across all sectors of higher education about how higher education can be equitable and excellent. This kind of dialogue should place greater emphasis on determining better measures for the quality of higher education—especially when it comes to teaching and learning practices as well as systems of advising—and finding ways to tailor education for each and every student.

Acknowledging Demographic Realities

A focus on each and every student requires a deeper understanding of the changing demography of the nation, as the United States is currently experiencing some of the most significant demographic changes in a century at the same time that inequality between groups is expanding rather than contracting.

The Salience of Race

The college completion agenda has had a limited focus on student demography, with institutional, state, and federal policies and programs concerned with how to accommodate and improve outcomes for an increasing proportion of college-going high school graduates. Yet much of these efforts have focused on students who are the first in their families to attend college, come from low-income families, or begin college academically underprepared for college-level coursework (ACT, 2011). An analysis of the language used in several of foundation reports about the completion agenda, however, suggests that demographic change is often discussed without reference to race. Considering the historical vestiges of race and racism in American higher education, it is important to examine how race is a factor in framing the college completion agenda.

The website of the Bill and Melinda Gates Foundation (2013), for example, says the following about their philanthropic work in higher education: "Our goal is to ensure that all low-income young adults have affordable access to a quality postsecondary education that is tailored to their individual needs and educational goals and leads to timely completion of a degree or certificate with labor-market value." Implicit in their stated goal is a focus on helping low-income students overcome barriers associated with class inequality. This is certainly a relevant issue considering the importance of education for labor-market outcomes. But what is not included in the Gates Foundation's statement about access to and success in higher education is reference to race and racism as structural factors that affect unequal educational outcomes (Bensimon, 2005). The term "structural" is purposefully used because it is indeed part of the process through which US federal policy, states, and practitioners in colleges and universities operate. Ching (2013) notes, for example, that while financial aid policies (e.g., Pell grants) exist to help support tuition for low-income students, no comparable policy exists for students of color. Further, racial and ethnic minorities have historically been legally prohibited from attending higher education institutions, whereas low-income students have not (Ching, 2013). These examples help to articulate why race needs to be at the fore of equity discussions or, at a minimum, part of the conversation. Yet, in looking across large-scale government and philanthropic policy priorities, there is generally infrequent reference to demographic data on race.

A Changing Demography: Context

The relevance of racial inequality is especially timely considering the United States is at the crossroads of tremendous demographic change. While the total US population more than doubled between 1950 and 2010—from 151 to 309 million, a faster rate of growth than any other industrialized nation in the world—it also experienced tremendous change with regard to its composition and profile. The US Census Bureau reports the majority of the increase in the US population

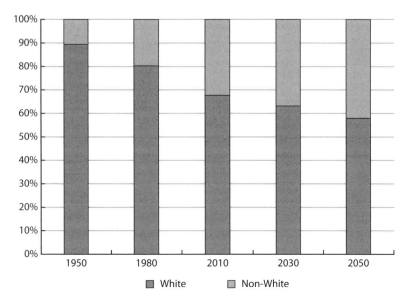

Figure 11.1. Actual and projected proportional representation of white and non-white populations in the United States, 1950–2050. *Note:* Figures for 1950 to 2010 are actual data; those for 2030 to 2050 are projection data. *Source:* US Census Bureau, Population Division.

is attributable to people who reported race as other than white. In 1950, about one in ten Americans was of a race other than white. By 2010, the share of the nonwhite population increased to about one in three (fig. 11.1). Projected changes in the population will render a new American "minority-majority" between the present day and 2050, with the white population projected to decrease to under half of the total population.

To further examine these demographic trends, it is important to look at the age distribution of the US population. William Frey at the Brookings Institution recently said of this phenomenon, "the white population is older and very much centered around the aging baby boomers . . . the future of America is epitomized by the young people today" (Ohlemacher, 2008). Frey said of America's youth, "they are basically the melting pot we are going to see in the future," an impact already being seen in the makeup of K–12 and higher education enrollment, especially in states like California, Hawaii, New Mexico, and Texas, as well as in Washington, DC, where minority populations have now exceeded 50%. In fact, about one in ten US counties currently have minority populations of 50% or greater, which is a 25% increase since 2000 (US Census Bureau, 2010).

Figure 11.1 depicts another demographic reality that cannot be underemphasized: the growth in minority groups. This change can be attributed largely to increases among Hispanics and Asian Americans and Pacific Islanders (AAPIs), with immigrants and their children being a significant factor in this demographic change (Teranishi, Suárez-Orozco, & Suárez-Orozco, 2011). In California, for instance, nearly all of the growth in the population between 2000 and 2010 can be attributed solely to Latinos and AAPIs (US Census Bureau, 2010). As of 2007, the foreign-born population doubled over the previous two decades to over thirty-eight million residents, representing 13% of the total US population (US Census Bureau, 2007). While the US population is projected to expand by 50% between 2010 and 2050, immigrants represent an estimated 82% of that growth (Passel, 2011).

Thus a critical analysis of the college completion agenda that calls for a focus on race and racial inequality is essential. Such a perspective shines a light on significant disparities that exist in educational opportunities and outcomes for marginalized and vulnerable populations. The changing demography of our nation must help to guide thinking about the higher education system and the nation's future more broadly.

Mitigating Racial Inequality

The shifting demographic landscape has a number of implications for directing more attention to equity in national education policy priorities. What researchers, policymakers, practitioners, and citizens do to rectify inequality in higher education is not only an essential component of the democratic mission of higher education, but a necessary one considering that the United States is in the midst of the most rapid demographic shift in history. It is within this context that the commitment of higher education to equity and social justice is instrumental and central to our higher education priorities.

While work is being conducted on a national level to reach equality of opportunities and outcomes for all students, researchers and policymakers must understand each of those groups individually in order to reach more widespread attainment goals (Teranishi, 2010). Unfortunately, one-size-fits-all practices of lumping together data for all students are often a mistake in that they produce policy choices and poor educational practices. According to Bensimon, Hao, and Bustillos (2006), "The reason for the absence of equity indicators is not lack of data, but that much of the available data are not disaggregated by race and ethnicity. Where the data are available, they are not reported in a manner that permits policymakers to make a quick assessment of the state of equity in higher education" (p. 157). The use of disaggregated data to inform educational practices is critical for achieving equitable outcomes in higher education and needs to be a deliberate and normalized practice at the institutional, state, and national level (National Commission on Asian American and Pacific Islander Research in Education, 2013).

Disaggregated data point to a widening gap between whites and racial minorities, as well as downward intergenerational mobility within racial minority groups. In some instances, the degree attainment gap has even grown over the past few decades. Analysis of data from the US Census Bureau reveals that between 1975 and 2005, four-year college degree attainment gaps for blacks and whites increased from 13% to 15%, the gaps between Latinos and whites increased from 15% to 24%, and the gaps between low- and high-income students increased from 31% to 62%. An effort to mitigate racial inequality is therefore timely and relevant to national priorities related to increasing degree attainment, which has been slow to change for some particular subgroups.

Disaggregated data also reveal that systemic social, political, and economic divisions have led to disproportionate gaps in educational attainment and workforce participation, and even downward intergenerational educational mobility for some minority subgroups (National Commission on Asian American and Pacific Islander Research in Education, 2013). Differences in intergenerational educational attainment can be seen in an age-cohort analysis of Pacific Islander subgroups compared to the national average. When comparing the educational attainment rates of 55- to 64-year-olds to 25- to 34-year-olds in the national cohort, a modest increase in bachelor's degree attainment can be seen (fig. 11.2). But data on Guamanians/Chamorro, Hawaiians, and Samoans show two disturbing trends: (1) the educational attainment of the younger generation of these populations is lower than that of the older generation, and (2) a widening gap exists between these Pacific Islander subgroups and the national average, thereby widening the attainment gap rather than closing it.

These trends of downward intergenerational mobility speak to the need for a concerted effort and a more central policy priority focused on racial inequality in higher education. It is also important to realize that this focus is not just relevant to the importance for the communities of color themselves, but also our nation as a whole. Consider higher education's historical commitment to helping produce an informed and engaged citizenry, which creates a more robust democracy for the entire nation.

If we as citizens are to take higher education's public purpose seriously, then what are the implications for the college completion agenda? A strong commitment to the public purpose of higher education suggests that colleges and universities

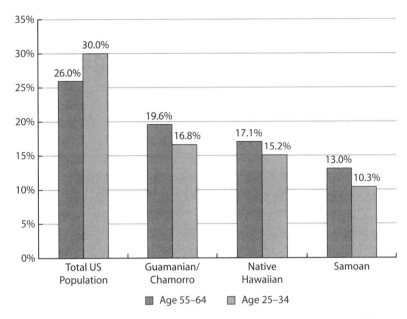

Figure 11.2. Age cohort analysis of college degree attainment for the total US population and selected Pacific Islander subgroups, 2008–10. *Source:* American Community Survey, Three-Year Public Use Microdata Sample, 2008–10.

actively work to mitigate disparities in educational outcomes for marginalized and vulnerable populations as a means to support the nation's democratic functioning. Achieving equitable outcomes in the college completion agenda requires policies and practices designed explicitly to reduce barriers currently facing young people from marginalized groups. Without an explicit approach to address these specific barriers, disparities between groups and the decline in the value and quality of higher education will persist, inhibiting progress for our higher education system as a whole.

Public-Private Partnerships to Mitigate Inequity

This focus on mitigating inequality means deeper, concerted understanding and responding to the barriers that contribute to inequitable outcomes for different student populations. Shifting toward such an approach requires a significant change in current priorities and practices at the federal, state, and institutional levels. In 2009, for example, the National Committee for Responsive Philanthropy found that fewer than one-third of education funders were directing funding to explicitly benefit marginalized communities, and only one out of ten foundations provided at least 25% of their grants to "advocacy, organizing and civic engagement" (Jagpal, 2009).

Now, to take a glass-half-full approach, we as authors would like to highlight promising partnerships and practices among policymakers, practitioners, philanthropy, and other key stakeholders to shift attention to equity in the college completion agenda. One partnership model that has been effective is a collaborative effort to build the capacity of minority-serving institutions (MSIs), including historically black colleges and universities, Hispanic-serving institutions, tribal colleges and universities, and Asian American and Native American Pacific Islander-serving institutions. Enrolling more than 2.5 million students annually—equivalent to one in five college students nationally—these institutions account for disproportionately large shares of undergraduate minority students (Gasman, Baez, & Turner, 2010). MSIs are an important sector of higher education as their numbers grow, fueled by the increase in minority students. This partnership has gotten the attention of policymakers, higher education advocacy organizations, and philanthropy as they recognize the relevance of MSIs to broader national priorities.

Conferring nearly a quarter million degrees annually, MSIs hold great potential for contributing to the broader goal of increasing college completion for the nation as a whole (Harmon, 2012). MSIs are considered places where investments can reach a critical mass of low-income minority students. Federal programs offer grants providing resources to address the unique challenges facing low-income students in college access and completion. Thus MSIs are a sector of higher education in which targeted investments can expand opportunities and improve outcomes for low-income minority students. A report from the Institute for Higher Education Policy (2012) states that "achieving college completion goals will take more than maintaining the status quo. Higher education will need to be innovative and open to alternative and diverse ways of approaching this issue. MSIs are already contributors to the national college completion goals and should be considered experts in the education of low-income, first generation, and underrepresented students."

But this approach is no "silver bullet." While MSIs hold great potential for contributing to broader higher education priorities, there is a need for the research community to parse where and how they have the most potential. Equally important is a research agenda in higher education that utilizes a critical lens to examine the distinctive impact of these institutions, particularly as they pertain to the use of federal grants and how they are leveraged to measure progress toward specific goals outlined for their funded programs.

In addition to the research community, strategic philanthropy can play a critical role in realizing the potential impact of MSIs. The MSI Funders' Group, for example, is a collective effort to understand and financially support MSIs and the students these institutions serve. The MSI Funders' Group aims to encourage innovative institutional practices, collaboration among institutions, transparency in outcomes, and accountability measures designed to increase student success—practices and outcomes that are critical for all postsecondary institutions (USA Funds, 2012). The core members of the MSI Funders' Group are the Lumina Foundation, USA Funds, the Kresge Foundation, and the Walmart Foundation, but the group also includes a number of other foundations that have participated in individual meetings.

Created in 2009 through a meeting at the Lumina Foundation, the MSI Funders' Group has meetings approximately three times a year that are hosted by different foundations and in many instances take place at MSI campuses. The group has invested substantially in efforts to support MSIs and the students they serve. The funding strategy has involved both individual and co-funded opportunities for foundations to support infrastructure development and programming at MSIs, as well as efforts to engage researchers, political leaders, funders, the higher education community, and the public. These forms of public-private partnerships are critical for a concerted effort to work toward equitable outcomes for minority students in higher education.

Conclusion

What has been effective in the college completion agenda is its ability to demonstrate the extent to which higher education is a key element of our domestic policy. What our education system does in the near future will determine our nation's long-term prosperity and our ability to compete in the global economy. Yet it is also important to recognize the nation's complacency with inequality and tolerance of a separate and unequal system of education. We need a catalyst to disrupt the status quo that can help our nation see the potential of a more accessible and equitable system of education. Equally important is the need for a movement that demonstrates the consequences of inaction. How we rectify inequality in education will determine our nation's future. The pursuit of this goal is not only an essential component of the democratic mission of higher education, but also a necessary one considering that we are in the midst of the most rapid demographic change in our nation's history.

Critical policy analysis has allowed us to better understand and articulate these inequitable conditions in higher education and the extent to which dominant policy frames respond to them. As a conceptual approach, critical theory has enabled us to address challenges associated with access, equity, and the stratification of postsecondary educational settings. We hope this chapter offered a forward thinking and proactive perspective on systemic cultural and political change through the application of critical policy analysis. We know that equity in higher education requires a significant shift in priorities and strategic planning. Using critical policy analysis, researchers, policymakers, and citizens can work toward effective policy solutions that include key allies and advocates from both within and outside of higher education to promote change in educational outcomes for students of color.

REFERENCES

ACT. (2011). *The condition of college and career readiness.* Washington, DC: Author.

Allan, E. J., Iverson, S. V., & Ropers-Huilman, R. (Eds.). (2010). *Reconstructing policy in higher education.* New York: Routledge.

Anderson, G. M. (2012). Equity and critical policy analysis in higher education: A bridge still too far. *Review of Higher Education, 36*(1), 133–42.

Bensimon, E. M. (2005). Closing the achievement gap in higher education. *New Directions for Higher Education, 2005*(131), 99–111.

Bensimon, E. M., Hao, L., & Bustillos, L. T. (2006). Measuring the state of equity in higher education. In P. Gandara, G. Orfield, & C. Horn (Eds.), *Leveraging promise and expanding opportunity in higher education* (pp. 143–64). Albany: State University of New York Press.

Bill and Melinda Gates Foundation. (2013). *Postsecondary success: Strategy overview.* Seattle, WA: Author. Retrieved from www.gatesfoundation.org/What-We-Do/US -Program/Postsecondary-Success.

Bosworth, B. (2010). *Certificates count: An analysis of sub-baccalaureate certificates.* Washington, DC: Complete College America.

Business Roundtable. (2009). *Getting ahead—Staying ahead: Helping America's workforce succeed in the 21st century.* Washington, DC: Author.

Carnevale, A. (2008). *College for all?* Stanford, CA: Carnegie Foundation for the Advancement of Teaching.

Carnevale, A., Smith, N., & Strohl, J. (2010). *Help wanted: Projections of jobs and education requirements through 2018.* Washington, DC: Georgetown University Center on Education and the Workforce.

Carnevale, A., & Stohl, J. (2013). *Separate and unequal: How higher education reinforces the intergenerational reproduction of white racial privilege.* Washington, DC: Center on Education and the Workforce.

Chase, M., Dowd, A., Bordoloi Pazich, L., & Bensimon, E. (2012). Transfer equity for "minoritized" students: A critical policy analysis of seven states. *Educational Policy, 7,* 1–49.

Ching, C. (2013). *Why race? Understanding the importance of foregrounding race and* ethnicity in achieving equity on college campuses. Los Angeles, CA: University of Southern California Center for Urban Education.

College Board. (2008). *Coming to our senses: Education and the American future*. New York: Author.

Gasman, M., Baez, B., & Turner, C. S. (2010). *Understanding minority-serving institutions*. Albany: State University of New York Press.

Harmon, N. (2012). *The role of minority-serving institutions in national college completion goals*. Washington, DC: Institute for Higher Education Policy.

Harper, S. (2012). *Men of color: A role for policymakers in improving the status of black male students in U.S. higher education*. Washington, DC: Institute for Higher Education Policy.

Iverson, S. V. (2007). Camouflaging power and privilege: A critical race analysis of university diversity policies. *Educational Administration Quarterly, 43*, 586–611.

Jagpal, N. (2009). *Criteria for philanthropy at its best: Benchmarks to assess and enhance grantmaker impact*. Washington, DC: National Committee for Responsive Philanthropy.

Kerr, C. (2001). *The uses of the university* (3rd ed.). Cambridge, MA: Harvard University Press.

King, P., & Mayhew, M. (2004). Theory and research on the development of moral reasoning among college students. *Higher Education: Handbook of Theory and Research, 19*, 375–440.

Lumina Foundation for Education. (2009). *Lumina Foundation's strategic plan: Goal 2025*. Indianapolis, IN: Author.

National Commission on Asian American and Pacific Islander Research in Education. (2013). *iCount: A data quality movement for Asian American and Pacific Islanders in higher education*. Princeton, NJ: Educational Testing Services.

NCHEMS. National Center for Higher Education Management Systems. (2010). *Closing the college attainment gap between the U.S. and most educated countries, and the contributions to be made by the states*. Boulder, CO: Author.

Ohlemacher, S. (2008, August 14). White Americans no longer a majority by 2042. *USA Today*. Retrieved from http://usatoday30.usatoday.com/news/topstories/2008-08-13-1800156177_x.htm.

Orfield, G., & Miller, E. (1998). *Chilling admissions: The affirmative action crisis and the search for alternatives*. Cambridge, MA: Harvard Education.

Passel, J. (2011). Demography of immigrant youth: Past, present, and future. *Future of Children, 21*(1).

Perna, L. (2005). The benefits of higher education: Sex, racial/ethnic, and socioeconomic group differences. *Review of Higher Education, 29*(1), 23–52.

Pusser, B., & Marginson, S. (2012). The elephant in the room: Power, global rankings and the study of higher education organizations. In M. Bastedo (Ed.), *The organization of higher education* (pp. 86–117). Baltimore: Johns Hopkins University Press.

Sabatier, P. A., & Jenkins-Smith, H. (1988). Policy change and policy oriented learning: Exploring an advocacy coalition framework [Special issue]. *Policy Sciences, 21,* 123–272.

Teranishi, R. T. (2010). *Asians in the Ivory Tower: Dilemmas of racial inequality in American higher education.* New York: Teachers College Press.

Teranishi, R. T., Suárez-Orozco, C., & Suárez-Orozco, M. (2011). Immigrants in community college: Toward greater knowledge and awareness. *Future of Children, 21*(1).

USA Funds. (2012) *Education partnerships.* Indianapolis, IN: Author.

US Census Bureau. (2007). *Selected characteristics of the native and foreign-born populations.* Washington, DC: American Community Survey.

———. (2010). *U.S. interim projections by age, sex, race, and Hispanic origin.* Washington, DC: Author.

White House Press Office. (2009, July 14). Remarks by the President on the American Graduation Initiative in Warren, MI. Retrieved from www.whitehouse.gov/the_press_office/Remarks-by-the-President-on-the-American-Graduation-Initiative-in-Warren-MI.

Zemsky, R., Wegner, G., & Massy, W. (2005). *Remaking the American university: Market-smart and mission-centered.* Piscataway, NJ: Rutgers University Press.

CHAPTER TWELVE

The New Stratification

Differentiating Opportunity by Race and Class at Community Colleges in the United States

GREGORY M. ANDERSON, RYAN P. BARONE,
JEFFREY C. SUN, AND NICHOLAS BOWLBY

Demographic shifts in the United States highlight the unequal distribution of access to higher education for an increasingly diverse populace. In fall 2013, the National Center for Education Statistics (NCES) reported that black and Hispanic college students enrolled at significantly higher rates at both community colleges and for-profit four-year colleges than public four-year colleges (NCES, 2013). The percentage of black students at public two-year colleges was 16%, and 28% at for-profit four-year colleges. By contrast, the percentage of black students at public four-year colleges was 12%. Similarly, the percentage of Hispanic students at public two-year colleges was 19% and 14% at for-profit four-year colleges, whereas the percentage of Hispanic students at public four-year colleges was just 13%. As the data suggest, societal barriers and bottlenecks still exist. Assuming that traditional public and private four-year institutions remain the highest-quality providers of postsecondary education, it is evident that the nation's system of access is not designed to meet the progressively complex needs of students who are working poor or low-income individuals from communities of color, often first-generation college goers. Thus we critically question policy actions about college access: Access to what?

As we discuss more fully below, government policies and sponsored initiatives such as foundation support for college completion have inadvertently exacerbated the access and quality conundrum. Much like a rising tide with levees at or exceeding capacity, a wave of unmet educational demand faces the nation. The ill fates that Lani Guinier and Gerald Torres (2003) forecasted are already appearing, such as the rationing of access (Rhoades, 2012b), skyrocketing default rates (US Department of Education, 2012), underemployed college graduates (Stone, Van Horn, & Zukin, 2012), and the emphasis on historically underfunded community colleges to solve the college access problems (NCES, 2013). These trends portend greater challenges ahead for policymakers, foundations, college administrators, and especially future college students.

Employing a critical approach that draws on the conceptual frameworks of equity and crisis management, we offer an interdisciplinary interrogation of the current policy rhetoric and projections about college access in light of the demographic shifts currently taking place and forecasted to present much more drastic changes in the near future. We further assert that the extant literature and policy solutions regarding the equity and opportunity challenges facing higher and postsecondary education in the twenty-first century have yet to address adequately either the serious pedagogical realities or severe resource constraints characterizing the stratified or unequal educational opportunities afforded to predominantly low-income and diverse students attending community colleges in the United States. Accordingly, our analysis, which challenges conventional policy approaches that quickly resort to technocratic solutions,[1] is primarily concerned with the educational experiences of students who are most economically vulnerable, disproportionally enrolled at community colleges, and significantly represented at propriety schools. Building off of earlier calls for a reexamination of educational access and opportunities (see, e.g., Nighaoui, 2007; Noguera, 2011; Yeakey & Bennett, 1990), this chapter focuses on the educational opportunities of the working poor and low-income students, who are disproportionately from communities of color and often first-generation college attendees.

To present our arguments, we have examined policy reforms aimed at public community colleges in part because of a growing congruence of approach and rhetoric shared by both government and major funding agencies touting technocratic solutions. These solutions most often revolve around strategies that present concrete evidence of educational progress as decisive indicators to the college equity dialogue. As such, these indicators appear to reduce time to degree or promote certification through credit recovery with the intention of fast-tracking a student body predominantly from communities of color and immigrant and low-income backgrounds into the labor market (Bastedo & Jaquette, 2011; Bowles, Gintis, & Groves, 2009; Goldrick-Rab, 2006; Goldrick-Rab & Pfeffer, 2009). We posit that, absent a significant and sustained investment in nonselective institutions, these "low-hanging-fruit" policy strategies may lead to unintended consequences and contradictory goals that uniformly fail to improve the overall quality of educational experiences of students who are most likely first-generation college attendees, low income, or individuals of color. This unintended and contradictory scenario is likely manifested in more apparent ways at two-year institutions, which are forced to compete for scarce state and federal funding.

Conceptual Framework

Critical theory guides this chapter; notions of competing equity and stratification, which are illuminated by insights from crisis management, offer a conceptual framework. Our use of critical theory directs us not only to critique the largely undissected US educational milieu and the associated neoliberal policy solutions, but also to offer recommendations as a site for resistance and transformation of the status quo. In addition to challenging conventional policy approaches in US education, we are similarly critical of the increasing methodological hegemony used to address important questions related to access, retention, and educational culture. Too often, epistemological and ontological assumptions remain unstated, thereby reinforcing a methodological status quo functioning to maintain oppressive systems (Gildersleeve et al., 2010; Guido, Chávez, & Lincoln, 2010). Most published literature in higher education tends to have predictable findings using conservative methods (Gildersleeve et al., 2010). Nonetheless, "educational leaders cannot afford to be complacent in this climate of educational inequity and let dominant arguments about higher education prevail" (Pasque et al., 2012, p. 7). We therefore encourage scholars and policymakers to embrace more transformative frameworks to inform equity-minded methodological approaches. Diverse methodological approaches present scholarly opportunities to help realize aspirational educational ideals for the success of all students in the leaky educational pipeline.

We believe that the combination of critical theory with a conceptual framework of equity and stratification offers a lens through which to view the proliferation of technocratic solutions in addressing long-standing educational challenges in the United States. Briefly, technocratic solutions apply a private sector cost-benefit analysis using a simple input/output quantitative measure to determine success in public education (Darder, 2005). This myopic approach is ill conceived and misapplied chiefly to community colleges and their open-access missions. We call for contestation and scrutiny into the technocratic policy rhetoric surrounding equity. Equity as a concept has largely supplanted equality-related discourses, reflecting a historically contextualized understanding that equal is not always equitable, and is often void of a commitment to social justice (American Association of Colleges and Universities, 2011; Espinoza, 2007). Despite growing rhetorical popularity, current US manifestations of meritocracy, color-blindness, and the master narrative of the American dream often mitigate longitudinal and social justice goals of equity (Akom, 2008; Anderson, 2005; Fine et al., 2003; Sun & Daniel, 2013). Whether discussing economic meltdowns, resegregation trends, recent

US Supreme Court decisions, or anti-immigration legislation, we are witnessing new distress signals of social stratification.

Crisis management organizational theories in the United States illuminate the social responses to such challenges, trends, and incidents. As a critical lens to examine policy rhetoric, crisis management uncovers the issue framing and social responses. Crisis management research has gained prominence in part because of public health concerns in the 1980s and has expanded to become an interdisciplinary framework for understanding organizational behavior (Simola, 2005). Similarly, this general approach has been applied to uncover political and cultural origins and unintended impacts of educational and labor policies in the United States (Skrentny, 1996).

When combining the lens of competing equity and crisis management, we contend that community colleges are increasingly serving the educationally advantaged at the expense of students from communities of color as well as immigrant and low-income backgrounds bereft of support mechanisms to enhance educational opportunities before entering the labor market. We explore how responses from both the federal government and large philanthropic foundations have advanced a policy narrative that, while contributing to the equity dialogue, does not sufficiently address the question of improving educational quality for poor and working-class students from communities of color and immigrant backgrounds.

Stratification and Community Colleges

From their inception, two-year institutions in the United States have served multiple purposes and missions (Bailey, 2002; Bailey & Morest, 2004; Cohen & Brawer, 2008). These missions have primarily featured two different trajectories for students. On the one hand, the origins of community colleges were firmly rooted in more career and vocational philosophies and objectives, generating associate and terminal degrees as well as certificates (Grubb et al., 1999; Grubb, Badway, & Bell, 2003). On the other hand, community colleges have also long served as transfer institutions for less resourced students seeking access to four-year institutions and the eventual acquisition of a baccalaureate degree (Cohen & Brawer, 2008). These two paths to a degree, forever synonymous with community colleges, are an expression of the pragmatic Dewey-inspired notion of the purpose of education and the aspirational, achievement-oriented ideology of the United States (Dewey, 1916, 1938). Dewey, a foundational public education scholar and ideologue of the 19th and 20th centuries, believed that through education "society can formulate its own purposes, can organize its own means and resources, and thus shape itself with definiteness and economy in the direction in which it wishes to move" (Dewey, 1897, p. 80). His aspirations for a democratic and accessible educational system (Dewey, 1897) helped lay a foundation for the estab-lishment of the first community college, Joliet Junior College founded in 1901.

For nearly a century, community colleges—depending on the economic and political conditions—have swung like a pendulum between these two possibili-ties and philosophies. Given their history, it should therefore come as little sur-prise that in the twenty-first century—with the country facing rapid technologi-cal innovation, globalization, vast financial instability, consistent poverty, major demographic change, and policy debate about college costs—community colleges have once again emerged as one of the core institutions undergirding US higher education policy.

Selective Policy Pathways

State-level analysis has revealed that low–socioeconomic status (SES) students are overrepresented in less selective institutions, chiefly community colleges with lower graduation rates, even when their academic abilities indicate that more highly selective universities would be a better match (Bowen, Chingos, & McPher-son, 2009; Tinto, 1973). Moreover, family income and parental education are both inversely related to the likelihood of attending a community college as opposed to a four-year college (Grodsky & Jackson, 2009). Four-year institutions, particu-larly highly selective ones, have therefore contributed little in the way of significant equity-driven solutions, as these universities and colleges continue to underen-roll poor and working-class students from communities of color and immigrant backgrounds (Anderson, 2005; Anderson, Sun, & Alfonso, 2006; Dowd, Cheslock, & Melguizo, 2008). As a result, "the exclusion of poor, working-class, and racial/ ethnic minority students from elite institutions reduces the probability that these students will enter positions of power in society" (Dowd et al., 2008, p. 444). Conversely, low-income students and students from communities of color (in-cluding those with immigrant backgrounds) are significantly represented in open-admission community colleges, and they are the most likely to leave higher education without earning a credential (Bowen et al., 2009; Goldrick-Rab, 2006).

Such "cooling out" of college aspirations is occurring in more stratified ways and much earlier in the educational pipeline, which is functionally a pyramid with gateways between each educational transition point (Anderson, Alfonso, & Sun, 2006; Sun & Daniel, 2013). Public education in the United States is more stratified on the basis of race, language, and SES today than it was in the 1950s, when the US Supreme Court heard the case of *Brown v. Board of Education* (1954) (see Darling-Hammond, 2010; Gándara, 2010; Oseguera & Astin, 2004; Rhoades, 2012a). In other words, what we are seeing is a new stratification in higher education, one that is nuanced and multipronged. Numerous factors in the aggregate cause this stratification and continue to generate inequitable educational pathways to success. The educational stratification that we consider utilizes a longitudinal view of the hierarchy of inequality over many generations in relation to efforts to enhance meaningful access to quality postsecondary opportunities (Duncan, 1968).

Over time, from a policy perspective, these efforts have moved significantly toward a more technocratic focus on achieving numerical targets that increasingly associate outcomes with success, without first adequately defining what constitutes a quality education and equitable experience afforded marginalized students. As a consequence, efforts to improve outcomes have ironically been placed aside to the preoccupation of an underlying and historical problem characterizing both public schools and two-year colleges: a chronic lack of funding by state and federal governments. In so doing, equity, although increasingly valued rhetorically in government and philanthropic reports, "is not measured in relation to educational outcomes for traditionally marginalized students in higher education" (Harris & Bensimon, 2007, p. 79). In addressing equity, the data tend to be fused with mean completion outputs, masking the demographic stratification and larger historical campus cultures designed by and for the dominant upper-middle-class voice (Museus & Jayakumar, 2012). The effect of such oversight is the continuing, unproblematized issue of educational equity in terms of the overall quality of educational experiences for poor and working-class students from communities of color and immigrant backgrounds.

Educational access is not a zero-sum game. As the data demonstrate, low-SES students have matriculated to postsecondary education at higher rates over the last four decades. Low-SES students are overrepresented in two-year colleges, however, and high-SES students are overrepresented in elite, selective universities (Bastedo & Jaquette, 2011; Lee, 2013). For example, only 3% of students from the lowest economic quartile enroll at elite universities (Carnevale & Rose, 2004). This socioeconomic tracking can be traced to postsecondary education, as students who attend schools with mostly high-SES students are 68% more likely to enroll at a four-year college than students who attend schools with mostly low-SES students (Palardy, 2013). What is revealing about these findings is that an emphasis on access has given way to a greater focus on targeted interventions to improve outcomes and reduce gaps as a way to address the framed crisis. As a result, the "underachievement of low SES students and students of color through the utilization of purported objective measures [continue to inadvertently] privilege high SES students and white students" (Darder, 2005, p. 215).

Few committed to an equity agenda would question the need for community colleges to improve graduation and transfer rates, especially in light of two-year institutions' tendency to serve as the primary vehicles for access to higher education for students of color and low-SES students. Yet a major concern regarding the positing of an outcome (increasing graduation) to address an underlying problem (attrition) is that such a policy approach presupposes the existence of a significant and sustained investment strategy to transform the ways students are taught, how they learn most effectively, and how to accurately and equitably assess their learning. Failing to attend to these critical and long-standing challenges at community colleges while positing ambitious goals is at best unrealistic, and at worst capable of generating contradictory and paradoxical policy outcomes.

The epicenter of the new stratification in higher education is community colleges, with their diverse and historically marginalized student bodies. Rhoades (2012b) is particularly critical of the trend of community colleges rationing access, citing California, Florida, Illinois, and Michigan as having collectively denied access to more than 400,000 interested students in 2012. This rationing of access has the most profound impact on low-SES students and students of color (Rhoades, 2012b). Because it appears that two-year institutions will continue to bear the brunt of responsibility for educating our most marginalized students in society, our approach is to draw critical attention to the policy fault lines and core challenges facing community colleges, beginning with remediation and developmental education.

Remediation and Developmental Education

Though often erroneously used interchangeably, "remedial" refers to remedying or correcting specific skill sets, whereas developmental education relates to developing or growing a competency area (Parker, Bustillos, & Behringer, 2010). Most community college students, 50%–60%, are required to take at least one developmental education course (Bailey, Jeong, & Cho, 2010; Bailey & Cho, 2010). Of these students who have graduated from high school or secured a general educational development (or GED) diploma, less than one-quarter complete a degree or certificate within eight years of community college enrollment (Bailey & Cho, 2010). College-level math proves particularly cumbersome, as three out of four students who enroll in a remedial mathematics course never progress out of the remediation sequence, which functionally serves as a gatekeeper—or perhaps more accurately as a metaphorical trapdoor (George, 2010). Not surprisingly,

Bailey and Cho (2010) assert that "addressing the needs of developmental students is perhaps the most difficult and most important problem facing community colleges" (p. 1).

The policy challenge related to remediation and developmental education is exacerbated when examining the immense costs associated with these programs. States spend tens of millions of dollars on remediation and developmental education, with rough national estimates suggesting over $1 billion spent annually (Bailey & Cho, 2010). But these expenditures do not accurately reflect the substantial costs that students bear. Opportunity costs, debt, and increasing student-loan defaults are components of the virtually immeasurable costs related to remediation and developmental education for students (Bailey & Cho, 2010). These factors are acutely devastating to the working poor and low-income individuals who are often from communities of color (Anderson, 2002).

Because successful solutions to the proliferation of the resource-intensive and largely unsuccessful remediation and developmental education are elusive, some historical contextualization is advised to capture contesting notions of equity. US colleges have engaged in remediation and developmental education virtually since inception; Harvard and Yale had such programs as early as the 1700s (Parker et al., 2010). In the early 1900s, the educational debate in the United States included stratification, though it revolved around a more fundamental question: Is it in the best interest of the country for all to have access to any discipline? Or, a view more poplar at the time, should new immigrants and low-income people be tracked into secondary vocational curricula? Rhoades (2012b) asserts that this fundamental and historical question is similar to today's debates, merely substituting "high school" for "community college." This contextualizing of contemporary issues with history is essential as educational leaders and policymakers engage in decisions that affect the future direction of US education and investigate and implement policy changes related to remediation and developmental education.

Standardized Testing

A key component inextricably linked to issues of remediation and developmental education in community colleges is the tool used for such placement and standardized testing leading to curricular stratification (Price & Roberts, 2008). Increasingly, prestigious programs at community colleges are erecting barriers to entry, seeking to avoid the enrollment of students with remedial and developmental education needs (Ludwig, 2011). As the crisis has elevated, one symptom of the technocratic climate in higher education is the proliferation of standard-

ized testing. Escalating tuition and an increasing focus and utilization of standardized tests are primary reasons for education stratification, as preparedness
remains the greatest predictor of college access and choice (Alon, 2009). Despite
the biases found in standardized tests, and the role tests play in creating education barriers for low-SES students, a comprehensive and critical examination
of the contemporary uses and impact of standardized tests has not satisfactorily
occurred in higher education (Alon, 2009). Although not purportedly used as an
admissions screening tool in open-access community colleges, these standardized tests nonetheless determine functional access to the college curriculum; the
exams thus function in essentially the same manner.

Despite the minimal oversight, the standardized testing industry has substantial influence on the dominant educational narrative in education. The rhetoric
of declining efficiency of public schools was similarly used in the early 1900s to
legitimate big business taking control of public education (Darder, 2005). Today,
many corporate leaders hold hostage the enterprise of public education in exchange for tax hikes and budget increases. Leaders advocate and mandate public
educational collusion with the standardized testing industry as a key lever in a
technocratic accountability movement couched by equity rhetoric (Darder, 2005).
As Darder (2005) asserts, "This veiled moralism that unwittingly permeates educational discourse and the acceptance of high stakes testing actually socializes
populations to accept uncritically the inferiority of the other and the need for
corrective action, in order to assure the participation of the majority within the
labor market as rightful citizens of this nation" (p. 221).

A compelling case for the intersection of community colleges as equity institutions, the influence of standardized testing as a crisis management response,
and stratification as an outgrowth is seen in the history and current status of
several state or metropolitan systems, including the City University of New York,
or CUNY (Anderson, 2002; Foderaro, 2011; Friedlander, 2010; Hilliard & Spaic,
2013; Lavin & Hyllegard, 2006). Founded in 1847 as the Free Academy of the City
of New York, CUNY was originally designed to give poor and working-class students access to high-quality education throughout the five boroughs of New York
City (Gallagher, 2010). From 1969 to 1999, CUNY's open-access mission resulted
in racial diversification of the overall student body, but it came with backlash over
concerns of low academic standards and decreased rigor (Friedlander, 2010; Gallagher, 2010; Lavin & Hyllegard, 2006). In response, CUNY adopted a system-
wide standardized testing policy in 1999; the policy functionally erected a barrier
to four-year university matriculation (Anderson, 2002; Tsao, 2005). Standardized
testing and the creation of admissions barriers, as seen with the newest institu-

tion in the CUNY system, the New Community College, function to create a two-tier system in CUNY largely based on race and SES (Dowd, Pak, & Bensimon, 2013; Foderaro, 2011; Meade, 2012; Pérez-Peña, 2012). Nonetheless, as Anderson (2002) and Diamond (2007) argue, the equity narrative within the high-stakes testing literature fails to address the need to focus on the educational learning environment as its central point of inquiry and primary site for intervention, investment, and reform.

Major Educational Funding Initiatives and the New Stratification

In the previous section, we articulated ways in which stratification has been exhibited among traditionally identified barriers to community college students when equity has been presented at the issue of concern but technocratic solutions have been the crisis management approach of choice. While presenting those traditional access barriers, we introduced elements of the new stratification as concretized in pathways policies, remedial and developmental education, and standardized testing. In this section, we further develop the concepts of the new stratification. Specifically, we examine how certain federal and philanthropic funding initiatives have contradictorily contributed to the oft-cited equity agenda.

Federal Funding Initiatives

Federal education reform agenda are inherently tied to reelection cycles and the political climate of the day, and they typically represent massive unfunded mandates pushed by technocratic philosophies related to accountability (Rhoades, 2012a). Policymakers are drawn to easy and quick solutions, as complexity is "difficult to sell politically . . . Untidy pictures do not lend themselves to simple solutions" (Eisner, 2002, p. 6). Federal higher education policies introduced by President Obama and the US Department of Education have recently rallied around the completion agenda. But these policies do not support educational quality concerns as part of holistic credential and graduation policies at community colleges (Tuckley, 2011). The push for degrees without sufficient attention to quality raises concerns that higher education may be furthering an overcredentialed workforce that is bereft of sufficient knowledge, skills, and abilities to address workforce needs. This credentialing dilemma will likely harm ethnic minority college graduates who are from working poor and low-income families without the professional networks to easily secure alternative employment if narrow and antiquated skill sets become stale. One might argue that the recently commissioned Equity and Excellence Commission within the US Department of Education (2013) will lead to sufficient educational reforms that close the achievement gap. But we contend that this group of twenty-seven members constituting the "transformational" team offers only a starting point through symbolic action. As constructed, it fails to maintain sufficient power to plan for scalability at the national level, flexibility in addressing local and cultural needs, and sustainability, especially through sufficient long-term funding.

Practically speaking, federal funding initiatives in education are mostly concerned with a P–14 view of education, and they fail to envision the more holistic P–20 view necessary for systemic reform. This failure to engage with necessary systemic reforms can be seen in the tendency to celebrate a few outliers for success (Giltner & Barber, 2013; Murray, 2011). The government frequently points to a handful of community colleges with impressive retention and graduation data without acknowledging the often-regional context for that success, including nonscalable resources (US Department of Labor, 2013). Similarly, federal policies have consequences that fail to properly address societal problems. In other words, while the policy goals themselves present worthy objectives, the lack of forethought and careful attention to what would be required to make these objectives a real and scalable possibility have been absent in the funding initiatives and policy mandates focused on college completion. Specific federal funding initiatives further exemplify this trend.

FEDERAL FUNDING POLICIES INFLUENCING HIGHER EDUCATION

Federal Policy Pronouncements and Selective Career Training Initiatives. The governmental "politics of projections" direct pronouncements regarding two-year institutions toward unrealistic goals for college completion (White House, 2013). For example, in January 2010 during his State of the Union address, President Obama explicitly mentioned community colleges, as he has done throughout his presidency, when he asserted that "we're also revitalizing America's community colleges . . . if we raise expectations for every child, and give them the best possible chance at an education . . . [by 2020] America will once again have the highest proportion of college graduates in the world" (Fuller, 2010). The strategies offered by the Obama administration in achieving these goals are quintessentially technocratic in nature. First, the Trade Adjustment Assistance Community College and Career Training Program is chiefly concerned with industry partnerships focused on workforce readiness, relying on a modest $500 million (White House, 2013). Second, Skills for America's Future, an initiative born out of the October 2010 White House Summit on Community Colleges, is a similar initiative based on private-public partnerships aimed at narrowly tailored worker technical skill development. Finally, in his 2013 budget request, President Obama proposed the Community College to Career Fund, an $8 billion investment in business partnerships to train workers in high-growth and constantly evolving areas such as health care and logistics (White House, 2013).

In the first year of the Obama administration, more funding was allocated to community colleges than in recent decades (Rhoades, 2012b). In so doing, however, the funding priorities have changed as they have "shifted from the Department of Education to the Department of Labor, and focused entirely on workforce development" (Rhoades, 2012b, p. 18). The focus on workforce development on its face is satisfactory, but functionally it serves to track low-income students and students of color into myopic and volatile vocational jobs. These graduates may be employed now, but their work skills will need retooling as technology and society evolve. This change illustrates that community colleges face limits in fulfilling other components of their equity-driven mission, and it demonstrates the tenuous nature of government-supported initiatives because they lack sustainability and capacity building to serve properly the needs of working poor and low-income students, who are also disproportionately from communities of color.

FEDERAL FUNDING POLICIES INFLUENCING P–12 EDUCATION

No Child Left Behind. P–12 education policies also illustrate the technocratic role of the federal government and the purported interests in furthering an equity agenda. The stated purpose of No Child Left Behind (NCLB) was to "ensure that all children have a fair, equal, and significant opportunity to obtain a high-quality education and reach, at a minimum, proficiency on challenging state academic achievement standards and state academic assessments" (NCLB, 2002). But criticisms of NCLB illustrate another equity issue; they are typically related to the tools measuring the quality of education and the lack of investment in improving quality (Sherman, 2008). Indeed, the federal government has consistently failed to provide the amount of funding NCLB requires (Driscoll & Fleeter, 2003; Duncombe, Lukemeyer, & Yinger, 2008; Minnici & Hill, 2007).

In addition, achievement is measured only by students' performance on annual multiple-choice reading and math tests. Teachers are subsequently compelled to teach "to the test" owing to the fear that their students will perform badly, resulting in the school's failure to make "adequate yearly progress" and potentially leading to their termination (Jennings, 2012). By teaching to the test, many students fail to receive a creative, personally relevant, and well-rounded curriculum (Beveridge, 2010; Jennings, 2012). Because of the intense focus on math and reading proficiency, fewer resources and time are devoted to subjects such as art, physical education, social studies, and science (Beveridge, 2010; Jennings, 2012). Finally, differences by state about the definitions and assessments of proficiency make it cumbersome to compare data on a nationwide scale.

In early 2010 and again on March 14, 2011, President Obama said he would seek to reauthorize NCLB, though as "flawed law" it would be modified to be similar to his $4.35 billion Race to the Top initiative discussed below (US Department of Education, 2010). Building on the call by researchers and other education stakeholders involving the need for policies to address the racial achievement gaps (Smyth, 2008), one of the stated key priorities within Obama's blueprint for reform is equity and opportunity for students of color and low-SES students. Nonetheless, as Sun and Daniel (2013) observe, even with policy mandates, an educational quality problem correlated with patterns of segregation exists, as the achievement data continue to demonstrate significant gaps in terms of race and income. Data suggest that segregated schools demonstrate probabilities of lower performance in reducing the racial achievement gap than integrated schools (Stiefel, Schwartz, & Chellman, 2007). Yet, recently, proactive policies aimed at integrating schools through diversity initiatives have failed in the courts (*Parents Involved in Community Schools v. Seattle*, 2007; US Department of Education, 2011).

Race to the Top. Race to the Top (RTTT) represents one of the most dramatic policy changes in the history of US education (Kolbe & Rice, 2012; McGuinn, 2012; Nicholson-Crotty & Staley, 2012). As an entrepreneurial policy that promoted federal access into school reform initiatives, the federal government incentivized states to chase a prize few could win, and as a result it has made a technocratic agenda attractive and prestigious. The program was created to push states to compete for funding rather than simply receiving disbursements based on a predetermined formula, so states must apply and be awarded RTTT funds. Funding is tied to states' actions toward five criteria: (1) designing and implementing rigorous standards, (2) attracting and retaining quality teachers, (3) maintaining data systems, (4) spurring innovation and using reported effective strategies to address struggling schools, and (5) demonstrating sustainability of reforms (White House, 2009).

Although these criteria emerge from selected successes as reported in educational research, the RTTT efforts present conflicting interests that may not produce the intended outcomes, especially for students at struggling schools (Kolbe & Rice, 2012; McGuinn, 2012). For instance, the teacher quality criterion seeks to link teacher compensation to students' test scores. Given resource constraints facing English language learning, special education, and general physical infrastructure improvements, underresourced urban schools, which often dispropor-tionately educate low-income students from communities of color and immigrant backgrounds, continue to face the greatest challenges to attaining educational gains. Concomitantly, teacher attraction and retention rates are also some of the weakest in such environments, leading to less qualified teachers being employed in the most underresourced and lowest-performing schools (Lankford, Loeb, & Wyckoff, 2002).

By introducing P–12 examples, our main point is to highlight how techno-cratic and market principles undergirding competition for scarce resources have uniformly failed to improve the overall quality of learning opportunities for the most marginalized students in the nation (Frankenberg, Siegel-Hawley, & Wang, 2011; Kolbe & Rice, 2012; McGuinn, 2012). The technocratic tendencies of P–12 policies strongly encourage business leaders, educators, and other stakeholders to collaborate to close the achievement gap (US Department of Education, 2009b). Nonetheless, past practices of this sort have led to the proliferation of educational management organizations and charter schools that feed into, rather than amelio-rate, stratification (Miron et al., 2010). For instance, the data are overwhelmingly less flattering when measuring the impacts on working poor, racial minorities, and immigrants—including those students who attend public schools that have re-ceived reduced funding as the introduction of charter school allocations dilute the available education funds (Frankenberg et al., 2011; Renzulli & Evans, 2005).

The RTTT also demonstrates a technocratic funding priority. The most evi-dent of this technocratic approach is the criteria referencing data-based decision making, or what the US Department of Education (2009a) calls "Supporting data systems that inform decisions and improve instruction." This criterion translates into requisite curriculum, including textbooks and specific subject matter, which are chosen on the basis of statistical data presumably derived from materials and approaches designed to produce the best test scores on national standardized tests. A data-driven approach to evaluating curriculum necessarily minimizes, or eliminates, school district and teacher discretion as well as state and local pref-erences and differences. Critics, both conservative and liberal, bitterly lament the loss of local and state control over curriculum and an ever-narrowing per-spective that nullifies critical human judgment and input while promoting edu-cational conformity.

Philanthropic Funding Initiatives

Stanley Katz (2012) of Princeton University once described the actions of large philanthropic organizations as akin to capital venture investors where grantees, like start-ups, "are required to specify measurable outcomes that can be achieved over the short term" (p. 12; see also Parry, Field, & Supiano, 2013). Given that perspective, it is not surprising that many philanthropic foundations are touting a technocratic approach that focuses more on numerical outcomes at the expense of addressing beneficiary experiences and improving the overall quality of teaching and learning. To a degree, such a shift is not surprising, especially when factoring in Katz's analogy involving venture capital and investments that are geared toward short-term (rather than long-term) goals associated with addressing age-old problems such inequality, racial segregation, corruption, and the inequitable distribution of resources. Yet these relatively predetermined quick-fix solutions may have no effect on narrowing the achievement gap. The Bill and Melinda Gates Foundation learned this lesson after a $2 billion investment to create small urban schools was deemed no more successful in terms of performance than their large-school counterparts (Ravitch, 2008).

Critical of large philanthropic foundations in the United States, Roelofs (2003) argues that foundations play a major role in directing a narrative and producing consensus. The power of foundations is understudied, and the nature of their gatekeeper and funding roles dissuade criticism. Moreover, they intentionally distance themselves from their corporate connections and claim neutrality (Katz, 2012; Ravitch, 2008). Similarly, Lederman (2012) observes that critics of the Gates and Lumina Foundations call them the "completion mafia" because they have purportedly "hijacked the national agenda for higher education and drowned out alternative perspectives" (p. 2). Roelofs (2003) takes this critique further by stating that, although foundations may intend to initiate changes seeking educational quality and true learning value, they tend to address symptoms through incrementalism rather than through a meaningful, comprehensive, and sustained institutional change strategy or agenda. Furthermore, the aspirational goals of large philanthropic foundations have political utility and galvanize funders to support a particular reform direction, such as the privatization of education, teacher effectiveness, or postsecondary workforce development.

According to Roelofs (2003), the scope of educational foundations cannot be overstated: "it is hardly an exaggeration to say that foundations have been the source of almost all innovations in education . . . using their normal methods of influence: Ideology, grants, litigation, policy networks and think tanks, and the revolving door" (p. 70). In effect, this process legitimizes a policy perspective, allowing the foundations and their sponsored centers to continue to function and flourish as well as influence and shape the educational reform agenda (Katz, 2012; Lederman, 2012; Ravitch, 2008). This tendency to legitimize a particular policy agenda or direction is especially salient in the sphere of US education, as a consistent feature of the P–20 environment is the a lack of federal authority and constitutional responsibility for ensuring equitable resources for all students regardless of their race, ethnicity, national origin, linguistic diversity, gender, socioeconomic statue, or zip code.

The Technocratic Agenda Moving Forward

An unproblematized reform agenda that spuriously correlates technocratic solutions with equity and social justice increasingly affects federal education policymakers, prominent US philanthropic foundations, and leaders in higher education. This agenda represents an economic strategy informed by the current manifestation of US free market capitalism (Singh, 2011). Such action is evident as seen through the US Department of Education privileging quantitative, quasi-experimental research to solve educational problems (Flinders, 2005). Flinders somewhat comically notes that "the Department of Education seeks to restore scientific research to a position it never lost for the purpose of gaining benefits it never achieved" (Flinders, 2005, p. 388). Similarly, Singh (2011) critically questions the relationship between what appears to be a growing obsession with enhancing data systems (particularly at the statewide and macro or interinstitutional levels) and policies to achieving equity.

At the macro level, neoliberal thinking supports a technocratic hegemony that centers privatization, efficiency, and economic rationality as the solutions to educational issues (Apple, 2001). Illustrating technocraticism in the higher education setting, Sullivan (2011) points to educational entrepreneurialism in activities in which educational administrators no longer direct policy in response primarily to student needs. Instead, college administrators feed into an emergent strategic planning model based on client/consumer satisfaction and accountability, which are hallmarks of profit-motivated private sector organizations (Dungy & Ellis, 2011). The technocratic agenda thus uncritically prioritizes outcomes as a means to improve the overall quality of learning opportunities afforded the most marginalized students. In so doing, there is a dangerous tendency to assume that, in addressing the symptoms of a system in dire need of transformation, we as a nation are seriously tackling and overcoming core problems that continue to plague quality and undermine equity. Because the model of US higher education has, for significant periods of time, been focused on universal public access, it would appear that an outcomes-based approach premised on accelerating time to completion and creating new pathways for success is an important and much-needed step forward. However, as quality educational opportunities continue to be rationed at the four-year level and now are also beginning to be tiered at community colleges, for-profit institutions have quickly emerged as free market alternatives to fill the gap between student demand and postsecondary supply.

The technocratic turn in policy, with its emphasis on mechanical solutions such as credit recovery schemes through improved data systems capable of identifying and recapturing institutionally polygamous and "swirling" students in the system, is in our view a slight-of-hand reform trick that occludes answering the hard and persistent questions concerned with equity and quality. There are many questions: For whom is mainstream US higher education set up to serve? What is the impact of neoliberal policies on the equity agenda? How are privilege, power, and oppression woven into the campus cultures in US higher education? How have mainstream educational foundations colluded with an oppressive educational status quo? What core competencies are required in the twenty-first century to ensure that postsecondary credentials, certificates, and degrees correlate most effectively with the new labor market opportunities of the US economy? What is the best way to deliver quality instruction to an increasingly diverse student body, and what kinds of investments are required to ensure equitable outcomes at community colleges? What safeguards must be built into higher and postsecondary education systems to minimize and punish—as opposed to inadvertently incentivize and tolerate—unscrupulous and predatory practices of some for-profits?

Recommendations

In an effort to address the critical questions raised above, we offer a few macro and micro recommendations as a way to begin to think more meaningfully and tangibly about postsecondary success in the twenty-first century.

RETHINKING THE METRICS: AN OPPORTUNITY TO DO THE RIGHT THING?

A technocratic culture that facilitates an overreliance on rankings, such as that of *US News & World Report*, must be problematized and analyses extended to include social justice and equity outcomes. As it currently stands, the metrics for such rankings actually function to dissuade universities from admitting high numbers of deserving, albeit marginalized, students so as to benefit most from selectivity measures that enhance status and prestige. Yet it would be naïve to suggest that standardization—whether in the form of quantitative testing, rankings, or other value-added metrics of effectiveness—will somehow magically fade into the educational sunset. At the same time, an obsession with metrics presents an opportunity.

MOVING THE TRANSFER AND ARTICULATION DIALOGUE: A HOLISTIC APPROACH

More selective institutions can increasingly backfill enrollment numbers with transfer students from community colleges, who are more likely to be from low-SES and immigrant backgrounds as well as from communities of color. Interestingly, transfer students are typically omitted from ranking measures (Dowd et al., 2008). As Dowd et al. (2008) suggest, "In a democracy, equitable access to elite institutions is critical to ensure public investments in higher education do not simply reproduce the existing class structure" (p. 467). The authors go on to suggest that "the number of low-income students concentrated in community colleges . . . provides a ready pool of potential transfers who . . . would increase their own human capital, contribute to closing the socioeconomic enrollment gap in higher education, and increase overall educational attainment in the U.S." (p. 449).

Elite institutions are likely not sufficiently incentivized to recruit and enroll low-income community college transfer students, and thus perhaps a more persuasive tactic is to focus less on the morality of enhancing access and instead appeal to institutional economics for less-selective four-year colleges and universities. We believe such an argument involves the cost-effective incentives afforded to four-year institutions confronted with a changing demographic featuring less resourced and increasingly diverse students, who are nonetheless qualified but unable to afford rising tuition. By admitting more community college transfer students into four-year colleges and universities, these institutions can generate considerable savings as time to degree is reduced, as well as the amount of institutional resources required to close the unmet financial aid need gap—a gap that increasingly forces qualified applicants to reject offers of admissions.

Thus it may be in the interest of four-year institutions, even the elite ones, to rely more on community college transfers to help manage a crisis undergirding the foundation of the higher education business model. This crisis is a product of a perfect storm of factors, which starts with the rapid change in demographics of students seeking access, who are from lower-income and diverse (linguistically, racially, ethnically, etc.) backgrounds, and culminates with the rising cost structure of universities and colleges that have traditionally stemmed the tide of growing expenses by increasing tuition. Given these competing factors, offsetting increasing expenses by making it too expensive for the "new" student bodies of the twenty-first century to afford access is not a long-term solution except for the incredibly elite, prestigious, and well-endowed institutions like Harvard, Stanford, and Yale. For the majority of higher education institutions, however, this storm is threatening to forever change the postsecondary landscape as for-profits and massive open online courses flood the market without the burden of traditional and inflexible operating expenses (permanent faculty, staff, benefits, expansive facilities, etc.).

Another possible and related action is statutorily requiring institutions to accept transfer students, an arrangement already seen in California, Florida, Illinois, and Washington (Dowd et al., 2008). But true appreciation from across institutions of higher education about the value of vertical transfers (i.e., from two-year institutions to four-year institutions) along with mechanisms that enhance the learning bridge between the two institutional types must augment the statutory requirement. That is, the mandate is insufficient without an intuitive and rationalized purpose—a well-articulated curriculum that blends both institutions. In a hostile legal and cultural climate, improving educational outcomes based on race and class is increasingly difficult, and thus mandates at the state level may represent a necessary policy lever for change if coupled with curricular integration.

But relying on macro circumstances to dedicate policy without also critically examining what support inputs are needed to assist transfer students in making good college decisions will only generate more contradictory and unintended consequences. To counter such consequences, we also suggest a concerted focus on providing more accessible information about college and financial aid specifically. While the federal government has placed a mandate for institutions to place college cost calculators on websites and in other institutional resources, families of first-generation college students struggle to make sense of these tools, and they confuse some students to believe that they may only be responsible for the net price. As Grodsky and Jackson (2009) note, "If we are to learn how information can be used to reduce stratification in higher education, we need to begin with a theoretically informed analysis of how information varies by social origins and what impact this variation has on college attendance and completion" (p. 2372). Moving beyond what most precollegiate programs tend to cover, we agree with others who posit that financial resources matter most in terms of information predicting educational attainment (Goldrick-Rab, 2006). Students—particularly those from low-income, first-generation college-going, and diverse backgrounds— are often dissuaded by the shocking "sticker price" of private universities and four-year colleges because information about financial aid is not readily available (Grodsky & Jackson, 2009).

ANOTHER LAYER TO INFORM THE SOLUTION: QUALITATIVE RESEARCH AT THE INSTITUTIONAL LEVEL

Empirical evidence from successful individual campuses can also help inform instructional, mentoring, and advising practices. Structured programming, intentional academic advising, and peer support, for example, are likely to have the biggest impact on student completion (Person, Rosenbaum, & Deil-Amen, 2006). Additionally, because there is no reliable national survey of the teaching techniques used in remedial courses at community colleges, the assumption is that drill-and-skill approaches are still dominant (Grubb & Associates, 1999; Levin & Calcagno, 2008). Therefore more work on pedagogy and best practices for teaching remedial and developmental education content is needed, and this line of research must consider, in a more complex manner than earlier research, the environmental variants such as the institutional type and surrounding cultural geography (Anderson, 2002).

Another related recommendation is that more asset-based qualitative studies are needed to critique, expand, and improve the current technocratic solutions (Dowd et al., 2013). This truly value-added inquiry provides rich data to qualitatively understand complex educational issues. Such a study, which is possible to replicate into a larger scale, recently looked at ten students who successfully transferred from community colleges to selective universities. The students noted the essential role played by college practitioners in positions of authority in the development of students' collegiate identity and subsequent likelihood to transfer (Dowd et al., 2013). The data in the small but seminal study informed one piece to a complex problem that quantitative research might not have uncovered absent the cultural digging associated with well-designed qualitative research. Dowd et al. (2013) share the important finding that, as the United States "aims to boost the number of college graduates and turns to community colleges to democratize education providing a gateway for low-status populations, it is clear that practitioners must be kept in mind as essential resources for student success" (p. 21). Campus administrators are important—and understudied—yet they represent assets for students in community colleges seeking to transfer to selective institutions who face countless structural barriers and discriminatory deficit-based beliefs related to race and SES (Dowd et al., 2013). Further, to avoid applying these lessons as a technocratic solution, we encourage campuses to examine the principles and general propositions of studies like this one. Then consumers of the research must craft policies and practices that fully appreciate their institutional context, operational assumptions, and values.

Conclusion

The impending crisis in US education has been documented for decades, with scathing critiques levied by Darling-Hammond (2010), Gándara (2010), and Kozol (1991) that demonstrate how the US education system is, in several respects, as segregated today by race and socioeconomic status as in 1954, when the US Supreme Court decided *Brown v. Board of Education*. At the higher education level, the technocratic reform agenda may have the unintended consequence of pushing demand to the bottom and restrictive success to the top. As Pasque (2010) aptly notes, "Educational leaders cannot afford to be complacent in this climate of educational inequity and let dominant arguments about . . . education prevail" (p. 7). Stated differently, without critical inquiry and insurgent analyses foregrounding equity and educational quality as *the* civil rights issue of the twenty-first century, we fear complacency will breed incrementalism and a perpetuation of the status quo.

Rather than focusing on the symptoms, we must now ask critical questions about the core functions and primary entry points of US postsecondary education, and especially community colleges. The conditions are ripe to ask such questions and to shift the discourse, presenting equity and quality not as separate concepts or mutually exclusive interests. Failing to rise up to the technocratic tide by succumbing to simplistic, low hanging fruit–type solutions that appeal to notions of equity and quality as aspirational expressions of outcomes without adequate substance may present effective sound bites at political rallies and swank fund-raising events. But in our view, such declarations should come with a consumer warning: buyer beware, as the contents may be damaging to our long-term health as a democracy and a nation of diverse citizens.

NOTE

1. The technocratic approach was first identified as a patterned societal reaction in the early 1900s, in which society valued laborers with scientific techniques such as engineers rather than business leaders and politicians. In simplified terms, the technocratic approach valued measured, numerical solutions and largely overlooked social ills that could not be easily presented in a formulaic manner.

REFERENCES

Akom, A. A. (2008). Ameritocracy and infra-racial racism: Racializing social and cultural reproduction theory in the twenty-first century. *Race, Ethnicity, and Education, 11*(3), 205–30.

Alon, S. (2009). The evolution of class inequality in higher education: Competition, exclusion, and adaptation. *American Sociological Review, 74*(5), 731–55.

American Association of Colleges and Universities. (2011, Fall). From the editor: A liberal and liberating education for all. *Making Excellence Inclusive.* Retrieved from www.aacu.org/compass/documents/MEINewsletter_Fall11.pdf.

Anderson, G. M. (2002). *Building a people's university in South Africa: Race, compensatory education, and the limits of democratic reform.* New York: Peter Lang.

———. (2005). In the name of diversity: Education and the commoditization and consumption of race in the United States. *Urban Review, 37*(5), 399–423.

Anderson, G. M., Alfonso, M., & Sun, J. C. (2006). Rethinking cooling out at public community colleges: An examination of fiscal and demographic trends in higher education and the rise of statewide articulation agreements. *Teachers College Record, 108*(3), 422–51.

Anderson, G. M., Sun, J. C., & Alfonso, M. (2006). Effectiveness of statewide articulation agreements on the probability of transfer: A preliminary policy analysis. *Review of Higher Education, 29*(3), 260–91. doi:10.1353/rhe.2006.0001.

Apple, M. W. (2001). *Educating the "right" way: Markets, standards, God, and inequality.* New York: RoutledgeFalmer.

Bailey, T. (2002). Community colleges in the 21st century: Challenges and opportunities. In P. A. Gram & N. Stacy (Eds.), *The knowledge economy and postsecondary education: Report of a workshop* (pp. 1–10). Washington, DC: National Academies Press.

Bailey, T., & Cho, S. W. (2010). *Issue brief: Development education in community colleges.* New York: Community College Research Center, Teachers College, Columbia University.

Bailey, T., Jeong, D. W., & Cho, S. W. (2010). Referral, enrollment, and completion in developmental education sequences in community colleges. *Economics of Education Review, 29,* 255–70. doi:10.1016/j.econedurev.2009.09.002.

Bailey, T. R., & Morest, V. S. (2004). *The organizational efficiency of multiple missions for community colleges.* New York: Community College Research Center, Teachers College, Columbia University.

Bastedo, M. N., & Jaquette, O. (2011). Running in place: Low-income students and the dynamics of higher education stratification. *Educational Evaluation and Policy Analysis, 33*(3), 318–39. doi:10.3102/0162373711406718.

Beveridge, T. (2010). No Child Left Behind and fine arts classes. *Arts Education Policy Review, 111,* 4–7. doi:10.1080/10632910903228090.

Bowen, W. G., Chingos, M. M., & McPherson, M. S. (2009). *Crossing the finish line: Completing college at America's public universities.* Princeton, NJ: Princeton University Press.

Bowles, S., Gintis, H., & Groves, M. O. (Eds.). (2009). *Unequal chances: Family background and economic success.* New York: Russell Sage Foundation.

Brown v. Board of Education, 347 U.S. 483 (1954).

Carnevale, A. P., & Rose, S. J. (2004). Socioeconomic status, race/ethnicity, and selective college admissions. In R. D. Kahlenberg (Ed.), *America's untapped re-*

sources: *Low-income students in higher education* (pp. 101–56). New York: Century Foundation.

Cohen, A. M., & Brawer, F. B. (2008). *The American community college* (5th ed.). San Francisco: Jossey-Bass.

Darder, A. (2005). Schooling and the culture of domination: Unmasking the ideology of standardized testing. In G. E. Fischman et al. (Eds.), *Critical theories, radical pedagogies, and global conflicts* (pp. 204–22). Oxford: Rowman & Littlefield.

Darling-Hammond L. (2010). *The flat world and education: How America's commitment to equity will determine our future.* New York: Teachers College Press.

Dewey, J. (1897). My pedagogic creed. *School Journal, 59*(3), 77–80.

———. (1916). *Democracy and education: An introduction to the philosophy of education.* New York: Macmillan.

———. (1938). *Experience & education.* New York: Kappa Delta Pi.

Diamond, J. B. (2007). Where the rubber meets the road: Rethinking the connection between high-stakes testing policy and classroom instruction. *Sociology of Education, 80*(4), 285–313. doi:10.1177/003804070708000401.

Dowd, A. C., Cheslock, J. J., & Melguizo, T. (2008). Transfer access from community colleges and the distribution of elite higher education. *Journal of Higher Education, 79*(4), 442–72. doi:10.1353/jhe.0.0010.

Dowd, A. C., Pak, J. H., & Bensimon, E. M. (2013). The role of institutional agents in promoting transfer access. *Education Policy Analysis Archives, 21*(15). Retrieved from http://cue.usc.edu/Dowd_Role%20if%20Institutional%20Agents%20in%20Promoting%20Transfer%20Access_EPAA_2013.pdf.

Driscoll, W., & Fleeter, H. (2003). *Projected cost of implementing the federal "No Child Left Behind Act" in Ohio.* Columbus: Ohio Department of Education. Retrieved from www.schoolfunding.info/states/oh/oh_nclb_coststudy.pdf.

Duncan, O. D. (1968). Social stratification and mobility. In E. H. B. Sheldon & W. E. Moore (Eds.), *Indicators of social change: Concepts and measurement* (pp. 675–719). New York: Russell Sage Foundation.

Duncombe, W., Lukemeyer, A., & Yinger, J. (2008). The No Child Left Behind Act: Have federal funds been left behind? *Public Finance Review, 36*, 381–407. doi: 10.1177/1091142107305220.

Dungy, G. J., & Ellis, S. E. (Eds.). (2011). *Exceptional senior student affairs administrators' leadership: Strategies and competencies for success.* Washington, DC: Student Affairs Administrators in Higher Education.

Eisner, E. W. (2002). *The educational imagination: On the design and evaluation of school programs* (3rd ed.). Upper Saddle River, NJ: Merrill Prentice Hall.

Espinoza, O. (2007). Solving the equity-equality conceptual dilemma: A new model for analysis of the educational process. *Educational Research, 49*(4), 343–63. doi: 10.1007/978-90-481-3221-8_9.

Fine, M., Anand, B., Jordan, C., & Sherman, D. (2003). Before the bleach gets us all. In M. Fine & L. Weis (Eds.), *Silenced voices and extraordinary conversations: Re-imagining schools* (pp. 113–32). New York: Teachers College Press.

Flinders, D. (2005). Multiple worlds, multiple ways of knowing: Elliot Eisner's contributions to educational research. In P. B. Uhrmacher & J. Matthews (Eds.), *Intricate palette: Working the ideas of Elliot Eisner* (pp. 127–38). Upper Saddle River, NJ: Pearson.

Foderaro, L. W. (2011, March 3). CUNY adjusts amid tide of remedial students. *New York Times*. Retrieved from www.mcc.edu/aqip/ap_dev_ed/dev_ed_CUNY _Article-Section-6B.pdf.

Frankenberg, E., Siegel-Hawley, G., & Wang, J. (2011). Choice without equity: Charter school segregation. *Education Policy Analysis Archives, 19*(1), 1–92.

Friedlander, J. N. (2010). From open admission to the honors college equal opportunities at the City University of New York. In F. Lazin, N. Javaram, & M. Evans (Eds.), *Higher education and equality of opportunity: Cross-national perspectives* (pp. 69–88). Plymouth: Lexington Books.

Fuller, A. (2010, March 30). Obama reaffirms support for community colleges at signing of student-loan bill. *Chronicle of Higher Education*. Retrieved from http://clips .corinthiancolleges.com/wp-content/uploads/downloads/2010/03/Chronicle-of -Higher-Education-Obama-Reaffirms-Support-033110.pdf.

Gallagher, K. (2010). Teaching Freire and CUNY open admissions. *Radical Teacher, 87*, 55–67. doi:10.1353/rdt.0.0067.

Gándara, P. (2010). Overcoming triple segregation. *Educational Leadership, 68*(3), 60–64.

George, M. (2010). Ethics and motivation in remedial mathematics education. *Community College Review, 38*(1), 82–92. doi:10.1177/0091552110373385.

Gildersleeve, R. E., Kuntz, A. M., Pasque, P. A., & Carducci, R. (2010). The role of critical inquiry in (re)constructing the public agenda for higher education: Confronting the conservative modernization of the academy. *Review of Higher Education, 34*(1), 85–121.

Giltner, T., & Barber, H. (2013, March 15). *U.S. education official applauds KCTCS efforts to educate and train students for high-demand jobs.* [Press release]. Retrieved from http://ashland.kctcs.edu/news%20and%20events/newsitem?id=%7B3f49c1d1 -f976-4298-9a79-f06b58a107d0%7D.

Goldrick-Rab, S. (2006). Following their every move: An investigation of social-class differences in college pathways. *Sociology of Education, 79*, 61–79.

Goldrick-Rab, S., & Pfeffer, F. (2009). Beyond access: Explaining social class differences in college student mobility. *Sociology of Education, 82*, 101–25.

Grodsky, E., & Jackson, E. (2009). Social stratification in higher education. *Teachers College Record, 111*(10), 2347–84.

Grubb, W. N., & Associates (1999). *Honored but invisible: An inside look at teaching in community colleges.* New York: Routledge.

Grubb, W. N., Badway, N., & Bell, D. (2003). Community colleges and the equity agenda: The potential of noncredit education. *Annals of the American Academy of Political and Social Sciences, 586*(1), 218–40. doi:10.1177/0002716202250226.

Grubb, W. N., Badway, N., Bell, D., & Catellano, M. (1999). Community colleges and welfare reform: Emerging practices, enduring problems. *Community College Journal, 69*(6), 30–36.

Guido, F. M., Chávez, A. F., & Lincoln, Y. S. (2010). Underlying paradigms in student affairs research and practice. *Journal of Student Affairs Research and Practice, 47*(1), 1–22. doi:10.2202/1949-6605.6017.

Guinier, L., & Torres, G. (2003). *The miner's canary: Enlisting race, resisting power, transforming democracy.* Cambridge, MA: Harvard University Press.

Harris, F., III, & Bensimon, E. M. (2007). The Equity Scorecard: A collaborative approach to assess and respond to racial/ethnic disparities in student outcomes. *New Directions for Student Services, 120,* 77–84. doi:10.1002/ss.259.

Hilliard, T., & Spaic, T. (2013). *Completion day.* New York: Center for the Urban Future.

Jennings, J. (2012). *Reflections on a half century of school reform: Why have we fallen short and where do we go from here?* Washington, DC: Center on Education Policy. Retrieved from www.cep-dc.org/displayDocument.cfm?DocumentID=392.

Katz, S. N. (2012, March 25). Beware big donors. *Chronicle of Higher Education.* Retrieved from http://chronicle.com/article/Big-Philanthropys-Role-in/131275/.

Kolbe, T., & Rice, J. K. (2012). And they're off: Tracking federal Race to the Top investments from the starting gate. *Educational Policy, 26*(1), 185–209. doi:10.1177/0895904811428975.

Kozol, J. (1991). *Savage inequalities: Children in America's schools.* New York: Crown.

Lankford, H., Loeb, S., & Wyckoff, J. (2002). Teacher sorting and the plight of urban schools: A descriptive analysis. *Educational Evaluation and Policy Analysis, 24*(1), 37–62. doi:10.3102/01623737024001037.

Lavin, D., & Hyllegard, D. (2006). *Changing the odds: Open admissions and the life chances of the disadvantaged.* New Haven, CT: Yale University Press.

Lederman, D. (2012, April 13). Foundations' newfound advocacy. *Inside Higher Ed.* Retrieved from www.insidehighered.com/news/2012/04/13/study-assesses-how -megafoundations-have-changed-role-higher-ed-philanthropy.

Lee, E. M. (2013). Elite colleges and socioeconomic status. *Sociology Compass, 7*(9), 786–98. doi:10.1111/soc4.12068.

Levin, H. M., & Calcagno, J. C. (2008). Remediation in the community college: An evaluator's perspective. *Community College Review, 35*(3), 181–207. doi:10.1177/0091552107310118.

Ludwig, M. (2011, January 21). "Tracking" revived at community colleges. *San Antonia Express News.* Retrieved from www.mysanantonio.com/news/education/article/Tracking-revived-at-community-colleges-969326.php.

McGuinn, P. (2012). Stimulating reform: Race to the Top, competitive grants and the Obama education agenda. *Educational Policy, 26*(1), 136–59. doi:10.1177/0895904811425911.

Meade, T. (2012). Dual enrollment lessons and the development of the New Community College at CUNY. *New Directions for Higher Education, 158,* 91–100. doi: 10.1002/he.20018.

Minnici, A., & Hill, D. (2007). *Educational architects: Do state education agencies have the tools necessary to implement NCLB?* Washington, DC: Center on Education Policy.

Miron, G., Urschel, J. L., Mathis, W. J., & Tornquist, E. (2010). *Schools without diversity: Education management organizations, charter schools and the demographic stratification of the American school system.* Boulder, CO: Education and the Public Interest Center.

Murray, P. (2011, September 26). *Senator Murray applauds investment in Spokane Community College skills training program.* [Press release]. Retrieved from www .highbeam.com/doc/1G1-268008834.html.

Museus, S. D., & Jayakumar, U. M. (Eds). (2012). *Creating campus cultures: Fostering success among racially diverse student populations.* New York: Routledge.

NCES. National Center for Education Statistics (2013). *The condition of education, 2013.* NCES Report 2013-037. Washington, DC: US Department of Education.

NCLB. No Child Left Behind Act of 2001, Pub. L. No. 107–110, §115, Stat. 1425 (2002).

Nicholson-Crotty, S., & Staley, T. (2012). Competitive federalism and Race to the Top application decisions in the American states. *Educational Policy, 26*(1), 160–84. doi:10.1177/0895904811428974.

Nighaoui, S. C. (2007). Affirmative action: Why we should consider reform. *Western Journal of Black Studies, 31*(1), 33–50.

Noguera, P. A. (2011). A broader and bolder approach uses education to break the cycle of poverty. *Phi Delta Kappan, 93*(3), 8–14.

Oseguera, L., & Astin, A. W. (2004). The declining "equity" of American higher education. *Review of Higher Education, 27*(3), 321–41. doi:10.1353/rhe.2004.0001.

Palardy, G. J. (2013). High school socioeconomic segregation and student attainment. *American Educational Research Journal, 50*(4), 714–54.

Parents Involved in Community Schools v. Seattle, No. 1, 551 U.S. 701 (2007).

Parker, T. L., Bustillos, L. T., & Behringer, L. B. (2010). *Getting past go: Remedial and developmental education policy at a crossroads.* Boston: Policy Research on Preparation, Access, and Remedial Education. Retrieved from http://inpathways.net/ Literature-Review-GPG.pdf.

Parry, M., Field, K., & Supiano, B. (2013, July 14). The Gates effect. *Chronicle of Higher Education.* Retrieved from http://chronicle.com/article/The-Gates-Effect/140323/.

Pasque, P. (2010). *American higher education, leadership, and policy: Critical issues and the public good.* New York: Palgrave Macmillan.

Pasque, P., Carducci, R., Kuntz, A. K., & Gildersleeve, R. E. (2012). Qualitative inquiry for equity in higher education: Methodological implications, negotiations, and responsibilities. *ASHE Higher Education Report, 37*(6).

Pérez-Peña, R. (2012, May 22). At CUNY, stricter admissions bring ethnic shift. *New York Times.* Retrieved from www.nytimes.com/2012/05/23/nyregion/at-cunys-top -colleges-black-and-hispanic-freshmen-enrollments-drop.html?_r=0.

Person, A. E., Rosenbaum, J. E., & Deil-Amen, R. (2006). Student planning and information problems in different college structures. *Teachers College Record, 108*(3), 347–96.

Price, D. V., & Roberts, B. (2008). *Improving student success by strengthening develop-*

ment education in community colleges: The role of state policy. Chevy Chase, MD: Working Poor Families Project.

Ravitch, D. (2008, November 19). Bill Gates and his silver bullet. *Forbes.* Retrieved from www.forbes.com/2008/11/18/gates-foundation-schools-oped-cx_dr_1119ravitch .html.

Renzulli, L., & Evans, L. (2005). School choice, charter schools, and white flight. *Social Problems, 52*(3), 398–418. doi:10.1525/sp.2005.52.3.398.

Rhoades, G. (2012a). The incomplete completion agenda: Implications for academe and the academy. *Liberal Education, 98*(1), 18–25.

———. (2012b). *Closing the door, increasing the gap: Who's not going to (community) college?* Policy Report 1. Center for the Future of Higher Education. Retrieved from www.insidehighered.com/sites/default/server_files/files/ClosingTheDoor_Embar goed.pdf.

Roelofs, J. (2003). *Foundations and public policy: The mask of pluralism.* Albany: State University of New York.

Sherman, W. H. (2008). No child left behind: A legislative catalyst for superintendent action to eliminate test-score gaps? *Educational Policy, 22*(5), 675–704. doi: 10.1177/0895904807307063.

Simola, S. K. (2005). Organizational crisis management: Overview and opportunities. *Counseling Psychology Journal: Practice and Research, 57*(3), 180–92.

Singh, M. (2011). The place of social justice in higher education and social change discourses. *Journal of Comparative and International Education, 41*(4), 481–94. doi:10.1080/03057925.2011.581515.

Skrentny, J. D. (1996). *The ironies of affirmative action: Politics, culture, and justice in America.* Chicago: University of Chicago Press.

Smyth, T. S. (2008). Who is No Child Left Behind leaving behind? *Clearing House, 81*(3), 133–37.

Stiefel, L., Schwartz, A. E., & Chellman, C. C. (2007). So many children left behind: Segregation and the impact of subgroup reporting in No Child Left Behind on the racial test score gap. *Educational Policy, 21*(3), 527–50. doi:10.1177/0895904806289207.

Stone, C., Van Horn, C., & Zukin, C. (2012). *Chasing the American dream: Recent college graduates and the great recession.* New Brunswick, NJ: John J. Heldrich Center for Workforce Development, Rutgers University.

Sullivan, B. (2011). From professional ownership to intentional coproduction: New competency demands. In G. J. Dungy & S. E. Ellis (Eds.), *Exceptional senior student affairs administrators' leadership: Strategies and competencies for success* (pp. 93–99). Washington, DC: Student Affairs Administrators in Higher Education.

Sun, J. C., & Daniel, P. T. K. (2013). Math and science are core to the IDEA: Breaking the racial and poverty lines. *Fordham Urban Law Journal, 41*(2), 557–98.

Tinto, V. (1973). College proximity and rates of college attendance. *American Educational Research Journal, 10*(4), 277–93.

Tsao, T. M. (2005). Open admissions, controversies, and CUNY: Digging into social history through a first-year composition course. *History Teacher, 38*(4), 469–82.

Tuckley, L. E. (2011). *Eight million more graduates by 2020? The impact of social stratification on undergraduate attrition in the U.S.* Washington, DC: Georgetown University.

US Department of Education. (2009a). *Robust data gives us the roadmap to reform.* [Press release]. Retrieved from www2.ed.gov/news/speeches/2009/06/06082009 .html.

———. (2009b). *Race to the Top program executive summary.* Washington, DC: Author. Retrieved from www2.ed.gov/programs/racetothetop/executive-summary.pdf.

———. (2010). *Blueprint for reform: The reauthorization of the Elementary and Secondary Education Act.* Washington, DC: Author. Retrieved from www2.ed.gov/ policy/elsec/leg/blueprint/publication_pg2.html.

———. (2011). *Guidance on the voluntary use of race to achieve diversity and avoid racial isolation in elementary and secondary schools.* Washington, DC: Office of Civil Rights, US Department of Education.

———. (2012). *Two-year official cohort default rates for schools.* Washington, DC: Author. Retrieved from www2.ed.gov/offices/OSFAP/defaultmanagement/cdr2yr .html.

———. (2013). *Equity and Excellence Commission.* Washington, DC: Author. Retrieved from www2.ed.gov/about/bdscomm/list/eec/index.html.

US Department of Labor (2013). *FY 2013 congressional budget justification employment and training administration.* Washington, DC: Author. Retrieved from www .dol.gov/dol/budget/2013/PDF/CBJ-2013-V1-07.pdf.

White House. (2009). *Fact sheet: Race to the Top.* [Press release]. Retrieved from www .whitehouse.gov/the-press-office/fact-sheet-race-top.

———. (2013). *Education: Knowledge and skills for the jobs of the future.* Washington, DC: Author. Retrieved from www.whitehouse.gov/issues/education/higher-education.

Yeakey, C. C., & Bennett, C. T. (1990). Race, schooling, and class in American society. *Journal of Negro Education, 59*(1), 3–18.

CHAPTER THIRTEEN

The Transformative Paradigm

Principles and Challenges

SYLVIA HURTADO

At a national meeting on retention, one researcher stated, "We are producing all this research for student success, but no one is working with campuses to implement our ideas." I thought the statement ignored the work of researchers who had been engaged with campus communities in turning ideas into action to improve student success. Thinking back, I now realize the decoupling of research and action occurs largely because of researchers' choice of paradigms, or worldviews, that distance them from the topics or communities that are the focus of research. Most higher education research, intended to focus on a practical and professional field, may lay claim to a transformative focus or express intentions for institutional improvement. Many studies ignore power dynamics in higher education contexts and do not address social justice aims, however, and those that do often leave implementation and interpretation of their results for practitioners to translate into local needs and uses. Fortunately, delineation of the various paradigmatic assumptions that drive research is now more explicit (Creswell & Plano Clark, 2011; Guba & Lincoln, 2005; Phillips & Burbules, 2000).

New understandings have emerged, identifying a transformative paradigm that several communities of scholars—including those who employ a feminist, critical race, queer, positive psychology, or resilience theory approach—reinforce (Mertens, 2003, 2009). Much of this scholarship arose independently from the social movements among specific communities, and this work extends what is now known as a critical postmodernist project taking root in educational research and practice that is not only about the deconstruction of power relationships "but also about active engagement in change and reform issues that seek to sever inequalities and other forms of social and cultural injustices" (Kanpol, 1999, p. 33). The transformative paradigm is intended to serve as an umbrella for all scholarly approaches that may employ different research methods but are rooted in a critique of power relationships, with emancipatory goals for individuals and transformative goals for institutions and systems of oppression.

But if much of the research in higher education does not fall squarely within these scholarly communities, and is interdisciplinary or borrows from many perspectives, how do we identify and promote more studies in higher education research that reflect a transformative paradigm? Scholars and evaluation researchers who adopt a transformative paradigm in the design and conduct of their research begin with an intentional plan to target an area for challenging the reproduction of inequality with a focus on social justice that "permeates the entire research process, from the problem formulation to the drawing of conclusions and use of results" (Mertens, 2003, p. 159). They create a mutual learning process between themselves and participants, or a similar approach that aligns with an ethic of inclusion, and a plan for action or empowerment that will advance social justice goals. In this approach, a researcher may work alongside campuses to define social justice aims, give voice to particular underrepresented populations, or help with research that generates strategies for institutional transformation. In this chapter, I show how the transformative paradigm differs from other paradigms in use in the field and provide examples in higher education with an eye toward expanding the characteristics and use of a transformative approach in higher education. The primary goal is to increase awareness of how higher education research can be effective in producing transformative research for achieving sustained social change. I conclude with emerging ways to advance the principles of transformative research in the field. We can raise the bar on research goals to create more transformative projects, and teach others how to do this work, as we strive for the larger goal of ensuring that institutions of higher education reflect and advance a just and inclusive society.

Distinctive Characteristics of the Transformative Paradigm

Unless higher education researchers are trained in the philosophical foundations of research, for the most part they are more intent on identifying a method and its appropriateness for a question rather than clarifying their own worldview and its implications for the research process and use of results. Yet the type of paradigm researchers adopt is often linked with their approach to a particular research question, which includes assumptions about the nature of reality (ontology); the extent to which the researcher makes explicit his own values or biases (axiology); the distance or relationship of the researcher to the communities being researched and nature of knowledge (epistemology); and ultimately the choice of technique for systematic inquiry (methodology). It is thus essential to create awareness and reflect on one's underlying assumptions in the research process and ultimate choice of method. In order to highlight the distinctive characteristics of the transformative paradigm, I summarize Mertens's (2009) ideas, adding my own observations about the kind of work this paradigm frames in contrast with different paradigms and their underlying assumptions, which are reviewed in detail elsewhere (Creswell & Plano Clark, 2011; Guba & Lincoln, 2005; Paul, 2005; Phillips & Burbules, 2000).

The transformative paradigm originated from the dissatisfaction of researchers and members of marginalized communities with dominant research paradigms and practices (Mertens et al., 2010). It has taken on different descriptions as it has evolved as one of several paradigms operational in the social sciences in general and education and psychology in particular. Building on the earlier work of Guba and Lincoln (1989) and Lather (1992), Donna M. Mertens (1998) noted four dominant paradigms: postpostivism, constructivism, pragmatism, and the emancipatory paradigm. Lather (1992) distinguishes educational scholarship that is intended to understand from research that is intended to deconstruct the status quo, and from work that is intended to emancipate individuals from forms of oppression. Emancipatory scholarship encompassed "critical neo-marxist, feminist, race-specific, praxis-oriented, and Freirean participatory" scholarship (p. 89). The emancipatory paradigm is distinct from all other worldviews in its recognition of power and oppression and the dynamic of resilience and resistance among oppressed groups in response to these challenges. Links between critical research rooted in poststructualism and emancipatory work subsequently became more integrated over time. (See Ropers-Huilman [1998] for an example of feminist research in higher education that is linked with poststructualism).

Several years later, Mertens (2005, 2009) revised the name of the paradigm from emancipatory to transformative, because this type of research was intended not only to liberate groups from oppression but also to emphasize the agency of these groups, and how researchers work in concert with these communities to achieve personal and social transformation. Creswell and Plano Clark (2011) use the term "participatory" rather than transformative (p. 42) for the paradigm that they credit Mertens for advancing, but it is much more. Mertens (2009) does not solely emphasize participation as a defining characteristic of the transformative paradigm as much as the central importance placed "on the lives and experiences of communities that are pushed to society's margins" (p. 48), the recognition of power that surrounds an investigation, and the relationship of the researcher to those that are the focus of the investigation.[1]

Although forms of participatory action research that prioritize conducting research *with* rather than *on* specific communities may promote a transformative paradigm (Heron & Reason, 2006), they must also possess other characteristics. A transformative worldview does more than simply involve participants in the research process; it also focuses on advancing social justice. The researcher must be conscious of the power differentials that exist in the research relationship and identify constraints of systemic oppression on behaviors and actions, even if participants are unable to name it or are themselves engaged in reinforcing it as internalized oppression. In fact, raising consciousness is often the first step in any transformative or liberation work in education (Freire, 1973; Ropers-Huilman, 1998; Zuñiga et al., 2007), and self-conscious action on the part of researchers can guide new methods (Zuberi & Bonilla-Silva, 2008).

The relationships between researchers and participants evolve over time and may begin with some distance as trust becomes established, particularly if they come from different worlds (e.g., disciplines, social identities and communities, privilege or status, levels of awareness) but are committed to the goal of social change. One of the ideal outcomes of a transformative investigation is mutual learning and reciprocal relationships, with the researchers learning from the wisdom of individuals engaged in a long-term struggle under unequal or oppressive conditions and research participants gaining new insight on their own lives and change efforts with the expertise of the researcher. While this may be an ideal relationship, there are other ways that participation can occur in a transformative approach, including listening to community members and working toward mutual engagement for social change. The International Association for Public Participation (2013) established a spectrum of progressive levels of public engagement relevant to research, decision making, and seeking solutions to social problems. This continuum goes from low to high levels of public impact, and activities range from informing, consulting, involving, collaborating, to empowering communities. Figure 13.1 adapts this model to designate a continuum of involvement with researchers and communities of interest. The ultimate goal of transformative research is more aligned with empowerment, although research studies may begin with other activities along the continuum. This continuum of engagement and impact stands in contrast to "drive-by" scholarship, which takes information from marginalized communities but rarely informs research participants about the findings and much less empowers communities to create change based on the research. This approach has created a distrust of researchers and resulted in a call to encourage researchers to become conscious of relationships and their status as an insider or outsider, particularly in communities with unique

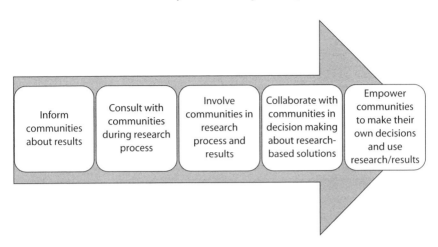

Figure 13.1. Continuum of researcher engagement with marginalized communities. *Source:* Adapted from the spectrum of public participation from the Association for Public Participation; see www.iap2.org.au/documents/item/84.

cultural traditions and worldviews (e.g., indigenous communities; Brayboy & Deyhle, 2000).

A consciousness and concern for marginalized communities is characteristic of researchers who adopt a transformative worldview. Mertens (2009) specifically states that "the transformative paradigm focuses on (1) the tensions that arise when unequal power relationships surround the investigation of what seem intransigent social problems and (2) the strength found in communities when their rights are respected and honored . . . the paradigm focuses on culturally appropriate strategies to facilitate understandings that will create sustainable social change" (10).

Other distinguishing features of the transformative paradigm include displaying concern for the vulnerability of populations in the research process, identifying the issues and the complex web of structural and individual factors that reinforce unequal outcomes, and using alternate frames and evidence that bring about greater awareness of educators' roles in maintaining the status quo or capacities for change. It is not enough to demonstrate differences and inequality—we have plenty of studies that show disparities and have even advanced the development of indicators in the social sciences to assess inequality (Hao & Naiman, 2010). But many of these studies fail to engender changes in society or higher education. Despite reports of how detrimental such disparities are to the larger social good, we can only conclude that the normative culture is invested in these inequalities in ways that complicate change. Researchers who use a transformative lens are typically engaged in a research process that helps educators and students divest from inequality embedded in norms and structures to devise solutions for social and institutional change.

Table 13.1 summarizes the basic tenets and beliefs that are characteristic of the transformative paradigm along the dimensions of axiology, ontology, epistemology, and methodology (adapted from Mertens, 2009; Mertens et al., 2010). In the dimension of axiology, the researcher working in a transformative paradigm is committed to a social justice agenda, applies respect for difference and values inclusion, and connects the research process and outcomes with social action. The researchers are aware of how their own values influence the research design, implementation, interpretation, and use of results—with a focus on solutions that will be beneficial to communities. Zuberi and Bonilla-Silva (2008) suggest that, as social scientists, "we must offer solutions that solve, and the world justifiably must demand not a lack of values and convictions, but rather the dedication to justice and ability to present the truth as we understand it regardless of the challenges it presents" (p. 12). Those engaged in high levels of participation with communities in the research process may also negotiate their values and beliefs and take participants' perspectives into account to refine the investigation. In contrast, postpositivist researchers assume that their own values do not affect the investigation or communities under investigation or take measures to eliminate bias. In the interest of maintaining objectivity, they strive to "let the dice fall where they may" when it comes to choice of method and claims of disinterest in results. But if one is not invested in the outcome, why would one be invested in implementation of the findings? Although researchers may claim that they are not invested in the outcome, most have hunches and intuition that guide their investigations. Further, personal, economic, and political interests drive the choice to become engaged in research and specific projects. In a constructivist paradigm, researchers make their own biases and values explicit in the research process as part of increasing the trustworthiness of a study, whereas pragmatists may include multiple stances on values (biased or unbiased; Creswell & Plano Clark, 2011).

In the dimension of ontology, transformative researchers recognize that power and privilege shape the nature of reality and reject relativism among multiple versions of reality, as not all versions of reality are equally legitimated in social contexts. For example, in a recent study, our research team's goal was to represent multiple realities based on different students' experience of the campus climate.

TABLE 13.1. Basic tenets of the transformative paradigm in research

Tenet	Description
Axiological assumption: ethics and values	Assumes respect for the cultural norms of diverse communities; promotes human rights and concern for vulnerable populations. Fosters an ethic of inclusion and connects the process and outcomes of research with a social justice agenda.
Ontological assumption: the nature of reality	Recognizes that privilege influences what is accepted as real; political, social, cultural, and economic lenses construct and shape versions of reality; and multiple versions of reality do not have equal legitimacy and must be critiqued in terms of their role in perpetuating inequality.
Epistemological assumption: the nature of knowledge and relationship of the researcher and participants	Recognizes power relations and dynamics; the "relationship between the researcher and participants is a critical determinant in achieving an understanding of valid knowledge within a transformative context" (Mertens et al., 2010, p. 198); building trust and communication is essential to understanding the culture. Ways of knowing can be linked with social identity or intersections of identity and positionality.
Methodological assumption: appropriate methods of systematic inquiry	Decisions on method involve an awareness of contextual and historical factors, considering forms of oppression. Multiple methods, techniques, and theories may be necessary. Relies on crystallization (multi-faceted perspectives and data sources) rather than triangulation, assumptions of heterogeneity rather than homogeneity, and is attentive to structures of opportunity and inequality, conditional effects (specific groups are affected differently by the same practices), and cultural norms in their influence on individuals and groups. Avoids an acontextual focus on individuals.

Source: Adapted from Mertens (2009) and Mertens et al. (2010) with my own additions to the basic tenets.

A campus administrator wanted an opportunity to weigh in on the study report to voice a concern about the potential to "misrepresent" the campus. Under this paradigm, hierarchies of power and privilege on campus are likely to influence any "singular" reality. Misrepresentation is unlikely if we carry out our work to convey authentically the experiences of students from multiple communities to bring insight into the heterogeneity between and within these communities. Contrasting the multiple versions of reality, and identifying those afforded the most privilege on campus, would help students, faculty, and staff on campus begin to understand how to move toward creating a more inclusive campus environment.

Versions of reality must be critiqued for their role in maintaining the status quo and oppression, also described as "speaking truth to power" (Zuberi & Bonilla-Silva, 2008, p. 13). Social psychologists have identified the use of hierarchy-enhancing myths as a strategy to resist change and maintain the legitimacy of unequal social relations (Sidanius, 1993; Sidanius et al., 2001). Transformative researchers identify legitimizing myths that permeate versions of reality, distinguishing normative realities based on privilege from realities based on oppression or marginalization. In other paradigms, postpositive researchers adopt a singular reality, constructivists provide multiple versions of reality identifying commonalties and divergence, and pragmatists may adopt both singular and multiple realities. Unless the researcher adopts a critical perspective, there is little consideration of the power hierarchies among realities in these other paradigms.

In terms of epistemology, scholars argue that we cannot study society or its problems from the outside because "we are part of the world and study society from the inside" (Zuberi & Bonilla-Silva, 2008, p. 12), and even question whether a neutral observer can get the facts right (Christians, 2005; Mertens et al., 2010). Researchers and the research context are part of the same privilege and power-based, racialized, class-based, and heterosexual norms that shape society. Zuberi and Bonilla-Silva (2008) argue for social scientists to adopt an epistemology of liberation, one that is conscious affirming of race and based on the notion of radical democratic pluralism that acknowledges and affirms differences as a way to build inclusion into social and political institutions. This is consistent with the epistemology articulated by critical race and gender researchers in education (Brayboy & Deyhle, 2012; Delgado Bernal et al., 2006; Yosso, 2005). Ways of knowing, or the epistemology of the researcher and the community under study, are negotiated in an interactive relationship and in efforts to improve understanding of the issues and solutions in the transformative paradigm. Transformative researchers derive empathic understandings of participants' ways of knowing to best convey their views, voices, and aspirations, sometimes aligning with and other times critiquing the multiple ways of knowing in the research context. Harding (1991) calls this strong objectivity. Its purpose is not to "merge the self with Other" but to "look back on the self in all its cultural particularity from a more distant, critical, objectifying location" (p. 151). She argues that systematic examination and critical scrutiny of background beliefs are essential ways of extending research and maximizing objectivity. In the spirit of the dynamic between subjectivity and objectivity, systematic forms of reflexivity are necessary to reflect on self and Other epistemologies in the research context (detailed in the last section of this chapter).

In contrast, postpositivist researchers assume they are value neutral, objective, and distance themselves from the community, issues, and action during and following the investigation. Their way of knowing is primary in the research process. Constructivists assume proximity and collect data where participants conduct their daily work to convey participants' ways of knowing, while practicality drives pragmatists in understanding "what works" (Creswell & Plano Clark, 2011, p. 42). In the latter case, different of ways of knowing may be acknowledged, but occasions may favor the epistemology of the researcher over the participants' in the process—as, ultimately, the researcher determines what works in the pragmatic paradigm.

Critical to determining a transformative paradigm are the underlying belief systems (described in table 13.1) that support the use of specific methods. The methodology or research process for the transformative paradigm is often focused on multiple methods and sources of data that reflect multiple theories or perspectives, referred to as a multifaceted knowledge approach focused on "crystallization" rather than triangulation (Mertens, 2009, p. 62), with attention to levels of sociohistorical context, social structure, culture, group-based identities, and their impact on individuals. Multiple methods and sources of data are necessary when evaluating individuals within and in relation to these multiple contexts.

Mertens et al. (2010) indicate that a qualitative approach is essential to the transformative paradigm but also often includes quantitative and mixed-methods techniques and approaches. Postpositive researchers use deductive approaches to test theory, posited a priori, using quantitative methods. Constructivists use qualitative methods to compare against established theory or to conduct primarily inductive analyses to generate new theory. Pragmatists may combine both quantitative and qualitative methodological approaches to understand what works.

Creswell and Plano Clark (2011) further distinguish the elements associated with different paradigms and implications for practice by suggesting that the rhetoric or language of research differs across these approaches. They state that postpositivists employ a formal writing style, constructivism uses a more informal style, pragmatists may use both formal and informal styles, and transformative researchers use "advocacy and change" language (p. 42). While there is more consensus regarding the standard format and language for research and presentation of findings among postpositivists than in other approaches, in general, there is more creativity about ways of using language and what a research product should look like in these other approaches. Transformative researchers use language that is not exclusive to scholars, but they are actively engaged in translating their findings to practitioners, using language that is effective for addressing policymakers, and empowering communities by incorporating local concepts and language. Mertens (2009), for example, connects evaluation with cyclical models found in indigenous communities to illustrate principles of transformative evaluation. Not all researchers identify their work in the transformative paradigm, however, which may be a result of dominant paradigms that dictate publication in journals, training in graduate programs, and notions of quality in research.

For example, some may avoid advocacy and change language because it is sometimes regarded as unscientific, derived largely from the beliefs that ground a postpositivist stance. In fact, critics go so far as to state that trends in advocacy research are to inflate the magnitude of the social problem or evidence supporting a position (Gilbert, 1997), potentially resulting in policy that "is neither effective nor fair" (p. 142). This view belies the politics surrounding investigations that deal with marginalized communities, as dominant groups may regard a research approach from the standpoint of nondominant groups as unworthy of public consideration or action. Sometimes researchers need to remove the cloak of invisibility that surrounds privilege (e.g., whiteness, heteronormativity), making what appears normal to some to begin to look abnormal from another perspective (Cabrera, 2014). Privilege essentially dominates norms and is embedded in common taken-for-granted actions, behaviors, and ways of living. Transformative researchers often name power and privilege at the individual, institutional, and systemic levels; highlight inequalities; and identify strengths that have been ignored or unrecognized among marginalized communities.

There is also a tendency to associate advocacy with poor research, but examples of poor research can be found in all paradigms, supporting issues on the right and left of the political spectrum. Research under the transformative paradigm that is oriented toward social justice can be structured with rigor so that the investigation is thorough, trustworthy, and inferences are supported, yielding new insights into complexities that have not been previously brought to light, while simultaneously advocating for communities that have been marginalized. Transformative studies often follow established and evolving conventions for conducting quantitative, qualitative, and mixed methods. I review such examples, illustrating transformative principles that shape studies in higher education.

Transformative Paradigm Studies in Higher Education with a Focus on Institutional Change

In identifying studies under the umbrella of a transformative paradigm, a synthetic review would include studies from many of the scholarly communities identified above, including but not limited to feminist, critical race, queer, disability, positive psychology, critical postmodernist, and critical resilience research. Because many higher education researchers may not see themselves as working primarily within these scholarly communities, or have developed their own approach based on multiple traditions that cut across social identity and forms of oppression, I focus on a few studies that advance the study of institutional transformation in ways that sustain social justice aims to illustrate the basic principles particular to the paradigm. I have selected studies that were large-scale (enhancing the generalizability of findings) or multiyear efforts and consisted of teams engaged in the research process and transformation efforts. Institutional change is the focus in these examples because institutions can be the link between individuals and societal change, and higher education institutions play a special role in advancing social progress (or reinforcing the status quo). In these studies, the authors clearly state the focus and purposes of the study as well as the debates or myths they intend to settle with new evidence. As they progressed through the different phases of the project, they were able to address multiple research questions; one study employed multiple methods in order to better address a range of research objectives. Many smaller-scale studies that focus on inequality or underserved populations also adhere to the transformative paradigm and can be linked with social action to further institutional change on a local level. I will return to this point in discussing ways to advance research under the transformative paradigm.

The Practice of Critical Dialogue in College Intergroup Relations

In the book *Dialogue across Difference: Practice, Theory, and Research on Intergroup Dialogue*, the authors focus on the purposes, implementation, and impact of critical intergroup dialogue on nine college campuses. It is a pedagogical practice to encourage mutual learning and communication skills that "can simultaneously acknowledge differences, inequalities, and conflicts as well as foster a capacity for collaboration and broad democratic engagement" (Gurin, Nagda, & Zuniga, 2013, p. 28). It is identity-based social justice education with the goal of empowering students with knowledge, skills, and values to navigate and transform a world plagued by conflict and inequality. Many of the campuses began dialogues on campuses as a proactive attempt to improve intergroup relations and the campus climate for diversity, but the educational objectives to produce citizens who can communicate, negotiate, and collaborate across social and cultural differences have increased in importance. While each of the campuses in this study had a dialogue program and many had conducted local assessments, as a collaborative group of practitioners and researchers, they believed they had much to gain from a rigorous study of a common dialogue curriculum/pedagogy across the campuses. The project was an opportunity to demonstrate how a curricular innovation could be adapted across campuses and generate replicable results, as well as how the pedagogy makes the best use of diversity as a vehicle for student learning toward educational objectives for a diverse and global world. From a sociohistorical view, the research occurred in the midst of continuing court cases with the potential to challenge the educational value of diversity, and the collaborators were intent on providing evidence about how diversity works in intentional education practice on college campuses. While these semester-long dialogues are typically designed to work across many types of differences on the basis of student social identities, the collaborative decided to focus on ten race/ethnicity dialogues and ten gender dialogues, and designated team members worked on implementing the same curriculum for these topics across the campuses—which in itself was a major fete to replicate in practice. Their mixed-methods approach to the study was focused on understanding mechanisms of change (communication and psychological processes) and student outcomes at the end of the dialogues and again one year later. While dialogue facilitators often use students' journals and reflective essays to tap into students' thinking and learning, the research approach also included analysis of coded video segments, interviews, and students' final papers. Most significantly, equally motivated students on the nine campuses were randomly assigned to a dialogue or control group composed of women of color, men of color, white men, and white women in equal numbers. All participants received surveys at the beginning of the semester, end of the semester, and one year following the dialogue. The entire study was designed to collect multiple forms of evidence in a multifaceted way to understand its impact, similar to the notion of crystallization using mixed-method techniques in this paradigm (Mertens, 2009).

There are several unique features of the study that place it within the transformative paradigm even though the collaborators came from various theoretical traditions associated with disciplines such as psychology, social work, social justice, and education. First, both researchers and practitioners shared values and epistemology that come from both research and teaching experience in engaging students in dialogue. There is a blurring of roles, as several of the researchers are also engaged in developing programs on their own campus, and those who are mostly practitioners work closely with the research and theoretical/conceptual base that underlies the practice. Both researchers and campus coordinators of dialogue programs had a strong mutual interest in learning about the practice to become more effective in its implementation and establish a common evidentiary base for the support of their programs.

Second, the practice of dialogue itself is designed to address power asymmetries in society through content, structure, and facilitation that empowers students as learners in recognizing privilege and oppression (their own and others'), asking questions, developing empathy, and sharing perspectives. It is focused on building dialogic skills and recognizing that socialization shapes the development of group-based identities, which are embedded in larger systems of power and privilege. Both practitioners and researchers are trained to identify how these asymmetries play out in the classroom in terms of students' personal stories, beliefs, and perspectives as well as how the latter are altered in the learning that occurs in dialogue that ranges from low-risk to high-risk activities in addressing conflict and hot social/political topics that generate differences of opinion.

The action goal for researchers and practitioners was clear: establish a strong evidentiary base that will help educators on college campuses implement and extend their intentional educational activities that address key societal challenges associated with diversity, equity, and democracy. Therefore there was a focus on what facilitators did as well as how and what students learned in the dialogues. Observations and interviews were coded into categories that reflected active cognitive processing and insights during engagement in the dialogue. Together with evaluation of quantitative measures of psychological and behavioral outcomes, the quasi-experimental aspects of the study helped to clarify how participation in dialogues across race and gender differences results in significant differences in twenty out of twenty-four outcomes compared with students who did not participate. They also document the diffusion of dialogue as an educational practice through institutes and collaborative activities with other campuses willing to learn and experiment with a similar pedagogical model. The study helped to link dialogue networks across campuses, sharing practical knowledge about the pedagogy and research results with additional campuses in training and the research community. At the individual level, with newfound awareness, students in the study worked on collaborative action projects of their own design, engaging in ally behaviors to improve their immediate campus or community environments. This extensive study reflects the complexity and possibilities in improving individual

and institutional change efforts as well as in coordinating research to inform practice and policies that sustain dialogue as a vehicle for creating awareness, skills,
and social action among students.

Grassroots Leaders and Institutional Transformation

Because not all researchers begin studies with such "insider" status or direct involvement as in the first example of the study of identity-based intergroup dialogue, I selected a second study that extends notions of power and institutional
change brought about by groups in higher education. Kezar and Lester (2011)
examine grassroots leaders among faculty and staff in higher education in their
book *Enhancing Campus Capacity for Leadership*. Building on social movement
theory, and their own previous work on alternative forms of leadership and collective action, they explore leadership that emerges from bottom–up rather than
top–down leadership, which has long been given credence in higher education.
Campus-based change agents and collectives have remained largely invisible because of the lack of positional authority and often marginalization in their efforts
to create institutional change and challenge the status quo. They begin the study
by disrupting a common assumption in higher education. They note, "there is a
system in place . . . that promotes the idea that heroic authority figures should be
the ones to make change" (p. 17). Their goal was to give voice, agency, and recognition to the challenges and successes of grassroots leaders who work to change
campuses, often without initial support of top or midlevel administration.

Women and people of color comprised many of the individuals and collectives
they studied, and though the focus was not on specific group-based identities,
they addressed identity as a component in the oppression and resistance strategies that crosscut and unify different groups under the umbrella of grassroots
leadership for institutional change. The researchers clearly valued the recognition of leadership across a variety of communities/contexts and were interested
in sustaining social change initiatives. Their focus on typical cases and a variety
of topics, rather than exemplars, helped to ground the study on common topics
that social change agents could learn from and increase their impact. Faculty and
staff in the study worked for change on such varied topics as student success in
science, technology, engineering, and math (or STEM fields); gender discrimination and sexuality; mentorship for student athletes, environmental sustainability;
Latino student success; and improving conditions for staff employees. Much of
the grassroots leadership activities were focused on creating greater equity for
various communities on campus and also on larger social issues.

Researchers began with the systematic selection of sites across five case-study institutions from different sectors, including a community college, liberal arts college, private research university, technical university, and regional public university. The grassroots leadership research team involved individuals similarly trained in qualitative methods. Documents and initial interviews helped to determine sites and multiple or nested cases of grassroots initiatives within institutions. *Enhancing Campus Capacity for Leadership* draws upon extensive use of documents, observations during weeklong visits or four site visits at each institution, and 165 semistructured interviews, including with eighty-four staff ranging from custodians to midlevel personnel in student affairs and eighty-one faculty from different tenure-track and nontenure ranks. Notes, interviews, and input from each of the team members generated a research report for each site. Care was taken to be attentive to internal hierarchies that inform perspectives and positionality within institutions. From a methodological standpoint, their attention to culture and historical context was also important, using documents and longtime participants at each institution that could clarify the historical context and provide further interpretation of events. In so doing, for example, they revealed how over time grassroots leaders achieved success in their initiatives—some after fifteen or twenty years. Grassroots efforts can prove to outlast the tenure of many top-level administrators in most of today's institutions.

What makes this a notable study under the transformative paradigm is their attention to power dynamics that surround each context, and their approach in honoring and respecting communities for their strengths in promoting a variety of issues that challenge the status quo on campus. The focus is thus not simply on institutional change but rather the identification of the forms of power operating within work contexts—an area that is largely unaddressed in studies in higher education (see chap. 3, this volume, by Brian Pusser). Kezar and Lester (2011) not only recognize traditional positional hierarchies but also detail how power is enacted by peers (e.g., bullying) and administrators at different levels (e.g., firing individuals) in resistance to change. They document agency and how grassroots leaders navigated the power dynamics of resistance and oppression. The study also uncovers information that reveals how grassroots leaders face unique institutional barriers in bringing about change, and how groups and individuals maintain their own resilience and strength as they persist in efforts. Further, they find that many of the challenges or forms of oppression were similar, as were strategies/tactics to navigate power, across institutional types. Grassroots leaders who use a strategic, tempered approach over time experience success and only revert to confrontation when facing an impasse. Retaining their own jobs to remain an advocate on campus was an important consideration in their grassroots approach, but participants also revealed how confrontational approaches (the old political model) sometimes "undoes their own work" (p. 26) in advocating for change. This finding resonates with Giroux's (1983) theory of resistance, which indicates that not all "oppositional behaviors" (among students) are meant to critique the established hierarchies or systems of oppression or are emancipatory. Some can be self-defeating. Kezar and Lester (2011) offer useful advice to help grassroots leaders become more successful and supported in their institutions, expanding conceptions and origins of leadership to address contemporary issues in higher education. As a result of the study, the researchers and participants alter the epistemology of leadership and advance practical knowledge about how to bring about and sustain social change on campus.

Advancing the Transformative Paradigm in Higher Education Research

The sample studies were selected for their unique focus on key principles that undergird the transformative paradigm, attention to quality in methodological choices and procedures, and evidence of change within institutions that are sometimes considered too big or impossible to change. The studies were multi-institutional and required a good deal of coordination and negotiation of values and worldviews among the research team as well as between researchers and study participants. The scale of these studies enhances generalizability of findings across institutions and individuals within them, but not all transformative paradigm studies must have such a grand scale. For example, several studies at a single campus or department have involved both researchers and groups of teaching faculty interested in studying their own curriculum reform efforts, using an action research approach with social justice aims (Mullinix, Sawyer, & Bishop, 2013; Peet, 2006). Other campus-based studies have focused on the critical resilience that empowers students from marginalized populations, taking into account the structural inequalities students encounter along educational pathways (Campa, 2010). Many more studies that begin on a local level can focus on transformation or generate research in the service of social change. To advance a transformative paradigm, I address the principles and challenges in the interrelated phases of conceptualization, design, implementation, and utilization of results and conclude with thoughts on further development of the transformative paradigm.

Many researchers begin studies with good intentions to help marginalized communities (or to help others better serve these communities) but lack social justice goals that permeate all phases of research. Identifying transformative research questions and theories is central in the conceptualization phase of the study; otherwise, researchers can default into blaming the victim, deficit language, or disempowering victim framing when it comes to members of marginalized groups. Honoring and respecting the cultural norms of study participants means identifying theories that recognize strengths and critical forms of resiliency within these communities. Even in extreme cases of socially reproduced inequality, domination is never complete (Giroux, 1983) and therefore there is room for alternative theory and solutions. Educational solutions based on social reproduction framing, for example, seek to remedy the deficits by using interventions that try to provide the social and cultural information missing from students' families that lack resources, rather than by addressing the real problem of power or resources in schools (Campa, 2010). Yosso (2005, 2006) acknowledges that inequality is reproduced and at the same time identifies the resources within communities and families that theoretically foster resistance and strength among Latino students in the educational process. In another example, the multicontextual model of diverse learning environments places student social identity at the center of practice and encourages research to address identity-conscious curricular and co-curricular educational practices, acknowledging that sociohistorical, political, and institutional climates for diversity inform outcomes and processes in college (Hurtado et al., 2012).

Another element of the transformative paradigm is the use and development of new theories and models that honor and respect the ways of marginalized communities. While such theory is innovative, it is rare to find this type of work to guide transformative designs because there is great conformity in not only dominant paradigms in the field but also theories supporting those worldviews that are reinforced in access to scholarly outlets, graduate training, and merit reviews of academic work. The challenge for transformative paradigm scholars is to push the boundaries of existing theory, expose how dominant theories do not serve marginalized communities, and devise new theories on the basis of the experiences of marginalized communities. Many theories under the transformative paradigm that have been based on marginalized communities also await further development (e.g., critical race theory, queer theory, intersectionality), and critiques of studies in relation to theory will help us advance approaches that consider marginalized communities in multiple and changing sociohistorical contexts. Using a critical research synthesis of higher education literature, for example, Nuñez (2014) extends a model of intersectionality that moves beyond a focus on multiple social identities to include multiple contexts that also address dimensions of power and historicity.

Another key framing approach within the transformative paradigm is to disrupt commonly held assumptions that perpetuate privilege and exclude or render groups invisible, illustrated in the grassroots leadership study example (Kezar & Lester, 2011). But a related challenge is that all human beings are subject to socialization from birth regarding prevailing assumptions about social identity groups, education, and knowledge fostered by social institutions (e.g., family, schools, graduate training) that reinforce myths legitimizing inequality (Harro, 2000). Transformative researchers can begin to interrogate prevailing assumptions as part of their research questions, and to also question their own assumptions about the nature of reality and knowledge through reflexivity as a step in study design and implementation. As a check on those assumptions, and also to provide transparency in design and build strength in the research phases, researchers are calling for and demonstrating the systematic use of techniques to encourage reflection at different phases of the research process (Collins, Johnson, & Onwuegbuzie, 2012; Papadimitriou, Ivankova, & Hurtado, 2013).

Peer debriefing, for example, is a method where a peer researcher poses questions to enhance consciousness about assumptions, clarify understanding of the research process, facilitate relationships between the researcher and study participants, or explore assumptions among individuals on research teams (Nelson et al., 2011). The technique has the potential to yield more "ethically and culturally responsive research" and to increase the confidence of novice researchers (Collins et al., 2012, p. 19). Other researchers use self-assessments or autoethnography to raise their level of reflection and awareness about the self and study participants in the research process (Mertens, 2009; Brayboy & Dehyle, 2010). Such techniques have great utility for advancing transformative studies but are not typically taught in graduate programs and are considered irrelevant to researchers operating under a postpositivist paradigm, where a key assumption is that the researcher is unbiased.

Conclusion

In order to build an epistemology of liberation for social and political institutional change (Zuberi & Bonilla-Silva, 2008), transformative researchers in higher education must be more explicit about how they include, as well as about the difficulties encountered, as they engage study participants from marginalized communities in different phases of the research process. To improve our understanding about how to turn research into action, we need good examples of involving participants in the design of the study, interpretation of findings, dissemination of results, or integration of findings into practice. In planning and designing studies, researchers can find intentional ways to ensure that results are useful by taking steps along the continuum of public engagement that ranges from informing communities about results to empowering communities to make their own decisions. In addition, ongoing studies can be modified to include more intentional action plans to increase the impact in the field, affirm educators' and students' experiences, and ensure that results are used to guide practices that can reduce inequality in higher education. Doctoral students writing dissertation proposals that have transformative intentions should be encouraged to include an action plan along some areas of the continuum to increase the use and impact of their findings.

In addition to increasing research designs focused on involving practitioners or marginalized communities in the development of the research or in its practical implementation, we need scholars with a transformative worldview to provide "translation" documents that make the work accessible to practitioners or communities who do not have time to read the literature or who lack the expertise to understand the implications of research for their work or own lives. Otherwise, the tendency is to adopt dominant theories and studies to guide practice despite the lack of systematic investigations or relevance for particular marginalized populations. Scholars operating under the transformative paradigm can provide more guidance from the research to help others serve marginalized communities or develop activities that raise awareness about educators' roles in reinforcing inequality and improving their work as change agents.

If the central goal is empowerment of marginalized communities, several other strategies can help turn research into action. For example, Project MALES uses mixed-methods research strategies to investigate the phenomenon of the Latino gender gap and then infuses their research findings into the development of an intergenerational mentoring model that focuses on Latino male educational success (see http://ddce.utexas.edu/projectmales/). In this case, the higher education researchers are engaging in translational research and action projects to address an educational crisis with Latino male success and attainments (Sáenz & Ponjuan, forthcoming). Helping to build resistance strategies among Latino males may be key for the success of individuals who can benefit from an intervention, and research on the mechanisms of oppression can help to transform racist, patriarchal, and heteronormative educational practices, structures, or policies that continue to constrain the educational progress of underrepresented men and women.

Until the development and scholarly discussion of the transformative paradigm, many researchers lacked a language for their work and capacity to articulate and make explicit their intentions to create and sustain social change. A liberating feature of the work under the transformative paradigm is that it constitutes a large umbrella for critical work in higher education and research inspired by social movements across multiple communities. The traditional divides between quantitative and qualitative methods are set aside to include research about what works best to achieve social justice aims. Many of the studies cited here are exciting examples of how scholars are advancing scholarship in the service of social and institutional change. Many more studies in higher education are associated with the central tenets and practices evolving under the transformative paradigm. As a community of scholars, we can further develop research under the transformative paradigm as an intellectual home for joining efforts to advance knowledge that will result in a more just and equitable society.

NOTE

1. Not surprisingly, the central tenets of transformative paradigm scholarship reflect principles that have guided feminist research over the decades as articulated by Harding (1987), expanded by Reinharz (1992), and subsequently extended by Ropers-Huilman and Winters (2011) in application to higher education research.

REFERENCES

Brayboy, B., & Deyhle, D. (2010). Insider-outsider: Researchers in American Indian communities. *Theory into Practice, 39*(3), 163–69.

Cabrera, N. L. (2014). Exposing whiteness in higher education: White male college students minimizing racism, claiming victimization, and recreating white supremacy. *Race Ethnicity and Education, 17*(1), 30–55.

Campa, B. (2010). Critical resilience, schooling processes, and the academic success of Mexican Americans in a community college. *Hispanic Journal of Behavioral Sciences, 32*(3), 429–55.

Christians, C. (2005). Ethics and politics in qualitative research. In N. K. Denzin & Y. S. Lincoln (Eds.), *The Sage handbook of qualitative research* (3rd ed., pp. 139–64). Thousand Oaks, CA: Sage.

Collins, K. M. T., Johnson, B., & Onwuegbuzie, A. (2012). *Promoting transparency in design and application of quality criteria in mixed research.* Paper presented at the annual meeting of the American Educational Research Association, Vancouver, BC.

Creswell, J. W., & Plano Clark, V. L. (2011). *Designing and conducting mixed methods research.* Los Angeles, CA: Sage.

Delgado Bernal, D., Elenes, C. A., Godinez, F. E., & Villenas, S. (2006). *Chicana/ Latina education in everyday life: Feminista perspectives on pedagogy and episte-mology.* Albany: State University of New York Press.

Freire, P. (1973). *Education for critical consciousness.* New York: Seabury.

Gilbert, N. (1997). Advocacy research and social policy. *Crime and Justice, 22,* 101–48.

Giroux, H. A. (1983). Theories of reproduction and resistance in the new sociology of education: A critical analysis. *Harvard Educational Review, 52*(3), 257–93.

Guba, E. G., & Lincoln, Y. (1989). *Fourth generation evaluation*. Newbury Park, CA: Sage.

———. (2005). Paradigmatic controversies, contradictions, and emerging confluence. In N. K. Denzin & Y. S. Lincoln (Eds.), *The Sage handbook of qualitative research* (3rd ed., pp. 191–215). Thousand Oaks, CA: Sage.

Gurin, P., Nagda, B. A., & Zuniga, X. (2013). *Dialogue across difference: Practice, theory and research on intergroup dialogue*. New York: Russell Sage Foundation.

Hao, L., & Naiman, D. Q. (2010). *Assessing inequality*. Thousand Oaks, CA: Sage.

Harding, S. (1987). Introduction: Is there a feminist method? In S. Harding (Ed.), *Feminism and methodology* (pp. 1–14). Bloomington: Indiana University Press.

———. (1991). *Whose science? Whose knowledge? Thinking from women's lives*. Ithaca, NY: Cornell University Press.

Harro, B. (2000). The cycle of socialization. In M. Adams et al. (Eds.), *Readings for diversity and social justice: An anthology on racism, antisemitism, sexism, heterosexism, ableism, and classism* (pp. 21–30). New York: Routlege.

Heron, J., & Reason, P. (2006). The practice of co-operative inquiry: Research "with" rather than "on" people. In P. Reason & Y. H. Bradbury (Eds.), *Handbook of action research* (pp. 144–54). London: Sage.

Hurtado, S., Álvarez, C. L., Guillermo-Wann, C., Cuellar, M., & Arellano, L. (2012). A model for diverse learning environments: The scholarship on creating and assessing conditions for student success. In J. C. Smart & M. B. Paulsen (Eds.), *Higher education: Handbook of theory and research* (Vol. 27, pp. 41–122). London: Springer.

International Association for Public Participation. (2013). *IAP2 spectrum of public participation*. Louisville, CO: Author. Retrieved from www.iap2.org/associations/4748/files/IAP2%20Spectrum_vertical.pdf.

Kanpol, B. (1999). *Critical pedagogy: An introduction* (2nd ed.). Westport, CT: Greenwood Press.

Kezar, A. J., & Lester, J. (2011). *Enhancing campus capacity for leadership: An examination of grassroots leaders in higher education*. Stanford, CA: Stanford University Press.

Lather, P. (1992). Critical frames in educational research: Feminist and poststructural perspectives. *Theory and Practice, 31*(2), 1–13.

Mertens, D. M. (1998). *Research and evaluation in education and psychology: Integrating diversity with quantitative and qualitative approaches*. Thousand Oaks, CA: Sage.

———. (2003). Mixed methods and the politics of human research: The transformative-emancipatory perspective. In A. Tashakkori & C. Teddlie (Eds.), *Sage handbook of mixed methods in social and behavioral research* (pp. 134–64). Thousand Oaks, CA: Sage.

———. (2005). *Research methods in education and psychology: Integrating diversity with quantitative and qualitative approaches* (2nd ed.). Thousand Oaks, CA: Sage.

———. (2009). *Transformative research and evaluation*. New York: Guilford Press.

Mertens, D. M., Bledoe, K. L., Sullivan, M., & Wilson, A. (2010). *Utilization of mixed methods for transformative purposes.* In A. Tashakkori & C. Teddlie (Eds.), *Sage handbook of mixed methods in social and behavioral research* (2nd ed., pp. 193–214). Los Angeles, CA: Sage.

Mullinix, B. B., Sawyer, R., & Bishop, J. S. (2013). *Unlocking educational futures: Weaving data in support of curricular development and decisions.* Paper presented at the annual meeting of the American Educational Research Association, San Francisco, CA.

Nelson, J. A., Onwuegbuzie, A. J., Wines, L. A., & Frels, R. K. (2011). The therapeutic interview process in qualitative research studies. *Qualitative Report, 18*(79), 1–17. Retrieved from www.nova.edu/ssss/QR/QR18/nelson79.pdf.

Nuñez, A. M. (2014). Employing multilevel intersectionality in educational research: Latino identities, contexts, and college access. *Educational Researcher, 43*(2), 85–89.

Papadimitriou, A., Ivankova, N., & Hurtado, S. (2013). Addressing challenges of conducting quality mixed methods studies in higher education. In J. Husiman & M. Tight (Eds.), *Theory and method in higher education research* (Vol. 9). *International perspectives on higher education research* (pp. 133–53). Bingley: Emerald Group.

Paul, J. L. (2005). *Introduction to the philosophies of research and criticism in education and the social sciences.* Upper Saddle River, NJ: Pearson Education.

Peet, M. (2006). *We make the road by walking it: The development of a critical consciousness from a psychosocial structuation perspective* (Unpublished doctoral dissertation). University of Michigan.

Phillips, D. C., & Burbules, N. C. (2000). *Postpositivism and educational research.* Lanham, MD: Rowman & Littlefield.

Reinharz, S. (1992). *Feminist methods in social research.* New York: Oxford University Press.

Ropers-Huilman, B. (1998). *Feminist teaching in theory and practice: Situating power and knowledge in poststructural classrooms.* New York: Teachers College.

Ropers-Huilman, B., & Winters, K. T. (2011). Feminist research in higher education. *Journal of Higher Education, 82*(6), 667–90.

Sáenz, V. B., & Ponjuan, L. (forthcoming). Latino males in education: Current trends and future outlooks on the growing gender gap in educational attainment. In R. Zambrana & S. Hurtado (Eds.), *The magic key: The educational journey of Mexican Americans from K–12 to college and beyond.* Austin: University of Texas Press.

Sidanius, J. (1993). The psychology of group conflict and the dynamics of oppression: A social dominance perspective. In S. Iyengar & W. McGuire (Eds.), *Explorations in political psychology* (pp. 183–210). Durham, NC: Duke University Press.

Sidanius, J., Levin, S., Federico, C. M., & Pratto, F. (2001). Legitimizing ideologies: The social dominance approach. In J. T. Jost & B. Major (Eds.), *The psychology of legitimacy: Emerging perspectives on ideology, justice, and intergroup relations.* Cambridge: Cambridge University Press.

Yosso, T. (2005). Whose culture has capital? A critical race theory discussion of community cultural wealth. *Race Ethnicity and Education, 8*(1), 69–91.

———. (2006). *Critical race counterstories along the Chicana/Chicano educational pipeline*. New York: Routledge.

Zuberi, T., & Bonilla-Silva, E. (Eds.). (2008). *White logic, white methods: Racism and methodology*. Lanham, MD: Rowan & Littlefield.

Zuñiga, X., Nagda, B. A., Chesler, M., & Cytron-Walker, A. (2007). *Intergroup dialogue in higher education: Meaningful dialogue for social justice*. San Francisco: Jossey-Bass.

Afterword

Critical research in higher education has generally been at the margins of the field, for reasons discussed throughout this book: the dominance of functionalist and rational choice approaches to scholarship and policy, the ways in which power shapes understanding and discourse, the patriarchal organization of institutions throughout the political economy, the embedded and entrenched patterns of understanding handed from one generation of scholars and practitioners to the next. And yet one must consider how there is still space for intellectual and social contest with such powerful norms in place. What is it that sparks the imagination of critical researchers and practitioners? What drives the imaginative questioning that gives voice to the oppositional narratives?

Imagination

A central lesson of this book is that critical approaches to higher education begin with acts of imagination, giving shape to a world different than the one we find now. Those imaginative acts, which stem from vision and knowledge, come into being through a commitment to realizing a positive change in the existing order. The contributors to this volume individually and collectively present visions of social justice in many forms that are fundamentally linked to the realization of equity through a variety of forms of knowing and knowledge. Through their work they invite students, scholars, and practitioners of higher education to follow their own imaginative intellectual paths with the knowledge that critical research can be done, is worth doing, and will make a difference.

Imagination is also central to the creation of a different set of institutions and policies in higher education. The chapters in this volume present models of more equitable organizations, remarkably different understandings of student engagement, new research paradigms, striking challenges to current and historical norms of understanding postsecondary practices, reinterpretations of language, and perhaps most importantly a belief that equity matters. All of this begins with a critical challenge, a leap beyond the status quo. That imaginative flight is central to critical approaches to higher education, and it is more than a little daunting.

The common animating force behind the critical work in this book is inequity. The higher education project—locally, nationally, and globally—has since its beginning struggled with inequities in missions, conflicting aspirations, discrimination, asymmetries of power, and at the heart of the matter contradiction. As a public good expressed through individual journeys and collective action, as a predominantly public and nonprofit project, higher education is both a personal and a political arena. As such, it holds enormous promise for transformation and faces tremendous pressure to serve dominant interests. Contradiction is a key source of imagination and inspiration, and a precursor to understanding the nature of contest. One can see the appeal to scholars and practitioners interested in redressing inequity of working through scholarship, teaching, organizational action, policy, and social movements. The recognition of inequity requires a transformative act of imagination: to name it requires the presumption that it could be something else, countenancing the proposition that the postsecondary arena, its institutions, and the world in which it is inexorably enmeshed could be more equitable. Yet the gulf between imagining a different universe and realizing the transformations that would bring the imaginary into being is wide. This book was designed to inspire and empower scholars and practitioners committed to equity, not to add daunting layers to the challenge. Taken together, the work here should sharpen awareness of the challenge to change at the same time that it offers tools, models, and visions of how to approach possibilities and challenges with authenticity and optimism. Depending on perception, a window either opens to a world of possibility or defines a boundary between interior and exterior space. This book is intended to do both.

Understanding Where We Begin

The process of change requires both a sense of what is to come and a clear assessment of where one begins. Throughout this book, the authors have argued that critical research requires close attention to the construction of what we understand as the status quo—the starting point of the personal, social, and institutional forces that shape higher education.

Standpoint

In various ways, *Critical Approaches to the Study of Higher Education* calls attention to the role of standpoints in research and practice, with particular attention to identities—of the scholar or practitioner, of the people or objects defined as subjects, of institutions or ideologies, and perhaps most importantly of the author. We consider identity to be a fluid construct, lived, defined, imposed in complex and historically mediated ways. Critical research requires defining one's own identity and standpoint and allowing for the possibility that powerful constellations of forces shape and reinforce the ways in which we define the identities and standpoints of ourselves and others, the nature of our vision, and the edges of our personal and scholarly horizons. This book intends to offer encouragement to contest such subjectivities by presenting alternative perspectives and possibilities and by offering tools for engaging with history, texts, institutions, and others in pursuit of new standing and understanding.

Sense Making

Just as a critical perspective sees identity as a product of subjectivities, norms of history, identity, and power dynamics, so too can the reading and interpretation of texts, language, and institutional practices be understood as products of hegemonic forces. The chapters in this volume turn attention to the gendered and racialized construction of mission, the mobilization of bias through repetition of dominant norms, and the ways in which symbols and policies shape inequalities throughout higher education. At the same time, the critical project itself must be open to critique, to contest, and to elaboration and development. With that openness comes the realization that the relationships between the self and another, between the status quo and change, between the powerful and the powerless are not binary processes; rather, they are multifaceted and dynamic, singular and plural at the same evolving moment.

Finding a New Way

The essays collected here share common threads and calls for transformation and deconstruction, bringing new light, innovation, unwinding, revision, reframing, and more. They also challenge some of the most fundamental ideas and models shaping the scholarship and practice of higher education: human capital, prestige hierarchies, the role of the state, functionalist research paradigms, organizational change, engagement, and institutional policy making, to name a few. Finding meaning beyond dominant norms of understanding is an essential element linking the research collected here. The desire to make change stems from recognizing the status quo and the norms that fasten it securely in place, as well as having the imagination to see it another way, and the will to bring another way into being. We intend for this book to offer space and encouragement for students, scholars, and practitioners to reclaim their personal, intellectual, and professional identities—and to question their own understandings and visions—in order to more effectively engage the beliefs, institutions, and policies that dominate our work and our world. In closing, we return to where we began, with a call to be critical, to question, to contest, and to change. Our hope is that the ideas, scholarship, and practices brought together here will support others in transforming higher education as a force for a more equitable and socially just society.

DERRICK P. ALRIDGE is a professor of history of education and program coordinator of the social foundations of education program at the University of
Virginia. His primary areas of scholarship are African American educational
and intellectual history and the civil rights movement. Alridge is currently
conducting research on the role of education and schooling in the civil rights
movement.

GREGORY M. ANDERSON is dean of the College of Education at Temple University. Anderson previously served as dean at of the College of Education at
the University of Denver and worked as the higher education policy program
officer for the Ford Foundation in New York.

RYAN P. BARONE is the assistant director for the Center of the First-Year Experience at Aims Community College and is an affiliated faculty member in the
School of Education at Colorado State University. He is interested in how critical postmodernism, higher education social justice leadership, two-year colleges, retention and success, men and masculinities, and social justice frame
qualitative research. Barone's publications cover topics including higher education demographic trends, sexual assault prevention, and historically white
fraternities. He received a BS from the State University of New York at Fredo-
nia, an MS from Colorado State University, and a PhD from the University of
Denver.

ESTELA MARA BENSIMON, EdD, is a professor of higher education and co-
director of the Center for Urban Education at the University of Southern California's Rossier School of Education. Her current research is on issues of racial equity in higher education from the perspective of organizational learning
and sociocultural practice theories. She is particularly interested in place-based,
practitioner-driven inquiry as a means of organizational change in higher
education.

ANNIE W. BEZBATCHENKO is a program consultant and former program
director at the Teagle Foundation. Now based in Toronto, she also works with
Storbeck/Pimentel & Associates on executive searches for foundations, colleges, and universities. She holds an MS from the University of Pennsylvania
and a PhD from New York University, both in higher education.

ROBIN M. BISHOP is an assistant professor of psychology at Mount Saint Mary's University. Her research interests include culturally responsive pedagogy, faculty development, effective teaching strategies for success of underprepared students, and achieving equity in student outcomes.

NICHOLAS BOWLBY is a doctoral candidate in the higher education program at the University of Denver. His research and scholarly interests are in the areas of college access for low-income students, student engagement, student satisfaction, and alumni involvement. As a graduate student, Bowlby has been involved in community service projects and graduate student leadership. He currently works at the University of Denver as the student engagement coordinator within alumni relations. Bowlby received a BA in speech communication from Southern Illinois University and an MA in communications from the University of Illinois at Springfield.

MITCHELL J. CHANG is a professor of higher education and organizational change and Asian American Studies (by courtesy) at the University of California, Los Angeles. Chang's research focuses on diversity-related issues and initiatives on college campuses. He has written over eighty publications, some of which were cited in the US Supreme Court's ruling of *Grutter v. Bollinger*, a case involving the use of race-conscious admissions practices. Chang received a National Academy of Education / Spencer Fellowship in 2001 and was recognized by the American College Personnel Association for outstanding research in both 2000 and 2008. In 2006, *Diverse: Issues in Higher Education* profiled him as one of the nation's top ten scholars. Chang has also been elected to serve as a board member for the American Educational Research Association and the Association for the Study of Higher Education.

ALICIA C. DOWD, PhD, is an associate professor of higher education at the University of Southern California's Rossier School of Education and co-director of the Center for Urban Education, whose mission is to promote racial-ethnic equity in postsecondary educational experiences and student outcomes. Dowd's research focuses on the political economy of postsecondary financing, governance, and research.

SHAUN R. HARPER is on the faculty in the Graduate School of Education, Africana Studies, and Gender Studies at the University of Pennsylvania, where he also serves as executive director of the Center for the Study of Race and Equity in Education. His research examines race and gender in education, equity trends and racial climates on college campuses, black and Latino male student success in high school and higher education, and college student engagement. Harper is author of over ninety peer-reviewed articles in such journals as *Review of Research in Education, Journal of Higher Education, Journal of College Student Development, Review of Higher Education,* and *Teachers College Record* as well as in other academic publications. His eleven books include *Student Engagement in Higher Education, College Men and Masculinities,* and the fifth edition of *Student Services: A Handbook for the Profession.* The American Educational Research Association presented him its 2010 Early Career Award and 2014 Relating Research to Practice Award.

JESSICA HARRIS is a doctoral candidate in higher education and student affairs at Indiana University. She received her BA in critical theory and social justice from Occidental College and her MEd from Pennsylvania State University. Her research interests include multiracial students in higher education, the influences of white supremacy and patriarchy in the collegiate experiences of women of color, and utilizing critical race theory as a tool to critique systems of oppression in higher education. Harris currently works as a project associate for the Faculty Survey of Student Engagement.

SYLVIA HURTADO is a professor and served as director of the Higher Education Research Institute at the University of California, Los Angeles, in the Graduate School of Education and Information Studies. Hurtado has published numerous articles and books related to her primary interest in student educational outcomes, campus climates, college impact on student development, and diversity in higher education.

MARION LLOYD is chief project coordinator at the General Directorate for Institutional Evaluation at the National Autonomous University of Mexico (UNAM). She is a member of the university's Higher Education Research Group and a regular columnist on international trends in higher education. She holds a BA in English and Spanish literature from Harvard University and an MA in Latin American studies from UNAM, where she is currently pursuing a PhD in sociology. For fifteen years, she was a foreign correspondent in Latin America and South Asia for various US publications, including the *Boston Globe, Houston Chronicle,* and *Chronicle of Higher Education.* Her research interests include equity and access to higher education, international university rankings, and comparative education policy, with a particular focus on Mexico and Brazil.

ANA M. MARTÍNEZ-ALEMÁN is a professor and chair of the Educational Leadership and Higher Education Department at the Lynch School of Education, Boston College. Her published work includes *Accountability, Pragmatic Aims, and the American University* and *Online Social Networking on Campus: Understanding What Matters in Student Culture.* Her scholarship has appeared in the *Journal of Higher Education, Teachers College Record, Educational Theory, Feminist Interpretations of John Dewey, Educational Researcher,* and the *Review of Higher Education.*

AMY SCOTT METCALFE is an associate professor in the Department of Educational Studies at the University of British Columbia. Her research interests include higher education policy; knowledge production; academic identity and subjectivity; gender, race, and ethnicity in education; and critical policy studies in education.

ANNA NEUMANN is a professor of higher education at Columbia University's Teachers College. Her research and teaching interests include the pedagogies of liberal education, teaching and learning in urban colleges and universities serving first-generation learners, professors and their intellectual careers, qualitative research strategies and methods, and doctoral students' learning of research and development as researchers.

IMANOL ORDORIKA is a professor of social sciences and education at the Institute for Economic Research, as well as general director of institutional evaluation at the National Autonomous University of Mexico. He received a PhD in social sciencies, policy, and educational practice from Stanford University in 1999. His research and publications have focused on power and politics in higher education (*Power and Politics in Higher Education*), globalization ("El central volumen de la fuerza" [The hegemonic global pattern in the reorganization of elite higher education and research], in *Knowledge Matters: The Public Mission of the Research University*), and international university rankings ("A decade of international university rankings: A critical perspective from Latin America," in *Rankings and Accountability in Higher Education: Uses and Misuses*).

AARON M. PALLAS is the Arthur I. Gates Professor of Sociology and Education at Teachers College, Columbia University. He has devoted the bulk of his career to the study of how schools sort students, especially the relationship between school organization and sorting processes and the linkages among schooling, learning, and the human life course.

LORI D. PATTON is an associate professor of higher education and student affairs at Indiana University. Her research focuses on African Americans in postsecondary contexts, critical race theory, college student development, and the influence of campus environments. Patton is best known for her research on culture centers and as editor of *Campus Culture Centers in Higher Education.* She also coauthored the second edition of *Student Development in Col-*

lege. Her recent research examines identity intersectionality among African American lesbian, gay, and bisexual students, and the experiences of black undergraduate women. Patton's larger body of scholarship has appeared in the *Journal of Higher Education, Journal of Negro Education, Journal of College Student Development, International Journal of Qualitative Studies in Education,* and *Teachers College Record.* The Association for the Study of Higher Education honored her with its 2010 Early Career Award and the 2008 Mildred E. Garcia Award for Exemplary Scholarship.

BRIAN PUSSER is an associate professor of higher education in the Curry School of Education at the University of Virginia and an affiliate of the Center for Urban Education at the University of Southern California. His research focuses on the organization and governance of higher education institutions, state and national postsecondary policies, and international higher education. He has authored or coauthored articles published in the *Journal of Higher Education, Educational Policy, Research in Higher Education,* and *Higher Education: Handbook of Theory and Research.* He is the co-editor of *Universities and the Public Sphere: Knowledge Creation and State Building in the Era of Globalization* and co-editor of the second edition of *Comparative Education* in the ASHE Reader Series.

KELLY O. ROSINGER is a doctoral candidate at the University of Georgia's Institute of Higher Education. Her research focuses on efficiency and equity outcomes of higher education policy at the federal, state, and institutional levels.

SHEILA SLAUGHTER is the Louise McBee Professor of Higher Education at the Institute of Higher Education, University of Georgia. Her scholarship concentrates on the relationship between knowledge and power as it plays out in higher education policy at the state, federal, and global levels. During the last fifteen years she has focused on topics such as intellectual property and statutes, commercialization of academic science and technology market mechanisms in higher education, and the dynamics of academic capitalism and the new economy.

JEFFREY C. SUN is a professor of higher education at the University of Louisville and a visiting scholar at the Ohio State University. He researches and writes in the area of higher education law. His publications have included venues such as the *Fordham Urban Law Journal, Journal of College and University Law, Review of Higher Education, Teachers College Record,* and the University of Pennsylvania's *Journal of Constitutional Law.* He serves on the board of directors for the Education Law Association and the Association for the Study of Higher Education. Sun received an MBA from Loyola Marymount University, a law degree from the Moritz College of Law at Ohio State University, and an MPhil and PhD from Columbia University.

BARRETT J. TAYLOR is an assistant professor of counseling and higher education at the University of North Texas. Taylor's research emphasizes the nature and effects of competition in higher education. He has approached this topic in several different ways, highlighting changes in the internal allocation of resources, organization of scientific research, and engagement in strategic communications.

ROBERT T. TERANISHI is a professor of social science and comparative education and the Morgan and Helen Chu Endowed Chair in Asian American Studies at the University of California, Los Angeles (UCLA). He is also co-director for the Institute for Immigration, Globalization, and Education at UCLA; a senior fellow with the Steinhardt Institute for Higher Education Policy at New York University; and principal investigator for the National Commission on Asian American and Pacific Islander Research in Education. He also recently served as a strategic planning and restructuring consultant for the Ford Foundation. Teranishi's research examines the causes and consequences of the stratification of college opportunities, with a particular interest in higher education policy priorities. His research has been influential to federal, state, and institution policy related to college access and completion.